Sure Signs

Stories Behind the Historical Markers of Central New York

BY

Howard S. Ford

© 2002 by Howard S. Ford. All rights reserved.

No part of this book may be reproduced, stored in a retrieval system, or transmitted by any means, electronic, mechanical, photocopying, recording, or otherwise, without written permission from the author.

ISBN: 1-4033-1485-3 (e-book)
ISBN: 1-4033-1486-1 (Paperback)

Library of Congress Number 2002105705

This book is printed on acid free paper.

Printed in the United States of America
Bloomington, IN

1stBooks – rev. 9/26/02

TABLE OF CONTENTS

INTRODUCTION ix

CHAPTER 1 1
        The Iroquois - they form a league - additional tribes - women's influence - the long house residence -clans - fierce warriors & their better nature - raising children - strategic location - Samuel de Champlain the fur trade and competition - the Hurons, Petuns, Eries, and Neutrals - Jesuits and coureurs de bois - Father Le Moyne and the mission to Onondaga - the eat-all-feast - Henry Hudson - New Netherland - the Dutch West India Company - Fort Orange - trading in Iroquoia - Cornelius May, Adrian Block - purchase of New Amsterdam - raids on Spanish colonies - the patroon system - governors Kieft and Stuyvesant - Rensselaer - the English take over - the first landed gentry - Governor Andros befriends the Iroquois - Robert Livingston and descendants - Oswego trading post

CHAPTER 2 21
        Charles II and William Penn - boundary conflicts - Penn, Quakerism, and the Iroquois- Talon - Frontenac, Marquette, and Joliet - La Salle - Governor La Barré backs down - Denonville - the Seneca towns - Frontenac raids Schenectady, Onondaga, and Jamesville - the conflict widens to New England and Acadia - fur flies in the upper Ohio Valley - the Palatine Germans in New York - Sir William Johnson - Fortress Louisbourg - Conrad Weiser and John Bartram at Onondaga - the Ohio Company - Céleron de Bienville and his Ohio River road show

CHAPTER 3 40
        Abbe Picquet's passion - Onondaga, a French Fort? Johnson quits - Moravian missionaries and smiths - Pickawillany - England gets in step - Molly Brant - French build Forts Presque Isle, Le Boeuf, & Venango - Washington protests for Governor Dinwiddie - French usurp fort building at Forks of Ohio - Washington's skirmish begins world war - the Walking Purchase and dirty deals - Pennamite Wars - Albany Congress - Johnson elevated - game plan - Braddock boondoggle - Mary Jemison - a Baronetcy from Lake George - Col. Bradstreet beefs up Oswego - Fort Bull & Battle Island - Montcalm outflanks Oswego - Gen. Webb panics & imperils - Gov Shirley replaced by Loudon - French fizzle at Fort William Henry - William Pitt now Prime Minister - Loudon at Louisbourg - Montcalm subdues Fort William Henry - His Indians rampage - Abercromby astounding at Fort Carillon - Gen. Amherst lambasts Louisbourg - building Fort Stanwix - Bradstreet turns tide and overwhelms Fort Frontenac

CHAPTER 4 59
        The campaign to take Fort Duquesne - building the Forbes Road - persuasion by Reverend Post - Grant's Highlanders ambushed & brutalized - Duquesne falls to Forbes - Stanwix builds Fort Pitt - Amherst renames Fort Carillon Ticonderoga - Major Robert Rogers raids Saint Francis - Sir William knocks out Niagara - builds blockhouse & Fort Brewerton - Generals Wolfe & Montcalm vie and die for Quebec - scurvy again - Montreal succumbs to Amherst - Canada now British - the stage for the Revolution prepared

CHAPTER 5 67
       British army land-grabbing - economy measures & Amherst's arrogance feeds Indian resentment - Pontiac's Conspiracy - forts Detroit, Pitt, & Niagara besieged; forts & garrisons at Michilimackinac, Sandusky, Preque Isle, & Le Boeuf wiped out - Devil's Hole - Bushy Run breaks siege at Fort Pitt - Pontiac abandons Detroit siege - Delawares and Senecas chastised at Canisteo - Amherst relieved of command - Croghan's gambit - Pontiac accepts peace at Oswego - King George III - the Proclamation Line - Fort Stanwix Treaty of 1768 - Treaty becomes moot by settlers and Revolution

CHAPTER 6 73
       The Stamp Tax - Charles Gravier's prophecy - colonial vexations - the Boston Massacre - Tea Party - the Quebec Act - Continental Congress - Joseph Brant - Skenandoah - Lexington, Concord, Ticonderoga, and Bunker Hill - the Invasion of Canada - congress courts Canada - Washington appointed head of Continental Army - Knox hauls cannon from Ticonderoga - British depart Boston - Mohawk Valley in feud - Loyalists flee to Canada - Common Sense - Declaration of Independence - Washington loses Long Island, New York, White - Plains gloom - battles of Trenton and Princeton - Gen. Schuyler readies central New York for war - Gen. Benedict Arnold buys time at Valcour Island - Burgoyne's Plan - St. Leger besieges Fort Stanwix - Oriskany ambush - Willett's raid - Arnold's hoax works - Bennington - Battle of Saratoga - Lafayette enlists - Brandywine and Germantown - Doctor Franklin, salesman extraordinaire - the French support the U.S.

CHAPTER 7 89
       Brant destroys Oneida Castle - Raids on the frontier - Cobleskill, Wyoming Valley, German Flats - Unadilla, Sheshaquin, Queen Esther's Town, Tioga, Oquaga Cherry Valley - Onondaga - the Sullivan-Clinton Campaign - Lake Otsego - Newtown - Kanadasaga and Chenussio - Boyd and Parker ambushed - Brodhead's raid - Indians flee to British at Niagara - the cold winter of 1779-80 - Brant chastens Oneidas and Tuscaroras - Indian raids resume - Marinus Willett pursues Ross' raiders to West Canada Creek - Walter Butler killed - Willett's last raid - Wars end - the Treaty of Paris - Treaty of Fort Stanwix, 1784 - the Iroquois lament - the Mohawks move to Canada

CHAPTER 8 109
       colonial land grants - more land grabbing - Governor Bellomont's reform - Sir William's land gains - Tory Land confiscated - post Revolution patents - the Military Tract - the Oneida, Onondaga, and Cayuga reservations - classical names - lively market and title tangle - French emigrés - the Asylum Company - Shequaga Falls in the Louvre - the founding of Greene - Frenchman's Island - Phelps-Gorham Purchase - Pulteney Purchase and Charles Williamson - Robert Morris and the Holland Land Company - the Pickering and Big Tree Treaties - the Wadsworth family - Seneca reservations

CHAPTER 9 128
       Elkanah Watson and the Western Inland Lock Navigation Company - preparing land and staking a claim - early settlers - Yaple, Dumond, and Hennepaw families - William Cooper, Abner Truman, Hugh White, Dominic Lynch - Chaumont and LeRay - the king of Naples and Spain - La Farge - liberalizing corporate, labor, and voting laws - Utica - the Holland Land Co., (east) - Boonville and Cazenovia - Eleazor Williams and the Oneidas - the Lost Dauphin - Watkins and Flint - slow expansion in central New York

CHAPTER 10 142
clearing land - cash crops, credit and barter - log cabins and furnishings - cottage industries - corn and other crops - livestock and predators - game and game laws - Seth Green, salmon, and trout - blacksmiths, peddlers, stagecoach drivers and newspapers get out the word - taverns, hotels, and homes - Skaneateles Lake admired by Timothy Dwight and other early commentary - the frosty summer of 1816 - lake effect - health and early medicine

CHAPTER 11 163
State authorized roads - trails into roads - turnpikes - Seneca Turnpike - lotteries for capital - Cayuga ferry evolves into Cayuga bridge - Turnpikes: the Great Western, the Susquehanna, the Ithaca & Owego, the Hamilton & Skaneateles pike - NY road pattern set by 1825 - state maintainenance of roads - plank roads - macadamized roads - bridges - Portageville Bridge - sleighs, wagons, carts, conestoga Wagons and horses - the Loomis Gang - stagecoaches - stage drivers John Butterfield, William Fargo, and Henry Wells - Wells College - Auburn - Hardenbergh Corners - Osborne, Metcalf, and Emerson - William Seward - Auburn Prison - Chief Logan - John D. Rockefeller - Seneca Falls - pumps and fire engines - Phoenix

CHAPTER 12 179
Handsome Lake, Cornplanter, and Quakers - Jemima Wilkinson, the Universal Friend - Joseph Smith and the Church of Jesus Christ of Latter Day Saints - Red Jacket's retort - the Oneida Community - Chautauqua

CHAPTER 13 190
The War of 1812 - General Dearborn's overall strategy - Old Sow at Sackets Harbor - loss of Detroit and the upper lakes - Henry Eckford from Brooklyn here to build ships - the first American Niagara invasion fails - Ogdensburg falls - an American beachead at York - Zebulon Pike and aide killed by exploding magazine - Chauncey takes Fort George - second British attempt at Sackets Harbor foiled by General Brown - Perry defeats British Navy on Lake Erie - General McClure burns Niagara on the Lake - Niagara Frontier destroyed by British - Battle of Lundy's Lane - Macdonough's victory at Plattsburg Bay - Washington, Baltimore, and the National Anthem - on the High Seas - "Don't Give Up the Ship" - New Orleans and Andrew Jackson - Wars conclusion inconclusive - Whitney's changeable parts

CHAPTER 14 204
Jefferson purchases Louisiana from Napoleon - Chancellor Livingston backs Fulton - the Clermont steams the Hudson to Albany - Cornelius Van Derbilt - state legislated 20-year monopoly held unconstitutional - competition soars, fares plummet - Nicholas and Lydia Roosevelt steam down the Ohio to New Orleans - they encounter historic earthquake - popularity of and improved steamboats - Vanderbilt termed Commodore controlling Hudson ferry and freight - Steam Ship Savannah sails and steams across Atlantic - S.S. Enterprise first steamship on the Finger Lakes - S.S. "Independence", "Highland Chief", and "Skaneateles" first steamships to succeed on Skaneateles Lake - after almost a century, steam excursion on the Finger Lakes was scuttled by the S.S. Frontenac fire, autos, and better roads.

CHAPTER 15 209
>the Erie Canal - DeWitt Clinton and political infighting - Geddes blazes canal route - squabble over route - frowned on by Jefferson and Madison - delayed by War of 1812 - war proves inland route to Lake Erie best - NY legislature votes money, dig begins - the first section, Utica to Montezuma - technology and the engineers - engineering features - economic boom ensues even before completion -Montezuma to Lockport - lock technology - Niagara to Lockport - Little Falls to Albany - Champlain Canal completed - Lafayette celebrated - jubilation over canal's completion - travel on the canal - cargos - western expansion - financial success - lateral canals - Province of Ontario builds Welland Canal - expanding the Erie - the Barge Canal - the Weighlock Building and Museum

CHAPTER 16 222
>beginning the B.& O. R.R. - Peter Cooper's "Tom Thumb" - the "Stourbridge Lion" - the "Best Friend of Charleston" - John Stevens' "John Ball" - the "DeWitt Clinton" - scrapped for "John Bull"- John Jervis uses wooden ties and invents bogies - rail improvements - sand for traction - rails cross NY - standard gauge - Erastus Corning and the NY Central - the Erie - rails reach Mississippi R. - cowcatchers - larger, faster locomotives - US Mail - cars by Pullman - coal replaces wood as fuel - telegraph, semaphores, switches - Civil War - Van derbilt's "Water Level Route" - Westinghouse" air brakes - standard cars and time - Robber Barons squabble for Albany line, other robbers - over 100 mph in the Central's "999"

CHAPTER 17 234
>Ebenezer Allen and the 100 Acre Tract - other early Rochester settlers - malaria - Colonel Nathaniel Rochester - canal boom - "Flour City" - bartering, currency, and early banks - nurseries - Rochester's clothing industry and Jewish colony make comfortable fit - Highland Park - Rochester Institute of Technology - the University of Rochester - Brockport College of Arts and Sciences - Flour City becomes Flower City - S.F.B.Morse and the telegraph, Hiram Sibley, and Alaska - the first automobile - Socony Oil and Everett - Bausch and Lomb, Pfaudler, Cutler, and Rochester Lamp - the father of Churchill's mother - Buffalo Bill - Syracuse and salt - Joshua Forman - Syracuse gets named - Salt starts Syracuse - Ochenang, Chenango Canal, Erie RR. boost Binghamton - D.L.& W.R.R. and "Phoebe Snow" - the Lester brothers - Henry Endicott, and George Johnson grows into everyone's shoes - the "Square Deal" - Elkanah Watson and James Le Ray found NY Agricultural Society - the State Fair - Jethro Wood's plow - Remington's rifle - McCormick's reaper - Geneva Experimental Station - Ireland's potato famine - Europe's loss, USA gain - Marcus Whitman, Oregon, the California gold rush, and the "Great Emigration" - the Patriot War - Civil War - Elmira - war's end and Lincoln's funeral cortege - Waterloo's Memorial Day - Taps - the Cardiff Giant - the Solvay Process spoils a lake - Crucible Steel and Camillus Cutlery

CHAPTER 18 258

Both sides in Revolution enlist slaves - Whitney's cotton gin and Borê's sugar granulator - Robert Carter's finding - Constitution limits slave trade - anti-slavery laws - Missouri Compromise - Kansas - Nebraska Act - $ 40,000 to return slave - birth of Republican Party - Nat Turner's insurrection - the Abolitionist's Movement - New York abolishes Slavery - the Underground Railroad - the Fugitive Slave Act - Uncle Tom's Cabin - Dred Scott - Harriet Tubman and Frederick Douglass - the Jerry Rescue - Gerrit Smith - Harpers Ferry - Lincoln elected, South secedes - William Seward - New York City considers secession - the Emancipation Proclamation - Thirteenth amendment

CHAPTER 19 270

education in central New York - state funding early textbooks - Blue Back Speller, Parson Weems, and McGuffey's Eclectic Reader - one room schoolhouse - Normal schools - academies, seminaries - free education - Hartwick, Colgate, and Cazenovia - Ezra Cornell - Land Grant schools - Willard State Asylum - Ithaca College - Lima Genesee genesis for Syracuse U - Genesee College, Cortland, and Oneonta - Elizabeth Blackwell invasive to medicine - Hobart, and Hamilton Colleges - Elmira College - the Reform Movement begins - Elizabeth Cady Stanton and Lucretia Mott - early voting laws - Susan B. Anthony - Amelia Bloomer, publicist - Earnings Bill of 1860 - Mrs. Anthony votes anyway - the opposition - the second generation steps forward - picketing the White House - harassment backfires - New York state votes right to vote - Harry Burns does the right thing - inventions soften inequality - suppressing alcohol brings on Income Tax

CHAPTER 20 285

Corning Glass Works - artisans at work - Charles Flint, company catalyst - Herman Hollerith - Thomas Watson understudies NCR's John Patterson and turns CTR into IBM - Ansco - George Eastman and Kodak - flexible film spools snapshots and movies - Rochester's nurseries grow and subdivide - James Fenimore Cooper's Leatherstocking Tales - Cooperstown - Isaac Singer and the Clarks - Farmers Museum - Baseball Hall of Fame - Rome - Jesse Williams' cheese - Utica and Woolworth's nickels, dimes, and skyscrapers - the Franklin automobile - L.C. Smith - the telegraph begets its competition - Alexander Graham Bell - trolleys and amusement parks - Syracuse streetlights - selling electricity - Crouse Hinds - New Process rawhide - Shubert Alley - Syracuse China - Pass and Seymour - Easy Washer - Dietz Lantern - Grover Cleveland - Elmira canals, the Erie, rails, shoes and fire engines - Elmira College and Mark Twain's Pilot house - Norwich: Bordens, violins, and Unguentine - Oswego power play - Baldwinsville, Port Byron, and Cortland - David Harem - central New York's wine industry - apples, hops, cabbage, rope walks, potatoes, and onions - teasels and Skaneateles - central New York dairies & ice - health spas - Clara Barton - Glen Haven Water Cure - Indoor plumbing - the Roosevelts retire to Skaneateles - legacies for the Twentieth Century.

HISTORICAL MARKERS GUIDE 306

Bibliography 391

MAPS

THE IROQUOIS AND THEIR NEIGHBORS 2

THE SULLIVAN-CLINTON CAMPAIGN 1 90

COLONIAL TRACTS & PATENTS and POST REVOLUTIONARY WAR TRACTS AND INDIAN RESERVATIONS. 127

THE WAR OF 1812 IN NEW YORK. 203

INTRODUCTION

Throughout New York state, as in many states, there are numerous historical markers tucked along the roadsides. The markers note the events of local, state, and national cultural interest that took place there; from sites of early Indian villages, early French, Dutch, and English explorations, French and Indian War campaigns, and Revolutionary War battles and skirmishes, including those relating to the War of 1812. As well, sites of log cabins, early churches, schools, grist and saw mills and other industry, including markers referring to "stations" of the Underground Railroad, and the locale of early social and religious reformers together with persons of cultural, military, and political interest are identified by these signs. The subject matter of the markers had its genesis before the twentieth century and for this reason, this narrative ends with the conclusion of the nineteenth century with a few exceptions.

In the twenty-one counties of central New York with which this book mainly deals, there were over a thousand markers put up beginning in the 1920s and continuing until 1959. Most are still standing and in good condition but road widening, accidents, and vandalism have taken their toll, leaving perhaps nine hundred survivors. The two foot by three foot cast iron signs are almost always fashioned with a dark yellow border and raised lettering set against a field of dark blue, the state colors. They serve in the same way as the headlines of a newspaper, alerting you to the subject, but for details you must read more deeply elsewhere.

Until recent years, there were far fewer cars and traffic moved at a slower pace, permitting drivers to pullover to read the signs. But as cities have spread, highways have been modernized, occasionally leaving no place to reset the markers, and today's stampede of traffic permits little leisurely investigation. These past interludes were fun, and learning what happened years before at celebrated sites about New York State in that manner was not only pleasant and effective, but often prompted more intense investigation. Reading the markers is still rewarding and fun, but much more difficult.

This book attempts to ease that effort and provide the stories behind the markers in chronological narrative form. As these stories unfold, the text of markers pertaining to that text appears. The book is limited to markers in the area from Monroe County south to the Pennsylvania line and east to include Otsego County and the upper Mohawk Valley. This defines most of the area of the Indian-Loyalist attacks on the New York frontier during the Revolution, from devastated Cherry Valley in the east to the rebel reprisals of the Sullivan-Clinton Campaign, culminating at the Indian towns of Newtown and Chennusio in the west. As you will see, many events that happened in adjacent areas were so interesting, that I couldn't resist their inclusion.

The Sullivan campaign, largely planned by George Washington, was the most significant military event in central New York, since it eclipsed the power of the Iroquois Confederacy and permitted the opening of the area to white settlement after the war.

Much of the history which affected central New York took place in such far-flung places as Quebec, Montreal, Louisbourg, Boston, Paris, Pittsburgh, the Niagara frontier, New York, London, Detroit, Philadelphia, Saratoga, and Albany. They are mentioned to put them in context with events which devolved in central New York, and to give continuity and more interest to the narrative.

Some of the story is background for how people lived in the early days of settlement. For example, the log cabin was not only the universal first frontier home in central New York, as elsewhere, but it became a symbol of toil, determination, and community effort to such an extent that presidential candidates for a hundred years laid claim to a humble birth in a log cabin in order to help establish their character. Many of the markers refer to sites of log cabins, tanneries, saw and grist mills, breweries, and shops of blacksmiths, carriage makers, wheelwrights, and gunsmiths, that we realize that people lived close to the people who served them. They knew intimately these artisans and generally how the articles were made. Today, the sales counter is still nearby but where, how it's made, and by whom is remote and obscure.

The nitty gritty of life and death was real and more stark than perceived today. Effective medical care was in its infancy. Those of us who have suffered maladies, accidents, and operations may not have survived in those days of limited and often un-scientific medical treatment. As the lucky heirs of those who suffered as medical practitioners learned, we now take many medical problems in stride.

This is especially true of medical treatment now ministered to the very ill and elderly who, like tender plants brought indoors before a frost, may continue to live for years.

Travel was certainly different: some people on stagecoaches were so fatigued with rough road travel they became sick, and could hardly stand when they stepped back onto terra firma. Compare this to Marshall McLuhan's comment on the current scene: "Travel, for the most part, is no longer travel; it is a process which has a beginning and an end, but virtually no middle. Travel is not an experience so much as a suspension of experience." Rail travel sought easy competition with the stagecoach and the Erie Canal, and central New York gave its name to the New York Central.

The markers noting the siege of Fort Stanwix do not have enough space to tell the story of Marinus Willett's raid on the siege line depleted by those loyalists and Indians who left to ambush Herkimer at Oriskany; or of Benedict Arnold's later ruse that had such an auspicious result there. These tactics so dispirited the loyalists and Indians that they fled St. Leger's stagnant assault and compelled him to abandon his siege which, in turn, helped undermine General Burgoyne's efforts at Saratoga. The victory over Burgoyne and his British Army finally merited official French support to Washington's army and led to the successful conclusion of the Revolution at Yorktown.

The markers cannot tell how obtaining a right-of-way to build a telegraph line by Rochester's native son, Hiram Sibley, led to the purchase of Alaska. Nor can they reveal that the ancient thirty-two pounder cannon, known as "Old Sow", was able to deter the British fleet in its attempt on Sackets Harbor with one of the enemies own cannon balls. (While researching material about the Revolution, I was surprised to read of another "Old Sow", this one an eighteen-pounder serving as a signal gun to warn Washington's men wintering at Morristown of any British sorties from their base on Staten Island). Possibly it was really the same cannon.

Not until the very last did I find support for my long-standing hunch that the term "snake oil", an elixir ballyhooed by traveling pitchmen to have magical medicinal qualities, is a contraction of Seneca oil that seeps from an ancient spring near upstate Cuba, and other regional wells, which the Indians did believe had medicinal value. In putting this book together it was difficult to resist adding such additional material even when I thought I had finished.

As the narrative focuses on a person or event, the appropriate marker, if one was erected, (even if no longer existent), has been inserted. The text of all the markers and their location is contained in the appendix and each of the county's markers are numbered Those marked with an asterisk indicate I could not locate the marker although I did not make the effort to find all of them. But you may find it; hopefully it was missing only because it was in the shop being renovated.

This book would have been much more difficult without the help of Philip L. Lord, Jr., archeologist and head of the State Historical Marker Program, a division of the State Education Department, who kindly advanced some good ideas and made available lists of the markers. The ladies at the Skaneateles Public Library were continually helpful to me and interested in the progress of the project. Nor can I help but be indebted to the authors of those volumes in the bibliography who painstakingly researched the information which I culled for inclusion in this book. I also found it exciting to haunt used bookstores and find volumes, often out of print, that seemed to serendipitously direct the course of my book.

Hank Schramm, a friend and author of a disproportionate number of books in my reading list, with good reason, was kind enough to read the entire manuscript when it was in very rough form, and still encouraged me to continue. My friend Dr. John Ayer, of Skaneateles, checked the section on frontier medicine for accuracy, and Don Sauer, a very civil engineer, also from Skaneateles, provided me with information on the early roads, many of which he modernized and re-paved during his career.

Golfing buddies, Dick Wedlich and Rich Gramsey stayed off the course long enough to read the same rough draft and make corrections of errors that shouldn't have been committed. My sister, the late Margaret Ford Taska, her husband Jarda, and my son William H. Ford, were free with approving comments, as well as critiques, for which I thank them. My wife, Ann Harris Ford, carefully read the work in its entirety, and in addition to keeping me fed and comfortable, spent considerable time and effort showing the "writer" the ways of style and how to write, a term that still seems too elusive and presumptuous for me to use. She also made more pleasant some of the photographic sorties by accompanying me in search of markers. I thank all of those mentioned for their gentle correction without causing me due embarrassment.

There is much more that could be included in this history of the region. It was difficult enough to not keep adding but I had to end the book someplace. For those who wish to know more, I recommend the volumes from which I have mined only a minimum. Local historical societies, such as ours in Skaneateles, have troves of detailed information and, of course, you must see the markers themselves.

Howard S. Ford

Skaneateles, N.Y. February 1, 2002

CHAPTER ONE

BOUNDARY OF INDIAN VILLAGE SITE PRIOR TO IROQUOIS DURING STONE AGE. OCCUPATION ABOUT 1000 A.D. EXCAVATIONS 1932-34 SHOW HEARTHS AND BURIALS

Cayuga County, 85
One mile east of Levanna

Any consideration of central New York history immediately invokes thoughts of the Indians the French called the Iroquois, or the Haudenosaunee (People of the Long House), as they call themselves. At first, the Iroquois League was formed of the Seneca, Cayuga, Onondaga, Oneida, and the Mohawk tribes located for more than four hundred years, in that order, east of the Genesee River and across the Finger Lakes almost to the Hudson River and edging south into present Pennsylvania.

According to the French explorer, Jacques Cartier, they were living along the St. Lawrence River, from the site of Montreal to Quebec, in 1535, when he encountered them. They were gradually pushed south by the more numerous Algonquians, but Canada was their ancestral land when they first formed the League. Some think this confederation took place about 1550; others say it was a hundred years earlier.

Legend has it that when they were warring among themselves, the great Dekanawidah was directed by Heaven to enlist the help of Hiawatha, an Onondaga, to visit the tribes to convince them that they should stop fighting each other and form a union to make them stronger and safe from outside attacks. When the Senecas were approached, they were hesitant to give up their sovereignty since they were a very proud, warlike people, and by far the largest tribe. But as they delayed, a total solar eclipse occurred. Noon skies turned dark as night which to them meant the Great Spirit was displeased with their recalcitrant attitude. They quickly decided to become part of the league after all and from that time the Five Nations of the Iroquois thrived.

Howard S. Ford

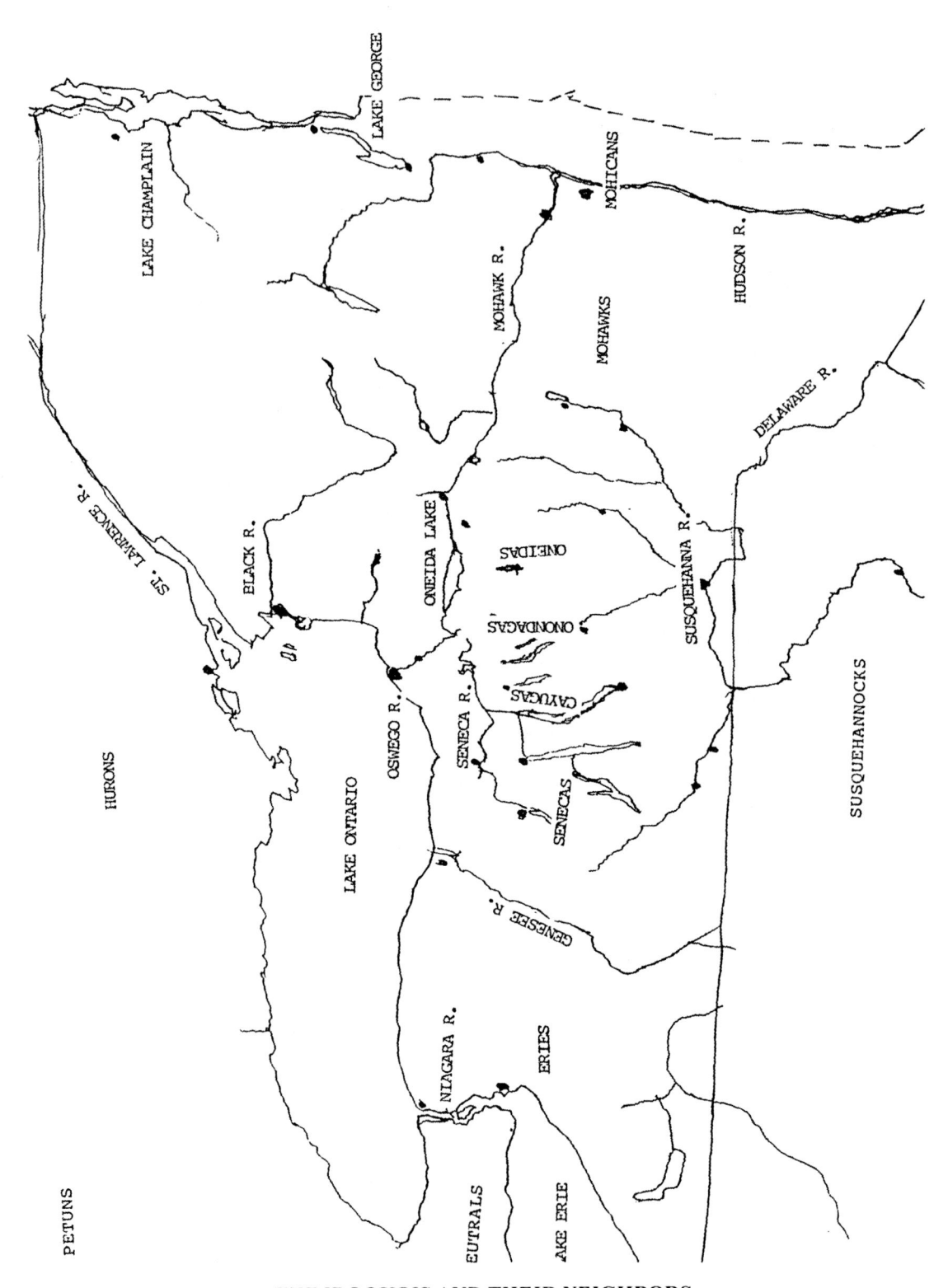

THE IROQUOIS AND THEIR NEIGHBORS

ONONDAGA NATION OF INDIANS SETTLED HEREABOUTS ACCORDING TO TRADITION SEVERAL CENTURIES BEFORE DISCOVERY OF AMERICA BY COLUMBUS, 1492.

Onondaga County, 10 * NY 57, 1 m. S. Three Rivers

Scholars reveal that there was, in fact, a total eclipse of the sun in 1450 placing the time the League formed. In 1715, the Tuscaroras, pressed by whites and the Catawbas, emigrated from the Carolinas and sought to join the League which, in time, was granted but as non-voting members and wards of the Oneidas, their sponsors. They brought with them the Sapony and Tutelos, who settled at the southern end of Cayuga Lake. Later the Stockbridge (the last of the Mohicans) and the Brotherton Indians (remnants of Connecticut, New Jersey, and Long Island tribes) joined, also under the patronage of the Oneidas. The Iroquois were now known as the Six Nations.

Women wielded great influence in this society, and though they were not ordinarily permitted in the men's councils, they nominated the chiefs, and could remove them, even execute them should occasion demand, and descent was matrilineal. The Iroquois had a council of fifty; the number of delegates from each tribe was determined by strength and numbers, and unanimous votes were necessary to go to war, again with the women's sanction, and to enact other important matters.

Families lived communally in long rectangular houses sided with elm bark called longhouses, which was emblematic of their Confederacy. Wide shelves for sleeping and for personal gear were placed one foot above the bare ground and five feet higher on the inside walls. In the early days, chimneys were unknown to them and smoke from the many fires had to find its way out, eventually, through small holes made for its exit in the roof. The inhabitant families, more often than not related, usually consisted of wife and husband, the wife's mother, un-married children, and daughters and their husbands, if the men were present. Confederacy and tribal bonds were strengthened by clans, whose totems such as the turtle, bear, wolf, deer, snipe, heron, etc., were carved, brightly painted, and placed on the long-house beckoning travelers of like lineage that they were welcome.

Women tilled the fields owned in common by the tribe and maintained village affairs, the men often being gone on extended hunting or fishing excursions or war forays. Men scorned work and prided themselves on their skills at hunting, fishing, and, particularly, making war. The Iroquois were the scourge of the northeast, making war on tribes from Maine to the Mississippi, from Hudson's Bay to the Carolinas.

Though the Iroquois were ferocious and could be fiendishly cruel to their enemies, a French Jesuit priest who was familiar with them in the mid-seventeenth century wrote, "no poorhouses are needed among them, because they are neither mendicants or paupers...Their kindness, humanity, and courtesy not only makes them liberal with what they have, but causes them to possess hardly anything except in common." Mons. De la Poterie spoke for them in his **History of North America**, viz. "When one talks of the Five Nations in France, they are thought, by a common mistake, to be mere Barbarians, always thirsting after human blood; but their true character is very different; they are the fiercest and most formidable people in North America, and at the same time as politic and judicious as well can be conceived. This appears from their management of the affairs which they transact, not only with the French and the English, but likewise with almost all the Indian Nations of this vast continent."

Children were taught to be independent and to not be intimidated by overbearing authority. They learned their cultural heritage and the importance of loyalty to the tribe and the confederacy. Boundaries of acceptable behavior were firmly understood without the necessity of harsh discipline, written laws, sheriffs, police, judges, and lawyers. They had a sense of right and wrong and violators were shamed, or ostracized until they could prove a willingness to abide by the tribe's standards.

The Senecas were the Keepers of the Western Door, the Mohawks Keepers of the Eastern Door, and the centrally located Onondagas, Keepers of the Council Fires and Medicine Bundles. In the early 1600s, the Iroquois were thought to number 5,500, but by the end of the century, because of adoptions of prisoners of war to offset attrition from war and disease, population increased to about 16,000.

SITE OF ANCIENT INDIAN FORT IN 1791 EARLY SETTLERS FOUND EVIDENCE OF THIS FORT HAVING BEEN IN USE FOR MANY YEARS

Chenango County, 38
Park in front of Oxford High School

The Iroquois were in a position of great power because of their organization, intelligence, bravery, audacity, and statecraft and their strategic location. The Mohawks, called Maquas by the Dutch, controlled the portages north to Lake George, Champlain and the St. Lawrence. With the Oneidas and Onondagas, they also controlled the route to Lake Ontario and the west from the Mohawk River via the Great Carrying Place (at present Rome) and the Oneida and Oswego Rivers; or from Onondaga Lake via the Oswego River. They had access to the south via the Hudson and by portaging from the Mohawk to Lake Otsego, the source of the Susquehanna, on to Chesapeake Bay.

The Senecas controlled Lakes Ontario and Erie through Irondequoit Bay and the Niagara River, and southwest via the portage from Lake Erie to Lake Chautauqua, down its outlet to the Conewango, joining the Allegheny River and south to the forks of the Ohio River. To the Iroquois, the Ohio included the Mississippi and the Allegheny. With the Cayuga the Seneca also had easy access to the Susquehanna by way of the Cohocton and Chemung Rivers and other tributaries.

NEAR THIS SPOT SAMUEL DE CHAMPLAIN ON OCTOBER 9, 1615 CROSSED THE RIVER AND DISCOVERED ONEIDA LAKE

Oswego County, 8
US 11 at Brewerton

In 1604, Samuel de Champlain sailed to the New World with the blessing of Henry IV and the more tangible backing of the Company for New France. Despite his reconnoitering the St. Lawrence River the year before, he made his first settlement on an island in the St. Croix river which feeds Passamaquoddy Bay, just east of present Maine. After suffering two harsh winters there, he sailed south close inshore along the New England coast to Cape Cod and repeated this search for a better location the following year, but the natives were restless and killed five of his men. Moving his small settlement to Port Royal did not prove successful either. So, in 1608, he sailed up the St. Lawrence to a narrow plain sheltered by a one hundred sixty-five foot bluff, which the Indians had called Stadacona but which he called Quebec.

Champlain's neighboring Indians were the Hurons whom he befriended. They were distant cousins of the Iroquois but had been natural enemies of these respected, but aggressive and feared people for uncounted years. The Huron, impressed by the French guns, wanted this firepower on their side, and persuaded Champlain to accompany them on a raid against the Mohawks in 1609. They clashed near where Fort Ticonderoga was later built, several Mohawk chiefs were killed by the guns, and the enmity between the French and the Iroquois began.

In 1615, Champlain, upon hearing from the Hurons of large seas to the west, made his greatest exploration. With the direction of his Indian guides, he labored his way up the Ottawa River to Lake Nippissing, and went down the French River to the great expanses of Georgian Bay and Lake Huron. Rather than return by way of Lakes Erie and Ontario, he took the short cut and went cross country via Lake Simcoe and a series of lakes which brought him to the Trent River and the Bay of Quinte at the foot of Lake Ontario. There a large congregation of Hurons persuaded him in making mischief with their enemies before returning to Quebec.

To further this project, he commissioned his Lieutenant Etienne Brulé to go into the country of the Susquehannochs at Carantouan (Waverly) to induce them to join the French in a raid on the Onondagas at Nichols Pond near the site of Cazenovia (some argue the raid was near Onondaga Lake). The Indians entertained Brulé, and agreed to join in the raid, but by the time the revelry wound down and they arrived at the Onondaga siege, the French had already given up their attack

Sure Signs: Stories Behind the Historical Markers of Central New York

and retired carrying Champlain, who had been wounded by two arrows, to Salmon River and Quebec.

CARANTOUAN
SPANISH HILL, 650 FT. SOUTH
WHERE ETIENNE BRULE, SCOUT
OF CHAMPLAIN CAME IN 1615.
THE FIRST WHITE EXPLORER
KNOWN TO REACH THIS REGION

Tioga County, 5
NY 17, west end of Waverly

His injuries prevented Champlain from making any more far-ranging explorations. In his stead, he again sent out Brulé, who ranged even farther and became the first white man to travel the Susquehanna River to its mouth. Champlain died Christmas day, 1635, having firmly established the colony despite the alienation of the Iroquois that was to plague Canada for so long.

SITE OF
CHAMPLAIN BATTLE
HERE CHAMPLAIN AIDED BY
HURON INDIANS ATTACKED THE
STOCKADED ONEIDA VILLAGE
OCT. 10-16, 1615

Madison County, 21*
Strip Road, 6 M. S of Canastota

The beaver hat was a fashion and mark of attainment in Europe. The main ingredient was available in every stream a Frenchman or an Indian might chance upon. Other furs such as martin, otter, and mink would serve, but beaver fur compacted better to make a more lustrous felt. The important thing about beaver was that men would go great distances to trap it, or trade with the

Indians for the pelts, learning in the process the rivers, plains, and mountains of a vast, intriguing continent, and the culture of its native people. Europeans were interested in furs, and both Iroquois and Huron were attentive to supply them in return for European-made tomahawks, kettles, knives, mirrors, beads, blankets, and a host of other products, particularly the musket.

After its own needs were met, each tribe wished to be the middleman in supplying tribes farther west. Distant tribes were usually in ferment and those armed with muskets found themselves with enormous advantage over their adversaries not yet in contact with white traders, sending disruptive turmoil deep into the continent.

Competition was fierce, and the Iroquois made war on their main rival, the Hurons, in the 1640s. They raided all the way to Georgian Bay and killed many, including the resident French Jesuit missionaries, Father Jean de Brébeuf and Father Gabriel Lalemant, both of whom died most cruelly. The surviving Hurons who were not taken back to the Iroquois towns to be either tortured or adopted into the tribe fled. Father Chaumonot, who worked with the unfortunate priests, escaped the destruction but led four hundred Hurons to a reservation that was set aside for them on the Île d'Orléans at Quebec. The Hurons were no longer a nation, and the survivors, who didn't join other tribes, fled to the Ohio valley and became known as the Wyandots.

The Iroquois, with genocidal frenzy, destroyed the Petuns, or Tobacco Nation, who lived southwest of Georgian Bay, and the next year, they decimated the Neutrals along the northern shore of Lake Erie. Both of these tribes were friendly to the Hurons and had given food and shelter to the survivors, provoking the Iroquois. The Eries, who lived west of the Genesee River and along the south shore of Lake Erie, also gave refuge to the surviving Hurons and were wiped out for their pains.

This grisly activity extended the Iroquois' range to include present western New York, and parts of Ontario, Pennsylvania and Ohio. In 1675, the Iroquois defeated the Andastes (the Susquehannocks) and Lenni Lenapes (the Delawares) tribes located in Pennsylvania and New Jersey, and began deriving tribute from them, still making the usual forays against Montreal and Quebec.

Sure Signs: Stories Behind the Historical Markers of Central New York

The Europeans viewed the Indians as very superstitious; it was their way of life. Every tree, rock, and animal had a spirit that the Indians believed could cause harm to them if not appeased in some way. In the opinion of the French Jesuits and Franciscans, they were ripe for the conversion of their souls to the Faith, and so the Black Robes, so called by the Indians, sought to Christianize all the tribes in New France which, to them, included the region now known as central New York.

These spiritually fervent and determined men went into the wilderness to bring the story of the Catholic faith to the "wild" men. Progress was slow and the converts did not always understand the theology, but because of gifts and patient kindness, Indians gathered at the missions. The priests tended the sick, and gave the last rites when their care was to no avail. These rituals caused the Indians to think the priests were the cause of death, and indeed, they may have been right since the Indians had little immunity to the white man's diseases. As a result, the Jesuits were at times subject to insult or worse, including extreme torture, as in the case of Fathers Francesco Bressani and Isaac Jogues. Both of them endured the worst that fire and mutilation can do to body and soul, yet both were so devoted, that even when they were rescued and returned to France, each again sought out their missions with the Indians, only to be martyred by them. Records of activities in New France were kept by the Jesuits in annual reports from 1632 to 1673. Much that we know of the region and the Indians is due to these **Jesuit Relations**, which when collected and published, came to seventy-three volumes.

The missionaries were on their own at the tribal villages but frequently they coexisted with a trading post or fort, and rivalry with the traders and the garrison caused resentment. Selling alcohol to the Indians was a sore point, as was the way of life adopted by the coureurs de bois (fur trade woods runners), who became indistinguishable from the Indians in manner and dress. The priests were intrepid explorers as well, and went everywhere the coureurs de bois went, and beyond at times.

The first missionary in western New York was Franciscan Father Joseph de la Roche Dallion, who set up his mission in the land of the Neutrals (near Lewiston) in 1626. The Seneca Indians showed him a spring near present Cuba, gushing an oil they thought had medicinal powers. This

Howard S. Ford

Seneca Oil was the first petroleum discovered in the New World, and much later, proved to be of the highest lubricating quality.

INDIAN HILL
WAS THE HOME OF THE ONONDAGA
INDIANS. LARGE POPULATION
LIVED HERE IN 1655

Onondaga County 66
town rd. at Indian Hill, SW of Oran

The first white settlement in central New York was by the invitation of the Onondagas, in 1654, of Father Simon Le Moyne. The following year, Fathers Dablon and Chaumonot came to the main Onondaga village, then located on a hill between the forks of Limestone Creek two miles south of present Manlius. They were shown the thriving area and taken to a spring thought by the Indians to be fouled by demons because of the salty taste. The Fathers found the spring attractive and erected their fort and Mission to St. Marie nearby on the eastern shore of Ganenntaa (Onondaga Lake).

FIRST MASS
IN NEW YORK STATE
WAS OFFERED ABOUT 300 FT. NORTH
OF THIS MARKER BY REV. J.M.
CHAUMONT, 1655, IN BARK CHAPEL

Onondaga County 64
Indian Hill on town rd. SW. of Oran

Encouraged, the French brought in additional people in 1656: five Jesuit Fathers under Father Ragueneau, ten soldiers under Zachary du Puys, and forty artisans and farmers. Included was Pierre Esprit Radisson, who had already been a captive of the Mohawks, and adopted by them. He had escaped, was recaptured and tortured, but escaped again, and now accompanied this mission

Sure Signs: Stories Behind the Historical Markers of Central New York

to the Onondagas. Later Radisson and his brother-in-law, Groseilliers, pursued the fur trade and explored all the way to Hudson's Bay. Their idea of building trading posts on Hudson' Bay, rejected by the French, was readily adopted by the English and gave birth to the Hudson's Bay Company.

INDIAN MOUND
JUST EAST OF HERE
KNOWN TO BE THE SITE OF
AN EARLY JESUIT MISSION

Cayuga County, 148
On Sesquicentennial Monument
lot, NY 90

The Jesuits were happy for the opportunity to spiritually influence the Iroquois. Father Chaumonot proceeded to the eastern shore of Cayuga Lake to start a mission there with Father René Menard presiding, while he went on to the Senecas to found another mission, and the following year to the Oneidas (Munnsville). Despite this diplomacy, there was much raiding back and forth between the French and the Iroquois who were interested in capturing any remaining Hurons from the French for slaves and torture victims. When the French in Montreal captured twelve Iroquois as hostages, it put a damper on depredations for a time, and probably saved the mission at Onondaga from being wiped out that winter. The French at the mission did not know how precarious their situation was until nearby captive Christian Hurons told them of the treacherous plans the Onondagas had in store for them.

The Indian's plan from the beginning was to invite the French to open a mission which they thought would lure refugee Christian Hurons from Montreal. They reasoned all could then be massacred in a big melee. The French taking of the Indian hostages had postponed this event. A new plan developed by the Iroquois (and confirmed by a converted Onondaga) was to capture Frenchmen and torture them in front of the walls at Montreal to gain release of the twelve hostages.

The small band of Frenchmen at Onondaga coolly formed an escape plan: to supplement four small canoes, they would build in secret two batteaux (in the fort's garret), each capable of carrying fifteen people and supplies. Essential to the plan was a scheme to exploit one of the Indians' more curious customs in order to divert and diminish their attention. This was the eat-all-feast at which guests were supposed to ingest everything served up to them, no matter how satiated they were, even to the point of nausea. This odd hospitality was for the purpose of deflecting dream demons from causing illness or some other adversity. The dictates of dreams could not be refused since they influenced much of Indian life.

On one occasion, an Indian dreamed of suffering a terrible death unless he and his group swam in a frozen river. They dove through a hole in the ice and hoped for an opening to escape downstream, but only a few survived. Now, a young captive Frenchman was told by the Jesuits to inform his Onondaga foster father that his dream doomed him to die unless the Onondagas gave such a feast, and a date was set for March twentieth.

The Indians accepted this dinner invitation, anticipating the gluttony they would enjoy, and the French garnered all the food they had for the day-long banquet and to supply their escape to Montreal. Gayly dressed Indians from neighboring villages came to join the fun and gorge themselves on food and drink, and to save the adopted young Frenchman. When guests protested further food offerings, the young man stressed that extreme indulgence was essential to save him. So the Indians ate on in discomfort, even though they were set on all the Frenchmen's later demise anyway.

More and more kettles of food were brought out of the fort accompanied by much noisy celebration. The comings and goings of many Frenchmen provided cover in the dusk for moving the loaded canoes and batteaux out to the beach. By midnight, overindulgence had climaxed to a comatose stillness, and all was ready. The Frenchmen closed the gates of the fort and shoved off onto the lake, breaking thru thin ice as they went until they reached open water, and then paddled furiously down to the outlet into the Onondaga River. They are said to have camped on an island (near Phoenix), and lightened their load by caching gold and cannon there.

As the hangovers from the excesses of the feast diminished, most of the Indians departed for their villages and resumed their usual business. Several days passed before the departure of the French was noticed.

Sure Signs: Stories Behind the Historical Markers of Central New York

TREASURE ISLAND
FRENCH COLONISTS CAMPED ON WEST ISLAND IN ESCAPING FROM ONONDAGA INDIANS IN 1658. SAID TO HAVE LIGHTENED THEIR WAR CHESTS AND DEPOSITED CANNON AND GOLD HERE

Oswego County, 21
NY 57 at Phoenix

Two weeks later, after almost constant paddling down the river and across Lake Ontario to the Saint Lawrence, all but three of the fifty-three French survived to reach Montreal. So ended the first mission to Onondaga. But an influential Onondaga sachem, Garakonti, had been impressed by Father Le Moyne and the Gospel, and three years later, Le Moyne happily accepted a return invitation.

A little over a month after Champlain had his fight with the Mohawks at Ticonderoga, Henry Hudson sailed his ship Half Moon up the river, later named for him, on behalf of the Dutch who had directed him to find a northwest passage to the Orient. During the pleasant month of September, Hudson tacked his way up river by wind and tide and got as far as the site of present Albany, whereupon he sent out men in small boats who reported back that there were rapids a few miles north. To Hudson, this clearly was not a path to the northwest passage and they turned south with the tide.

The Dutch traded with the Mohicans, who at that time claimed the area and were receptive, in contrast to the Wappingers, the Raritans, and other tribes whom Hudson had found on his upstream voyage. They had been at first friendly and curious when he entertained them in his cabin with wine, but had become light-fingered and unruly which brought about fatal clashes. Now, blocked by rapids, and trading over, Hudson turned around and sailed back down on the tide to the ocean to continue his quest.

Imagine what it must have been like sailing in past Sandy Hook, up the Narrows, and to have seen Manhattan Island in its virginal state; then continuing north, with the palisades bordering the river looming 300 to 500 feet high to the west and the river spreading out to form the majestic Tappan Zee before it narrows past Stony Point. Farther on, the Catskills rise 4,000 feet in the western distance, and the Taconics, not quite as high, are beautiful on the sunrise side of the river. Unsullied, this expanse was covered with magnificent stands of maple, native chestnut, pine, spruce, oak, and virgin forest as far as the eye could see, a fecund and primitive loveliness.

Europe had squandered its forests to the extent that, at the time of the Spanish Armada only twenty years before, both England and Spain had to go as far as the Baltic to obtain the timber to build their fleets.

When Hudson returned to Europe, his backers were disappointed that a quick and easy route to China hadn't materialized. But they were enthralled that beaver and other pelts could be bought cheaply for a few trade goods from a people still living in a stone-age economy.

Within twelve months, five ships a year were sailing the Atlantic to satisfy the market for goods the Indians could either not make themselves, or as cheaply, such as iron pots, or wampum beads that the Dutch learned to make in quantity. By 1613, a few shacks were built on Manhattan Island, and a year later, a small fort called Fort Nassau was built on Castle Island on the upper Hudson. Within four years this outpost was washed away by floods, but, in 1624, the Dutch West India Company, which had been granted a trading monopoly by the Dutch government, built another and more substantial post near the site of Albany and called it Fort Orange.

Soon Dutch traders reached out to the Mohawks a short distance to the west. The earliest we know of was a Kleynties who with two others ventured up the Mohawk visiting the Mohawk castles (palisaded towns), as far as Canajoharie. From there, they cut south to Lake Otsego, and followed its outlet, the Susquehanna River, downstream to the Wyoming Valley. They then turned east to the upper Delaware, were captured by Indians, and spent the winter in the Catskills before being ransomed in 1616.

In 1634, Harmen Myndertsen van den Bogaert went up the Mohawk to open trade with the Oneidas and Onondagas southeast of Oneida Lake. The Dutch had now been trading muskets to the Mohawks for twenty beaver pelts each, and the Iroquois thus armed, became an even more formidable enemy to the French. It is estimated that they had about three hundred muskets by 1643, which is about the time they began to use them against the Hurons, the competing middlemen in the fur trade. The English later succeeded to this profitable trading "agreement", which not only made lots of money but armed the Iroquois making them an invincible force to have on your side.

The Dutch attempted to do some colonizing and fort building in the Delaware Valley and in Connecticut but without much lasting success. (Some say Jersey mosquitoes vanquished one Dutch garrison). Still, the cape at the southern end of New Jersey was named after Cornelius May, and Adrian Block left his name on an island off the eastern end of Long Island. Of more consequence, the Dutch are said to have paid the equivalent of twenty-four dollars for Manhattan Island, but historians are not sure to whom. It was certainly to a band of Indians, but whether they were the previous residents, the Manahatta, or the Canarsies, or merely a group passing through on their way to the fishing grounds off Long Island is anybody's guess.

The Swedes also founded a colony centered around the site of present Chester, Pennsylvania in 1638, and appointed as the first governor Peter Minuit, who when in the earlier employ of the Dutch, had purchased Manhattan from the Indians. But the Swedish colony was taken over by the Dutch after seventeen years.

The colony of New Amsterdam at Manhattan was required by the Dutch West India Company to maintain at least twenty warships for defense. Behind this policy was also the idea of staging raids on Spanish commercial shipping. In 1623, twenty-six Dutch warships under Piet Heyn set out for and captured San Salvador, capital of Brazil. This was so profitable, that three years later they again went south and sank twenty-six more ships, capturing all but a few of the merchant fleet that had been convoyed. In 1628, this same company squadron, again under Piet Heyn, set forth once more and captured another Spanish merchant fleet and the annual Silver Fleet, all of which brought in booty of about sixty million dollars.

In 1629, the West India Company, disappointed with the small number of people staying to farm and trade at the colony, created the patroon system, a method to spur settlement of New Netherland at little cost to itself. The system improved the personal fortunes of some of the directors enormously by granting them large and favorable tracts of land if the necessary number of tenants (fifty) was obtained within four years.

Two patroonships were granted on the North River (the Hudson), two on the Connecticut River, and two on the South River (the Delaware). The patroons were given grants of sixteen miles of river frontage eight miles deep or more. After six years, the only surviving patroonship centered on Fort Orange (Albany), and belonged to Kiliaen Van Rensselaer, an Amsterdam diamond merchant who had agents buy his land from the Mohicans (he never crossed the Atlantic). He soon expanded the tract to both sides of the river and to the now Massachusetts line, developing a seven hundred and fifty square mile dynasty which he called Rensselaerswyck.

The Rensselaer family was able to attract immigrants to work the land, but the standard lease terms became oppressive; the hard work the lifetime tenants put into improvements reverted to the patroon and little improved the tenant's lot or that of their heirs. Indeed, the rent to the heirs was increased because of the property's increase in value. Of course, the tenants were forced to buy their supplies at the patroon's store, and have their grain ground at his mill; violators were evicted.

An early governor of New Amsterdam, William Kieft, launched an Indian war that was as brutal on the part of the Dutch as by the Indians, perhaps more. He crossed the Narrows to Staten Island and massacred eighty Indians and later made a village raid in present Westchester county killing 500 more. When he received complaints from bounty hunters that severed heads were too cumbersome to redeem, he substituted scalps to qualify for the bounty. He was replaced in 1647 by vile-tempered Peter Stuyvesant, a peg-legged domineering autocratic veteran of South American wars, who ended the carnage and governed so that Dutch-Indian friction was kept to a minimum.

The white population of the colony, including the Jersey side of the harbor, in 1654 was about two thousand, most of them on Manhattan. Even then, it was a cosmopolitan mix from all nations, creeds, and backgrounds, high and low. In the city of New Amsterdam one in four houses was a tavern, the streets were mere dirt paths, and cows and goats grazed the weeds on the small parade ground inside the fort's parapet. The ten-man garrison may have felt doubly secure from Indian attack behind the palisade across the island from the North to the East River where Wall Street is now.

In 1664, the English, who had been distracted by their own Civil War and the troubles under Oliver Cromwell, decided that territory between their settlements in New England and Virginia should not be intruded upon by the Dutch at New Amsterdam. So Colonel Richard Nicholls sailed into the harbor with four warships and suggested to Peter Stuyvesant, that the Dutch surrender. This was agreeable to the general populace but not to Stuyvesant who was for resisting. The good burghers pointed out to him the sad state of their fortifications, which the Dutch West India Company had been too penurious to improve, and argued that to resist would only postpone the inevitable. They prevailed upon him to surrender which, after a week of dickering, he finally did.

No shots were fired; the colony of New Netherland, from the Connecticut River to the Delaware, was turned over to the English intact (New York's governors governed New Jersey until 1738). It was a smooth transition, with taxes reduced and property rights retained by the Dutch. King Charles II magnanimously gave the new province to his brother, James, Duke of York and Albany, who later became King James II. Within a month, the canny British had made a treaty with the Iroquois at Albany.

Colonel Nicholls was appointed governor for four years and drew up the Duke's Laws, which were acceptable to the duke in England, since they did not allow representative government. Nicholls was liked, even by the Indians, in contrast to some Dutch governors, who had many a serious Indian war, often over no more important problems than farm animals straying into Indian territory where they were shot as fair game. Nicholls also started a race course at Hempstead, and being an afficionado of the sport, contributed a cup for which races are still held.

He was succeeded in 1668 by Francis Lovelace, who, to his mortification, was out of town seeing to the readying of the first Boston-New York post road when a Dutch fleet sailed into New York harbor in August of 1673, and recaptured the fort there as easily as the English had nine years earlier. The new Dutch governor, Anthony Colve, rebuilt the city's fortifications the following year, and armed the walls with 190 cannon to protect by land and sea.

Because of the Treaty of Westminster between the English and the Dutch the next year, the province reverted to the English, and in 1674, Major Edmund Andros became the new Governor. He realized early in his administration how important a close alliance with the Iroquois was for the

Howard S. Ford

defense of New York, and that he, as the representative of the King of England, should encourage the Indians to rely upon him as the source of support and supplies.

As lands were granted, favorites under the English became manor landlords, notably the Livingstons, the Jays, Philipses, Van Cortlandts, De Lanceys, Beekmans, Schuylers, Morrises, Verplancks, Ten Broecks, and the Hardenberghs. These families tended to intermarry, concentrating wealth and political power even more. Tenant resentment of their hapless conditions periodically broke out in uprisings along the Hudson, but the feudal system survived the English takeover, even the promises of the American Revolution, and the odious conditions were not relieved until the 1840s.

In 1675, the Iroquois were uneasy; increased Jesuit activity in their area had resulted in more and more of the tribe being converted and emigrating to Canada. Almost half the Mohawks were lured away to the Caughnawaga's camp across the river from Montreal. The Caughnawaga Mohawks or "praying Indians", became so numerous due to the blandishments of the Jesuits in the last half of the seventeenth century that a group called the St. Regis split off and formed a village up river seventy miles.

TOTIAKTON
SENECA TOWN OF 120 CABINS
WAS LOCATED HERE
BURNED BY DENONVILLE, 1687
JESUIT MISSION, 1668-1683

Monroe County, 10
East side Plain Road, South
Of Rochester Junction

In the west, Father Fremin had established La Conception mission (Rochester Junction) among the Senecas in 1668. The mission of St. Jean was established nearby (Lima), St. Michaels (East Bloomfield), and St. Jacques at present Boughton Hill, all within five years. Moreover, the Mohawks were still smarting from a French expedition in 1666 which wiped out five of their towns. This demonstration of force persuaded numerous Indians to consider peaceful living under the Cross.

This Canadian emigration also had the effect of taking fur trade business away from Albany, so it was necessary to create a compelling reason for the Iroquois to rely on the English, particularly the province of New York. Governor Andros soon made a point of traveling upriver deep into Iroquois country to have a conference at one of the upper Mohawk Valley towns. Mohawks, Oneidas, Onondagas, Cayugas, and Senecas were there, and the ceremonies consisted of the usual agenda of exchanging presents, solemn speeches accompanied by the deliverance of wampum belts for emphasis (and for the record), and the ceremonial smoking of the polished redstone calumet.

Andros accomplished his objective better than he knew, for except for isolated instances such as the Seneca's brief defection during Pontiac's rebellion and the Oneida's to the rebels in the Revolution, the Iroquois were loyal allies, as it suited them, with the British for one hundred years. To emphasize the importance of good Iroquois relations, Andros also created a Board of Commissioners of Indian Affairs.

He appointed Robert Livingston, a young Scot reared in Holland, as his first Secretary of Indian Affairs. Livingston, formerly secretary to Rensselaerswyck, quickly learned the intricacies of the Confederacy and the trade. His marriage to Alida Schuyler, widow of his employer, helped secure his position which enabled him to amass great wealth. He remained Secretary of Indian Affairs for over forty years.

In 1700, at a conference at Onondaga Castle, he suggested the strategic importance of a fort at the mouth of the Oswego River to counter the French in their commercial and military activities. A trading post was established there in 1722 soon followed by the first Fort Oswego in 1727, which proved to be an important bastion for the colony over the next century in the wars with the French, the Indians, and the British.

His last conference with the Iroquois was at Onondaga in 1721 when he was almost seventy years old. Livingston understood the strategic necessity of the Iroquois alliance to "keep bright the friendship chain". Because of his knowledge of the Indians and trade with them, he made a fortune

Howard S. Ford

and acquired over time 160,000 acres in Dutchess and Columbia counties, collectively known as Livingston Manor.

Livingston created a family of generations of prominent statesmen, jurists, and diplomats. His great grandson, another Robert R., was a member of Thomas Jefferson's committee that drafted the Declaration of Independence, and of the peace commission ending the Revolution. He also negotiated the Louisiana Purchase and later financed Robert Fulton and the development of the first successful commercial steamboat, the Clermont (named after the family home). Others in the family promoted the formation of King's College, later re-named Columbia University; one was an original trustee of what became Princeton; one was an aide-de-camp to General Andrew Jackson, and another was a Justice of the United States Supreme Court.

CHAPTER TWO

Charles II of England, in 1682, reluctantly paid William Penn a long overdue debt owed his late father, Admiral William Penn, who had gained renown defeating the Dutch navy in 1665 as well as gaining the island of Jamaica for the realm. In lieu of the ƒ16,000, Charles granted Penn a proprietary colony, consisting of lands extending west of the Delaware River from the fortieth parallel north to the forty-third, and named it Pennsylvania in honor of his father. This conflicted with New York's southern boundary since most of the Mohawk Valley and all the Finger Lakes would have been in Pennsylvania. Not until 1789 was the New York-Pennsylvania boundary settled at 42° North. (Pennsylvania's southern boundary with Maryland came to be finally settled in 1769 when the Mason-Dixon survey line, named after the surveyors, was finished).

Penn was a hands-on owner, unique among large land owners, since he left England in 1682 to visit his vast possessions for several years and began immediately planning for the colony's settlement and platting the layout of Philadelphia. For six years, Penn had been one of the twelve proprietors, mostly Quakers, of West Jersey across the Delaware before coming into possession of Pennsylvania. His Quaker philosophy reflected on the colony in that he bought land fairly from the Lenni-Lenapi or Delaware Indians (named after the Delaware River, in turn named after Lord De La Warr, first royal governor of Virginia), rather than acquiring it through sharp dealing, and while he lived (to 1718), the Indians were treated decently.

As his father had been, William Penn was on excellent terms with Charles II and his brother, the Duke of York. Nevertheless, fifteen years earlier in 1665, when he had become a Quaker, he wrote about religious toleration and other liberal doctrine for which he twice spent time in the Tower of London. He now wished to put his beliefs in practice. He gave Pennsylvania a government democratic for the times and based on justice, charity, freedom of religion, and trial by jury, with the people having self rule.

Penn also believed that the use of force did not settle international or domestic problems, that criminals should be reformed, and that treason and murder were the only reasons for executing them. Rather than severe penalties, punishment was lenient, designed to prevent crimes and to rehabilitate the prisoner: it worked, serious crime was at a minimum. These conventions, largely unpracticed in Europe and some colonies, attracted many Quakers and others interested in liberal and fair government.

He also wanted to purchase land from the Iroquois, who by now dominated the region of the Susquehanna. Part of his idea was to deflect the Great Lakes fur trade from Albany to his colony, via the Susquehanna and its northern tributaries. The Albany merchants were much relieved when, after plying the chiefs with greater than normal gifts, they heard that the Iroquois would not sell all the land Penn wanted, but would honor their commitment in their deed to the Duke of York.

As the English took over from the Dutch, Louis XIV had been taking renewed interest in New France. To build forts and protect the farmers in their fields, and subdue the Iroquois, he promised to send the Carignan Salières, a crack regiment of 1300 veteran soldiers. And in order to make the colony pay for itself, the king sent Jean Talon, a friend of his financial minister, Jean Colbert, as Intendant under Governor Tracy, to spruce up Quebec's economy. Talon fostered immigration and immediately showed good sense in correcting a severe shortage of women by arranging for a contingent of French women, "daughters of the king", to be shipped over and let nature take its course. He also founded a brewery, a tannery, cleared more land for settlement, brought in horses, and encouraged ship building. The population, which had been slightly over 3200 (two-thirds of them men) when he arrived in 1666, doubled in the six years of his administration. In 1666, the French, with 1700 men, subdued several Mohawk strongholds, and peace and the establishment of missions followed. The King decided Talon's talents should not be wasted on Canada and promoted him to be valet of the king's wardrobe and recalled him to Paris.

The new governor of New France, Louis de Baude Comte de Frontenac, arrived on the scene in the fall of 1671, and to gain favor with the Indians and a competitive edge in the fur trade, invited the Iroquois to attend an important meeting to be held at Cataraqui, at the outlet of Lake Ontario. Frontenac and his entourage left Quebec in early June and traveled in state up the St. Lawrence in two gaudily painted armed barges, each rowed by sixteen men. This cavalcade, convoyed by sixty canoes, dazzled the habitants of New France which then amounted to about 6,000, most of whom farmed on the river banks between Quebec and the newer village of Montreal.

The Indians were anxious to size up the new governor of Canada and to view the spectacle he had prepared for them. But he kept them waiting, taking more than six weeks to arrive from Quebec as he examined the colony's people and problems and to make his debut before the Indians as grand as possible. Finally, he appeared in resplendent cavalier uniform amid flourishes and thrumming drums one early morning, his troops mustered in two lines forming a colorful gauntlet all the way to the Indian encampment. Unlike the Indian gauntlet lines of a thrashing mob between which white captives were forced to run for their lives, the sixty chiefs were respectfully escorted to Frontenac's tent flanked by guards in full dress uniform on both sides, and the ceremony began. The gauntlet similarity was not wasted on the chiefs.

Frontenac's strong voice conveyed to them an avuncular manner, and he spoke of peace. But he also implied that the brunt of French power would be brought to bear if he was irritated. As Frontenac spoke, his military engineer had men working on the new palisaded fort which went up rapidly. In two weeks, the fort was practically completed, reinforcing the new governor's message to the Iroquois chiefs. The fort was not for military purposes, he insisted, but was to serve as a trading post, and to save the Indians from having to go all the way to Montreal with their furs.

The Iroquois chiefs agreed to peace, even with their customary enemies, the Hurons and Algonquins, and kept the peace for Frontenac's ten-year first term as governor. Though new to Canada, Frontenac had gauged well the Indian appetite for pomp and ceremony. Frontenac later complimented himself when writing Colbert "that if the principal chiefs had not been gained by his flatteries and presents, not a single Frenchman would have been left in Canada." He also gained the enmity of the fur trading establishment by eclipsing their location at Montreal with the new fort at what is now called Kingston. This quarrel with his French competitors in the trade was to plague Frontenac for the rest of his term, and to hamper the explorer and trader, La Salle, by reason of the governor's friendship.

Under Frontenac's direction, Louis Joliet, a young experienced woodsman, and Father Jacques Marquette were encouraged to explore farther west. Guided by Indians familiar with the Mississippi valley, they headed into Green Bay, on Lake Michigan's west shore to ascend the Fox River past Lake Winnebago. At a certain trail, they carried their canoes and supplies a mile around swampy ground (at present Portage) to the Wisconsin River and resumed paddling, ever south-westward. In several days, they passed the point of Prairie du Chien and caught the powerful surge of what the Indians called the Father of Waters, the Mississippi River, becoming the first Europeans to do so.

Grateful for the additional propulsion, they admired the vastness, the flora, the fauna, particularly the large herds of dark humpbacked "cows" on the open prairie, and savored the excitement of this adventure. They marveled at the volume of water added to the main stream by the Illinois, the Missouri, and the Ohio rivers. Weeks later when they reached the mouth of the Arkansas River, they were advised by Indians there that they were only ten days from a large salty sea but that there were unfriendly tribes farther down. Satisfied that the Mississippi did not flow into the Pacific and Spanish territory but to the Gulf of Mexico and that they had opened up new lands for New France, they returned north on the Mississippi. But to add to their knowledge of the river systems, they tried a different return route by paddling up the Illinois River to the Des Plaines River where a short carry took them to the stunted Chicago River and Lake Michigan.

SITE OF INDIAN VILLAGE
TECHIROGUEN
VISITED BY LE MOYNE 1654
AND BY LA SALLE 1673

Onondaga County, 2*
US 11 at Brewerton

BURNING SPRINGS
CHARTED ON EARLIEST MAPS
OF NORTH AMERICA AFTER
LA SALLE'S VISIT AUGUST 1669
CAUSED BY ESCAPING NATURAL
GAS, ONCE MYSTERY TO VISITORS

Ontario County, 1
Case Rd. 1m. NW Bristol Ctr.

In 1679, Robert Cavalier Sieur de la Salle was intent on reaching the mouth of the Mississippi despite political opposition and competition in Montreal for the fur trade. On an earlier trip, he and Fathers Galinee and Dollier had traveled up the St. Lawrence and across Lake Ontario to Irondequoit Bay, and sought out one of the main Seneca villages near present Victor. Here they had heard of a great river which flowed southwest—a possible passage to the south seas and China. They also visited the burning spring, still flaming, near Bristol. At this village, La Salle obtained Seneca leave to portage around Niagara Falls, and on Lake Erie to build the Griffon, the first sailing ship on the upper Lakes, as well as a fortified warehouse below the falls (Lewiston).

The ship foundered—no one knows where—on its way to meet him where the St. Joseph River enters Lake Michigan. When the ship did not appear, he canoed up the St. Joseph, portaged where South Bend is today to the Kankakee River, and down the Illinois River to near present Peoria where he witnessed the Iroquois exercise their fury on villagers of an Illinois Indian town. La Salle built a fort before winter and began to trade with other Illinois and Miamis. When in February, 1680, he heard that his creditors had confiscated his warehouse of furs and supplies in Montreal, he had to scrap his immediate plans and start the long cold trudge back overland to protect his interests, making the journey in 65 days to Fort Frontenac. With the help of Governor Frontenac, one of his main backers, he recovered his furs and supplies.

La Salle's Seigneury, or estate, was located near the rapids ten miles up the river from Montreal. His neighbors knew he was as yet unsuccessful in fulfilling his intention of finding the way to China and the Orient, and with sarcastic derision, they called the place Lachine. La Salle later used the Lake Michigan-Illinois River route and went all the way down the Mississippi to discover that the river did, in fact, empty into the Gulf of Mexico. He declared the land drained by the Mississippi and its tributaries to be French territory, and named it Louisiana in honor of Louis XIV.

To secure his claim, La Salle went to Paris in 1684 to see the king personally to get funds and the authority to build a fort near the mouth of the Mississippi. He did get the royal backing, but on his return, he mistook Matagorda Bay for the mouth of the Mississippi, and bad luck, including shipwreck and near starvation on the Texas coast, dogged him all the way. (La Salle's ship was found in 1999, mired in the shallow muddy bottom of Matagorda Bay, with the number of cannons and their embossed foundry dates providing positive identification). Finally in 1687 near the Trinity River in Texas, with La Salle and the few survivors desperately struggling to reach the Mississippi, he was murdered by some of his own disaffected men.

The successor to Frontenac, in 1682, was La Févbre De La Barre whose limited military experience and minor victories over the English as Governor of Cayenne, left him poorly prepared for confrontation with the Iroquois with regard to both military skill and statecraft. The English, under the new Governor Dongan, had been stirring up the Senecas, Cayugas, and Onondagas, and selling them guns and powder. However, most of the Senecas were busy warring with the Illinois and disrupting the fur trade and left Quebec or Montreal, for the moment, free from attack.

In the spring of 1683, La Barre had some boats built, ostensibly preparing to make war on the Iroquois, but rather than using the boats in a military offensive, he employed them to get a personal foothold in the fur trade. That year, it became more urgent to curb the Senecas and invitations were sent to the chiefs. To La Barre's distress, the Indians never showed up. Charles Le Moyne, a respected trader and patriarch of a famous French Canadian family, was sent to use his influence to coax the most important men of the tribe to attend, and forty-three chiefs did finally come to Montreal. La Barre asked the Senecas to desist in attacking the tribes of the Upper Lakes, a request that was spurned. Little happened, but La Barre, in an attempt to ingratiate himself with them, put La Salle, a trading competitor, in jeopardy by agreeing with the Iroquois that La Salle was selling arms to the Illinois, Miamis, and other enemies of the Iroquois, and that he, as governor, did not sanction this.

An attack by the Senecas on a flotilla of La Barre's trade canoes stirred him to take action against them in the spring of '84. With a force of 1200 he proceeded up the St. Lawrence, tarried at Montreal, and by the time he arrived at Fort Frontenac, many of his men had become sick with malaria and dysentery, diminishing his effective fighting force. The original idea of a chastising attack had to be changed to a conference at which he would attempt to intimidate the Indians.

At La Famine, a seasonal fishing village at the mouth of the Salmon River, the Onondagas, the Cayugas, and the Oneidas patiently heard him out (the Senecas haughtily refused to attend). La Barre complained of their raiding and disarming the western Indians of arms and ammunition the

French had given, and of their introducing the English into France's trading grounds. He warned that if these incursions were not stopped, La Barre would make war on the Iroquois.

Garangula, an Onondaga orator and chief, spoke forcibly when he defended their raids and the disarming of the French allied Indians. Iroquois sovereignty gave them the right to conduct themselves as they wished, he said, regardless of both the French or the English, and the French threat of war was a hollow boast since they knew that sickness had weakened the French army. He asserted that it was more likely that they could "knock the French on the head" rather than the other way around. In the end, La Barre conceded and promised not to attack, the Indians made no concessions, and the inglorious conference ended La Barre's campaign.

La Barre had also sent word to the upper lake forts for traders Duluth, Perrot, and La Durantaye to assemble a force of Huron, Ottowa, Sauk, Fox, and Menominee Indians to assist his Frenchmen in the now aborted attack. Now, word was sent to the group at Niagara which had had to be cajoled to come so far to fight the Iroquois was to return home without the expected booty. La Barre's grandiose stand against the Indians was a fiasco, and French influence with the Iroquois, and the tribes of the upper Great Lakes, was at its low point. La Barre was soon recalled to France.

When his replacement, the Marquis de Denonville, arrived at Quebec, scurvy had taken 150 of the 500 soldiers aboard, and more were hospitalized. His instructions were specific: to stop the political bickering over the fur trade, to rebuild France's prestige, especially with the western tribes, and to thwart English designs on the region south of the Great Lakes claimed by France. He tried polite correspondence with Dongan, whom he knew was also Catholic, to persuade the English to stop trading in the area. The courtesies failed, and Denonville became enraged when he heard of two heavily armed trading flotillas from Albany passing through Seneca country that season on their way to Michilimackinac, where Lakes Huron, Superior, and Michigan join.

Like La Barre, Denonville wished to chasten the Seneca, and planned an attack in secret so that not even Father Jean de Lamberville at the Onondaga mission was notified, even though the efforts of the Jesuits were one of Canada's best buffers against the Iroquois. Again, Duluth, Perrot, La Durantaye, and Tonty were recruited to muster the western tribes in force. The lure of booty to be captured from the two English trading flotillas when they reached the upper lakes was also persuasive in this expedition. They were to hold the tribes at Niagara until Denonville gave the signal to proceed. (Henri de Tonty had been the late La Salle's most trusted and invaluable lieutenant who had much clout with the Indians, partly because of an iron hand that replaced one lost to a grenade in the Sicilian Wars. His father was an Italian financier who moved to France, and is known to history as the inventor of a form of life annuity scheme called a tontine).

Denonville was so resolved to destroy the Senecas that he attacked two friendly Christian Indian villages near Fort Frontenac to forestall intelligence of his plans from reaching the Senecas and made thirteen chiefs prisoners to be shipped down the St. Lawrence and pressed into service on His Majesty's galleys in the Mediterranean. One of them escaped to Onondaga to reveal this treachery and the plans for the imminent attack. When the Iroquois discovered Denonville's intentions, they asked the English at Albany for help and received powder and lead but no soldiers.

FORT SITE
HERE DENONVILLE'S FRENCH ARMY
LANDED TO INVADE THE SENECA
COUNTRY; JULY 12, 1687, 400
MEN WERE LEFT TO BUILD FORT;
BATTLE AT VICTOR, JULY 13,1687

Monroe County, 7
Sea Breeze Bluff, Lake Ontario

LA SALLE ROAD
ROUTE USED BY THE FRENCH
ARMY OF DENONVILLE TO
DESTROY SENECA INDIANS AT
TOWN SOUTH OF VICTOR, N.Y.
JULY 13, 1687

Monroe County, 15
NY 96, a mile east of Bushnell Basin

When he had gathered his force of 2000 French and Indians, Denonville set sail from Fort Frontenac. As he neared Irondequoit Bay, Tonty's force appeared in the west, and the joint landing was perfectly made. The Marquis built a temporary fort, garrisoned to protect his fleet of batteaux, and moved south to the Seneca towns. The Indians retreated before him, leading him into an ambush, but Denonville was able to repulse them. He did not engage them again but as he approached, the Indians set fire to and abandoned their towns near the present villages of Victor, East Bloomfield, Lima, and Rochester Junction. After the mayhem, Denonville retired northward, stopping at a cluster of ponds (Mendon Ponds) for the refreshment of his men.

WAR SITE
DENONVILLE'S ARMY OF 3000
FRENCH AND INDIAN ALLIES
CAMPED HERE 23 JULY 1687
RETURNING TO IRONDEQUOIT
AFTER RAZING SENECA TOWNS

Monroe County, 11*
Mendon Ponds Park

When he returned to his boats, the Marquis sailed west to Niagara where he built the first Fort Niagara and provisioned it for eight months. Winter and the Senecas kept the one hundred-man garrison confined, blocking any delivery of more supplies. In the spring, a friendly band of Miamis inquired at the fort, and getting no reply, broke into find ten barely-alive men, the rest having died of starvation, scurvy, or the cold.

Denonville considered his campaign supremely successful, but because of his duplicity, it was just the opposite. The Senecas rebuilt their towns at new locations, which remained until the time of the American Revolution, and the common food supply of the League carried them through the winter. Unlike Denonville, they were considerate of de Lamberville by hiding him away from any young warriors seeking vengeance.

But the Senecas did not forget this and other French atrocities. The following summer, 1500 braves attacked the settlement of Lachine and again in November, with seething ferocity, killed over a thousand men, women and children without mercy. The French were so dismayed that they planned to abandon and blow up the fort at Cataraqui but the fuse burned out after their departure and the Iroquois became richer by twenty-eight barrels of powder and other stores as well as taking possession of the fort. New France became imperilled and close to famine since it had lost and would lose more habitants who were mostly farmers. For fear of attack by small raiding parties, the survivors could not plant or bring in a harvest and the French prestige with the western tribes, upon which the fur trade then depended, was at its nadir.

As much as a curmudgeon as he was, Frontenac, now seventy, was considered by Louis XIV to be the man to set things right, and he was returned to Canada the same year that the contest for the north of North America began when England declared war on France in 1689.

Denonville's original plan to conquer New York, though approved by the king, had been shelved but was now to be reactivated. A force would take Albany via the Lake George-Champlain corridor, and move on to New York. Non-Catholics would be deported except artisans, who were to be enslaved and stripped of their property, which would be given to imported Canadian and French settlers. This conceit called for an army of only 1500 men and two warships to defeat a colony of 18,000. When New York was overcome, the New England colonies were to be similarly conquered!

Frontenac first had to pacify the Iroquois, and rebuild Canada's prestige and goodwill with the Upper Lakes tribes to retain their trading business and be able to rely on them for future military ventures. It was an uphill task partially because the Indians had a taste for English goods, which were better made and far cheaper than those made by the French. Frontenac decided to use Indians along with whites to jointly attack unfortified white settlements for the first time, a practice that became standard on both sides from then on.

The Black Robes helped persuade the Indians to go along on these forays, convincing them that God was on their side, and would favor them against non-Catholics. Ten crowns were offered the Indians by Frontenac for scalps, but this was later reduced and more offered for prisoners, white or Indian, men, women, and children. (The Indians soon learned to cut a scalp so that it looked like two, and some of the western tribes were even able to make part of a buffalo hide look like a scalp.) Frontenac tried to soften the Iroquois by bringing back and releasing Denonville's captive chiefs so that they would be inclined to make a truce with him but the Iroquois demanded that he destroy the fort at Cataraqui which he refused. Despite this setback, the grand plan to attack Albany and New York was initiated in the winter of 1690. The French and their Indians snowshoed up frozen Champlain and Lake George carrying everything they would need to sustain them for a month, then changed their minds and attacked Schenectady instead, killing many, taking prisoners, and burning most of the town. Other parties attacked Salmon Falls, on the western edge of Maine, and Casco Bay (Portland) with the same results. Then the plan to attack New York was dropped.

Albany trader Peter Schuyler, with a force of New Yorkers, retaliated by trying to take Montreal and New Englanders attacked Quebec by sea, but both missions failed even though Sir William Phipps from Massachusetts captured Port Royal in Acadia.

The English and colonials were mostly non-military men, unskilled in warfare, leading equally unskilled and untrained farmers, tradesmen, and artisans. By contrast, the French had regiments trained in Indian warfare and were often led by experienced army officers like Frontenac. The Iroquois, to offset attrition from the effects of epidemics and war, had adopted many captives into the tribes; by 1694, almost half the Onondaga chiefs and two of the Oneida's were Frenchmen.

In 1696, Frontenac made one last raid despite his seventy-four years, this time in relative ease since he traveled by boat and in the summer. Leaving Cataraqui, his 1600 Frenchmen and 460 Indian raiders crossed Lake Ontario in four hundred batteaux with four small field pieces to the mouth of the Oswego River and paddled to the falls (Fulton) ten miles upstream. Fifty braves lifted the batteau with Frontenac seated in his chair, carried him around the mile of rapids, and resumed their course upstream.

When batteaux could no longer be used, the warriors carried the old campaigner in his armchair lashed to poles, as in a sedan chair, through the woods to the main Onondaga village, then near Jamesville. But the forewarned Onondagas had burned and vacated their village leaving behind a very old man who wished to glorify his final hours.

Howard S. Ford

—600 FEET
SITE OF INDIAN TOWN
ONONDAGA
1684–1696
DESTROYED AT TIME OF
FRONTENAC'S INVASION 1696

Onondaga County, 25*
NY 91, 1½ m. S. of Jamesville

Destroying crops and food stores, the invaders also tortured the old man who taunted them, according to his culture, even as they burned him alive. Seven hundred Frenchman went east to destroy a village of the Oneidas who were unable to negotiate peace to save their village and crops. The plan to "pacify" the Iroquois was not successful. The raid backfired: the French lost their harvest for lack of men at home.

The English arrived too late to help defend the Iroquois villages but from their own supplies carried the Indians through to stave off starvation that winter. Frontenac died at about the same time as King William's War ended (1697), the first of a series of grisly wars between the English and the French for the domination of the continent. Policy changed; the French avoided stirring up the Iroquois, remembering the retaliation at Lachine. Besides, there was a profitable smuggling operation in English goods between leading Albany traders and those of Montreal along the Champlain- Lake George corridor. Neither side wished to disturb this arrangement, winked at by both authorities, and so the northern New York border was quiet for a long time.

In 1702, Queen Ann's war began. In the European phase of the war, the Duke of Marlborough, also known as John Churchill (Winston Churchill's ancestor), was winning victories at Blenheim, Ramillies, and Malplaquet over the forces of Louis XIV.

Here, the French Canadians concentrated their raids on small unprotected towns on the New England frontier where the prospect of resistance was negligible. French officers led parties of French "bushlopers", Abenakis (from Maine), and Caughnawagas. In 1704, the famous raid on Deerfield, Massachusetts, took place in the middle of a severely cold winter, securing many captives, and raids were made on Wells and Pemaquid in Maine, as well as other small towns and isolated cabins. They all followed the same pattern of killing, pillage, burning, taking prisoners, and misery.

(The Caughnawagas were Mohawks converted by local French missionaries and brought north to live at the mission across the St. Lawrence from Montreal so as to be far removed from the pagan influence of their relatives. Increasingly, many of them were younger white captives who refused repatriation, preferring the easy routine of the Jesuits and Indians there. A famous resident was Kateri Takawitha, born in 1656 at Auriesville on the Mohawk, daughter of a Mohawk and a captive white mother. At sixteen she was drawn north, sought baptism, and became a nun. She died in 1690 with such a reputation for devotion that ailing people were healed by visions of her and she was recommended for canonization in 1844 and beatified in 1980).

Another naval attempt on Quebec failed, but since the previous treaty gave Port Royal back to the French, it was retaken, and now called Annapolis Royal, in honor of Queen Anne, perhaps to make it stick this time. And so it did: when the treaty to the War of Spanish Succession (as the larger related war in Europe was called) was signed in 1713, Acadia, as well as Newfoundland and fur trading posts on Hudson Bay, was retained by the English. With Newfoundland and Acadia, flanking the mouth of the St. Lawrence, in English hands, guarding against French ships destined for Quebec and Montreal became much easier. Cape Breton Island, however, remained French.

In the 1750s the population of the English colonies, stretching along the Atlantic coast from Maine to the Carolinas, but hemmed in by the Appalachians, was over a million compared to the entire population of Canada, concentrated mostly along the St. Lawrence River between Quebec and Montreal, of 55,000.

The system of northern rivers and the Great Lakes was beneficial to French explorers and traders. It was much easier to travel a long distance by water with 1500 pounds of trade goods in a batteau than haul a string of packhorses through mountains with the same load. The elevation of the most lofty Great Lake, Lake Superior, 1,000 miles to the west, is only 602 feet above sea level or 356 feet above Lake Ontario, with 165 feet of that represented by Niagara Falls. Westward expansion for the French was much easier by water than for the English faced with the Appalachian Mountains.

By 1725, the French had even advanced several hundred miles up the Missouri River and built a fort to trade with the Osage Indians. (The Ozark Mountains got their name from "aux arcs", i.e., on the way to the Arkansas Indians). Within fifteen years, Louis-Joseph Vérendrye got as far as present Pierre, South Dakota, and there deposited an inscribed lead plate declaring the event and French dominion to all who cared.

Of more importance, as English traders began trickling into the upper Ohio valley to trade with the Miamis, Mingos (emigrant Senecas and Cayugas), and the displaced Delawares and Shawnees, they attracted many Indians away from the French trade. Their pack trains displayed better made goods from Pennsylvania, Virginia, and the Carolinas and at much cheaper prices. This severely threatened French trade and expansion. Closely involved in the trade, Louis Thomas de Joncaire, Lieutenant of Marines who had strengthened the Fort at Niagara and who was to found a dynasty of his own, exploited his close relationship with the Senecas and established Fort des Sables on the shore near Irondequoit Bay. To counter this competition, the English took Robert Livingston's advice, and opened a trading post at Oswego only a few years later, in 1722, and made it into a fort within five years.

FORT DES SABLES
A FRENCH TRADING POST
BUILT BY JONCAIRE NEAR
THIS SITE IN 1717 AS A
SENECA LINK TO NEW FRANCE
AROUSED BRITISH IRE

Monroe County, 8
Sea Breeze Bluff, Lake Ontario

In 1711, the British government wished to increase the production of naval stores for the fleet, and Governor Hunter of New York wanted more laborers to improve trade in the colony. With the aid of Queen Anne, he secured a government grant of ƒ10,000 to import 3,000 Palatine German refugees, mostly from London, who had fled their war-ravaged homes on the lower Rhine River and contracted for their labor. Their willingness to work for less was disrupting the English labor market and causing riots. They were settled at Livingston Manor and at other large estates along the Hudson.

The working arrangements didn't work out, and most of the Palatines dispersed, some nearby to found the towns of Newburgh, Rhinebeck, and Germantown. Others moved west to the Schoharie and Mohawk valleys, where the Mohawks sold them land on easy terms. Their presence increased the population of the colony of New York about ten per cent, and many of their descendants left a significant mark on our history: men such as John Peter Zenger, who won his landmark trial against tyrannical Governor William Cosby for freedom of the press, and Conrad Weiser and Nicholas Herkimer, of whom more later. Palatines who went south came to be called Pennsylvania Dutch, along with other German immigrants attracted to that benign commonwealth.

Another destined to become a significant personage arrived in 1738 from im-poverished conditions in Ireland at the invitation of his uncle, Peter Warren, who had worked his way up to Captain in the Royal Navy (and heightened his status by marrying into the De Lanceys, a family of noted traders up to their ears in furs, smuggling, and politics). He was to manage his uncle's 14,000 acre estate and trading post near Fort Hunter and the lower Mohawk Indian town of Teantantologo, where Schoharie Creek enters the Mohawk. William Johnson was twenty-three, hard-working, smart, and fascinated by the Indians' customs and culture. He joined them hunting, dancing, and in their ceremonies, which he learned as if he had been born one of them.

Above all he treated them fairly at the trading post and elsewhere, an unheard of practice. The other traders would most often let the Indians buy items and consume a jug of rum or brandy for which they had little natural tolerance. When the Indians sobered up, the trader overcharged them for all they had allegedly bought. Johnson abhorred such practices and saw a great future for himself by dealing honestly.

Gaining experience, he purchased property nearby on the north side of the Mohawk, where he opened a trading post of his own and wrote his uncle about his intentions. His business soon thrived, drawing trade from his uncle's complex. He enjoyed the highest influence with Palatines, many of whom became his tenants, customers, and advocates, as well with the Iroquois, and was soon adopted by the Mohawks as Warraghiyagey, "a man who undertakes great things". For advice, Johnson gravitated to Tyanoga, or Hendrick, a venerable Mohawk chief whose stature in the tribe and with the whites had resulted in his being selected years before, along with three other chiefs, by Peter Schuyler to visit London where they had been celebrated by government ministers and presented to Queen Anne.

Largely on the advise of Cadwallader Colden, cognoscente, politician, and published chronicler of Iroquois history, Governor George Clinton, who had not met Johnson, made him Superintendent of Indian Affairs. Johnson's appointment proved to be one of the most important, not only to New York, but to the northern colonies because the continued friendship of the Iroquois (and their tributary Indians) was necessary for the English to have on their side. It was certainly necessary to not have the Iroquois favoring the French. He built Mount Johnson to accommodate his increasing number of tenants, to reflect his success, and to entertain numerous guests, red and white. As well, he opened his own trading posts at Fort Oswego and at Oquaga.

The French built Louisbourg, a massive stone fortress on Cape Breton Island, to guard the entrance to the St. Lawrence river and which became profitable for privateers to use as a protected base to prey on the New England fishing fleet. At the instigation of Governor Shirley of Massachusetts, William Pepperel, a colonial, and the same Peter Warren, now commodore of His Majesties' Royal Navy, planned the capture of this place. It was considered a mad scheme with no possibility of success. But in an unusual example of cooperation between colonial militia and British Regulars, the siege was conducted with a minimum of foul-ups. Six weeks of bombardment by land and from the ships succeeded in taking the fort. Cunning allowed the French flag to fly to induce French ships, unaware of the surrender, to approach and be captured. Pepperel was rewarded with the first colonial baronetcy by the Crown, and the newly promoted Admiral Warren gained over ƒ20,000 in prize money. But the assault and disease killed about 1,000 New Englanders and it was costly in treasure to them as well. In 1748, the Treaty of Aix-La-Chappelle ended the War of Austrian Succession (King George's War on this side of the Atlantic), which included a paragraph requiring Britain to return Louisbourg to the French in exchange for the state of Madras in southern India. This soured many New Englanders on the government in London. At the same time, the war trained many Americans in the arts of war. The dissension and military experience prepared the way for the more significant wars to come.

One of the Palatines was Conrad Weiser who was born in Wurttemberg, Germany in 1696 and came to New York with his family when he was fourteen. Their group was one of those settled at Livingston Manor. Several years later when the project was abandoned, many Palatine families moved and bought land from the Mohawks at German Flats and environs, thirty miles west of the settlement line. The Weisers spent a winter living in the home of a Mohawk chief before moving again to the Schoharie valley. Soon, Weiser left home, and spent the next fifteen years living with the Mohawks learning their language and customs. He married a Palatine girl and later moved to Womelsdorf, west of Reading, where his homestead still stands.

As the official interpreter and agent representing Pennsylvania, he became a close friend of Shikellimy, a French-Canadian captive of the Oneidas who had become a chief and was delegated by the Iroquois Council at Onondaga to ensure the allegiance of the Pennsylvania Indians (mostly Delawares and Shawnees) and to act as envoy between the Confederacy and the Proprietors of Pennsylvania. Weiser was to attend treaty conferences between the leaders of the middle colonies and the Iroquois, meeting in Albany, Philadelphia, Lancaster, Easton, Carlisle, or Onondaga.

In 1743, Weiser was accompanied by John Bartram and his friend, Lewis Evans (a surveyor and geographer whose detailed maps were later used by General Braddock and migrating colonists). Bartram was a self-taught botanist in Philadelphia whose fame arose from collecting plant specimens in the wilderness, cultivating them in his botanical garden (the country's first), and selling them in the colonies and England to the cream of inquiring professional and amateur gardeners. He kept a diary citing geographical and botanical details of this trip from Philadelphia to Shikellimy's home at Shamokin (Sunbury, Pennsylvania) on the Susquehanna, and on to Tioga, Owego, the Tioughnioga River, Tully Lakes, and the heights of present Pompey, arriving at the village of Indian Orchard, or Cachiachse, overlooking Butternut Creek valley.

While Weiser and Shikellimy were conferring with the sachems, Bartram and Evans went to Onondaga Lake and the springs there, and boiled down a gallon of brine to yield a pound of salt. They also went on a trip to Oswego, noting as they left the sand hill west of the Onondaga Lake outlet (which much later became Long Branch Park). They then passed the confluence of three rivers, and stopped downstream at the falls. The village there existed primarily for the purpose of transporting goods and batteaux around the rapids, and a fair number of people made their living this way. Of course, this village was the great ancestor of Fulton.

They continued to Fort Oswego Bartram described as a trading castle on the west side of the river, built twenty feet high of stone so soft he could carve his name with his pocketknife. There they were entertained and went swimming, but he wrote that the water was too cold, especially for late July. He gathered seeds of a brilliantly scarlet-flowered mint and sent them to his London agent who named it Oswego Tea.

Weiser's mission from the governors of Pennsylvania and Virginia was to make amends for a foolish attack by some Virginia soldiers on a small Iroquois war party, traveling the historic Great War Road in the Valley of Virginia, on their way to ravage the Catawbas in Carolina. Over a period of a week of convivial discussion, banqueting, distributions of gifts, consumption of ceremonial rum, and smoking of the calumet, the breach was healed, and an indemnity paid for the deaths of the warriors. Weiser's journal reveals the hospitable and friendly manner in which this took place with chiefs he and other officials had known a long time. The Iroquois were highly regarded by the whites, but they knew how to play Britain and France to their own advantage.

The Ohio Company, whose investors were mostly Virginia gentry interested in land speculation and the fur trade, was chartered in 1747 and received its first grant of land from the Crown in 1749. It sent an experienced and articulate frontiersman, Christopher Gist, to scout the region a year later, an activity soon known to the French.

It was now a fact of wilderness life that the tribes could no longer live without the tools they bargained for from the Europeans and their decisions about war were often based on this need. Traders from Canada had been doing business along the Ohio and its tributaries for close to a century. But in recent years the Canadians were beginning to feel the effects of competition from English traders whose wares were not only better made and cheaper, but easily available since they were setting up trading posts and depots in the upper Ohio Valley.

In 1749, Captain Pierre Joseph de Céloron de Bienville was sent to put and end to these incursions and to promote the commercial and political interests for New France. He proceeded with his flotilla of thirty-three canoes up the St. Lawrence, crossed Lake Ontario and portaged around Niagara Falls into Lake Erie. When he came to a certain cairn on the south shore, he made the carry to Lake Chautauqua, and paddled out its outlet to Conewango Creek and the Allegheny River. Down the Allegheny (called the Ohio by the Indians) a hundred or more miles, the flotilla reached the Forks of the Ohio and then coursed La Belle Rivière, the beautiful Ohio.

On this odyssey Céloron's mission was to impress the tribes with the power of France, the advantages of dealing with them rather than the English, and to declare France's ownership. Like Vérendrye, he buried lead plates at appropriate locations, each with an inscription glorifying the King and France's dominion.

He stopped at each Indian village on the river to preach to and cajoled the crowds that gathered and, like a good salesman, noted their response. Then a tin sign, embossed with the Royal Arms, was nailed to a large tree, and a hole dug nearby for the designated inscribed lead plate. The village sachem would invariably state, in conformity with delicate diplomacy, that the tribe would be happy to trade with the French and would drive the English out of their country.

The French were not fooled by this expression of native cooperation which the exigencies of the moment required. There were some tense moments, and it became obvious that the Indians resented this arrogant intrusion of the French, and were happy with their English suppliers. Céleron dutifully sought out other Indian villages up the Muskingum, the Scioto, and other Ohio tributaries. His reception at Pickawillany (present Piqua), far up the Miami River where 4,000 Miamis were hosting other tribes and a group of English traders, began to become ugly and the worst of any. He quickly quit the town, portaged to the Maumee River to reach Lake Erie, and returned to Montreal.

Céloron reported to the new governor, the Marquis de la Jonquière, that the expedition failed to impress the Indians. Disappointed, the governor became determined to build more forts to secure French trade and military dominance in the Ohio Valley.

CHAPTER THREE

Abbé Francois Picquet, a zealot who, in 1749, had built the mission of La Presentation at the mouth of the Oswegatchie River (Ogdensburg), hated the English with a fanaticism equal to his passion for the Church. He converted many Onondaga and Cayuga Indians, teaching them that Christ was a Frenchman who had been crucified by the English, and that the King of France was the eldest son of the wife of Christ. Picquet and his Indians four years earlier had raided and destroyed the blockhouse and town of Saratoga. The Abbé warmed to ideas of attacking Fort Oswego, which was a thorn in his side, since it attracted Indians to trade from as far away as lakes Michigan, Superior, and Huron to by-pass French posts farther east. Governor Duquesne had said that Picquet was worth more than ten regiments.

To outwit the English, Picquet attempted to buy land from Red Head, chief of the Onondagas, to build a post near their main village. This could be disruptive to the Confederacy since Red Head did not have the League's sanction to conclude a sale. In order to preclude this or any future sale, William Johnson suggested that the League deed to him the prized land two miles deep around Onondaga Lake including the proposed post site. The League agreed to this.

Johnson paid ƒ350 for the land and promised to not improve it, or if he sold it to the Crown, the same covenants would apply. He offered it to the Crown for his cost, but the Crown refused his offer. Up to this time, 1751, he had dug into his own pocket to manage Indian affairs, and because of this penurious attitude on the part of Albany and New York officials, and Crown refusals to back him up on other important matters dealing with the tribes, Johnson resigned as Superintendent of Indian Affairs. To the Iroquois, the acceptance of Johnson's resignation was tantamount to a rejection of their English alliance at a time when the French were intensely trying to woo their influence.

A year earlier, two Moravian missionaries, the Reverends Cammerhoff and David Zeisberger, visited Onondaga from Bethlehem, Pennsylvania by way of the Cayuga towns, pausing overnight at Owasco and Skaneateles lakes. They were well received by chief Canassatego who granted their request that the two be allowed to live at Onondaga to learn the language. After returning home,

Sure Signs: Stories Behind the Historical Markers of Central New York

Cammerhoff died. Coincidentally, the chief died soon, too. Two years later Zeisberger and two others left Bethlehem for Onondaga via New York to make good on accepting the chief's hospitality to study the Onondaga language. Zeisberger came twice more for the season of '53, and again for '54 through '55, with different associates each time. These visits were in preparation for establishing a mission, but Zeisberger became enmeshed in the coming conflict as did other Moravians and their mission never materialized.

SAINT JOHN'S BEACH
BISHOP FREDERIC CAMMERHOFF
AND DAVID ZEISBERGER,
MORAVIAN MISSIONARIES,
BUILT THE FIRST SKANEATELES
SHELTER ON THIS SITE 1750

Onondaga County, 81
U.S. 20, ¼ m. East of Skaneateles

There was clamor for smiths at the Indian towns for keeping their pots, traps, and other hardware, especially muskets, in repair. Johnson had responded to this need as yet another way of retaining the Iroquois on the British side. The French, not to be outdone, catered in the same manner and many Indian towns had rival smiths. Meanwhile, the Ohio Valley Indians ignored Céloron's threats and the English traders remained. This soured the French with the prospect of losing more business. The English presence there was especially irksome to Charles Michel de Langlade, a young ambitious trader who felt he had been slighted at Pickawillany, and wished to revenge himself on "Old Britain", the Miami chief, the English traders, and the town.

Orders had been given to Céloron to arrange the destruction of Pickawillany, considered the showcase of the English trading posts, and Langlade persuaded him that he was the man to do it. With a force of over 250 Chippewas and Ottawas, and a dozen French troops, Langlade descended on the town of now over 8,000 Miamis and other tribes (men, women, and children), and English traders, including the successful trader, George Croghan. The chief, "Old Britain", and many others were brutally killed as were several traders, and five traders were captured and sent to Montreal. The Pickawillany villagers were told that if they continued to trade with the English they would all be killed, and then the attackers set the village and warehouses afire. The allegiance of many western tribes then swung back to the French.

September 2, 1752 was the day that England, by Royal Proclamation, had set for finally coming around to doing what the rest of Europe had done in 1582: it scuttled the Julian calendar set by Julius Caesar, which had served western civilization well for 1800 years. But because of being slightly out of sync in the timing of the earth's relationship with the sun, the Old Style calendar (and the planting schedule) was now off by eleven days. So all the days up to September 14th were also scuttled, and the new more precise Gregorian calendar was put in service and called New Style.

At about this time, Johnson met sixteen-year-old Molly Brant, daughter of a powerful Mohawk family, who charmed Johnson and became his second, but not only, wife a not uncommon practice with traders. (Johnson was also known to have accepted feminine hospitality throughout the tribes). As Johnson added to his estate, first with Fort Johnson, a residence with necessary fortifications, and again with the more grand and well-appointed manor house, Johnson Hall, Molly presided over his table as hostess to diplomats, generals, nobility, Indian chiefs, traders, and friends.

Soon after the return of Celoron's expedition, the French began building a fort at Presque Isle (Erie, Pennsylvania), and another twenty miles south called Fort Le Boeuf. The trading post at the nearby Seneca village of Venango, was taken over and converted to another but smaller fort. In the absence of Johnson as Superintendent of Indian Affairs, this French threat in the west, compounded with the probable disaffection of western Indians who could draw away the Iroquois with them, prompted Albany to appoint an Indian council, although it took two bumbling years to do this.

Governor Dinwiddie of Virginia thought the three forts were a threat to the interests of the Dominion of Virginia in the upper Ohio Valley (and the interests of the Ohio Company of which he and the first families of Virginia were stockholders). He chose twenty-one year old George Washington, another stockholder, with Christopher Gist to guide him, as emissary to the commander at Le Boeuf, Captain Jacques Legardeur de Saint-Pierre, to protest this invasion of English territory.

Sure Signs: Stories Behind the Historical Markers of Central New York

Over a sumptuous dinner Legardeur replied to Washington that Governor Dinwiddie should instead make his feelings known to the new Governor of Canada, the Marquis de Duquesne, and that Legardeur would remain there at his post until Duquesne gave him orders to vacate.

Washington and Gist, now deserted by their Indian guides, and having abandoned their lame horses, made their way alone back down the treacherous ice-choked Allegheny River, in which their raft overturned so that they had to swim to an island to dry out and warm up. They fought blizzards, eluded waylaying Indians, and re-crossed the mountains to arrive in Williamsburg a month later, in mid-January, 1754. Washington noted that even though the Ohio Company had a post nearby, where Wills Creek joins the Potomac (Cumberland), a more strategic location would be at the Forks where the Allegheny and the Monongahela joined to form the Ohio River.

Dinwiddie asked Washington to write up a report and had it published complete with Washington's rough map of the journey. The report was also printed in London, and young Washington quickly became a well known hero on both sides of the Atlantic. Shortly after Washington's return, Dinwiddie sent out another group under the command of William Trent, a trader from Philadelphia and Trenton, and brother-in-law of Croghan, to follow up Washington's suggestion and build a fort at the Forks of the Ohio. The importance of a fort there occurred to the French at the same time, and a thousand Frenchmen appeared in mid-April to eject Trent and his men from their partly completed structure. On their way back to Williamsburg, Trent's group was intercepted by Washington leading a small force on its belated way to reenforce Trent.

Washington hastily built a necessarily inadequate palisade which he called Fort Necessity, poorly sited at a place called Great Meadows. After a skirmish with a small French patrol, the captured commander, Jumonville, was tomahawked by the leader of Washington's Indians. Both sides jockeyed around in the area for several months, with the French benefitting from reenforcements under the command of Coulon de Villiers, ironically, the brother of Jumonville. Washington's backup forces finally arrived also, and if it weren't for the French wrongly hearing that many more were still on the way, Washington and his small army could have been wiped out.

Villiers attacked the poorly protected fort resulting in thirty of Washington's men killed and seventy more wounded. He sent a flag of truce suggesting that Washington had no choice but to surrender. He refused. Villiers sent a second offer and, realizing the futility of his situation, Washington capitulated to honorable terms, but a later and more careful translation of the surrender terms held him responsible for Jumonville's shameful death.

This first taste of combat for Washington concluded in humiliation and defeat. As well, the action was the initial clash between troops of France and Great Britain in what became a world-wide conflict that was called the French and Indian War on this side of the Atlantic and the Seven Years War worldwide. The date was July 4, 1754.

The proprietors of Pennsylvania, mindful of Conrad Weiser's age, appointed Daniel Claus and sent him north to Fort Johnson to learn the complexities of Iroquois culture and diplomacy and to be prepared as a replacement. Young Claus surprised his sponsors with praise for Johnson whom he confirmed had full sway with the League that had refused to deal with the newly appointed Indian commissioners in Albany. Claus soon became a deputy of Johnson's and eventually his son-in-law.

Fifteen years earlier, in 1737, the Penn descendants, hard-pressed by creditors, saw an opportunity to exploit an ambiguously worded and unconsummated 1686 treaty with the Delawares known as the Walking Purchase. The Penns doctored the treaty but retained the provision that the tract on the Delaware River would be defined by how far a man could walk in a day and a half. The path began near Newtown and ran northwest, parallel to the Delaware several miles distant. The Penn's agent cunningly chose three trained runners, rather than one walker, and cleared the way of obstructions. Sixty-four miles (just past the site of Jim Thorpe) was covered by the most enduring runner. This extended the line beyond a sharp northeast bend in the river so that the boundary running northeast ran sixty miles back to the Delaware near Minisink Ford. The Delawares were defrauded of half a million acres leaving them seething with resentment at this chicanery.

The Iroquois Council, to whom the Delawares sought redress, chose to confirm the Penn claim, and the Delawares and their brother tribe, the Shawnees, had no choice but to move the short distance to the Wyoming Valley along the Susquehanna.

One of the legacies of the Stuart Kings was the sowing of confusion due to their flamboyantly vague charters. Connecticut's charter, like many, ambitiously ran to the Pacific, arguably including the Wyoming Valley, due west in Pennsylvania. If Connecticut's claim was upheld, speculators would drive out the already displaced Delawares and Shawnees, and likely alienate Ohio Valley Indians into the arms of the French. Johnson was asked to mediate the validity of a deed Connecticut speculators had had signed by some unauthorized Delawares they had gotten drunk, not an unusual occurrence. He came down hard for the Delawares, the Onondagas, and the proprietors of Pennsylvania by declaring the Connecticut deed fraudulent. (The speculators still disagreed and political and physical skirmishes, known as the Pennamite Wars, ensued over several decades between the interested parties in both states).

The French, in an effort to alienate the Iroquois from the English, exploited these and other unjust land-grabbing on the part of the English, and the English knew they should remedy these abuses of the Indians for strategic reasons, if not as a matter of equity. This immediate threat of the French alienating their Indians prompted the commissioners to action. So in 1754, the Board of Trade and Plantations in London instructed Governor De Lancey of New York, to invite delegates from the colonies north of the Potomac to meet in Albany with the Iroquois to address these concerns, but only seven of the colonies sent delegates.

As the conference began, Johnson approved Hendrick's eloquent presentation of the Indian position which complained of land frauds and of Albany merchants selling arms to the French and their Indians, that neither France or England had any right to be in the Ohio Valley, and that William Johnson should be reinstated to replace the unsatisfactory Indian commissioners. The usual gifts were handed out, and the chiefs, having made their grievances known officially, departed the official, but not the unofficial congress. Several land deals were made "in the bushes" which transferred title to the lands of the Wyoming Valley, (under the signatures, among others, of Chief Hendricks, Conrad Weiser, and Benjamin and William Franklin), and western Pennsylvania in which boundaries were unclear, causing grievances later on.

The Albany Congress continued in session and also agreed to form a union of the colonies to act on mutually beneficial policy. This idea had been considered by the colonies before, but for economic and political reasons it had never jelled. Even Canassatego, the Onondaga chief, had at the 1744 Treaty at Lancaster, suggested that the colonies form a confederacy for strength as the Iroquois had done.

The colonies' concerns were to establish a uniform policy in dealing with Indian affairs, take control of future western settlement, the raising of a standing colonial army, and the building of forts on the frontier. Taxes would have to be raised from the colonies and a permanent congress, similar to the Iroquois Council, created. Delegate Benjamin Franklin and the commissioners wholeheartedly endorsed these proposals. Unfortunately, back home the colonial assemblies failed to ratify colonial unification.

FT. HENDRICK
1754-1760
BRITISH POST GUARDING
MOHAWK CASTLE. NAMED FOR
KING HENDRICK KILLED
AT LAKE GEORGE, SEPT. 1755

Herkimer County, 8
NY 5S at Indian Castle

Thirty years later, a publisher was about to republish Franklin's "Reasons and Motives for the Albany Plan of Union" and asked Franklin if he wished to make changes. Franklin remarked that if the plan or something like it had been adopted, the mischief leading to the Revolution most likely would not have occurred and there would not have probably been any reason for separation from the Mother Country.

Some unified action did come about after this but not in the manner proposed by Franklin. The crown rejected the idea of provinces treating with the Indians as in the past, and instead, installed royal officials to oversee dealings with the tribes. William Johnson was appointed Supervisor of Indian Affaires for the Six Nations and their allies, this time not accountable to the colonial governors or assemblies and with his activity paid for directly from the Royal Treasury. Johnson had to quit the fur trade to insure that his actions would be unbiased regarding either the Indians or the colonies.

At the same time London appointed General Edward Braddock, a long-time career officer and crony of the duke of Cumberland, (son of King George II, "butcher" of Culloden nine years earlier and head of the army hierarchy), to be Commander-in-Chief in North America, and sent him to Virginia with command over four regiments of regulars, plus two provincial regiments raised by Governor Shirley of Massachusetts.

Braddock's orders were to recover territory lost to France at Forts Duquesne and Niagara, gain control of Lake Ontario, take Crown Point, a French fort on Lake Champlain, and to destroy Fort Beauséjour in Acadia. Unknown to him, Lieutenant Colonel Monckton with a force of New Englanders had already taken the Acadian post, re-naming it Fort Cumberland, and expelled the Acadians (an event memorialized in Longfellow's **Evangeline**). All these objectives were important, but gaining control of Lake Ontario first would block the ability of the French to supply Forts Duquesne and Niagara and leave them to die on the vine. This was the importance of Oswego, and the colonials proceeded to strengthen the fort there and at the Great Carrying Place between the upper Mohawk and Wood Creek on the route leading to Lake Ontario.

Braddock assembled his army of 2,300 men at Alexandria to begin the march up the gentle hills of the Potomac Valley to Wills Creek where he built a fort and named it Fort Cumberland. From here he had 110 miles to go over increasingly mountainous terrain with heavy artillery, 150 heavy wagons, and 500 pack horses. This last stretch was the Nemacolin Trail, hacked out of the wilderness by Thomas Cressap and Nemacolin, his Delaware guide, five years before, which Washington and Gist had used. (US 40 closely follows this route). Drilling and blasting, cutting trees and laying logs corduroy fashion over swamps, removing stumps and bridging streams—all was done to make a twelve-foot wide road for transporting the heavy equipment.

In the first five days, they made only fifteen miles, so they left behind most of the baggage train to come along at its own pace, and made much better time thereafter.

When they were within ten miles of the fort and exhausted from having come this far under such trying conditions, they were ambushed by 250 French and 600 Indians firing from behind trees and rocks. The regulars, taught to not break ranks, staid in formation and made excellent targets for the enemy. But after three hours of this, many of Braddock's men panicked and, in the confusion, only 459 came through unscathed. Sixty-three out of eighty-six officers were casualties, and 977 of almost 1,400 noncoms and enlisted men were also killed or wounded. Braddock had five horses shot out from under him before dying from his wounds, and Washington, also in the thick of it, lost two horses, but as in all his battles, he led a charmed life and was not wounded. Among the survivors were Daniel Morgan, Adam Stephens, Charles Lee, Horatio Gates, as well as Washington, all of whom became rebel generals in the Revolution. Also surviving were Thomas Gage who became General in Charge of British Forces in Boston until after Bunker Hill, Christopher Gist, Dr. Jonas Craik (Washington's life-long friend and one of the doctors who attended him when he died), Daniel Boone, and George Croghan, now a deputy to Johnson. There were only sixteen French casualties and, at the most, forty Indians were killed. The whole expedition, recalled Benjamin Franklin years later, "gave us Americans the first suspicion that our exalted ideas of the prowess of British regulars had not been well founded."

The atrocities perpetrated by the French and Indians on the people of western Pennsylvania now increased and reached as far as the east bank of the Susquehanna.

One of those atrocities was a raid in the early spring of 1755, on the family of teen-age Mary Jemison, that had settled near Gettysburg. Four Frenchmen and six Shawnees waylaid them at their farm, killing a neighbor, and rounded them up to be marched to Fort Duquesne. Years later Mary related that the second or third night out, her mother, expecting death for herself and her husband, told her to remain strong, to not forget them or her prayers, or how to speak English, and to not try to escape. She knew her mother was saying good-bye; she never saw her parents or brothers again.

She was led along the trail to Fort Duquesne where she was traded to two Seneca squaws who treated her kindly. A few days later she and the Shawnees, with the scalps of her family at their belts and the two squaws, went down the Ohio River in a canoe ninety miles to a small Seneca village where she was washed and given new Indian clothes. The Seneca squaws befriended her, taught her what she needed to know, and adopted her into their family to replace a brother who had been killed in the battle with Washington at Great Meadows.

In time, she was married to a Delaware brave whom she resisted at first, but as he was kind and had many other virtues, she came to love him and eventually have a son by him. Her new family decided to relocate to the Genesee River region, so with her nine month old son and her Indian "brothers", she hiked from the Ohio country to the Genesee only to find that her husband had died while on a separate trip.

In the earlier years of her captivity, Mary had several chances to be returned to the whites, but her "sisters" prevented this, and by the time of the Sullivan raid on the Genesee country, she turned down another chance, satisfied with her way of life (and perhaps recognizing the difficulty of being accepted back by the whites). In turn, the Seneca so loved and respected her that when the Big Tree Treaty was to be signed in 1797, they asked her what land she wanted, and made sure that it was deeded to her by the treaty. She had married again, Hiakatoo, a chief thirty-six years her senior who was cruel and ruthless in war but kind and generous at home, and lived a happy life with him, bearing him six children before he died at well over a hundred. She lived the rest of her life on the bottomland along the Genesee that was given to her by the Senecas. It is still called the Gardeau tract and can be viewed from an overlook off the main road in Letchworth State Park.

Mary Jemison died in 1833 in Mount Morris, ten years after recounting her story to Dr. James Seaver, a local clergyman. Her memoirs detail the Seneca way of life, and insight of the effect on them of the whites, the wars, and the treaties.

SITE OF
DE-YU-IT-GA-OH
(VALLEY BEGINS TO WIDEN)
SENECA INDIAN VILLAGE
THE SPRING USED BY
MARY JEMISON IS NEARBY

16*
Livingston County
On Squawkie Hill Road about
2 miles south of Leicester

A cabin she built for her daughter when she was over sixty years old testifies to her resourcefulness, as does her life. (The cabin and a council-of-war cabin from Caneadea were moved years later by philanthropist William Pryor Letchworth to a small hill near his home, Glen Iris, and a statue of Mary toting her infant was erected close by).

In addition to being appointed Superintendent of Indian Affairs for the northern department, Sir William Johnson was now made Major General over militia from New York, New Jersey, and New England. The battle plan called for him to capture Crown Point on the west shore of Lake Champlain. In mid July of 1755, he left Albany up the Hudson with a flotilla of heavy artillery, 3,500 mostly untrained men, and Mohawks including his friend, King Hendrick and Hendrick's thirteen-year old grand-son, Joseph Brant. After fifty miles they disembarked, where Johnson assigned a detail to rebuild old Fort Lyman. He then crossed the height of land to the head of the beautiful lake that Father Isaac Jogues had, over a hundred years earlier, aptly named Lac Sacrement, and promptly renamed it Lake George, in honor of King George II. Johnson made sure that this information was included in the first dispatch to London.

At the same time, word arrived that Baron Dieskau, in command of French militia, was moving south from Crown Point. He was on his way with only half his men to attack the lightly manned and half-completed Fort Edward. His Indians refused to move against the fort armed with artillery but Dieskau managed an ambush against an advance thrust by Johnson. Chief Hendrick and a senior officer, Colonel Ephraim Williams, led the charge, and were both killed in this ambush. Colonel Williams had been prudent enough to draw a will before leaving Albany; one of its provisions created the college later named for him.

This advance force made an orderly retreat, giving Johnson's men at the head of the lake enough time to put up a barricade of wagons, tree trunks, and boats to protect them and the cannons they had lugged so far. The French came on against murderous fire of grape shot and musket balls, which cut a swath through their ranks, making their brave attempt hopeless.

The battle of Lake George was inconclusive in that even though Baron Dieskau was captured and his men lost the field, Johnson did not follow up and cut off their retreat by taking their boats at Ticonderoga. Nor did Johnson take Crown Point.

The French began building Fort Carillon at Ticonderoga, and the English completed Forts Edward and William Henry (named for grandsons of the king—another despatch).

Compared to Braddock's defeat only months before, the Battle of Lake George, despite it flaws, was considered an important victory in the colonies and London saw to it that Johnson was made a baronet and given the sum of ƒ5,000.

Another objective of the British war plans was to strengthen Oswego, which, as important as it was both militarily and commercially, had been neglected and allowed to decay. In the spring of 1755, reinforcements arrived and more than 300 ship-wrights also came to build a fleet of small warships. The first was a forty-foot galley to be manned with oars and armed with a light cannon.

HERE THE ANCIENT CARRY PASSED SOUTHWARD TO FORT NEWPORT AND WOOD CREEK

Oneida County, 58*
W. Dominick & Jay Streets, Rome

A new fort was built on the west side of the Oswego River, and for the first time, a fort was built on the east side of the river as well, both sited on higher ground. Winter came on before either could be finished. The weakest link in the Albany-Oswego supply line was the carrying place, so Fort Williams was built at the east end at the headwaters of the Mohawk (Rome) and Fort Bull, more a warehouse than a fort, was put up four miles west on Wood Creek that winter.

Poor planning resulted in inadequate provisions; many men died and the survivors barely endured to spring. It didn't take long for the French to find out about this new construction; in late March of 1756, Governor Pierre Vaudreuil sent out through the Adirondacks a guerilla force on snowshoes under his brother's command, which wiped out Fort Bull and all the supplies and killed thirty-eight. Few survived.

General Shirley of Massachusetts put off his expedition to take Niagara, even though an Indian spy had slipped into the fort and reported that the walls were so rotten that they could be pulled down and that the garrison numbered only a hundred.

Captain John Bradstreet had been put in command at Oswego, with an excellent war record including a part in the taking of Louisbourg, and charged the place with new energy in the spring of 1756. He built many batteaux to supply Oswego from Albany, and resumed ship and fort construction after a winter so cold, all one could hope for was to survive. Two ships of fair size were being constructed, but French and Indian spies relayed all this to Montreal, and time began to run out for the English colonials.

In July, Colonel Bradstreet, a Nova Scotian and regular officer who obtained his commission by merit rather than purchase, and young Phillip Schuyler, scion of a leading York state family, with a company of men, were taking empty batteaux back to Albany when, nine miles south of Oswego, they were attacked by a force of French and Indians under Coulon de Villiers. They holed up on a small island, staving off the onslaught until reinforcements arrived to drive the attackers off, but they lost over sixty men. Captives revealed that the French had plans to soon destroy Oswego. (The island is now called Battle Island, and the battle is commemorated by both a bronze plaque mounted on a boulder and a challenging New York State golf course).

Louis Joseph, Marquis de Montcalm now arrived to be commander of all French troops in North America. He had with him three able assistants: Colonel Bourlamaque, the Chevalier François de Lévis, and Louis Antoine de Bougainville, his aide-de-camp. Bougainville was young and gifted with an inquiring and disciplined mind. (He later became an admiral, circumnavigated the world accompanied by naturalists and astronomers and explored the south seas a decade before James Cook's similar exploit. Two straits in the Pacific and an island in the Solomon Islands were named after him, and he introduced the tropical vine, bougainvillea to Europe). He was with Montcalm wherever the action was, and kept a careful and detailed journal.

General Montcalm, forty-four, had been in the army all his adult life. A shrewd observer and strategist, he quickly realized the significance of Oswego and Ticonderoga, and wasted no time organizing his campaign. Technically, Montcalm was under the orders of Governor Vaudreuil who had laid out a broad strategy, but Montcalm's military achievements and charm soon made him the recognized leader of Canada.

His first success was the destruction of both forts at Oswego. They had not been completed in time, and the rebuilt forts, supplies, ships, and batteaux, all went up in smoke. Montcalm was new to making of war with Indian allies and unprepared for their acts of brutality in the excitement of battle and its aftermath, although the usual prospect of plunder had induced the Indians' participation. Almost 100 wounded and other prisoners were massacred by the Indians as Montcalm and his troops looked on, helpless to arrest the cruel and gruesome action.

General Daniel Webb, in his dilatory attempt to relieve Oswego, only reached the great carrying place, panicked, and destroyed both forts there. Fortunately for inland settlements, Montcalm retired to Canada. But the loss at Oswego and the carrying place forts, left "Fort" Johnson, Johnson's mansion, and a blockhouse there with some artillery, the main bastions of defense. The upper Mohawk valley was exposed to an attack by the French, amazingly deferred a year, at German Flats (Herkimer).

1755-1756
FORT WILLIAMS
GUARDED
UPPER MOHAWK LANDING
BURNED IN A PANIC
BY BRITISH GEN. WEBB

Oneida County, 52*
Bouck St., btw. E Whitesboro
& E. Dominick St., Rome

London was unhappy with General Shirley's efforts as Commander of American Forces, and in the summer of 1756, Cumberland replaced him with another crony, Lord Loudoun, appointing General James Abercromby and General Daniel Webb as interim commanders until Loudoun could arrive on the scene.

Loudoun trained both his regular troops from England and the provincials rigorously, and he recognized, as Braddock refused to, the value of a fighting force that could fight in the woods, Indian style. This meant taking advantage of natural cover, and aiming their shots at a Frenchman or

Indian, rather than haphazardly at a mass of the enemy as in the European manner. Loudoun also improved the supply system and the intelligence service.

War between France and England couldn't be contained and erupted in Europe, and William Pitt became Prime Minister. Largely due to Pitt's management, the English eventually won the Seven Years War, which ranged across North America, the Caribbean, Europe, and to India, with Great Britain, Prussia, and Hanover (King George's electorate) on one side and France, Austria, Russia, Saxony, Sweden, and after 1762, Spain on the other. Cumberland was removed; his commanders lacked victories and he, himself lost his army and the (family) Electorate of Hanover without firing a shot.

An attempt to take Louisbourg by the English failed for reasons that would have been hard to overcome by any commander: many ships of the French fleet happened to show up in the harbor earlier than expected, and, in addition, they had the bad luck to have to contend with constant fog and a hurricane that dismasted twelve of their ships—the fortunes of war. Loudon let his forces languish in Acadia until the prospect of help from the fleet disintegrated, and then sailed his army back to New York.

Governor Vaudreuil had in February sent men, again under the command of his brother, across the ice of Lake Champlain and Lake George to strike Fort William Henry at the head of the lake. But the element of surprise was lost, and they had no heavy artillery with which to shell the fort. Aside from burning many English batteaux that would be needed the following summer, the expedition was a fizzle.

In late July of 1757, Montcalm with 8,000 men proceeded from Fort Carillon south up Lake George by canoe and batteaux to Fort William Henry. With the necessary heavy artillery to successfully lay down a siege, they began the usual program of digging zigzag trenches along which they would move the guns close enough to blast down a wall from a protected position. Of course, they were resisted by the English, but it was a foregone conclusion that the fort would fall. The French offered honorable terms after three days of bombardment, and in good faith the English surrendered.

Again, Montcalm did not control his 1,800 western and Abnaki Indians, who began to hack at the wounded in a hospital tent with their tomahawks, and then at the retreating unarmed English prisoners as they marched out of the fort. Montcalm seamed helpless with his soldiers to restrain the frenzied and rum-soaked red men running amok, but it was a bloodbath that put a stain on his character. Various estimates range as high as 1600 killed outright, and that 200 prisoners of the Indians were marched off to Montreal to be later redeemed for rum and supplies.

Now Albany and even New York City felt vulnerable, but the French went no farther; their objective had been only to knock out an enemy base of operations.

So far, the war had gone very badly for the colonials, but one bit of irony developed. The western Indians who perpetrated the carnage at Fort William Henry, starting with the helpless in the hospital, were not aware that many were sick with smallpox. They carried the latent disease back home with them, and having little natural immunity to this infection, became victims themselves. They also contaminated their home villages, and a very large number of the Potawatomies died of the epidemic.

Lord Loudoun was reprimanded for the failures at Fort William Henry and Louisbourg the year before, and replaced by General James Abercromby. The English war objectives for 1758 were to try once again to capture Louisbourg, to take Fort Carillon and to advance north down the Champlain Valley to seize Fort Duquesne.

General Abercromby and his second in command, Viscount George Howe, and their flotilla of 900 boats from Nantucket and Cape Cod, advanced down the sparkling waters and islands of Lake George in fine weather in July. The soldiers landed at the foot of the lake, and unlimbered their legs when they began the final march along the short outlet, and approached Fort Carillon nearby at the head of Lake Champlain. Lord Howe, who was highly regarded by high and low and thought to be the brains of the expedition, was, inauspiciously, shot and killed on patrol in the first skirmish.

Montcalm had had his 3,000 men cut all the virgin timber across the point of Ticonderoga and stack the untrimmed logs with the sharpened branch ends facing outward for a barricade. The cleared field now exposed any assault party within a hundred yards of this abatis to murderous fire. Abercromby directed his forces from too far from the scene of action and made grotesquely bad judgements in his use of men and equipment. From the beginning, he could have blasted the log barricade, and then the walls of the fort itself had he ordered the heavy artillery, brought all this far, hauled up the slope from the barges. Instead, wave after wave of Abercromby's regular troops futilely advanced against the French abatis only to be shot down. With casualties of 1,610 out of almost 6,400 men, Abercromby withdrew to Fort William Henry, abandoning his supplies and baggage to the French garrison which had been destitute.

The colonies were appalled that this large English and colonial force, with all the planning and treasure that had gone into the expedition, could have been defeated and lost so many men. At the moment of truth, Abercromby had been guilty of both incompetence and cowardice. A nadir in military performance had been reached.

The French at Louisbourg, having resisted the earlier English attempt, mainly because of the vagaries of men and nature which had been favorable to them, realized their vulnerability, and reinforced the defenses to make it the strongest fortress of North America. The English fleet patrolled the coast and, despite continued fog and storms, captured most of the French supply ships trying to run their blockade.

With most of the French fleet occupied in Spain or elsewhere, the naval advantage was England's. Sir Jeffrey Amherst, appointed by William Pitt, began the siege June 1st and, benefitting from experience gained from so many previous assaults, and with the help of Brigadier General James Wolfe and 11,000 men, subdued Louisbourg by the end of July. Pitt did not wish to have such a formidable fortress remain standing and ordered the huge edifice razed to the ground. A naval blockade of the St. Lawrence, Quebec, and Montreal could now be much more effective.

FORT STANWIX
AND
REVOLUTIONARY
SKIRMISHES

Oneida County, 50
Mill & Whiteboro Streets, Rome

At a council of war in the early summer of 1758, the order for the construction of a strong fort to guard the "Great Carrying Place" was given. At the same council, Lieutenant Colonel Bradstreet was given orders to take Fort Frontenac, a mission he had advised for two years. Brigadier General Stanwix was put in charge of constructing the fort he had designed, and Bradstreet had charge of 123 large batteaux and 95 whaleboats. While Stanwix began building the fort, Bradstreet's force of 3000 men, of whom ninety-five percent were provincials, cleared fallen trees from Wood Creek, then paddled the length of Oneida Lake, and camped six miles downstream near Three Rivers. When his seventy Iroquois found out that it was to be a raid on Fort Frontenac, they bowed out.

SITE OF
STOCKADED FORT
1758-1759
ABOUT 60 FEET SQUARE
CONTAINING THREE STOREHOUSES
BUILT BY COLONY OF N. Y.

Oswego County, 30
NY 57 at Three Rivers

The next day, they temporarily reduced the number of men in each boat, and shot the rapids (at present Fulton), covering the mile of rough water in three minutes! Only a few mishaps and an hour and a half later, they arrived at Lake Ontario. From there they moved northeast and stayed close to shore, glad of the calm August weather since the open boats were heavily laden with supplies and cannon. Thirteen days from the carrying place and they were at Fort Frontenac.

Now, it was the French who had been lax and incompetent. The stone fort, which guarded Lake Ontario and the lifeline to all the western forts, including Fort Duquesne, had been neglected and many of the guns could not be brought to bear. Bradstreet had four twelve-pounders and four eight-inch howitzers, but he didn't have to prolong the siege against the inadequate force of 110 French, including women and children. They resisted for two days - sufficient to surrender with honor - with only two French killed and minor wounds sustained by Bradstreet's men. Of the entire French Lake

Howard S. Ford

Ontario fleet of nine gunboats captured, he burned all but two which he loaded with a vast amount of captured armament and supplies including truck for trading with the Indians, depriving the western French forts of the same.

Bradstreet's men did as much damage as they could, and not wishing to waste cargo space, sent the French captives marching back to Montreal to create a credit for prisoner exchange. They themselves hastened back to Stanwix since the expedition had been audacious enough to not count on any more good luck. This secret and competently carried out mission was important all out of proportion to it's cost. Lake Ontario now was under English control so that supplies to Fort Duquesne and the other western French forts could be cut off, insuring their fall.

**BLOCKHOUSE
60 RODS EAST OF
THIS POINT STOOD
FORT ERECTED BY
BRITISH IN 1759**

Oneida County, 98
NY 13 in Sylvan Beach

CHAPTER FOUR

Inept military efforts by Washington, Braddock, Webb, Abercromby, Shirley, and Loudoun, and the terror inflicted earlier at Pickawillany swayed Ohio Valley Indian's allegiance to the French, and hundreds of Senecas aligned with them as well. Fear grew that If the nearer Iroquois followed suit even the eastern seaboard would be imperiled.

Fort Duquesne's strategic location at the forks of the Ohio enabled the French to use the Indians as a formidable force to push back British boundaries during war and was a tremendously profitable market during peace. Alienating the Indians from the arms of the French and taking the fort was the next order of business. Brigadier General John Forbes was put in command of the re-attempt to do this in the spring of 1758.

His promotion was based on merit rather than being a crony of the Duke of Cumberland, no longer the Captain-General. He had proven his courage serving under Lord Loudoun, was dedicated, and an avid student of military sciences. The campaign required skill in supplying the expedition and building a road which would extend more than two hundred miles over the rugged Alleghenies through a tangle of virgin forest. Building forts at intervals on the road would provide warehousing and quartering for the garrisons needed for the siege of Duquesne and guarding the supply line. Forbes wanted to extend the road from Philadelphia tapping supplies there rather than using Braddock's road from Alexandria. Virginians, including Washington, pressed him to use the southern route citing the lesser expense of repairing an existing road and because of its commercial value to them in opening the Ohio Valley to settlement after the war. But Forbes won out; he would use the Philadelphia pike and make a road out of the path from the Susquehanna used by the pack-trains of the traders on their way to the Ohio Valley; it would be forty miles shorter and he would not have to cross the Youghiogheny River.

Forbes, in contrast to most British regular officers, believed in making war Indian-style; he was also fortunate in having as his second in command his friend and Swiss-born Lieutenant Colonel Henry Bouquet, whose ability and support was essential as Forbes health deteriorated as the campaign progressed. Bouquet and his Royal Americans arrived in Lancaster early April joined by

Howard S. Ford

Lieutenant Colonel Archibald Montgomery and 1000 Highlanders in June, soon followed by artillery and stores. Washington, in charge of the third column, marched his men (making a total of 6000) a month later to Raystown where Fort Bedford was being completed on the path earlier laid out by George Croghan. Under Forbes, it was being made into a road from Harris' Ferry through Carlisle, Shippensburg, Chamber's Fort, and Fort Loudoun. (The road later became the foundation for US 30, the Lincoln Highway).

By early September, more than a month of toil cleared and prepared the road over formidable Laurel Mountain to Loyalhanna Valley where they erected Fort Ligonier. As the road builders neared Fort Duquesne, Forbes became so weak that he fell behind and had to be carried in a litter. Major James Grant, with Bouquet's blessing, made a feeler thrust with 800 of his Highlanders in hopes of seizing the fort but was ambushed by French-led Indians and 300 of his men were killed or captured and some brutalized later at the fort. Bouquet was able to calm his men, avoiding the disastrous panic that had shambled Braddock's campaign, and shielded the laborers with a vanguard and flankers against numerous attacks which still claimed sixty more of his men.

A Moravian missionary, Christian Frederick Post, had been for fifteen years a trusted friend of many of the Delaware and Shawnees, who were victims of the fraudulent Walking Purchase and had been shoved from their ancestral lands. In the spring, he was asked by the Pennsylvania governor and a few of the Delaware chiefs to travel to the Wyoming valley to persuade them to change their loyalty from the French. His success merited going a second time to convince the Ohio Delawares. They agreed to meet with eastern Delawares, the Cayuga and Seneca, the governors of Pennsylvania and New Jersey, the Penn Proprietors and their underlings, Conrad Weiser, leading pacifist Quakers, George Croghan, Johnson's deputy, and Reverend Post at Easton in October 1758. Forbes kept in touch with the treaties progress.

They all had their dignity and turf to uphold and axes to grind. The sore point of the Walking Purchase was ignored (but ever present), and to counter its bad effects, the Penn agents were persuaded to relinquish a large tract in western Pennsylvania, though it had been bought legally, back to the Iroquois who would continue to allow the Delawares and Shawnees to live and hunt there. The Indians agreed to withhold their support from the French fort, which was on short rations, and agreed to release white captives. George Croghan, with Johnson's authority, stated that Britain would, from that day on, consider land west of the mountains the Indian's exclusive territory. The main issue of peace was settled a month before the defense at Fort Duquesne collapsed. Fort Duquesne's fall was partly due to Post's brave and successful parleys as well as the alluring promises of Croghan.

Heavy fall rains hampered road building and Forbes, who had caught up to his army in the field at the Loyalhanna, was considering halting the campaign for the winter. In early November, French captives revealed that the fort was under-manned. The tentative plan for closing operations for the winter was scrapped and Forbes and his officers decided to press the attack since the time seemed ripe.

When they were camped only ten miles from the fort on the night of November 24th, they heard an awesome explosion which the next day was still spewing smoke. The French had blown up the fort and abandoned it to the English. Settlers became much safer on the frontiers of New York, Maryland, Pennsylvania, and Virginia, as the French concentrated on defending Niagara, Montreal, and Quebec. Unfortunately, General Forbes was so ill that he had to return to Philadelphia where he died shortly after the first of the year at age forty-nine.

SITE OF
BRITISH CAMP
SIR JEFFREY AMHERST WITH
TEN THOUSAND TROOPS WAS
HERE 1760 ENROUTE TO
CANADA TO CRUSH FRENCH
POWER IN AMERICA

Oswego County, 29
NY 57 at Three Rivers

One of General Amherst's first acts was to direct General Stanwix to build a new and secure fort at the forks of the Ohio, in 1759, naming this one Fort Pitt. He sent Brigadier Prideaux to take Fort

Niagara, using Oswego as a staging point, and ordered him to build a new fort there when he returned. General Wolfe was assigned to move up the St. Lawrence and take Quebec. Amherst delegated himself to subdue Fort Carillon at Ticonderoga and Fort St. Frederic at Crown Point. It took him four days of cautious siege to take Carillon but, all along, the French plan was to sacrifice it and withdraw after an indifferent defense.

As at Duquesne, the French had left a lighted fuse in a powder magazine, which exploded but caused little damage other than destroying the barracks and killing some horses. They also blew up Fort St. Frederic, and withdrew to the foot of Champlain at Isle-Aux-Noix for a defensive stand. The only way for Amherst to pursue safely was to build a small squadron of batteaux to transport men and supplies, and enough small warships to outgun the small French fleet which still had the run of the lake.

Amherst also repaired both forts, and renamed Fort Carillon for its point of land, called by the Indians Ticonderoga.

In mid September of 1759, he moved his batteaux and warships north, and the French crews scuttled three of their four warships, leaving Amherst in control of Lake Champlain. When he then heard that Wolfe had taken Quebec, he halted operations for the winter, rather than moving on Montreal that year. The only really daring act that season was Major Robert Rogers' Regulars's retaliatory attack on the St. Lawrence village of the St. Francis Abenakis, who had been harassing the New England frontier. Rogers' force destroyed the village, and killed 200 Indians, but even so, only a third of the Rangers got back safely.

Fort Niagara was undermanned, and upon hearing the English were coming, Commander Chevalier Pouchot requested reinforcements from Fort Venango and points west. The British, under the command of Brigadier Prideaux, came up the Mohawk to Oswego where they met with General William Johnson and his Iroquois.

The combined force then continued to Niagara, and began the dreary digging and artillery volleys necessary to a siege. To the Indians this was not warfare, and they stayed out of it on both sides, awaiting the outcome.

When Prideaux was killed by a random shell fragment out of one of his own mortars, Johnson took command without contention from the regular British officers, an unusual show of respect for a colonial.

The siege had been in progress two weeks, when 1,600 French and Indians arrived from the west, and began their attack on Johnson's rear. Johnson's men had time to erect a breastwork of logs, and waited until the enemy was very close and, with the presence of the Iroquois on the flank, returned a furious fire that decimated the relieving force. Johnson convinced Pouchot that he should surrender, gave him honorable terms, and remembering Fort William Henry, made sure that the French were able to embark for New York, safe from Indian meddling and plunder.

FORT BREWERTON
ORIGINAL EARTHWORK
OF FORT ERECTED BY
BRITISH IN 1759

Oswego County, 5
US 11 at Brewerton

In Prideaux's absence, the French, including Abbé Picquet and his Oswegatchie Indians from La Presentation, tried to take Oswego, but were repulsed. Amherst then called for Brigadier Thomas Gage to come west to replace the fallen Prideaux, and build a new fort at Oswego. A blockhouse was built where Wood Creek enters Oneida Lake. That same year, another fort was built at the western end of the lake and named after its builder, Major George Brewerton. The only action the fort saw was the result of resentment shown by the Indians at having a favorite fishing spot taken over by the British; they raided the post garden of vegetables several years later. A smaller fort was erected to guard the portage at Oswego Falls.

The French at Quebec felt secure because of the bastion's location on the north shore point of the Saint Lawrence, and the high cliffs above the river that would have to be scaled to reach it. Searching out the river channel would also impede the British fleet sailing upstream. (Captain James Cook was to survey the channel the following year). However, Admiral Charles Saunders skillfully navigated his twenty-two warships and 119 troop transports up the river, and encamped 9,000 men on the Isle d'Orleans in sight of Quebec by the end of June, 1759.

Within a few weeks, men and artillery were deployed on both sides of the river, and a devastating artillery barrage began. The English were also able to get a few warships upstream past the city, and cut off river communications with Montreal.

At the end of July, British troops made an attempt on a redoubt at Montmorency, a few miles below Quebec. Instead of waiting for other troops working their way into position, they decided to go it alone up the steep 200-foot bank, but withering fire from above, and a sudden drenching rainstorm made climbing the muddy slope impossible. They lost 500 men in the struggle.

Several other actions were taken in the vicinity, one forty miles upstream, all desultory. The armies were sizing up each other, but it was now early September. Wolfe was not a healthy man and seemed in the throes of confusion and remained aloof. But he sought the advice of his senior officers who suggested that another attempt be made two miles above the city to draw Montcalm out. A diversionary movement was made downstream; the ruse worked, and Wolfe, under cover of darkness, deluded a few guards and personally led his men up the steep 200-foot bank unopposed. Against orders, his adjutant, General Isaac Barré (who was to argue for America's cause as a Member of Parliament in a few years), sent up more men strengthening Wolfe.

The French thought this action was the diversion, and before they realized the truth, 4,500 redcoats and several cannon were on the Plains of Abraham. Montcalm's forces of about equal strength met those of Wolfe, in European style, formation marching directly against formation. As they closed on each other, the French fired first, but they were out of effective range. Wolfe was in the front line, leading his men, and was struck by a musket ball that proved fatal before the day was over. At forty yards the British fired, injuring many, and, pressed on with a bayonet charge, forcing the French to break ranks and flee. Montcalm was also wounded as he was leaving the battlefield, and survived Wolf only by hours.

Bougainville arrived later in the day from upriver, saw there was little he could do, and marched his men back several miles to await developments. Much of the French army around Quebec panicked, abandoned their equipment, and retreated.

Generous terms were given and Quebec surrendered. But Bougainville and Lévis still had armies intact, and Montreal remained in French possession.

Quebec city was a shambles from two months of shelling, and food supplies were dwindling. Brigadier General Murray, loaned money to a French commissary to help feed the inhabitants; redcoats shared their rations with Quebec habitants, helped bring in the harvest, and unpleasantness between conqueror and conquered was reduced. Everyone was busy, cutting wood, grinding grain, repairing fortifications, and preparing for winter and the inevitable assault by the French the following spring. The British still did not know how to avoid scurvy: 700 of them died and many more became sick and unable to function. Over 200 years earlier, Cartier had had the same problem with scurvy when he wintered on the St. Lawrence, and the Indians taught him the use of a tea made with spruce needles. The British troops tried it now and it worked.

In the spring of 1760, after suppressing a partisan assault at Quebec, British forces began to converge on Montreal: 10,000 men under Amherst were joined by William Johnson with 1,300 Indians from Oswego. General Murray with 2,500 men, four warships and other supply boats, worked their way up the St. Lawrence; and Haviland with 3,000 troops from Crown Point, forced Bougainville on Champlain to retreat from Isles-Aux-Noix before him and Murray. They all arrived at the same time in early September, ringing Montreal with an intimidating army that brought about a surrender without firing a shot. Governor Vaudreuil, the last French governor of New France, surrendered September 7, 1760.

The terms of capitulation on the civilian population were generous, but those given the military were harsh because of the atrocities the French and Indians had inflicted at Fort William Henry and Oswego. The war was virtually over in Canada, but the final division of who came out with what still had to be decided by the fighting in Europe and the terms of the victor. The French Navy was no longer effective. The blockade of France and Canada by the British Navy together with the cost of the war was very damaging to French commerce and cut the availability of supplies in both Europe and Canada. In 1763, the Treaty of Paris was signed, and France gave up all of Canada and territory she claimed east of the Mississippi. A faction in Parliament wanted the victor's prize to be the much more valuable sugar-rich French West Indies rather than cold Canada, (the fisheries off the

Grand Banks were more valuable) but Pitt prevailed. Two small groups of islands, Miquelon and St. Pierre, used for fishing off the southern coast of Newfoundland, still belong to France. Louisiana had not been the scene of the war, and so was not a factor in the treaty; France soon deeded it to Spain, her ally, to compensate her for the loss of the Floridas (to England) and Minorca.

Great Britain tried to saddle a portion of the expense of the French and Indian War on the American colonies, who resisted and fought a revolution partly because of these impositions. The arrogance and superior attitude exhibited by the regular officers to the colonial American officers and men, and their sorry record of military "invincibility" sobered American leaders and prepared a seedbed of resentment that the folly of several succeeding administrations in London fed and ripened.

In France, heavy taxes needed to meet the cost of the war in North America and elsewhere, together with lavish court expenses over the next thirty years, helped incubate the French Revolution. The world was never to be the same.

CHAPTER FIVE

When the British took over the French forts, they enlarged them and granted the surrounding land to officers, traders, and other favorites as was customary with them. This land-grabbing contrasted with French policies and caused consternation to the Indians, particularly the Senecas who had been told by the British that they would occupy the forts only long enough to defeat the French. New rules for licensing and governing Indian traders also were set in place, but Sir William had no prosecutorial powers and trading abuses continued.

The Indians had been used to receiving lavish gifts and other niceties periodically from the French for the use of their land, but Amherst had contempt for the Indians and treated them arrogantly. He withheld gifts, including the distribution of ammunition for hunting which was necessary for the Indians to avoid starvation. Sir William and Croghan warned him of the dangers of such arbitrary rules but the general insisted on ignoring Indian sensibilities, and years of pragmatic dealing with them was brushed aside.

Some of the local French took advantage of this situation to fan the embers of long-simmering Indian enmity for the British by persuading Pontiac, an obscure Ottawa chief, and leaders of other western tribes that the French king would send an army up the Mississippi to destroy the British and they would all share the spoils. With these rumors circulating, it was easy for Pontiac to co-opt their hatreds and shape a loosely formed confederation to implement his plan to drive the British out.

The fighting of the French and Indian War had been over only three years when Pontiac made his move in May of 1763, and tried to storm Fort Detroit from the inside using a clever and deceptive scheme. His Indians were to enter the fort as on any normal trading day, but with muskets sawn short so that they could be hidden in the braves' and squaws' clothing. A given signal would trigger the attack. Major Gladwin, commander at Detroit, was forewarned of a possible plot so it failed, but Pontiac kept his force of many tribes surrounding the fort, and prevented supplies from getting in.

Simultaneously, Forts Pitt and Niagara were attacked and besieged. Within a month, the smaller forts at Michilimakinac, Sandusky, Preque Isle, and Le Boeuf were overwhelmed and many in the garrison were wantonly and brutally slaughtered.

To Pontiac's chagrin, the British were able to break the blockade and resupply the Detroit fort by using an armed schooner which forced its way past opposing canoes and delivered arms and food to the fort's water gate. Pontiac then realized that the weakest link in the chain of supply was the portage around Niagara Falls. In mid- September, a small force of Indians ambushed an armed and escorted supply train above the Devil's Hole rapids of the river with devastating results to the porters and the guards. Another attempt to bring supply transports the length of Lake Erie was swamped by a severe storm, dampening British hopes that the fort could be re-supplied before winter.

Colonel Bouquet's victory at nearby Bushy Run relieved the four-month siege of Fort Pitt. No doubt, the smallpox epidemic which was spread to the Indians at a parley by giving them infected blankets from the fort hospital reduced their numbers. As well, the arrival of November and the Indian's need to hunt to provide for winter thinned the number of Indians surrounding both forts Pitt and Niagara.

Pontiac's coalition of Ottawas, Wyandots, Ojibwas, Delawares, and Potawatomies weakened more rapidly when the French army did not appear. When Pontiac learned that the French had signed the Treaty of Paris and were not going to come to his assistance, he aborted his siege of Detroit at the end of October, 1763, and his confederacy weakened even more. His hopes for the following spring wilted when he learned that the French forts in the Illinois country would be invested by the British and his source of weapons and ammunition would dry up.

The Delawares had lured the Senecas into supporting Pontiac and both tribes were raiding settlements in western Pennsylvania. Sir William Johnson persuaded the Senecas to bow out of the action by sending three parties, headed by his son, John Johnson, Henry Montour, Crohgan's interpreter, and Johnson's brother-in-law, Joseph Brant, to destroy Delaware villages in the region of Canisteo, long the hangout of renegades, red, white, and black. The Delawares fled to sanctuary in Ohio to live among the Shawnees and Miamis, the Senecas deserted Pontiac, and young Brant counted his first coup to become a warrior. Sir William was proud that he had been able to keep the other five nations of the League from joining Pontiac's rebellion.

He then announced to the less war-inclined lake Indians that he was willing to meet with them at Niagara to discuss their grievances and the resumption of trade, which many now desired. Bouquet and Bradstreet subdued the Shawnee and the Miamis in Ohio and obtained the release of two hundred captives, including some French, and with winter almost at hand, persuaded them to cease fighting and harassing the frontier.

KANESTIO CASTLE
INDIAN VILLAGE BURNED 1764
BY CAPTAIN ANDREW MONTOUR
AND A PROVINCIAL FORCE

Steuben County, 5
NY 21, Canisteo

Several months after London heard of the devastating attacks on the forts, General Amherst asked to be recalled. The victor over rival-nation France, was perceived by some as being outgeneraled by the savage, Pontiac, and was replaced by Major General Thomas Gage, who in turn would have his ultimate humiliation at Lexington and Concord, and Bunker Hill.

With Johnson's blessing, the peripatetic and energetic Croghan sailed to London to obtain permission to seek and parley with Pontiac which was granted by a government desperate to not add any more expense to that already incurred in the French war by this new one with the Indians. With this authority and the help of his many Indian friends, he sought Pontiac in the wilds of Illinois, mollifying all Indians he came upon. By chance, he encountered Pontiac who had already concluded that he could not prevail, would have no one but the British to rely on for supplies in the future, and so should sue for peace, the sooner, the better for the Indians.

Johnson contrived to be overly respectful to Pontiac at the treaty ceremony held in 1766 at Oswego by following Croghan's advice "to ruin his influence with his own people". Indeed, the British attention and favors to Pontiac created jealousy among the chiefs and made Pontiac's star set as rapidly as it had risen.

In terms of casualties and property loss to the British, Pontiac's Indians won hands down. But Pontiac's attempt to organize a confederacy of tribes strong enough to stop white westward expansion failed and wouldn't be tried again in any meaningful way for thirty years when Little Turtle, understudied by Tecumseh, made his attempt.

Three years later at Cahokia, across the Mississippi from the beginnings of St. Louis, a Peoria Indian stabbed Pontiac on the street in the belief he was doing a service to the tribes. The assassin soon learned that the tribes, including his own, disagreed with that assessment, and he fled in desperation to hide inextricably in the hollow of a large (but not large enough) tree where he died of starvation.

King George III was twenty-two when he became king in 1760, and young for his years, he had not learned to read until he was ten. Reigning was difficult for him, and choosing wise ministers was equally hard; he had six of them in the first ten years of his reign. Then, he appointed Lord North who directed the folly of the next dozen years until the British defeat at Yorktown finally discredited North's administration.

Folly was compounded when Lord Germain, a favorite of the king became North's secretary of state in 1775. The confusion of orders dispatched from London preceding the Saratoga campaign is attributable to him. King George's reign endured sixty years, the last ten of which he was determined by doctors to be mad. But the king had had to contend with Pontiac's Conspiracy, the American Revolution, the French Revolution, Napoleon Bonaparte, and the cruel rebelliousness of his sons.

With the friction between Indians and settlers becoming more aggravated, the king proclaimed the lands west of the Alleghenies closed to immigration in 1763. Sir William and others in London had suggested this policy to pacify the Indians and to avoid thinly settled and indefensible areas, if western expansion continued, in favor of heavier populated, defensible settlements east of the Proclamation Line. Exclusion of colonists from western settlement was justified, but it was resented by the those who had plans for western expansion. It also defied enforcement.

London was also concerned that governing already unruly colonials far removed from the coastal cities would be difficult and costly.

As Pontiac's rebellion was winding down, people on the frontier began to again migrate into the upper Ohio Valley. The Indians became agitated and numerous local Indian meetings were held to determine action against this most recent violation of the British promise to restrain whites from settling west of the Line. Croghan informed Johnson that the Indians were planning a much larger congress to organize resistance but it was postponed until the following spring. To circumvent such a meeting, Johnson urged the Iroquois that they should preempt the congress and hold it in their home domain since they were universally regarded as the "senior" Indian nation.

In September of 1768, the Fort Stanwix Conference attracted over 3000 Indians from most of the tribes east of the Mississippi as well as traders, governors, land speculators, and politicians from the colonies. But Johnson and Croghan, with the Board of Trade and the Iroquois, had already negotiated a sale by the Iroquois of all their subjugated land south of the Ohio, down to the mouth of the Kanawha River, to the British for ƒ10,000. The Confederacy wanted to part with this land to divert the white expansion to take place well south of their New York domain. For the British, owning this land gave them more control over westward expansion even though now the line would extend farther west and south before returning to the crest of the Appalachians. It was more land than for which London had planned.

PROPERTY LINE
WESTERN BOUNDARY OF
CIVILIZATION FIXED BY
FORT STANWIX TREATY
NOV. 5, 1768. WITNESSED
BY SIR WILLIAM JOHNSON

Oneida County, 65*
NY 12 north of Waterville

The land companies, traders, and frontiersman thought their futures were improved, but the Shawnee, Delawares, and Mingos, who had been allowed to live and hunt on Iroquois land, were again humiliated by the "senior" nation and had to move again to north of the Ohio. The Iroquois awarded Johnson and Croghan large tracts of land in central New York for past and present services.

GEORGE CROGAN
INDIAN AGENT–LAND SPECULATOR
LIVED IN PIONEER LOG HOME
LOCATED HERE 1769–1770.
GENERAL JAMES CLINTON'S
HEADQUARTERS IN 1779.

Otsego County, 18
On Main Street, Cooperstown

Following the Fort Stanwix Treaty, the line ran from Fort Stanwix along Unadilla Creek south to near the site of Hancock, then to Owego and to Williamsport (settled 1772). It then ran westward cross-country to the head waters of the West Branch of the Susquehanna to the Delaware-Shawnee town of Kittanning on the Allegheny and down that river and the Ohio to the mouth of the Kanawha River, then back to the Appalachian ridge (near Roanoke). Within a short time, land companies, with an eye for dividing up the land among themselves, gained influence with the highest levels of government in London, cutting officials in on expected profits to garner grants. Samuel Wharton and William Trent, traders from Philadelphia and Washington, Franklin, Croghan, and many other top people were on the verge of seeing their efforts fulfilled when the passage of the Quebec Act, in 1774, slammed the gate shut on their prospects. But by this time, over 30,000 settlers moving west by way of the Forbes and Braddock roads had pre-empted the hopes of the land companies in the Ohio Valley, making moot any legalistic efforts to dislodge them. The early addition of Kentucky (1792) and Tennessee (1796) to the original thirteen states of the United States were the outgrowth of this resolute migration.

Within a very few years the Royal Proclamation Line became academic.

CHAPTER SIX

To meet the large cost of the recent wars and to build and garrison forts to enforce the Proclamation line, a series of taxes were imposed on the colonies. One of the first was a tax on publications such as playing cards, licenses, deeds and other papers. The tax varied with the item; two pounds for a college diploma to a half penny for a half-sheet pamphlet. To show the tax had been paid, a stamp was required. (At the time, Charles Gravier, comte de Vergennes, French ambassador to Turkey, later to become France's Foreign Minister, astutely predicted that the absence of France in Canada would result in the colonials no longer needing the mother country's protection but that they would be called on to pay for it, and would reject this burden for independence). Britons paid total taxes of twenty-six shillings compared to one shilling levied in the colonies. Delegates from nine colonies met in New York to protest that only their own legislatures should be able to tax them. The tax was highly objectionable but, as well, the revenues were to be used in part to pay the governor's salary. Colonial legislatures over the years had insisted on paying the governor his salary in order to have a degree of control over him. This control would now be in jeopardy and the attempt at interference was resented. The outcry was so intense that Parliament promptly repealed the tax that Benjamin Franklin scorned as "that Mother of Mischief".

But at the same time, Parliament passed the Declaratory Act asserting the government's right to levy taxes on the colonists, and imposed a series of duties on glass, lead, paint, paper, and tea. This caused even greater outrage, and the government and king were furiously criticized in the American press. Colonial merchants then refused to import from English manufacturers, aware that English merchants would pressure Parliament to repeal the tax. Again, London responded and the duties on all of these were repealed, except for tea, to emphasize the government's authority. Ten thousand British regulars were imposed on Boston's 22,000 residents to insure compliance and many were quartered in private homes against the owners' will. Resentment flared at London's arrogance and later, the crude insolence soldiers showed Boston families. Samuel Adams formed the Sons of Liberty with young invigorated men, and the idea caught on in many towns to protest insulting and foolish government decrees whenever they could harass and embarrass local government officials.

The Navigation Acts had been passed a hundred years earlier to insure that the mother country would profit from the commercial activities of the colonies, but at the same time not suffer competition from them. This put the colonies at a disadvantage, treating them more like a conquered people than as equals. The acts were amended occasionally as home country industries sought favor and advantage. Lack of enforcement enriched enterprising colonials.

For example, New England had developed trade with Portugal, by sending them barrel staves for the making of wine casks, in return for Portuguese Madeira. Under the acts, the same wine had to be bought through English merchants for higher prices, so the market for barrel staves and Madeira both withered. Exports also had to clear through England so that English merchants would get their cut. The same tampering affected the important sugar, molasses, and rum business, drying up markets.

Suspected law breakers would now be tried not locally, but in Halifax without a jury, and very likely receive a guilty verdict. "Taxation without representation" rang through the colonies, and the government reacted by creating harsh penalties including dissolving the legislature. Those who lived inland and were not directly affected by these restrictions, understood the problems of those in the port cities, reasoning that such harsh conditions could be imposed at will on any industry or region.

With all the English troops in Boston, a clash with the civilians was bound to happen. In March, 1770, a small crowd harassed a guard and a snowball-throwing incident snowballed into redcoats firing a round at the taunting crowd, and five of the rowdies were killed and converted into heros by the time super-patriot Sam Adams finished his eulogy. The British captain and his men were ably defended by Josiah Quincy and John Adams (a cousin of Sam's) and acquitted. To avoid further incidents, the redcoats were recalled to Castle William located on an island in Boston Harbor.

When the fortunes of the East India Company turned down, the government gave it the monopoly over tea in the American colonies to prop up the company, and fixed the price to undersell even the smuggled product. But Crown-sanctioned monopolies were frowned on because they exhibited favoritism and privilege, and the common resentment united the colonies in their opposition. Even staunch loyalists disliked the government's action.

On December 16, 1773, Boston Sons of Liberty dressed as Indians (Mohawks they were called), threw hundreds of casks of tea overboard; tea was also dumped in New York harbor and left to go stale in warehouses in Philadelphia and Charleston. English author Horace Walpole commented, "The Americans have at least acted like men. Our conduct has been that of pert children; we have thrown a pebble at a mastiff and are surprised that he was not frightened."

In reprisal, England closed the port of Boston so that not even a ferry could cross the bay. Food and other supplies could enter the city only across narrow Boston Neck. More regulars were sent to enforce the rules until the tea and the taxes it would have generated were paid for. This applied to Boston only, but other towns showed their continuing sympathy and support by defying the government and supplying Boston with food.

Other laws were enacted in London to strip Massachusetts colonists of their rights, and to protect the Crown's officials from punishment for overzealous prosecution. The attorney general, judges, sheriffs, and justices of the peace were to be named only by the governor. Juries were to be filled by the governor's appointed sheriff. Town meetings could be held but only by permission of the governor, and the agenda had to be approved by him. These so-called Intolerable Acts affected only Massachusetts but the other colonies feared that they could always be applied to them as well. No one thought to bow under pressure and comply. Yankee dander was up.

Adding insult to injury, the Quebec Act was declared to restore pre-war rights to French Canadians. The act provided for non-interference with the affairs of the Roman Catholic Church, and extended the boundary of Quebec south to the Ohio River. Both provisions caused concern. The colonists, both north and south, had for at least twenty-five years made plans for western settlement and trade in the Ohio Valley; with the winning of the French and Indian War these plans were coming to fruition. Any law with a hint of favoring Catholicism caused anxiety by reminding them of the atrocities of England's history of oppressive and inconstant religious stance over a state religion. Highly coveted rights gained over many years of strife were perceived in jeopardy.

Not least in the list of irritations was the arrogance and condescension shown by the British personally for the Americans over many years. Even loyalists resented this.

London couldn't have planned better to get a unified rebellious response. Committees of Correspondence were organized, another Sam Adams' idea, to pass crucial information between the colonies and engendered more cohesion than was ever mustered before. In 1774 at Williamsburg, the germ of the idea of independence began to be considered by some legislative leaders. A colonial congress was proposed for the fall in Philadelphia.

John Sullivan from New Hampshire, son of indentured Irish immigrants and a self-made lawyer who hated the British, made the opening remarks, summarizing the objectives of the congress: "to devise, consult, and adopt measures to secure and perpetuate their rights, and to restore that peace, harmony, and mutual confidence which once subsisted between the parent country and her colonies." Accommodation with Great Britain, not independence, was still the agreed upon theme.

By the meeting's adjournment, it had been agreed that colonial rights were the right to life, liberty, and property, to assemble, and to have exclusive power over taxation and internal policy. Many of Parliament's acts were declared illegal; the colonies would exert economic sanctions until they were repealed. All imports from England were to cease by December 1, 1774, and enforcement procedures were planned.

Sir William Johnson knew that revolution was coming: he was on the side of the Crown, and advised the Iroquois League to be. But Johnson collapsed and died July 11th, 1774 while addressing an Indian conference at Johnson Hall. When his son-in-law, Guy Johnson, assumed Sir William's office, at Johnson's testamentary suggestion, no one was certain which way the Indians would turn. Joseph Brant and a few other Mohawks were closely allied to the British, but the rest of the Iroquois were undecided. Brant, whose fine education at Dr. Eleazer Wheelock's school in Connecticut (later moved to Hanover, New Hampshire and renamed after Lord Dartmouth), had been sponsored by Sir William for whom Brant later served as secretary, went to London the following year for almost six months. He received flattering attention from the elite, was a guest of James Boswell for a few days, sat for his portrait painted by Romney, and was overwhelmingly impressed by the power of England and its unimaginably large population.

The Americans told the Confederacy at councils that they wanted the Indians to stay out of the conflict, that it did not affect them, and that they should stay neutral. Despite this, some of the Oneidas and Tuscaroras were persuaded by their missionary friend, Samuel Kirkland, and the elderly Oneida war chief, Shenandoah, (aka Skenandoah), to favor the Americans. Later, in addition to providing spies, guides, and raiding parties during the Revolution, Shenandoah went so far as to have his men deliver grain to Washington's desperately needy troops at Valley Forge. Washington later expressed his gratitude by naming the beautiful Valley of Virginia after his venerable ally.

The Senecas, Cayugas, Onondagas, and Tuscaroras were subjected to many harangues by John Butler and other loyalist large landowners in the Mohawk valley, but stayed neutral for several years until British Brigadier Barry St. Leger mustered them to join his forces at Oswego just before laying siege to Fort Stanwix.

In April, 1775, British regulars, under General Gage's orders, marched out to confiscate arms and ammunition reportedly stashed by the rebels just outside Boston. They were also to take wealthy ship owner and merchant, John Hancock, into custody charged with smuggling, (openly admired by his countrymen for being so adept at it), as well as Sam Adams for rabble-rousing. The "shot heard round the world" from Lexington and Concord triggered the taking of Fort Ticonderoga by Ethan Allen and Benedict Arnold in May. The Battle of Bunker Hill followed in June, supposedly a victory for the British but, as one English wag said, "Any more victories like that and we wont have any men left to carry the news of victory home."

In the fall of 1775, Generals Benedict Arnold and Richard Montgomery brought their separate armies toward Canada, Arnold through the wilds of Maine, and Montgomery along the historic Champlain corridor. Montgomery took Montreal and moved down the St. Lawrence to link up with Arnold at the edge of Quebec. Both expected many disaffected Canadians to join them but few did. Montgomery charged a city blockhouse in a snowstorm New Years' eve, and a blast of grapeshot wiped out him and his unit. Arnold was wounded in the leg in a similar attack nearby the same night.

A delegation from Congress, confident of persuading Canadians to side with the Americans, proceeded that spring from New York along the Hudson, Lakes George and Champlain to Montreal. It consisted of ailing septuagenarian Benjamin Franklin, Charles Carroll of Maryland (who became the last surviving signer of the Declaration of Independence), his brother, John Carroll who became the first Roman Catholic Bishop of the United States, and Samuel Chase (later a Justice of the US Supreme Court). At Montreal, the bigotry of the colonists in their resistance to the Quebec Act the previous year was not forgotten by the leading French Canadian Catholics who were more comfortable under British rule than they had been under French bureaucracy. It was clear that there was no hope of Canadian collusion. Soon the word spread that the British fleet was sighted sailing up the St. Lawrence and the delegation's plans as well as Arnold's long siege of Quebec had to be abandoned.

In Philadelphia, Congress appointed George Washington to lead the Continental forces, and he hastened to Cambridge to head a ragtag army already mustering to oppose the British under General William Howe, who had replaced Gage after the Bunker Hill fiasco. Needing artillery, Washington ordered Henry Knox, a Boston bookseller, to round up enough men to bring the recently captured artillery back from Ticonderoga. This would be a big enterprise any time, yet in the middle of January, he maneuvered fifty-nine pieces over Lake George and Hudson River ice before snaking them in the snow along what roads there were from western Massachusetts. To the British amazement, the big guns and breastworks were set up overnight on Dorchester Heights overlooking Boston and the British fleet; the ensuing bombardment was intimidating enough to force the British to evacuate Boston, taking many grateful loyalists with them. (A sustained barrage couldn't have been carried out for lack of gunpowder. To appear well supplied, Washington had had gunpowder barrels filled with sand, and the British never spied this out). John Sullivan marched his men into the city as the British departed, and celebrated the recovery of Boston and St. Patrick's Day, 1776.

Feeling in the upper Mohawk Valley and the Palatine district was largely in sympathy with the Bostonians in resisting King George's repressions. That the Crown was willing to use Indians against the colonists, converted many a loyalist into a rebel. Feeling was so bad that General Gage had written Sir Guy Johnson from Boston suggesting that he should leave the valley for his own safety. Sir Guy and his family, Joseph Brant, Tory John Butler and his son Walter, and others then left for Oswego, but Sir John Johnson, Sir William's son, did not attempt to leave. Philip Schuyler, a well-to-do Yorker landowner and veteran of the French and Indian War, now General and commander of the Northern Department of the Continental Army, feared some mischief, and had Sir John and his wife taken prisoner and hauled off to Albany.

Both were soon freed and allowed to return to Johnson Hall. Then, in the fall of '76, Sir John fled with thirty other loyalists and a group of Mohawks to head northeast through the woods to Crown Point and Montreal. His now ailing wife was left at home, but was again confined at Albany by Schuyler as hostage for Sir John. (Some contend that Raquette Lake, was so named because of the many raquettes, i.e. snowshoes, later found there after being abandoned by the fleeing Johnson party during a thaw).

Late in 1775, Parliament passed the Prohibitory Acts, thus declaring war against the colonies, giving them the status of a foreign and, by implication, an independent nation. This gave momentum to the idea of independence espoused so fervently by John Adams and the pamphlet, **Common Sense,** written by Thomas Paine, an articulate Quaker vouched for by Doctor Franklin and newly arrived from England.

The Declaration of Independence, authored by Thomas Jefferson and his committee of five (who referred to the recently drawn Virginia Declaration of Rights), cited a list of regal offences, defied King George and Parliament, and announced the intention of separating from the mother country. Within a few weeks of July fourth, the colonies were notified of the national purpose so carefully considered and eloquently stated.

But those noble words had to be backed up with adequate force, unfortunately lacking. General Washington, with the new Continental Army, lost the Battle of Brooklyn late that summer. Yet he managed, under cover of night and an early morning fog, to steal his entire army across the East River to Manhattan, evading General William Howe's more numerous troops and the British fleet, under the command of brother Admiral Richard Howe, if only temporarily. Washington did the best he could with what he had: a hasty retreat to White Plains, followed by a loss there, saved his small army. When Forts Lee and Washington, straddling the Hudson, capitulated, he decided to retreat again, this time across New Jersey to the western shore of the Delaware River.

New York City was now in the hands of the British as it would be for the rest of the war, and enthusiasm gave way to doubt. A hastily assembled army of merchants, farmers, and artisans on short enlistments, was up against one of the most powerful armies known. With the army, Thomas Paine's **Crisis** summed up that "the summer soldier and sunshine patriot" were a real concern in those "days that tried men's souls".

But the day after Christmas, Washington's troops crossed the Delaware and took the 1500-man garrison at Trenton by surprise, and the Hessian soldiers' bacchanalian yule revelry there was heavily paid for. Several days later, Washington eluded British General Cornwallis by vacating his bivouac at night but leaving fires burning to appear still encamped to delay British pursuit till morning. He then gained a victory at Princeton and skedaddled off to Morristown where he and his army holed up for the winter. It wouldn't be the last time Cornwallis had egg on his face. Doubters diminished, currency climbed in value, enlistments extended, and low morale moderated.

General Schuyler's spy network passed intelligence back to Albany of the formation of Sir John Johnson's Royal Greens and John Butler's Rangers in Montreal, and of Brant's Indians in force at Oquaga on the upper Susquehanna. Accordingly, Schuyler deployed Colonel Goose Van Schaick to Johnstown, and Colonel Elias Dayton to the mouth of West Canada Creek, with orders to build a fort there (Fort Dayton), and to make repairs to the aging Fort Stanwix.

In the summer of 1776, British General Sir Guy Carleton brought his force to the Richelieu River and built a fleet of small ships intent on taking Ticonderoga at the head of Lake Champlain. As Carlton's ships passed Valcour Island, near present Plattsburg, General Arnold and his small fleet of hurriedly-made batteaux moved out to harass them, and was able to keep it up for two days before his boats were sunk, burned, or scuttled. It was enough to discourage Carleton, and such British plans were put off for the year, gaining valuable time for the Americans.

"Gentleman Johnny" Burgoyne, sometime playwright and man-about-town, had been in Canada that winter (1776-77), and formulated his **"Thoughts for Conducting the War from the Side of Canada"**. He personally presented his plan to King George and Lord Germain; both approved it. The plan was threefold: to move a force under his command south from Canada along the Champlain corridor to take Albany; for General Howe to move an equally imposing force north from New York. And to avoid being flanked from the west and to destroy the farms of the Mohawk valley that supplied food to the rebels, Brigadier Barry St. Leger was to command a force from Oswego, take Fort Stanwix, ravage the valley, and link up with the other two forces. The idea was to separate the unruly New Englanders from the rest of the colonies. The British would divide and conquer.

General Howe, Supreme Commander of His Majesty's forces in New York City, was not informed of his part in it; the dispatch, by neglect of Lord Germain's office, was not sent to him. As well, the rebels had expected Burgoyne's plan and spied out the details. That spring of 1777, General Schuyler sent Colonel Peter Gansevoort and his second in command, Lt. Colonel Marinus Willett, with 750 men and the necessary artillery, to rebuild and strengthen Fort Stanwix.

In early summer, Barry St. Leger landed his forces near the mouth of the Salmon River, and marched them to Oswego to join forces with 1,000 Indians under the Seneca chiefs, Gucinge and Cornplanter, and Joseph Brant with his Mohawks, doubling his strength. The Indians were favored with gifts and supplies, and learned of the confrontation between Brant and General Nicholas Herkimer and his Tryon County militia at Unadilla a month earlier. At parley, there, Brant and his Indians scented a trap and ignored provocation by Herkimer, and did not rise to the bait. This was thought a good omen by the Indians.

1/4 MILE
TO HISTORIC
CARR FARM
MEETING PLACE OF BRANT'S
INDIANS AND TORIES
1770—1778

Chenango County, 3
NY 8, 6 m. north of New Berlin

Most of the Indians had been determined to stay neutral except that the presents and the rum made it easy for them to be cajoled to come "watch" the British reduce the fort at the great carrying place. John Butler's Rangers and Sir John Johnson's Royal Greens were eager to march south and exact revenge for being forced to abandon their thriving farms, businesses, and possessions in the Mohawk Valley.

Howard S. Ford

St. Leger finally began his march in the last days of July, and Thomas Spencer and Silas Towne, Oneida spies, left Spy Island near Texas Point to reach Gansevoort with the vital military details in time. By August third, St. Leger reached Fort Stanwix only hours after the fort had been reinforced with 200 men and more supplies. St. Leger deployed his forces in siege formation, and began lobbing cannon shells at the fort. He had spurned the suggestion to bring heavier artillery, and his light cannon did not have much effect on the heavier rebuilt log walls.

At the same time, General Herkimer had gotten word of St. Leger's move, and began mustering 800 militia to go to the relief of the fort.

SILAS TOWNE
REVOLUTIONARY HERO
HERE OVERHEARD PLANS OF
ST. LEGER'S ARMY WHEREBY
PATRIOTS SAVED FORT STANWIX

Oswego County, 13
CR, on shore of Lake Ontario
4 miles north of Mexico

When word reached Joseph Brant from his sister, Molly Brant, in Canajoharie, that Herkimer planned to cross the Mohawk at Deerfield (across the river from present Utica) and would be coming along the river's south shore to relieve the fort, many Senecas went with Brant to stop him. Brant knew the perfect ravine there to stage one of the most notorious ambushes in American history.

On August 6, Herkimer and his men met cruel fame when 1,000 muskets in the hands of Johnson's Royal Greens, Butler's Rangers, and Brant's Indians blasted them from behind trees and bushes by the small brook several streams north of the Indian village of Oriska. The fighting, much of it hand-to-hand, began about ten in the morning, and soon the melee moved out of the ravine on to the wooded flat nearby.

Herkimer directed their method of fighting by having two men take cover behind a tree instead of one. When one fired, the other would be ready to shoot the Indian running in to tomahawk what he thought was only a single vulnerable man. After that, the first man would be reloaded, ready for the next threat. The general was wounded in the leg but settled himself under a tree with his pipe and continued to direct his men. The fighting lasted about two hours until a drenching and violent thunderstorm dampened everyone's gunpowder and further fighting. Sporadic shots resumed when the rain slackened but finally stopped entirely in mid-afternoon.

Losses were more than either side expected. The Indians suffered twenty-three chiefs and sixty-eight warriors dead, and an equal number wounded. They could ill afford this. Of the British, thirty-three were killed and forty-one wounded. The rebel militia suffered over 500 dead, half of them at the battle, and the other half, including General Herkimer, died of their wounds after they had returned to Fort Dayton.

ORISKANY BATTLEFIELD 1777 PUBLIC WELCOME

Oneida County, 46
NY 69 at Oriskany Battlefield

Even though Herkimer's relief column did not reach the fort and took a terrible drubbing, the ambush set the stage for weakening the resolve of the besiegers. Adam Helmer and two other fast runners had been sent at night by Herkimer from Deerfield to tell the fort that help was on the way. When they arrived at Stanwix, the runners told of the many Indians they had evaded in the woods on the way. The men at the fort had also noticed a significant reduction of the besiegers, and decided to make a sortie from the fort against the now-weakened segment of the encirclement threatening them.

Lieutenant Colonel Marinus Willett led 250 men out to surge against Sir John's almost vacant encampment. They pillaged weapons, clothing, camp equipment, food, personal ornaments, good luck charms, and finery, including Sir John's personal and official papers and equipment, and the like left by the Indians and rangers who had gone to participate in the ambush. Seven wagons were filled three times before they retired with this booty back to the fort.

DURING SIEGE OF FORT STANWIX AUG 1777 MAIN BRITISH CAMP WAS BETWEEN THIS POINT AND THE BLUFF TO THE SOUTH

Oneida County, 63
E. Bloomfield Street & Roosevelt Ave.

Sir John had tried to persuade St. Leger on several occasions to give up the siege of the fort in favor of ransacking the valley. Had he succeeded, there was nothing to stop him, with Herkimer's militia decimated and in disarray after the ambush and their return to Fort Dayton. But St. Leger was stubborn and insisted on taking Fort Stanwix. The siege continued.

The situation looked grim for the Americans at the fort when Willett sneaked out the sally port, under cover of a rainy night, to reach General Schuyler forced south by Burgoyne a hundred miles east. In his retreat, Schuyler had been using his outnumbered forces to slow Burgoyne's advance by having his men wreck bridges and fell trees so that they crossed and locked in place, making roads impossible to pass and time-consuming to clear.

Meanwhile, two braves on the British side, had been asked to escort a white girl, Jennie McCrea, to safety. In an argument, one of the Indians in his rage tomahawked the girl and returned with her beautiful auburn hair bloody and hanging at his belt. Word of this electrified the whole region and augmented Schuyler's forces as nothing else could. By now, Schuyler had fallen back to Stillwater on the Hudson. His men, mostly New Englanders who resented serving under New York State leaders, had lost what faith they had in him, and begrudged the relief force that Willett requested.

General Schuyler decided that Fort Stanwix should be saved if possible, and sent 800 men under Benedict Arnold with additional supplies up the Mohawk. Meanwhile, a group of Tories and loyalist soldiers that had left the siege line to go recruiting in German Flats, was captured in

Shoemaker's Tavern there. Among them was Walter Butler, son of John Butler, leader of the Royal Rangers, and Hon Yost Schuyler (no relation), a simple-minded boy of the village and nephew of Nicholas Herkimer. As spies, they were to be sent to Albany and shot, but Yost's mother and brother pleaded for Hon Yost's life, and, in accommodation, General Arnold hatched a ruse.

SHOEMAKER TAVERN
BUILT BEFORE THE REVOLUTION
GEN. WASHINGTON HAD DINNER HERE
UNDER TREE ON HIS VALLEY TOUR IN
1783. WALTER BUTLER CAPTURED
HERE; LATER ESCAPED ALBANY JAIL

Herkimer County, 13*
NY 5S at Mohawk

Since the Indians were known to believe that the mentally unbalanced were divinely directed, Arnold ordered Hon Yost to "escape" to St. Leger and to give him and his Indians an exaggerated account of the size and power of Arnold's relief force on the way. He was also to say that they carried many new weapons, were to give no quarter, and were only a matter of hours away. For good measure, a friendly "fleeing" Indian was to arrive at the siege line a few minutes later to tell them of Burgoyne's "defeat" with heavy losses. Hon Yost's brother's life was hostage to the success of this mission. They shot holes in his coat to give credence to the story and sent him on his way.

As Hon Yost fled into the enemie's lines, spouting his rehearsed story, panic began to mount. St. Leger's Indians had had several bad omens recently, starting with their excessive casualties at Oriskany, and the later loss of clothing, the medicine bundles and personal items because of Willett's raid. (Indians preferred fighting almost naked, so the theft of their clothes left behind left nothing to keep them warm at night). Finally, the soldiers had shelled Fort Stanwix for over two weeks with no results, and no plunder to show for it as had been promised. All their effort was for naught and they would be overwhelmed by this large body of Americans due to arrive any minute.

No further discussion was necessary, and Indians and soldiers alike left the area, looting St. Leger's stores as fair compensation for their troubles, eager to reach safety and the boats beached at the eastern end of Oneida Lake. On August 22nd, the siege of Fort Stanwix was abandoned, enabling Arnold's relief force, together with many of the besieged, to go to the aid of those fighting Burgoyne at Saratoga.

General Schuyler had now fallen all the way back to the Mohawk River where he was relieved of command in favor of General Horatio Gates. (Gates and Burgoyne had started their careers in the same regiment of the British army thirty-two years earlier).

In contrast to Schuyler's demotion, Burgoyne was emboldened by learning of his recent promotion to Lieutenant General. But within days his luck changed. He learned of St. Leger's fiasco at Fort Stanwix and to expect no help from him, and lost more men when Colonel Baume and his Germans were ambushed in their attempt to obtain the rebel supplies at Bennington by Brigadier General John Stark's New Hampshire militia.

Rebel General Lincoln had retaken Fort Ticonderoga, cutting Burgoyne's supply line. Redcoats from New York City had marched north and taken the lower Hudson River Forts Clinton and Montgomery before burning Kingston, the capital of the new state of New York in October, but advanced no farther and returned to their base. Burgoyne realized that neither General Howe or Howe's second in command, General Henry Clinton, had plans to come all the way north from New York this late in the campaign to consummate the grand war plan. (Clinton had spent part of his boyhood in New York when his father had been royal governor of the province).

Many of Burgoyne's German mercenaries had become casualties or deserted, and most of his Indians had left because of harsh treatment and their hapless surprise when they saw the increasing rebel opposition. Burgoyne had no scouts as he marched down the river road between the Hudson and the bluffs known as Bemis Heights on his right. The battle ground was a mix of woods, open fields, brambles, and deep ravines.

The Battle of Freeman's Farm resulted in twice as many casualties lost to Burgoyne as to General Gates, and afterward, Burgoyne suffered more desertions while Gates rapidly gained recruits, impelled by the tragedy of Jennie McCrea, to defend their homesteads. After several serious engagements, Burgoyne began to retreat into the trap prepared for him. Benedict Arnold, who had vehemently argued with Gates on strategy, gained the day with his unauthorized charge on the enemy and hastened the British defeat (ruffling Gate's feathers even more).

Burgoyne surrendered on October 17, but not before military necessity forced him, he said, to burn to the ground General Schuyler's elegant farm house and barns Burgoyne had been using as his headquarters. Horatio Gates, Benedict Arnold, Daniel Morgan, John Brooks, James Wilkinson, Henry Dearborn, John Glover, John Fellows, John Stark, and the Polish engineer, Thaddeus Kosciuszko (who built the fortifications), all enhanced their reputations at what became known as the Battle of Saratoga.

With Washington still at Morristown and able to harass, perhaps prevent him from marching south to occupy Philadelphia, General Howe had departed New York with a flotilla of barges loaded with Hessians and British troops for an undisclosed destination, unaware that he was supposed to be an important part of Burgoyne's campaign. But on August 22, he and his army arrived at the northernmost reach of Chesapeake Bay at the Head of Elk (Elkton, Maryland) to disembark and make for Philadelphia. Washington guessed his intent and had his generals there to meet him.

After the success at Trenton and Princeton, many European but mostly French, aristocrats, following the then current fad of flaunting high titles and battle honors, offered their services to the Continental Army through diplomat Silas Deane in Paris. Some had nothing to offer except arrogance garnished with a supercilious attitude, and demanded high-paying command positions; but others were genuine and valued.

Marie Joseph Paul Yves Roch Gilbert du Motier, Marquis de Lafayette, wished neither pay or command, only to serve with George Washington whom he highly admired. The two struck up a warm and lasting friendship when Lafayette met Washington for the first time near Philadelphia in the early fall. He was just in time to join with Nathanael Greene, Anthony Wayne, John Sullivan, and Casimir Pulaski, to fight a losing defense of Philadelphia near Chadds Ford against generals Howe, Cornwallis, and von Knyphausen at the Battle of Brandywine where Lafayette took a bullet in the thigh. The embattled and outnumbered rebels had to give way before General Howe's troops.

In Philadelphia, Congress realized its danger, and moved first to Lancaster, then to York for safety. The British occupied Philadelphia, but two weeks later, Washington and his men proved themselves by taking the offensive at nearby Germantown, and almost succeeded. Victory slipped their hands in a fog, but they proved to the world and themselves that they were now seasoned against the professional and veteran British army. They endured the winter just west of Philadelphia at Valley Forge.

The Comte de Vergennes, France's Foreign Minister, who some ten years earlier had predicted America's turn to Independence, observed Britain's predicament with satisfaction. Wishing to exploit the conflict with her colonies without engaging France in the war, the count had devised a subterfuge to worsen England's entanglement and obtain some satisfaction for the humiliation imposed on France at the 1763 Treaty of Paris. France had lost not only Canada, but their forces in India had also succumbed and the vastly lucrative Indian trade was lost to France as well. In May of 1776, with the help of effervescent Caron de Beaumarchais, confidant of the king, accomplished musician, and author of the plays, "The Barber of Seville", and "The Marriage of Figaro", on which Mozart and Rossini and Mozart based their music, the Count had set up Rodrique Hortelez et Cie, a false trading company, to secretly funnel arms and ammunition to the Americans.

With the victory at Saratoga (partially due to French arms), the count judged that America had a chance of achieving victory, certainly of wounding Great Britain. In Paris, Benjamin Franklin, Silas Deane, and Arthur Lee were enabled by the Saratoga triumph to finally persuade the count and Louis XVI to officially back the American's against France's historic enemy. (The wily Franklin had exploited the French concern that the Americans might accept conciliatory terms offered by Britain, restoring, rather than diminishing the British Empire).

The agreement stated that in the event of war between England and France, the United States would support France; neither country would make peace without the consent of the other. Six months later, Charles III of Spain, Bourbon uncle of Louis XVI, became a party to this agreement.

France had its axe to grind and got its revenge. The United States obtained its independence.

CHAPTER SEVEN

After the siege of Fort Stanwix was raised, Brant and his Indians deliberately attacked and destroyed the Oneida village of Kanowalohale (Oneida Castle) nearby in retaliation for the Oneidas acting as scouts for Herkimer. They no longer joined in sieges with the British. Instead they fought using tactics that worked for them; raiding vulnerable villages and quickly withdrawing to minimize their losses—they hit and ran.

ONEIDA CASTLE
CHIEF VILLAGE OF ONEIDA
TRIBE OF INDIANS
MEMBERS OF
IROQUOIS CONFEDERACY

Oneida County, 95
NY 5 in Oneida Castle

The Indians licked their wounds that winter and spring saw guerrilla war on the frontier begin. At the end of May 1778, Brant led his Mohawks from Oquaga to Schoharie Creek to lure soldiers away from Cobleskill and into an ambush. The tactic worked as usual and the small town of twenty homes was burned and thirty-one people killed.

At the same time, John Butler's Royals strode out from Niagara to Chenussio, Kanandaigua, and other Indian villages gathering Seneca, Cayuga, and Onondaga recruits as they progressed toward the white frontier. When they reached the navigable waters of the Kanisteo River, 900 Indians had joined the 400 loyalists. There they divided: one group made dugouts to float most of the party downstream, the other under Gucinge of the Senecas began marauding toward the Susquehanna West Branch and south along that river in a circuitous and devastating sweep before linking up with the others at Tunkhannock downstream on the north branch of the river.

Howard S. Ford

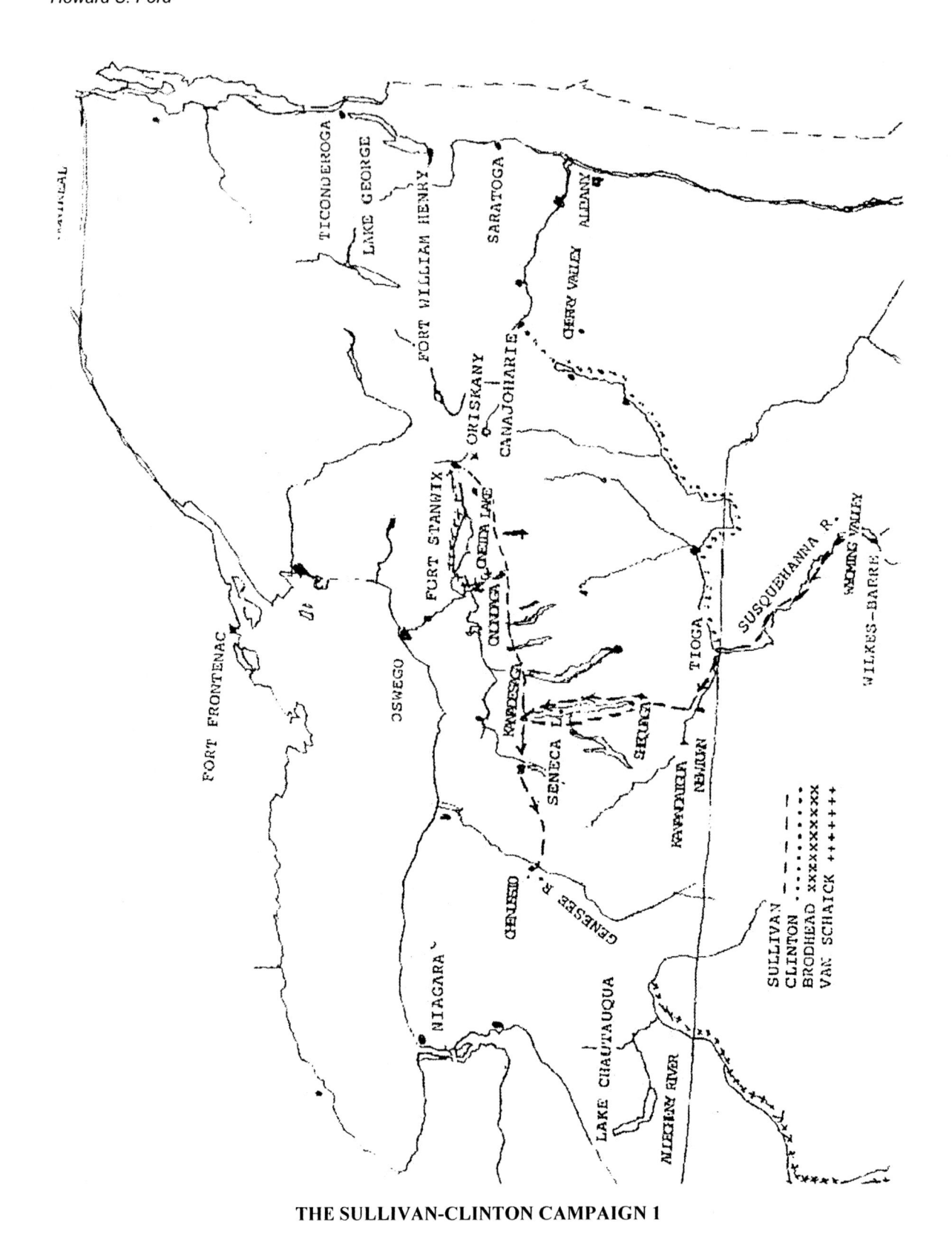

THE SULLIVAN-CLINTON CAMPAIGN 1

HERE INDIANS AND TORIES USED PINE TREES TO BUILD CANOES FOR TRANSPORT TO WYOMING – WYOMING MASSACRE JULY 3, 1778

Steuben County, 7*
CR, 1 mile north of Hornell

On July third, this overwhelming force divided and descended on the people at the small forts at Pittston, Forty Fort, Wilkes-Barré, and Wyoming. These towns were settled by emigrating Connecticut Yankees on land they still contended belonged to Connecticut (owing to loosely worded charters). They had named one town in honor of two members of Parliament who had defended the American cause early on, Jack Wilkes and Isaac Barré. Most of the able-bodied men had reported to the Continental Army, leaving only relatively small garrisons in each fort to protect the area.

The soldiers at Forty Fort misjudged the size of Butler's party as Butler hoped they would. Taking the initiative against their officer's advice, they left only a small force to protect the women and children at the fort and advanced on the seemingly small enemy company of loyalists and Indians. In the face of this, the enemy withdrew leading the Americans into an ambush by a much larger force.

TRAIL OF SCOUT ADAM F. HELMER ENTERING MOHAWK VALLEY TO WARN GERMAN FLATS OF APPROACH OF BRANT'S INDIANS, SEPT. 17 1778

Herkimer County, 11
NY 5S at Mohawk

Howard S. Ford

The Wyoming Valley Massacre claimed 300 killed of 450 soldiers, with many more wounded. The women and children and the elderly were not molested for the most part but they had to flee because most of their homes and barns were burned. Refuge was eastward across the mountains back to Stroudsburg, Lehigh, Easton, and west to Fort Sunbury for survival.

Andrustown, north of Lake Otsego six miles, was attacked in late July and Nanticoke, Pennsylvania in late August. German Flats (Herkimer) was hit in early September, but with little loss of life because of Adam Helmer's famous twenty-four mile run from Edmeston to warn people in time. They flocked to Forts Dayton and Herkimer for safety, but at the end of the raid only two houses, the church and the fort, were standing on the north side of the river, and three houses on the south side. These frontier attacks were all hit-and-run led by Joseph Brant from his base at Oquaga on the Susquehanna.

The loyalty of the Oneidas was questioned by local Americans. So in late September, the Oneidas made a raid of their own on the important Tory towns of Unadilla and Butternut burning buildings and garnering livestock and other plunder, and taking five captives, rather than scalps, at each place.

Later when Brant was out raiding in the upper Delaware Valley and away from his base at Oquaga, the Americans struck back. A force of 260 from Fort Defiance at Schoharie went south under Colonel William Butler (no relation to Tory John) and wiped out Oquaga and other Indian towns nearby. On the way back, they burned what was left of Unadilla with its sawmill and gristmill. From Fort Sunbury by the mouth of the West Branch of the Susquehanna, Colonel Thomas Hartley and Colonel Zebulon Butler (no relation), with 217 men, destroyed the three important Indian villages of Sheshaquin, Queen Esther's Town, and Tioga, with small loss to themselves. Most of these Indian houses were fine homes with chimneys, glass windows, and wood floors.

From Niagara, another force of 200 whites and several hundred Indians, this one commanded by Walter Butler, (who only recently had escaped from an Albany jail) began to move east through the Seneca, Cayuga, and Onondaga towns enlarging their strength to 600 under Gucinge and Little Beard. Chief Big Tree of Conesus and Red Jacket (a young articulate Seneca sachem who prized a red jacket given him by a British officer), warned them that they eventually would be overwhelmed by the unending numbers and weapons of the Americans, and that they should make peace. But the hatred of the Indians had been unleashed and nothing could stop their fury.

Much farther east, they were intercepted by Joseph Brant and his 250 Mohawks who were still smarting from the loss of their homes at Oquaga. The two groups joined, making over a thousand on their way to attack the village of Cherry Valley.

Colonel Ichabod Alden was confident that the residents at Cherry Valley had nothing to fear because of the 300 Massachusetts troops he commanded there. The villagers had just completed building a fort under the direction of Lafayette; only days before were openings cut in the parapet to give firearms and two cannon a field of fire. Local Oneidas had reported that a large number of Tories and Indians was camped at Tioga and that their quarry was Cherry Valley. Alden did send two scouting parties out but one of these parties was taken captive as they slept, and the other reported nothing unusual.

2/5 MILES WEST TO SITE DUNLAP HOME DESTROYED AT TIME OF CHERRY VALLEY MASSACRE NOVEMBER 11, 1778

Otsego County, 5
US 20 at Cherry Valley

Butler's men deployed in the woods surrounding the town waiting for his signal to attack after dawn. Rain that day turned to snow at night, and to sleet and fog in the morning, obscuring their movements. Two Indians near the road couldn't wait and each took a shot at a settler on his way to town in midmorning. This confused Butler's people, since the signal was to be three shots, not two. Though wounded, the settler rode into town yelling, "Indians!" all the way. This triggered the attack and Butler's Royals, Little Beard's and Gucinge's Senecas, and Brant's Mohawks rushed the town, shooting, shouting, and shedding terror and mayhem on the startled townspeople.

Howard S. Ford

It was like a small civil war because many of the Mohawks and Butler's men had known people in town for years. Brant and Butler knew the Wells family, had even dined under their roof, but it was too late to save them; all thirteen were slaughtered (as were most of the garrison's officers who were Wells' guests) in the first rush, and the large and beautiful well-furnished house was burned. Brant was not the leader of the Cherry Valley raid, but he did manage to protect another family well-known to him by appropriating their house for his own to deter other Indians.

In all, forty-two soldiers and thirty-two civilians were killed. Sixty were taken prisoner and marched off southwest down the Cherry Valley Creek trail—naked or ill-clothed and burdened with their captor's plunder—to Kanadesaga, Chenussio, and other towns far to the west. Thirty-two of the thirty-three homes and thirty-one barns were burned along with the smithy and the grist mill. So passed November 11th, 1778.

On the following April twenty-first, Colonel Goose Van Schaick and Colonel Marinus Willett, both veterans of the siege of Fort Stanwix, and 558 men who had lost family and homes to Indian depredations, descended on the inhabitants of Onondaga and destroyed their frame and log homes and the longhouse where the council fires of the Iroquois had been burning for over 200 years. They came from Fort Stanwix, crossed Oneida Lake, camped across the outlet from the ruins of Fort Brewerton, and made their surprise attack with the vanguard of sixty Oneidas led by Chief Hannyerry.

FRENCHMAN'S ISLAND CAMPSITE OF VAN SCHAIK'S EXPEDITION ON RETURN FROM ATTACK ON ONONDAGA APRIL 22, 1779

Oswego County, 4
NY 49, ½ mile east of Constantia

The five-and-a-half day campaign accomplished its purpose with no American casualties. Fortune favored forty or so Onondagas who had decided after the first of the year to side with the Americans and had departed to live with the Oneidas and Tuscaroras. Of the Onondagas who were still in the village, twelve were killed and thirty-three taken prisoner. Their food supplies were destroyed as were their homes.

This assault on a major Onondaga town was ordered by General Sullivan, the first action of what became known as the Sullivan-Clinton Campaign. The campaign was authorized and designed in large part by George Washington. As his orders stated: "It is proposed to carry the war into the heart of the country of the Six Nations, to cut off their settlements, destroy their next years' crops, and do them every other mischief which time and circumstance will permit."

He appointed Major General John Sullivan (military courtesy required the commission to first be offered to General Gates who declined the appointment, as was expected) to head the campaign and authorized him to draw 5000 Continental Army troops from other regions, a large percentage of the available troops. The New Jersey, Pennsylvania, and New Hampshire Brigades reported to Easton, Pennsylvania on the Delaware to prepare for what was expected to be a long and hazardous march through the virgin and hilly wilderness. The New Hampshire Brigade arrived first in order to hack the road out of the difficult Pocono Mountain country to Wilkes-Barré.

The Fourth or New York Brigade under Brigadier General James Clinton at the same time proceeded up the Mohawk River to Canajoharie where they portaged batteaux and supplies twenty difficult miles to Lake Otsego. There they waited for orders to move down the Susquehanna and destroy Indian villages en route, until they joined with Sullivan and the main force at Tioga where the Chemung joins the main river.

One of Sullivan's primary problems was to get adequate supplies to Easton and Wilkes-Barré to sustain his 3,500 men for three months. Essential staples that had spoiled and similar problems detained the start of the trek north but the delay enabled the troops to complete the widening of the existing Indian trail. On June eighteenth, they got under way from Easton, finally launching this campaign of devastation.

Five days later they arrived at Wilkes-Barré, only to be delayed again because of continuing supply problems. Sullivan could not move the army again until a large number of wagons, horses, military supplies, and foodstuffs arrived. On July 31 the army and 1200 pack horses, 120 boats loaded with artillery and supplies, and 700 cattle to feed the troops belatedly moved out, crashing and trumpeting their way to Iroquoia. Sullivan sent word to Clinton at Lake Otsego to begin moving downstream.

The summer had been a dry one so General Clinton had prudently built a dam at the lake's outlet to raise the water level high enough to float heavily loaded batteaux down the shallow first ten miles of river. By August sixth when he received word from Clinton, the lake had risen more than three feet. Clinton ordered the dam broken and the next day over 200 manned batteaux floated down river as in a spring runoff, accompanied by 600 men marching alongside on both shores.

CLINTON'S DAM
DAM OPENED AUGUST 9, 1779
2000 MEN AND 200 BATEAUX
WENT DOWN THE SUSQUEHANNA
Otsego County, 20
Lake St., Cooperstown

As it moved downstream, the army destroyed the Indian towns of Oneonta, Otego, Aleout (a Tory town), what was left of Unadilla and Oquaga, Conihunto, Shawhiangto (Windsor), Ingaren, Otsiningo, Choconut, and Owego. Meanwhile, Sullivan's brigades in Pennsylvania traced the Warriors Trail along the east shore of the Susquehanna, cutting across loops wherever possible and heralded their presence every morning and evening with a signal cannon. (PA 92 north from Pittston to Tunkhannock, then US 6 to Towanda, and north on US 220 to NY 17, and west at Waverly is the approximate trail).

Indians taking occasional pot shots at those on the line of march and injuries sustained by a few small groups when they left the trail constituted all the fighting to this point. The first Indian town Sullivan came upon was Newtychanning (near Towanda); it had been freshly abandoned and there was no resistance. They burned the houses and crops and moved on, passing the remains of Sheshaquin and Queen Esther's Town destroyed by Hartley the previous fall, and arrived at Tioga August 11th. Building a supply depot, Fort Sullivan, while they waited for Clinton, helped while away the time. A detachment went north twelve miles and destroyed the town of Chemung, also recently abandoned but for a few braves. Here, they had their first serious encounter with the Indians, suffering seven killed and fourteen wounded.

OF THE SULLIVAN-CLINTON ARMY ON ITS CAMPAIGN AGAINST THE BRITISH AND INDIANS OF WESTERN NEW YORK IN 1779

Schuyler County, 22*
NY 14, just south of Montour Falls
The standard sign seen along the routes of Generals Sullivan and Clinton.

On August 22, Clinton's and Sullivan's armies joined, celebrated their success so far, and rested for the expected fighting still to come. They resumed the pace and by August 29th, when they had gone about fifteen miles up the Chemung, they came to the base of a steep hill that looked right for an ambush. Scanning the hillside with a telescope revealed warriors and breastworks cleverly camouflaged. The order was given to quickly deploy behind what cover was at hand; and to not follow after any small ostensibly weak band of the enemy that might appear. This Indian ruse that led to ambushes had worked so well in the past was not to be allowed any success here.

Sullivan devised a pincers and flanking strategy, with a diversion of artillery and rifle fire in front, that was so effective Brant's, Sir John Johnson's, and Butler's men barely had time to escape the closing trap and retreat north.

The Americans lost eleven dead and thirty-two wounded; the British and Indians lost seventeen dead and an unknown number wounded. But the Indians lost several chiefs: Rozinoghyata of the Onondagas; Kayingwaurto, Gucinge and Queen Esther (Montour) of the Senecas; and Captain John of the Mohawks. And most of all, they lost heart. The Battle of Newtown, as Sullivan called it, was later realized to be decisive; from here until Sullivan's men reached Chenussio, there was very little fighting.

NEWTOWN
SO NAMED BY GENERAL SULLIVAN
OCCUPIED BY BRITISH
AND INDIANS
DESTROYED BY GENERAL
SULLIVAN, AUGUST 30, 1779

Chemung County, 1*
NY 17, 1 mile west of Lowman

After the battle, the village of Newtown was burned and the crops of squash, potatos, beans, cucumbers, watermelons, turnips, tobacco and corn, all near ripe for harvest, were ruined. A small detachment followed up a stream and burned the town of Rumonvea near present Big Flats, and the main army did the same to Kanawaholla (Elmira). Sullivan then turned the army north away from the Chemung River to reach the larger town of Shequaga (Montour Falls), called by some Catharine's Town, after Catharine Montour, sister of Queen Esther. They followed down Catharine Creek, got bogged down in a swamp, and several miles short of Seneca Lake they came upon the abandoned village, fires still burning under kettles of food. Again, all was laid waste except for a small plot of corn they reserved for the army's return, before resuming the march up the east side of Seneca Lake.

The small lakeside villages of Peach Orchard, Appletree (Valois Point), and Kendaia (Pontius Point), with crops and orchards, were all destroyed in the Indian's absence as the army progressed to the northern end of the lake. Fear of an ambush was always present, especially as they forded the Seneca River outflow at the lake's northeast corner, and again as they marched west on the beach straddling the foot of the lake and the swamp, but no Indians were seen. They passed a small cluster of what appeared to be Indian summer homes overlooking the long fetch of the lake before coming to the comely major Seneca city of Kanadesaga (just northwest of the site of Geneva).

SITE OF KANADESAGA
CHIEF CASTLE OF
THE SENECA NATION
DESTROYED SEPT. 7, 1779
IN GEN. JOHN SULLIVAN'S
RAID

Ontario County, 8
CR.1/4 m. west of Geneva

It was composed of sixty well-made frame homes, such as they would find in a white eastern city, with forty other log homes and quonsets, all surrounding several acres of grassy park where over twenty years before, Sir William Johnson had erected a block-house and fort. The city was surrounded by neatly tended vegetable gardens which, in turn, were enclosed by extensive orchards and fields of corn.

Kanadasaga was destroyed without opposition, as was Kashong seven miles south on the west side of Seneca Lake and Skoyase (Waterloo) seven miles to the east. The army was again unopposed in this laborious ravaging, and was apprehensive of a large battle when they determined to move west against the principal town of the Senecas, Chenussio, or Little Beard's Town, (Cuylerville) as some called it.

TORY QUARTERS
SITE OF MILITARY DEPOT
UNDER COMMAND OF
COL. JOHN BUTLER
DESTROYED SEPT. 1779 IN
SULLIVAN EXPEDITION

Ontario County, 16*
US 20 & NY 5, shore of Seneca Lake

The nightly mountain dews became frost in the early days of September, and everyone wished to conclude the expedition soon before snow and cold enveloped them. The twenty-three fine homes of Kanandaigua had to be burned as well as the crops, and at this point (now US 20A), they turned southwest to arrive at Honeoye with its twenty homes at the outlet of its lake. Sullivan split his forces here so that any excess equipment could be deposited and guarded at the sturdiest of the Indian houses, and the rest of the army would travel unencumbered except for necessaries to subdue Chenussio. The house was fortified and the rest of the town burned.

At the next encampment, past Hemlock Lake and just north of Conesus, Sullivan ordered Lieutenant Thomas Boyd to take a half dozen men to scout out the area around Chenussio in case a trap was planned.

General Sullivan moved west, first striking the town of Gathsegwareohare where a hundred young warriors made a stand until a few howitzer shots dispersed them. The next day the town and crops were burned and they crossed the Genesee River to approach the largest Seneca town.

Chenussio consisted of 128 homes set willy-nilly around a large two-story long-house and, in turn circled by about 12,000 bounteous acres of fields and orchards. It was a beautiful wide valley with lush crops and was to be remembered by many a farmer-soldier with appreciation and longing for land like this of his own. According to Mary Jemison, the Senecas declared that these fields were here before they had settled there, and had been cleared by "the old ones", so that the Senecas never had to fell a tree in order to plant their crops.

FIRST HOME
BUILT BY A WHITE MAN
CAPT. ROSWELL FRANKLIN
IN CAYUGA COUNTY 1789
HE WAS AN OFFICER IN
SULLIVAN–CLINTON CAMPAIGN

Cayuga County, 68
W. side of NY 90, Aurora

All had been abandoned except for Sara Lester and her sickly child, who had been captured at Nanticoke the previous November. (Her child soon died and she later married Captain Roswell Franklin. The couple became one of the first to settle Aurora, New York). The next day it took an army of 4,000 men eight hours to destroy all this verdant husbandry. It went against the grain to ravage so much of what the squaws had obviously tended with care and skill.

BOYD–PARKER TORTURE TREE AND BURIAL MOUND. WESTERN LIMIT SULLIVAN'S EXPEDITION 1779. SENECA VILLAGE LITTLE BEARD'S TOWN

Livingston County, 19*
US 20 & NY 39, ½ m east of
Cuylerville

Boyd and his two dozen men (he took more than was ordered) were caught in an ambush intended for the main army. A few escaped, but the rest, except for Boyd and Sargent Michael Parker, were killed and badly mutilated; especially bad was the fate of Chief Hannyerry. Boyd and Parker were later found in a horrible state of mutilation, much of which was done while they still lived. They were buried on the spot next to a tree, now huge, where a small park commemorates their tragedy.

Sullivan now announced that they had accomplished what they had come so far for and it was time to go home. The army retraced its way to Kanadasaga where Sullivan sent a large detachment under Lieutenant Colonel Henry Dearborn a few miles east to destroy the Cayuga villages on the west side of Cayuga Lake and also sent Lieutenant Colonel William Butler to similarly work his detachment up the east side of Cayuga. Sullivan also ordered Lieutenant Colonel William Smith to finish the destruction of Kashong, and assigned Colonel Peter Gansevoort to take a detachment to the lower Mohawk towns and arrest the male Mohawks there. (Gansevoort took the Seneca trail now made into a highway and known as the Seneca Turnpike through present Seneca Falls, Auburn, Skaneateles, Onondaga Hill, and Canaseraga (Chittenango) to Fort Stanwix).

FORD ACROSS WASCO OUTLET ON GREAT IROQUOIS TRAIL USED BY COL. PETER GANSEVOORT WHO ENCAMPED HERE SEPT. 21, 1779

Cayuga County, 113
Owasco Lake outlet bridge

At about this time, the Commandant at Fort Pitt, Colonel Daniel Brodhead, had come back from a 400 mile quick march up the Allegheny River, destroying several Seneca and Mingo towns and their crops, and keeping the Indians off balance as to where the next invasion of their country might occur. Of the 600 men on the raid no one was injured.

Sullivan's army returned to Kanawaholla where the General sent other detachments to wipe out the towns as far as Painted Post. As the expedition returned, many horses succumbed to the strain and poor fodder. (The Indians who later returned to their former grounds, placed the horses skulls in rows on the ground and the spot was later called The Valley of the Horseheads.)

A general celebration was held for the success of the expedition and the good news that Spain had finally become a signatory to the alliance with France and the United States against Great Britain. The tide of war was turning and these men were going home. General Sullivan marched his army to Morristown, where the rest of the Continental Army with Washington settled in to winter quarters. Sullivan then resigned from his long army service and soon was elected to Congress.

The hostile tribes fled to Niagara and the charity of the British that fall because they could do nothing else. Twelve hundred homes of 3,000 families had been destroyed with all their corn, their orchards, their vegetables. Their lives were in further jeopardy because the winter of '79-'80 turned out to be one of the most severe of the century. (The Hudson froze over so thick that cannon could be hauled over the ice from Staten Island to New York City and, farther south, even Chesapeake Bay at Annapolis was frozen so that wagons could be drawn across to the Eastern Shore.)

The Indians were encouraged to start hamlets outside of Niagara along Buffalo Creek to relieve the crowding, but many died of the cold, starvation, malnutrition and disease. Wildlife also succumbed to the severe season in large numbers, making hunting difficult but essential to feed a family and supplement the British hand-outs.

Despite the devastation of the Seneca, Cayuga, and Onondaga villages, the Sullivan Campaign was not wholly successful. Iroquois wrath became more savage and, with the help of the loyalists, proceeded to bathe the frontier in tears and blood. Loss of their towns, crops, casualties and culture made them implacable enemies of the Americans, not just participants on the King's side. Many of their chiefs and sachems were dead and few remained who knew the precise words and procedures of their ceremonies without which they felt at a loss in such time of need. They also developed a strong resentment of the British for bringing them into the war and for what they thought was an inadequate defense of their country.

The Onondagas, who a year earlier had gone over to the Americans and to the Oneida towns, now returned and went to Niagara, angry at the destruction of Onondaga the previous April. The Oneidas were continually threatened by Brant and others, and some fled to Niagara; others to upper Mohawk valley towns where Philip Schuyler, as Indian Commissioner, offered them shelter in old barracks at Schenectady. As feared, not only Kanowalohale, but other Oneida and Tuscarora villages were destroyed by Brant. Over 400 Oneidas and Tuscaroras stayed on the American side and went to Fort Stanwix for relief. The Confederacy was rent wretchedly by this dissension.

Early in February of 1780, war parties departed from Niagara to exact vengeance on the frontier towns of New York and Pennsylvania. Schoharie, Ballston, Canajoharie, Saratoga, Skenesboro, Fort Ann, Fort George, and Stone Arabia were all sacked. It was so bad, Governor George Clinton said, "Schenectady may now be said to become the limits of our western frontier." Despite its apparent success, the Sullivan expedition did not halt Indian depredations but increased the destruction to much of the state of New York; those not attacked were still fearful that they would be and made sacrifices helping those who had no food or shelter.

After the winter, in 1781, the raids resumed; one raid by Delawares went as far east as the Hudson River. Others hit Derlach near Otsego Lake, Canajoharie again, Minisink Ford, Fort Hunter, and Shamokin. Even General Schuyler's Albany mansion was entered in an attempt to kidnap the general and the family was attacked. They miraculously came through unharmed (a hatchet mark on the stair railing attests to such a near thing). However, a guard was wounded and another made prisoner.

One of the last British raiding parties left Oswego, a week after General Cornwallis' surrender at Yorktown, to again lay waste the Mohawk Valley. Six hundred Rangers, Royal Yorkers, and Indians under Major John Ross plundered all the way to Warren's Bush just south of the Mohawk with many farms, homes, livestock, and recently harvested crops destroyed.

A RAIDING FORCE LED BY MAJOR ROSS AND WALTER BUTLER WAS HERE ATTACKED BY COL. MARINUS WILLET'S PATRIOT SOLDIERS

Herkimer County, 23
CR 3 miles SE of Gray

When they turned north to make for their base at Carleton Island, they were intercepted by Colonel Marinus Willett near Johnstown. They fought and then became separated, but Willett with 400 whites and sixty Indians caught up with Ross's party when they had just forded West Canada Creek. An Oneida brave took a chance shot across the stream and killed Walter Butler, known for his cruelty and a long-time target for rebels, but pursuit was not attempted because the weather turned bitter. In November, Schoharie was hit one more time. And in the spring, Indians burned the mill at Little Falls.

Oswego had been neglected by both sides, and that spring the British under Major Ross with Joseph Brant took over the fort and made repairs. On July fifth Brant set out with almost 500 Indians for the frontier. He was quickly recalled by Ross who had received orders to stop all hostilities due to the peace treaty in progress in Paris.

ONE MILE EAST
COLONEL MARINUS WILLET ROUTED
BRITISH-TORY FORCE OCT. 30, 1783
ALONG WEST CANADA CREEK
WALTER BUTLER, TORY LEADER
WAS KILLED BY AN ONEIDA

Oneida County, 45
Fairchild Road, north of

Despite the treaty process and the imminent end of the war, Colonel Willett recognized the importance of Oswego as a base of operations and supply depot in any further campaign against the British. He obtained permission from General Washington to attempt an attack on the place, and in early February of 1783 left Fort Herkimer for Oneida Lake and the Oswego River traveling on sleighs over the ice. When only four or five miles from the fort, the ice was no longer strong enough and he and his men went ashore, relying on an Oneida scout to guide them through the woods. Incredibly, they became lost over the next six hours (perhaps they were caught in a white-out), and could not find the fort until dawn lost them the element of surprise. They then called off the expedition and returned to Fort Herkimer with the guide under arrest. As it turned out, aborting the mission made no difference since the Preliminary Articles of Peace had been signed November 30th, over two months earlier. Hostilities ceased and the final treaty assured independence.

The Iroquois were largely ignored as a party of interest in the treaty that ended the Revolution. Because of a change in administration after Yorktown, Great Britain ignored its stated policy of protecting Indian lands, an inducement that had served to recruit the Iroquois as allies in the Revolution. This disregard put the British army officers and Indian administrators, who had to deal with the Indians on a daily basis, in a very embarrassing position to defend a policy over which they had no control. Only two members of Parliament spoke against the new Shelburne government for its abandonment of the Indian lands as a dishonorable breach of faith, but they were shouted down by a country weary of war and unhappy about losing the American Colonies.

General Frederick Haldimand, in charge of His Majesty's forces in North America, refused to honor the treaty provisions that required the British to give up the forts on the Great Lakes. He argued that holding them would calm Indian fears and prevent reprisals, as well as force the Americans to honor treaty provisions relating to the loyalists. The forts at Detroit, Niagara, Oswegatchie, and Oswego were thus not available to the Americans for treating with the Indians (and would be a source of contention for the next twelve years).

The conference was to be held at Fort Stanwix, but was delayed until early September 1784 so that the Indians could bring in their corn. Some legal wrangling ensued between New York and Congress, and between such legal minds as James Monroe and James Madison over jurisdiction. The New York Commissioners met with the Indians first, settling little except establishing civility between them and the Indians.

The Federal Commissioners met with the Indians a month later, asserting their bargaining position and the United States' sovereignty over all Indian lands. Many whites had had their eyes on and wished to confiscate the Indian lands in New York State but George Washington and Philip Schuyler prevailed and the Iroquois retained most of their New York domain. The Indians were at a great disadvantage because not only were they were allies to the losing side and their interests had been ignored by the Treaty of Paris, but also because there was great dissension among the tribes, and sickness back at Niagara prevented many leading sachems from attending. The commissioners let the Indians read the arbitrary treaty but refused to give them a copy.

In short, there were no negotiations, only laying down the terms for the cessation of hostilities: the return of prisoners, and the giving up of New York land by the Indians south and west of Niagara to the Pennsylvania line and the Ohio lands west of Pennsylvania. Pennsylvanians then made demands of their own, taking a large portion of northwest Pennsylvania from the Senecas, all for

$5000 in trade goods. When made known back at Buffalo Creek, the negotiations of the chiefs were much criticized, and the Six Nations refused to ratify the Treaty. But it was a done deal.

Anxious to cash in on supplying the British and the remnant of their Indian charges at Fort Niagara with beef, a family of drovers risked the slow trek from New Jersey in 1787. After crossing the Delaware, they followed Sullivan's trail along the Susquehanna to Tioga, passed Seneca Lake to Kanadesaga, then wheeled westward through Canandaigua, Canawaugus (Avon), via the great bend of Tonawanda Creek (Batavia) to Niagara. Though this was the country of the Senecas who only a few years earlier were wrathful enemies, the head drover's son wrote years later that they made several droves a year, and in subsequent years, and were always treated well by the Indians. He also recalled that the tribes habitually exacted a select steer, willingly given, from each drove for crossing their territory, and the drovers invited the Indians to a barbeque each fall to celebrate a successful working relationship.

Even though a provision of the treaty specifically stated that "The Oneida and Tuscarora nations shall be secured in the possession of the lands on which they are now settled", the Indians gradually lost their land. They lived too close to encroaching settlements and as early as 1785 the State of New York began negotiations to buy their land. Most of the Oneidas and Tuscaroras moved to Wisconsim in the 1820s. By 1842, only a small area south of Sherrill remained in Indian hands.

Philip Schuyler, who had been Commissioner for Indian Affairs, accurately predicted the future of the Indians and the ability of the whites to acquire their land. "As the whites settled land closer and closer to the Indians," he said, "game would become scarce and their hunting would degenerate and no longer sustain them, forcing them to sell off some of their land at low prices. Eventually, the Indians would abandon or sell all for very little and drift away to join western tribes where they would be accepted." This conflict of economies and cultures was just as devastating to them as the war.

In Canada, the British finally made some recompense to those Indians who suffered property loss as a result of the war. Joseph and Molly Brant, for example, received almost ƒ1450. In 1784, Brant was also able to negotiate with General Haldimand for a tract of land in Ontario six miles on either side of the Grand River, from its source to Lake Erie, for the relocation of most of the Mohawks and Indians from other nations of the League. The Fort Hunter Mohawks preferred to be established on a separate tract near the Bay of Quinte.

As for the acknowledged loyalists, their property was confiscated and patriot passion prevented many from returning to their homeland and homes. Some fled to Upper Canada (Ontario province), Brunswick, and Nova Scotia. Others sought residence in the Bahamas and Bermuda and a few returned to the British Isles.

The Indians had chosen the losing side but would have lost their land in any event. They were victims in the path of a massive migration of whites determined to establish themselves coast-to-coast in North America who would tolerate no interference with this "manifest destiny", a phrase not coined for another sixty years.

CHAPTER EIGHT

Land grants were applied for and made to favored persons along the colonial frontier before the Revolution, many in the Mohawk Valley. The governor made the grants after the grantee took several steps: he had to secure permission to buy from the Indians, warrant to survey the land, and secure a second warrant from the governor directing the attorney general to prepare the patent, etc. Each step involved a government official and high fees resulting in considerable enrichment of the officials, judges, and lawyers. One authority states that as a rule of thumb for most governors, one third of each grant was reserved as his share.

COXE'S MANOR
31,470 ACRES OF LAND
ALONG THIS SUSQUEHANNA VALLEY
WERE GRANTED TO DANIEL COXE
AND ASSOCIATES BY THE CROWN
OF ENGLAND. JANUARY 15, 1775

Tioga County, 10
NY 283, 2 ½ m. west of Owego

The grantee had to negotiate with the Indians and, because Native Americans considered land for its use and enjoyment versus European ideas of exclusive ownership, misunderstandings abounded, even if the white purchaser was aboveboard in his dealing. Many Indians thought they were only allowing whites the use of their land, and not parting with ownership or use by themselves, especially since the amount they received in the deal was often trifling.

Thomas Dongan, governor from 1682-88, provided his friend, Robert Livingston, with 160,000 acres and another 90,000 acres to Frederic Philipse. Governor Fletcher, 1692-98, made substantial grants to some thirty favorites, including 86,000 acres to Stephen van Cortlandt, 205,000 acre Highland Manor to Adolph Phillipse, and twenty miles of Hudson River frontage eight miles in depth to Henry Beckman. These tracts were all on the east side of the Hudson.

Fletcher's successor, Richard Coote, the Earl of Bellomont, was an honest man who even dealt fairly with the Indians and was aghast at Fletcher's extravagance. He reported to London that the settlement of the colony was retarded because immigrants went to other colonies where they could buy land outright rather than rent. He inspired outraged opposition from the landed gentry when he questioned patent procedures and recommended that all patents of more than one thousand acres be divided.

The most notorious was the Dellius grant made by Fletcher for 620,000 acres on the Hudson River and engineered by Peter Schuyler, Indian trader and mayor of Albany. Bellomont successfully challenged the patent on the basis that the Wappinger Indians had been swindled by the time-honored practice of getting them drunk. Other fraudulent methods were dealing with unauthorized Indians and ambiguous purchase agreements, such as the Walking Purchase, and another deal that provided "as much land as covered by an ox hide". To the Indians amazement and chagrin, the hide was cut into an incredibly long thin strip for a large enclosure.

Bellomont died after only three years in office, and to the relief of aspiring manor holders, was succeeded by governors Cornbury, Cosby, and Clarke who repeated the venality of their predecessors until freely available land began to run out. One of the results of Bellomont's reforms was limiting patents to 2000 acres per person, but speculators named servants and tenants as partners, who, after the deal was completed, relinquished their ownership to the main patentee.

Sir William Johnson knew how to acquire large acreage because of his favored position with the Iroquois and in New York politics, as well as with the London government. After his initial purchase where he erected Fort Johnson, then sumptuous Johnson Hall, and later laid out the beginnings of Johnstown, he wangled large tracts on the Mohawk, the Susquehanna, both sides of Charlotte River, and Onondaga Lake amounting to 500,000 acres.

St. John de Crèvecoeur recounted in his **Journey into Northern Pennsylvania and the State of New York:**

"'One day,' Sir William Johnson told me, 'old Nissooassou came to my home and said:

"'O father, last night I dreamed that you gave me a fine scarlet-coloured suit, trimmed with gold, with a hat to match.'

'You don't say!'

'Yes, on my word as a Sachem,' he replied.

'Well, then, you shall not have dreamed in vain, for I shall present you with them, and gladly.'

'The next day,' continued Sir William, 'having invited him to dinner, I saw my chance, saying:

'Henrique, I, too, had a dream last night.'

'What did you dream father?' he asked me.

'That in the name of your tribe, you gave me a small piece of Tienaderhah, known as Acerouni.'

'In terms of acres, how much land does this include?'

'Ten thousand,' I replied.

'After a few moments of thought, he said to me:

'Well, you shall not have dreamed in vain either, for I shall give you this little piece of land: but don't take it into your head to dream any more, good father.'

'And why not, Henrique? Dreams are involuntary, aren't they?'

"'You dream too hard for me and soon you wouldn't leave any more land for our people.'"

The largest single tract in New York was Cornbury's grant to Major Johannes Hardenberg and six associates of land bought from the Esopus Indians for ƒ60 in 1708 comprising most of what became Delaware, Greene, Ulster, and Sullivan Counties.

In 1705, the Oriskany Patent, extending from Rome to Oriskany, was granted to five colonial officials but later was confiscated by New York State during the Revolution because the then owners were Tories. Six-hundred ninety-seven acres of this tract were sold to Dominic Lynch who founded there what later became Rome. Forty-three thousand acre Cosby Manor, the area from Frankfort to Yorkville, owned by Governor Cosby early in the century, was sold in 1772 to Philip Schuyler, John Bradstreet, and others. After the Revolution, the area developed rapidly and became the city of Utica.

William Franklin, last Royal Governor of New Jersey and son of Benjamin Franklin, (and to his father's later sorrow, a noted loyalist), George Croghan, deputy to Sir William Johnson, and a group of Quaker merchants from Burlington, (then one of the two alternating New Jersey capitals), had acquired from the Oneidas and Mohawks 100,000 acres from the west shore of Lake Otsego to Unadilla Creek (the proclamation line), when attending the 1768 Fort Stanwix Treaty.

By the end of the Revolution, William Franklin had been exiled in England, Croghan had died bankrupt, and the other owners and creditors were either ruined, dead, or scattered, and their papers in disarray. In January 1786, William Cooper of Burlington, a wheelwright turned successful merchant, and a backer, Andrew Craig, acquired some of the Otsego Patent at depressed prices from desperate owners, and the rest at a manipulated sheriff's auction in Canajoharie.

Other grants in Tory hands including those of Guy and John Johnson, heirs of Sir William (parts of the towns of Remsen, Marcy and Trenton), and the Right Honorable Henry Lord Holland (Holland Patent), also reverted to the state. General Thomas Gage, Commander of British Forces at Boston during the battle of Lexington and Concord, owned the bulk of what later became the Town of Deerfield. He saved it from confiscation by transferring title to his father-in-law, Peter Kemble. Land at Oquaga which had belonged to Joseph Brant and Sir William, as well as other land along the upper Susquehanna belonging to Tories was also confiscated by the state.

After the war, the state rewarded many worthies by granting them large parcels of land. Sixteen thousand acres were given to General Baron von Steuben (Town of Steuben) who had reorganized and trained Washington's men at Valley Forge. Marinus Willett, second in command at Fort Stanwix during St. Leger's siege, was granted a large parcel in northern Oneida county. Thomas Machin, who had erected the heavy chain across the Hudson River at West Point to prevent the British fleet from sailing troops upriver and later served in the Sullivan Campaign, also received a large area which became Boonville and Forestport. Jellis Fonda, who passed information from his trading post regarding Tory activities to Philip Schuyler, and risked his life many times in the war, was rewarded with 40,000 acres near Rome and Western.

George Clinton, as the first governor of the State of New York, purchased a large area from the Oneidas in the southern part of Oneida County and in Madison and Chenango counties. He also bought 6000 acres jointly with George Washington from Marinus Willett a mile south of Kirkland, and sold it to one Nathaniel Griffin in 1790.

STEUBEN GRANT
OF 16,000 ACRES BY THE
STATE OF NEW YORK, JUNE 27, 1786
FOR SERVICE IN THE REVOLUTION
HE CLEANED 60 ACRES NEAR HERE
FOR HOMESITE (1788-1793)

Oneida County, 79
CR west of Steuben Memorial

In 1791, Nicholas and John Roosevelt, together with George Scriba, a New York merchant, purchased 500,000 acres in what are now Oneida and Oswego counties, but they sold their interests to Scriba a few years later. (This is the same clan of Roosevelts that spawned the Oyster Bay Roosevelts - Theodore Roosevelt and his niece Eleanor - and the Hyde Park Roosevelts - Franklin D. Roosevelt).

WASHINGTON TRACT
THESE LANDS ARE PART OF
PARCEL OF GROUND DEEDED
TO NATHANIEL GRIFFIN BY
GEORGE WASHINGTON AND
DEWITT CLINTON IN 1790

Oneida County, 33
NY 233, 1 1/2 m. S. of Kirkland

While secretary to John Adams when he was our first ambassador to England, Col. William Smith, a former aid to Washington, married Adams's daughter, Abigail, in London, in 1786. Later, Smith persuaded English investors to join him in purchasing 270,000 acres of now southern Madison and northern Chenango counties. The Smith's moved there 1807, but Abigail died of cholera while visiting her parents in Boston; he passed on three years later.

UNADILLA RIVER
LANDS WEST OF RIVER CEDED
TO N.Y. STATE BY INDIANS IN
A TREATY MADE BY GOV. GEORGE
CLINTON AT FORT SCHUYLER,
SEPTEMBER 22, 1788.

Chenango County, 20
NY 8, 2 m. south of New Berlin

Sherburne, Smyrna, Hamilton, Eaton, and other towns grew out of this purchase. (The carriage house of the formerly elegant New York Smith mansion, now among dingy buildings shadowed by the Queensboro Bridge, has since been restored by the Colonial Dames of America and serves as their headquarters).

WEST HILL– 1802
COLONEL WILLIAM S. SMITH,
AID TO WASHINGTON, OWNED
150,000 ACRES HEREABOUT IN
1791; MARRIED ABIGAIL ADAMS.
BURIED AT REAR. DUE NORTH

Chenango County, 40
NY 80, 2 m. NW of Sherburne

Like the grants made in the colonial years which were divided into almost perpetual leaseholds, all these tracts of land were obtained by wealthy and well-connected speculators but, unlike the colonials, they were encouraged by the state with tax concessions to develop the region and to resell to smaller holders.

One of the last of a long line of patroons, Stephen Van Rensselaer, died in 1839 at age 75. At the death of a patroon previously, the land devolved to the oldest son under primogeniture, a law going back to the days of feudalism. With new laws, the manor of Rensselaerswycke, not much

Sure Signs: Stories Behind the Historical Markers of Central New York

changed from its maximum dimension, was now split up among his ten children. Within fifty years, due to deaths, financial reverses, remarriages, and sales, the 700,000 acres had been broken up several times and the many parcels were in the hands of diverse strangers.

In 1787, the New York Genesee Land Company was created by John Livingston, Major Peter Schuyler, Dr. Caleb Benton and others to obtain Indian lands and to establish their own republic in western New York. Since purchase of land by individuals from Indians directly was then illegal, the company obtained 999 year leases from the Senecas of much of their land. Canadians, including the former Tory, John Butler, and the Mohawk chief, Joseph Brant, also became a part of this plot, and at Kanadasaga, the Canadians and the Americans met with the Iroquois to arrange the details. Governor Clinton came down hard on this plan and instigated legislation making such leases illegal. The company tried to enlist public enthusiasm for the creation of a separate state, but the petitions were largely ignored and the idea died.

To induce men to enlist and fight in the Revolution, the states, including New York and the Federal Government had promised grants of land to be made available after the war to men who had met the terms of their enlistment. In 1782, even before the war was over, the New York State legislature allocated a Military Tract for the veterans—like most states, New York was cash poor but rich in soon-to-be acquired real estate. The Tract was in the now Adirondack counties of Franklin, Essex, and Clinton, but there were no takers because the thin soil and short season were unfavorable for farming. This tract was withdrawn by the State and a second made ready in central New York. By various treaties from 1785 to 1789 with the Oneidas, Onondagas, and the Cayugas, the state acquired much of their land to constitute the veterans bounty lands.

ONONDAGA RESERVATION ESTABLISHED IN 1788, THE ONONDAGA INDIAN NATION FOUNDED THE IROQUOIS LEAGUE

Onondaga County, 51*
NY 175 at Onondaga Hill

RESERVATION OF CAYUGAS SOLD TO THE STATE 1789 A BODY OF TUSCARORAS WERE THE LAST OF THE IROQUOIS TO OCCUPY THIS POINT

Cayuga County, 146
On Farley's Point

The Oneidas retained a reservation extending from the southeastern shore of Oneida Lake, but had sold several thousand acres to Peter Smith, (one-time partner of John Jacob Astor, and father of reformer Gerrit Smith) who built his home at Peterboro. The Onondagas's reservation of a hundred square miles then included all of the present city of Syracuse. The Cayuga's reservation, also a hundred square miles, lay like a horse-shoe clasped on both sides of Cayuga Lake from about Aurora north to the Seneca River.

Simeon DeWitt, Surveyor General of the State (and Governor Clinton's nephew), began surveys to lay out twenty-six townships (two more townships were added later) comprising the counties we know today as Seneca, Cayuga, Cortland, and Onondaga and portions of the adjacent counties of Wayne, Oswego, Schuyler, and Tompkins. The land was made available to the veterans in early 1791 by the drawing of lots.

Each township was six miles square and composed of thirty-six 600-acre lots with land set aside in each town for churches, schools and roads. Privates and noncoms were entitled to 600 acres; lieutenants, 1200 acres - with larger acreage according to rank, increasing to 5500 acres for a major general.

Robert Harpur, Assistant Secretary of State was given the task of naming the towns since DeWitt's map identified them only by number. His interest in the classics inspired him to name the towns after Greek, Roman, and Carthaginian generals, politicians, poets, and an early Greek physician. Marcellus, Cato, Sempronius, Romulus, Aurelius, Manlius, Vergil, Homer, Cicero,

Pompey, Fabius, Tully, Lysander, Brutus, Camillus, Hannibal, Cincinnatus, Ulysses, Solon, Scipio, Hector, Galen, and Ovid thus lent their names to the towns waiting to be settled. English poets and philosophers were not neglected: Dryden, Locke, and Milton were applied as well as Junius, a nom de plume for a never identified pre-Revolutionary English political writer and critic.

Syracuse, Rome, Utica, and Ithaca were community names that came later, applied by the residents themselves. The Lewis and Clark Expedition must have inspired Mandana for the Mandan Indians encountered up the Missouri River, and Navarino, Borodino, and Waterloo by the Napoleonic wars. Penn Yan was a compromise arrived at between Yankee and Pennsylvania settlers there who were dissatisfied with Snells Town. Later, Harpur himself was not overlooked - Harpursville and Harpur College in Binghamton are named for him.

Many veterans sold their allotments for next to nothing to well positioned speculators, made privy to veteran lists, who later became rich. A lively market ensued between uninterested or cash-poor veterans and others wanting to acquire this land reputed for its ability to grow lush crops. Some sold their lots several times, causing much chagrin to those who cleared and improved what they thought was theirs, only to find that they had defective title and had to defer to the proven claimant. Real estate courts were tied up until 1803 before all these titles were untangled.

During the French Reign of Terror, royalists, aristocrats, and the well-to-do were liable to be shorn of their estates and imprisoned; indeed, before it was over, more than sixteen thousand, nobles and commoners alike, were subjected to the impersonal and dreadful decapitating machine newly invented by Dr. Guillotin. The lucky ones smuggled themselves out of the country, usually with little or none of their wealth.

Louis Marie Vicomte de Noailles, scion of 400 years of nobility and a leading member of the King's court, (and brother-in-law of Lafayette), had served with honor at Yorktown. Despite his proposal in 1789 to the States-General to abolish all titles and feudal rights of the ancien régime, his record with the revolutionary Americans, and his Republican sympathies, he had to flee France for his life several years later.

Arriving in Philadelphia, he became a partner of William Bingham, a leading merchant, politician, and owner of vast lands in Maine and on the Susquehanna, including a village later named after him.

Another eminent refugee arriving in Philadelphia was Antoine Omer Talon, (descendant of Jean Baptiste Talon, Intendant under Canada's Governor Tracy), a commoner who had risen to chief justice and one of the King's advisors. Mons. Talon was smuggled out of Marseilles in a large wine cask by his friend, Mons. B. Laporte, a wine merchant who accompanied him to America.

Philadelphia was already crowded with refugees, not only from France, but from Santo Domingo, where black insurrectionists were fighting to reclaim their country. De Noailles and Talon wished to find a suitable site for the safe and secluded settlement of their countrymen. Robert Morris, called "the financier of the American Revolution", owned large tracts of land in New York and northern Pennsylvania; making it available to the émigrés as The Asylum Company was a way to pay back France for its essential help in the American Revolution and make a profit at the same time.

The first settlement nestled on flat alluvial ground already under cultivation by squatters on the North Branch of the Susquehanna just south of present Towanda. The town was laid out with plans for a boulevard to be flanked by two-story log homes, complete with chimneys, glass windows, and wide porches. Shops, several inns, a mill, a wharf, and a smithy were built, with two larger homes constructed first for the looked-for day when Queen Marie Antoinette could be rescued from her jailors.

Occasional visits by French royalty and statesmen reinforced the belief that their former status would be regained and were cause for celebration. De Noailles arrived with the first colonists but soon returned to Philadelphia where he managed the financial affairs of the colony. In 1794, the well-known Charles Maurice Talleyrand, former Bishop of Autun, now bellwether politician and diplomat, visited for two months, a guest of Monsieur Talon, and then continued his tour of the country. The Count de Maulevrier and the Duc de Rochefoucauld-Liancourt, made Asylum a stop on their separate tours. Both kept journals from which much of this material originated. Late in 1797, the young Duc d'Orleans, and his younger brothers, the Duc de Montpensier and the Count de Beaujolais, stopped by on their way from Niagara, via Canandaigua and Elmira on a protracted tour of the United States.

The émigrés were not used to heavy toil and knew little of farming, but the enclave endured. Their shops contrasted with the usual frontier trading posts since they carried stocks of luxury items

Sure Signs: Stories Behind the Historical Markers of Central New York

similar to what they had been used to in Paris. By 1796, the peak, there were about fifty log homes in all, and about two hundred habitants. After a day of hard work, men and ladies pleased themselves by dressing in formal attire for an evening of music, cards, or dancing in the former "Queen's Mansion" in an effort to recapture Parisian pleasures.

As hard as they worked, the residents of Asylum did not prosper financially or in spirit. They sorely missed France and yearned to return. In 1802, when Napoleon issued an edict granting émigrés the right to petition for repatriation and recovery of their property, they celebrated for days, singing, dancing, and toasting the future.

Most of the émigrés returned to France. They arrived in time to be subject to compulsory conscription by Napoleon a year later. Within a year, Asylum was abandoned. Monsieur Laporte and a M. Hemet remained and were able to buy the property of their departed townsmen cheaply. They became successful farmers, and agents for Morris and his associates. De Noailles left his successful business in Philadelphia and took a command under Rochambeau (the younger), in Santo Domingo and was mortally wounded in a naval battle in 1804. Morris became bankrupt when credit and the market for his land here and elsewhere collapsed. Mons. Laporte lived in the Queens Mansion until 1846 when it was demolished. A bronze marker on a boulder recalls the story of the hamlet, now called Frenchtown.

But the young Duc d'Orleans loved to paint and capture nature at its best on canvas. One of his favorite views was of Shequaga Falls (Montour Falls), and his painting of the scene, rendered years later, hangs in the Louvre in Paris. The Duc, or as he is better known, Louis Philippe, went on to become the last King of France in 1830 (with the help of the aging Lafayette), until the Revolution of '48 deposed him.

Captain Joseph Juliard, already retired from command of a merchant ship to marry a lady from New Haven, Connecticut and live out of the fray, became attracted to the émigré colony on the Chenango River. As they arrived, the hamlet's residents, who had endured a winter of severe privation, were about to flee the area in favor of moving to Asylum, and he quickly bought up the entire settlement. He and his family settled there for good, and his descendants can still be found in the area. The town was later named in honor of General Nathanael Greene.

Howard S. Ford

SHE-QUA-GA
"TUMBLING WATERS'
A SKETCH NOW IN THE LOUVRE
MADE ABOUT 1820 BY
LOUIS PHILIPPE
LATER KING OF FRANCE

Schuyler County, 24
Genesee Street at Montour

Mons. Devatines, a cultured gentleman from Lisle, fled the violence of the French Revolution in its earliest phase. Seeking a haven in America, and new to the art of fleeing, he impoverished himself with needless expense and foolish speculations. He heard of an island in Oneida Lake near Scriba's settlement of New Rotterdam (Constantia), and there settled for seclusion, in 1791, with his wife, two children, and his few remaining personal items, including his most prized possession, a fine library.

For five years the family strenuously cleared twenty acres on the island, and planted a large garden, profuse with flowers, vegetables and fruits. They sold their produce to the villagers on shore in whose company they felt socially squeamish. Despite this, they enjoyed mutual assistance from the settlers and became fast friends of the Oneidas nearby. These accomplishment under difficult conditions were satisfying to Mons. Devatines who consoled himself by perusing the volumes in his collection.

However, after several years of this regimen, seclusion soured to intellectual isolation; they longed to escape menial toil and again enjoy the social graces they had known at home in the ambience of their countrymen. As the Revolution waned, friends in Albany contributed to a fund to enable the Devatines, now five in number, to return to France. The island has retained its moniker, Frenchman's Island, to this day.

The hoped-for rapid settlement of central New York was delayed for several other reasons besides the veterans title tangle. There were many conflicting land titles between the states because of overlapping Royal grants running westward often without limit, and these had to be reconciled. The British failed to honor their commitment to abandon forts at Michilimackinac, Detroit, Niagara, Oswego, and Oswegatchie until 1796, and fear of what mischief they might promote with the Indians of Pennsylvania, Ohio, and those who had drifted back to New York left many prospective settlers hesitant to move west. General Mad Anthony Wayne's victory in 1794 over the tribes in Indiana Territory at the Battle of Fallen Timbers relieved these anxieties and settlement began to gain momentum.

Western New York was claimed by Massachusetts because Charles I, in 1629, made a grant to the Massachusetts Bay Company which extended to the Pacific Ocean, while his son, Charles II, in 1664, granted some of the same land to his brother, the Duke of York and Albany (later to become James II.) This and other disputes were settled at the Hartford Convention in 1786 with Massachusetts giving up its claim of sovereignty and New York agreeing that Massachusetts had the right of preemption over land west of the seventy-seventh meridian (the preemption line), which passes through Sodus Point and along the western edge of Geneva and the Military Tract.

PREEMPTION LINE
BOUNDARY DRAWN BETWEEN
MASSACHUSETTS AND NEW YORK
DECEMBER 16, 1786
CAUSE OF LONG CONTROVERY
IN WESTERN NEW YORK

Ontario County, 14
US 20 & NY 5 at western edge
Of Geneva

Preemption Road, just west of Geneva, still marks that boundary. Preemption meant that Massachusetts could sell that land subject to the Indian title. Massachusetts claimed a second tract on the Susquehanna called the Boston Ten Towns, (located south of the Military Tract between the Chenango River and Owego Creek and now part of Tioga and Broome counties) which was treated the same way, and later sold to speculators for twelve cents an acre. The northwest corner of the Boston purchase is about two miles east of Slaterville Springs.

WEST OWEGO CREEK, N.W. BOUNDARY 'BOSTON PURCHASE' 230,400 ACRES OF INDIAN LAND CEDED BY NEW YORK TO MASS. 1787, TO SETTLE BOUNDARY DISPUTE

Tompkins County, 13
Cr 2½ miles east of Slaterville Springs

In April of 1788, Massachusetts sold the tract of 6,000,000 acres (all of New York west of the Pre-Emption Line) for ƒ300,000 to two well-connected Massachusetts land speculators, Oliver Phelps and Nathaniel Gorham, and their associates. The shrewd and persuasive Phelps lost no time in bargaining with the Indians to obtain title to 2,600,000 acres of the tract between the line and the Genesee River, and parlayed for more west of the Genesee. The purchase from the Indians cost $5000 cash and $500 annually "forever".

Phelps and Gorham managed to sell some parcels, but sales were slower than expected, and a change in governmental financial policy had an adverse affect on their ability to pay the first of three annual installments. To relieve their financial obligations, they relinquished to Massachusetts two-thirds of the original purchase, that part west of the Genesee they had not settled with the Indians. A year later, they sold 1,250,000 acres to Robert Morris. In turn, Morris had his financial problems which forced him to sell to an English land syndicate headed by Sir William Pulteney of Bath, England.

PHELPS-GORHAM PURCHASE
PIONEER LAND OFFICE
WESTERN N.Y. ESTA. HERE
1789
HOME SITE OLIVER PHELPS
IST JUDGE OF CO. 1789-93

Ontario County, 6
US 20, NY 5 & 21, between Niagara
& Ontario Streets. Canandaigua

The tract stretched from the western boundary of the Military Tract to the Genesee River and south to the Pennsylvania line. The syndicate appointed Charles Williamson, a Scot and retired British Army officer (who had spent the war as a prisoner near Boston) as their agent in residence. He platted towns, and gave them names such as Lyons, Geneva, Charlotte, and Bath. With flair and enthusiasm, he sponsored a fair in 1793 at Williamsburg (NY 63, 3 miles south of Geneseo), including a horse race, attracting entries from as far away as New Jersey, Maryland, and Virginia. He built roads to the navigable waters of the Susquehanna for access to Philadelphia and Baltimore, and to Pultneyville on Lake Ontario; built grist mills, sawmills, a sumptuous hotel, even an opera house to bring the musical and theatrical arts to the wilderness.

Geneva, formerly Kanadasaga, was where Williamson preferred to stay, at his newly-built Geneva Tavern, where he reserved rooms. Laying out the town to take advantage of the lake vista from the bluff, he sold lots on either side of South Main Street, but prohibited building on the lake side in order to preserve the view.

He induced many prominent families from Virginia and Maryland to pull up stakes and move from their established plantations to the region. The Fitzhughs, the Nicholas's, and the Roses brought wealth, slaves, and Episcopalianism with them.

The Nicholas's bought the area of White Springs Farm, the site of Ganechstage, one of the relocated Seneca villages after the Denonville raid. The Roses made their home on the hill where later the magnificent Rose Hill Mansion was built, since rebuilt and preserved overlooking the Geneva shore of Seneca lake.

FIRST ROAD IN WILLIAMSON BUILT BY CHARLES WILLIAMSON IN 1794 CALLED THE OLD SODUS ROAD BETWEEN PALMYRA AND SODUS BAY

Wayne County, 29
US 104 at East Williamson

Williamson and this infusion of wealthy southerners helped change Geneva from what Elkanah Watson said of it in 1791, "a small unhealthy village", and what someone else a year later said, "Geneva consists of about twenty log cabins, three or four frame buildings, and as many idle persons as can live in them." Years later, on another trip, Watson revised his comment to, "Geneva is now not only an elegant but a salubrious village, and distinguished for the refinement and elevated character of its society."

Unfortunately, Williamsburg did not mature as Williamson had hoped. He had hired agents abroad to recruit settlers to further develop the community. The Hamburg agent was indifferent to quality workers, and sent over a gang of street idlers who had little experience with the work required. (It was not uncommon in Europe for men to be impressed into involuntary servitude, and later sold at dockside to work off their bond-age over several years.)

SITE OF WILLIAMSBURG FIRST SETTLEMENT IN COUNTY ESTABLISHED 1792 BY CHARLES WILLIAMSON

Livingston County, 12*
NY 63, 3 m. south of Geneseo

The men violently objected to the hard conditions and the arrangement didn't work. Williamson's interest shifted, the project was abandoned, and within a few years, the hoped-for metropolis melded back to wilderness.

All this development on the part of Williamson cost a great deal with no return to the investors. Because of the expense, the Pulteney directors replaced him in 1801 with Robert Troup, a Federalist lawyer who at least recovered the investment of the principles through debt collection and curbing expenses. By the time of the Civil War, the company had done no better than break even and the land office was closed.

Morris made money on his sale to the Pulteney interests which encouraged him to buy the land west of the Genesee that Phelps and Gorham had turned back to Massachusetts. For ƒ100,000 he acquired about 4,000,000 acres. He retained a reserve of 500,000 acres in the eastern section of this tract and sold the balance to the Holland Land Company in 1796, the syndicate of Dutch investors which had already entrenched itself at Cazenovia, Boonville, and Barneveld.

Two friends of Morris's were investors in this reserve and had been rivals in politics since the War. In 1804, they contended for the last time across the Hudson from New York in a duel in which Aaron Burr fatally wounded his rival, Alexander Hamilton, former Secretary of State and the son-in law of elderly General Schuyler. Morris' attempt to acquire title from the Senecas had been delayed until the Indian question on the western frontier was resolved by the Battle of Fallen Timbers. That year (1794), the Pickering Treaty Council at Canandaigua gave assurance to the Senecas from George Washington—through his agent, Timothy Pickering—that they were secure in their lands. Nevertheless, title from the Senecas was secured in 1797 by Morris' son, Thomas, (acting as resident agent for his debtor-prison bound father), at the Big Tree Treaty held near Geneseo.

Cornplanter, Red Jacket, Handsome Lake, Farmer's Brother, Fish Carrier, and Little Beard were some of the signatory Seneca leaders present at the council. One of the commissioners for the United States was Jeremiah Wadsworth from Connecticut, a Commissary General in the Revolution, whose nephews, James and William, acquired extensive acreage in the region at a sheriff's sale (a major part of which had been Morris' reserved tract). The Wadsworth family has retained fifteen thousand acres of the beautiful Genesee Valley, maintaining a balance of woods, pasture, and land under cultivation which they can view from Hartford, the ancestral mansion at Geneseo.

Generations of Wadsworths have gained fame through positions of leadership in the military, the United States Congress, the diplomatic corps, business, and animal husbandry, mainly breeding and racing thoroughbreds.

ABOUT 1/4 MILE WEST
TREATY OF
BIG TREE
SITE OF MEMORABLE TREATY
RELEASING SENECA TITLE TO
3,600,000 ACRES OF LAND
SEPTEMBER 15, 1797

Livingston County, 11*
NY 63 at Geneseo

For the land west of the Genesee, the Senecas received $100,000, which was to be invested in stock of the Bank of the United States for their benefit, and were left with ten reservations totaling 350 square miles. Over the next several decades they sold all but four of these tracts, retaining Cattaraugus, seventeen miles along Cattaraugus Creek; Tonawanda, seventy square miles; Alleghany, forty miles long and a mile wide on both sides of the Allegheny River including Salamanca village; (most of the reservation is now inundated by water backed by Kinzua dam); and the square-mile Oil Spring tract near Cuba. The Tuscaroras have their reservation near Niagara Falls.

INDIAN CABIN
NEARBY IS THE SITE OF
LAST CABIN IN THIS TOWN
OCCUPIED BY THE SENECAS,
BEFORE THEIR REMOVAL TO THE
BUFFALO RESERVATION, 1826.

Livingston County, 37
NY 436, 4 miles west of Nunda

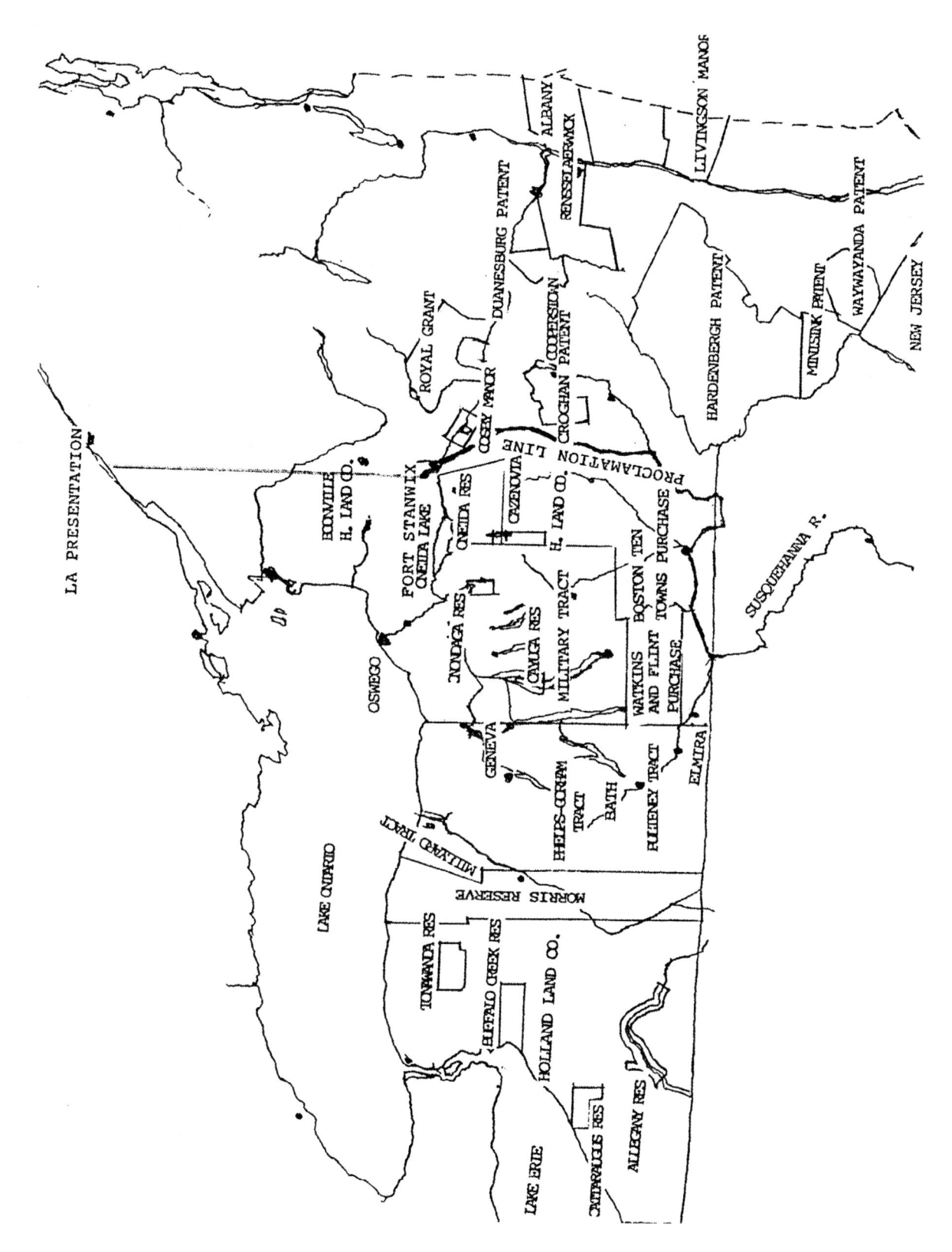

Sure Signs: Stories Behind the Historical Markers of Central New York

COLONIAL TRACTS & PATENTS and POST REVOLUTIONARY WAR TRACTS AND INDIAN RESERVATIONS.

CHAPTER NINE

Settlers fleeing years of harvesting rocks from New England soil made their way to central New York up the Mohawk, portaged at Fort Stanwix to Wood Creek and Oneida Lake, and continued on to Three Rivers and upstream along the Seneca River to the Finger Lakes. Low water levels and other obstructions sometimes made this travel difficult and the idea of a canal began to develop in the minds of several men, notably Elkanah Watson, who throughout his life was enterprising, resourceful, and widely traveled.

In the fall of 1777 when he was nineteen, Elkanah was sent by John Brown, a Providence merchant, with $50,000 sewn in his clothes to deal with a company agent in Charleston, South Carolina. This was not an easy task with the British in his path busy burning Kingston on the Hudson and the altercations at Brandywine and Germantown which he had to thread. So successful was he in this mission that Brown next sent him to Paris with important dispatches for Benjamin Franklin. During his five years in France, he was fascinated by the canal system there and in Holland. When he returned to America he hiked a tentative canal route westward from Albany to the environs of Oneida Lake and printed a report to promote a canal.

The year 1791 saw Watson and a small group of potential investors explore this route through central New York as far as Geneva. The journal he kept all his life noted that as his party rounded a point to enter Cross Lake upstream on the Seneca River, they spotted a grove of huge and stately beech trees, their trunks all carved with the names of previous travelers-graffiti in the wilderness of 1791!

A year later, Watson, General Philip Schuyler, and backers representing the Holland Land Company, the Pulteney interests, and Le Roy Bayard & Company, created the Western Inland Lock Navigation Company. Hiring English engineer William Weston, the company built a small canal and five locks at Little Falls to by-pass a three-quarter mile section of the Mohawk River where it dropped thirty-nine feet.

INLAND CANAL
BEGUN 1792
AND SECOND
ERIE CANAL
COMPLETED 1844

Oneida County, 54*
S. James & E. Whitesboro Sts.
Town of Rome

In 1797, two miles of canal were completed connecting Lake Ontario via Wood Creek with the Mohawk at Rome. At Herkimer, another short canal bypassed some rapids with two locks. Wood Creek and the Mohawk were cleared of obstructions so that shallow-draft Durham boats, sixty feet long and carrying sixteen tons, could replace boats that held only a ton and a half. At the same time, the investor formed a similar company to join Lake Champlain and the St. Lawrence River by canal to the Hudson.

The cost of hauling goods from Albany to Seneca Lake dropped from $100 a ton to $32. Even so, the companies did not prosper, and were taken over by the state in 1820. But building the locks and canals was a pioneering feat of engineering for the area that gave impetus and technical foundation to the promoters of the Erie Canal.

PORT WATSON
NAMED AFTER ELKANAH WATSON
BUSY RIVER PORT 1800–1850
SITE SHIP YARDS, ROPE WALK,
FACTORIES. "ARKS' CARRIED
CARGOES TO PENNSYLVANIA

Cortland County, 4, bridge at Port Watson St.

Some early settlers passed along the Indian trails, but usually they were traveling without family to build a cabin and make a small clearing. Often as not they would journey in the winter, preferring sleds to transport them rather than wheels which could mire in mud in other seasons.

The best areas for settling were the recently vacated fertile clearings, usually bottom lands, used by the Indians and picked up by knowing speculators. Only small brush that had grown since their departure had to be removed in order to prepare the field and plant a crop. The Yaple, Dumond, and Hennepaw families, happening on the "ancient maize lands of the Cayugas" at Ithaca, returned the following year to sow seed and build their homes, only to find that their agent had failed to properly register their claim at Albany. They had to abandon this preferred location but relocated nearby.

The quickest and easiest way to make a clearing for growing a crop was the Indian technique of killing the trees by girdling them and letting in the sunlight, the trees could be cut down later. After planting a crop the settler would go back home to return with his family, their milch cow or other farm animals, and additional furnishings and tools.

ORIGINAL LANE USED BY FIRST SETTLERS; YAPPLE AND DUMOND NEAR STATE ST; HENNEPAW ON CASCADILLA CREEK

Tompkins County, 57
East Buffalo St., Ithaca

The trip could take a month or more, and many had to spend the nights along the trail making what shelter they could. A few cabins along the road were styled as "taverns", but not many travelers wanted to risk sleeping with strangers in the same bed usually ridden with fleas.

It was common for first and even second-time settlers to fail in making a go of it, despite the hard work and the making of improvements which accrued to the benefit of succeeding homesteaders.

When William Cooper bought his land at Lake Otsego he laid out lots, built a gristmill and sawmill at what became Cooperstown, and went back to Burlington to fetch his family. Wise entrepreneurs would clear the land before selling it which made it more likely that the settlers would survive the agonizing period between planting and harvest when all food had to be brought in or bought. Anticipating difficult times for his settlers in the early years, Cooper generously provided them food and the means of survival and eventual prosperity. One April, a fortuitous run of shad up the Susquehanna saved them from sure starvation.

Despite Cooper's brusque manner, he was well liked and became the county's first judge. Many sugar maples favored his land and Cooper believed that all the country's sweetening needs could be met by syrup refined from the sap of the maple tree. But his strong Federalist political opinions came into disfavor after the turn of the century, and he was murdered, hit from behind by an unknown assailant after leaving a Federalist meeting in Albany.

Abner Treman saw service in the Battle of Stony Point under Mad Anthony Wayne, and was with Colonel Henry Dearborn destroying the Indian villages on the west side of Cayuga Lake in the Sullivan Campaign. He knew the location he wanted in the Military Tract and was fortunate in obtaining it. He and his family arrived near Taughannock Point in February of 1793 with all they owned on a sled. They stayed a few nights as guests in the cabin of a settled neighbor while they built a lean-to in which to live until they could build a cabin for themselves. The cabin must have been well built because it served as their home for the next seventeen years. Treman built and operated a grist mill, but his main income came from occasionally selling off part of his land, and the town of Trumansburg (the post office misspelled it) grew up around him. Treman had come in over the new road—built by Joseph Chaplin - which was surveyed to run from Oxford to Bath by way of Dryden and Ithaca.

Hugh White, Revolutionary veteran from Connecticut, settled along Sauquoit Creek, in 1785, and with Zephaniah Platt, Melancthon Smith, and Ezra L'Hommedieux, founded Whitestown, just west of Utica. Many other Yankees immigrated and in 1809, Dr. Seth Capron and Benjamin Walcott from Rhode Island formed the Oneida Manufacturing Company, backed by local and Albany financiers, for making cotton and woolen cloth. The Walcott family was one of the first to have a medical plan for their employees and also provided them company housing (for less than $20 a year). Soon, others

Howard S. Ford

founded a woolen factory in Oriskany and the industrial development of the upper Mohawk valley began.

> SAMUEL WEYBURN
> SETTLED HERE IN 1790
> THE HOSPITALITY OF HIS LOG
> CABIN HOME SAVED LIFE OF
> ABNER TREMAN, REV. SOLDIER
> CAUGHT IN BLIZZARD 1793-94
>
> Tompkins County, 77
> Taughannock Falls State Park

> SITE OF
> WOOLEN MILL
> ERECTED IN 1810
> BELIEVED TO BE THE 1ST
> IN AMERICA TO MANUFACTURE
> FABRICS FROM RAW MATERIAL
>
> Oneida County, 106
> NY 69, Oriskany

Nearby Lynchville could have grown faster had New York City merchant Dominic Lynch not insisted on leasing lots. As Governor Bellomont had observed a hundred years earlier, people, especially Yankees coming through, wanted to buy land, not rent. The community changed its name to Rome and incorporated in 1819, the year the Erie Canal was built to course a half mile south of the city.

When Benjamin Franklin was in Paris seeking French support for the American Revolution, the French were eager to help the United States in order to wound England, but reluctant to officially recognize the upstart country for fear of provoking an untimely war with the English. So Franklin sought wealthy and influential intermediaries to gain the ear of the French Court.

Jacques Le Ray de Chaumont had made several fortunes trading with the West Indies and the American colonies, enabling him in to cap his congeries of estates in 1750 with the purchase of the famous Château de Chaumont sur Loire (built in 940) from which he stylized his name. Member of the king's council, overseer of the king's forests, advisor to Louis XVI on commercial matters, and commissary officer of the French Army, Chaumont wielded considerable influence with the king and key officials.

Of a benign nature, he improved the lot of the peasants on his estates and was beloved by them (which during the worst of times was to serve him well). Chaumont admired the celebrated and ingenious Doctor Franklin, somewhat his counterpart in America, and the American cause. For nine years he gave Franklin and the American legation the free use of a town house, and the hospitality of his table at his estate at Passy, between Paris and Versailles. Of the most importance, he introduced Franklin socially to the court. From his own funds, he advanced two million francs for arms to the colonies through playwright and agent Beaumarchaise's fictional trading company, and outfitted a squadron of ships for another guest at Passy, John Paul Jones.

By war's end, Chaumont had seriously depleted his funds for America's cause, which prompted him to send his eldest son, James Le Ray, to America to negotiate recovery from a penurious Congress. James was partially successful (mainly due to the attention of his avuncular friend Franklin), but his task took five years. During this time he wed a New Jersey girl, was introduced to leading businessmen by Governeur Morris (a close friend and U.S. ambassador to France), and became a U.S. citizen.

Several years after James had returned to France in 1790, he was sought out by William Constable, a survivor of the bankrupt land syndicate involved in the Macomb Purchase (present Lewis, and most of Jefferson, Franklin, and St. Lawrence counties), whom he had met in New York. Constable interested Le Ray and his associates in buying substantial tracts in the North Country.

Le Ray employed Quaker Jacob Brown (who later led the defense of the region in the War of 1812, becoming general in chief of the U.S. Army), as his agent to develop the area and to accommodate French aristocrats to whom he had sold land. Roads, mills, stores, and wharves were built, and another agent, Doctor Beaudry, built for Le Ray an impressive four-columned mansion, with flanking wings similar in appearance to Jefferson's Monticello, at Leraysville, on the edge of present Fort Drum. Le Ray wished to live the life of a benign feudal seigneur, as his father had in France. Cape Vincent and Alexandria Bay were named for his sons and the town of Theresa for his daughter. In each town, a fine stone home was constructed for its namesake.

Le Ray's and his father's affairs in strife-torn France required his personal attention and kept him from returning to the North Country until 1802, when he stayed for a year. But over his lifetime, he was able to stay for much longer periods, twenty-eight years in all. He sold 10,000 acres to a group of Pennsylvania Quakers who named their settlement Philadelphia (it is this Philadelphia whose dairymen developed the famous Philadelphia cream cheese). Though a strict Catholic, he donated land to the Baptists, Quakers, and Presbyterians in addition to the gifts he made to the Catholic churches in Clayton, Cape Vincent, and Belfort.

Following Napoleon's defeat at Waterloo, James arranged to meet Joseph Bonaparte (the former King of Naples and then Spain, so appointed by his younger brother, Napoleon), and sold him 27,000 acres of North Country as a retreat. The deposed king, calling himself the Count de Survilliers, had his hunting lodge and a summer home at opposite ends of what he called Lake Bonaparte, and, happier in his garden than he ever had been as king, he installed his mistress at Evan's Mills while his wife chose to remain in Italy. The experience of one winter at his residence in Natural Bridge convinced him to stay at his regal palace on a thousand-acre bluff overlooking the Delaware River in Bordentown, New Jersey until spring was certain.

Then he and his caravan of a coach and six leading wagons filled with guests, retainers and their baggage and supplies, enriched merchants and tavern owners en route as the party frolicked along the Mohawk Valley and up the crude Black River Turnpike on the way to Natural Bridge. Well-to-do French shared the social season with the former king and established local estates, enlarging the French enclave and Le Ray's prosperity. When Louis Phillipe assumed the throne in 1830, the erstwhile king was happy to return to France, and sold his property three years later, most of it to John LaFarge, of whom more later.

Sales and rentals of Le Ray's 350,000 acres rapidly continued to increase until by 1832, income had decreased to a trickle, and the Le Rays, too, departed for France, leaving their properties to be managed by agents. Ironically in 1832, James Le Ray founded, with the former peripatetic but still active Elkanah Watson, the New York State Agricultural Society, and was elected its first president the year of his departure. (The two could easily have met fifty-five years earlier when Watson was sent with dispatches to Franklin in Paris.) The Le Ray land office in Carthage stayed open till 1914.

OLD FRENCH ROAD BUILT BY FRENCH COLONISTS, 1790 ON WAY TO SETTLE CASTORLAND; FIRST ROAD TO NORTH COUNTRY FOLLOWING AN IROQUOIS WAR TRAIL

Oneida County, 16
NY 12, 1 mile SE of Boonville

Jean de Le Farge (anglicized to John La Farge) was a French soldier who escaped from black revolutionaries in Santo Domingo, and later made his fortune as a blockade runner between France and England during the Napoleonic wars. He bought land in the North Country from the estate of an Indian trader who had tricked the Oneidas into deeding him the land ("to fulfill a dream") called Penet's Square after the devious trader. The northwest corner of the tract was on the St. Lawrence at Clayton. La Farge had continued to add to his holdings, including the purchase of two-thirds of Joseph Bonaparte's land when the ex-king departed for France. Late in life he married a cultured sixteen year-old French girl from New York, but, four years of feeling snubbed by the local social circle in LaFargeville became intolerable to her. She insisted they move to New York causing La Farge to sell all his considerable property.

Besides leaving his name to La Fargeville, he left a son, John, who became a famous artist and church muralist. Painting religious murals led him to become even more famous working in stained glass, for which achievements he received the Legion of Honor from the French government. He married Margaret Perry, granddaughter of Oliver Hazard Perry and great granddaughter of Benjamin Franklin.

Howard S. Ford

His artistic bent was passed on to his son and three of his grandchildren, one of whom was Christopher Grant La Farge, a church architect well known for his designs, particularly the Cathedral of St. John the Divine in New York. One of the architect's sons was Oliver La Farge, the popular anthropologist, and author of numerous books, including **Laughing Boy** (about Navaho life), for which he won the Pulitzer Prize in 1929.

As the new country grew, it shuffled off the restraints and conventions of colonial government in favor of new laws and policies to infuse a latent energy into the economy. In 1811, New York state encouraged investment by passing laws granting corporations limited liability, legal person status, perpetual life, and the means for tapping outside money to increase business capital, the mechanisms for issuing shares of stock. Corporations could obtain their charter from the secretary of state rather than having to have a special law enacted in order for them to engage in business. The state made no attempt to regulate the corporations, but left the question of their rights, privileges, and responsibilities to be worked out by the courts. The New York Stock Exchange grew from a handful of brokers on Wall Street in the early 1790s and acted as a catalyst in the amassing of capital for ambitious and expensive enterprises such as the new spinning and weaving mills.

Even after the Revolution the colonial system in which trade associations required heavy initiation fees for apprenticeship persisted. But by 1825, this practice, that had resulted in closed clubs of artisans, was discouraged by law, as was indentured servitude. This opened opportunities to all those who were freemen, i.e. those who were made eligible to vote at that time (1804). To vote, one had to be a white male freeholder of real estate worth twenty pounds, or pay annual rent of at least forty shillings. At this time, groups of workers began to organize to protect themselves from unfair labor practices.

In 1788, Major John Bellinger settled near the ford of the Mohawk, close to old Fort Schuyler built by the British 28 years earlier. He was soon followed by Peter Smith and his partner, John Jacob Astor, from Waldorf, Germany, (who soon moved on to bigger enterprise). Moses Bagg, a blacksmith, arrived in 1794, and built a tavern next to his smithy, launching the family's future business. Samuel Hooker was hired by the Holland Land Company in 1797 to build York House on Whitesboro Street, which endured until fire destroyed it in 1966. Named in 1796 after the

Carthaginian port city, Utica became a market town, a banking center, and an active textile manufacturing center, with the canal and, later, rail lines bringing coal from Pennsylvania to fuel further growth.

The Holland Land Company wished to exploit the manufacture of sugar and syrup from maple trees on a year-round basis. The company directed Gerrit Boone, its agent of a small parcel it owned north of Rome, to try his hand at this, but of course, Mother Nature grants success to this activity for only a few weeks in late winter. Boonville, named after him, is neighbor to Barneveld, another small parcel belonging to the company; however, Holland Patent refers to the Right Honorable Henry Lord Holland, the colonial patentee, not the Dutch company.

BAGG'S TAVERN
ORIGINALLY A LOG HOUSE
FOUNDED 1794 BY MOSES BAGG
WASHINGTON, LAFAYETTE
HENRY CLAY & GEN. GRANT
WERE GUESTS HERE

Oneida County, 92
Genesee and Main Sts., Utica

BOONVILLE
SETTLED 1795; NAMED FOR
GERRIT BOON; NATIVE OF LEYDEN,
HOLLAND, AGENT OF HOLLAND LAND
CO. TOWN FORMED 1805; VILLAGE
INCORPORATED 1855

Oneida County, 19
NY 12D, Boonville

John Lincklaen, a retired officer of the Dutch navy and another of the company's field agents, had been attracting settlers to the 120,000 acre strip that ran from Ohwagena (Cazenovia Lake) south to the site of De Ruyter (named in honor of the famous Dutch admiral), which he purchased in 1792, and named after the company's general agent in Philadelphia, Theophilus de Cazenove. The village of Cazenovia, located on the lake and the Cherry Valley Turnpike, prospered as evidenced by the imposing federal-style 1807 mansion, Lorenzo, built for Lincklaen's family and commanding a magnificent view at the head of the lake. Jonathan Denise Ledyard, brother-in-law and adopted son of Lincklaen, married a Strawbridge, (successful, and still operating Philadelphia merchants), and succeeded to resident agent and owner of Lorenzo.

FIRST COUNTY SEAT
THIS BUILDING ERECTED FOR
COURT HOUSE 1810, COURTS
HELD 1812-17. SOLD TO
METHODISTS 1818. CONFERENCE
SEMINARY ESTABLISHED 1824.

Madison County, 1
Seminary St. between Sullivan & Lincklaen
Cazenovia

In 1836, he and two others built the Lincklaen House, which still provides meals and lodging to travelers. The Lincklaen heirs donated Lorenzo to New York State in 1968. Managed by the Parks and Recreation Commission, it is open to the public.

When a young girl, Eunice Williams was captured by the French and the Caughnawaga Indians as they raided Deerfield, Mass in February of 1704. She elected to remain with the Indians and raised a daughter. Her granddaughter married Chief Thomas Williams (Indians took their wives' names), and as both parents agreed to have their son, Eleazor, receive a white education, they left him with a Williams' relative in Massachusetts in 1800, (the Williams family persistently but unsuccessfully tried to persuade Eunice and her descendants to return to the white settlements).

The son became a voracious reader and an eager student of a Reverend Hale, and with him traveled to various Indian missions.

During the War of 1812, he dissuaded the Caughnawaga and the St. Regis Indians from joining the British, and later was wounded at the battle of Plattsburg. Though brought up a Roman Catholic in Canada and educated by Congregational ministers to be a missionary among the Indians, he came under the influence of Bishop Hobart, who appointed him a lay minister to the Oneidas at Oneida Castle in 1816. He soon learned the Oneida language, built a mission chapel for them, and was successful in quickly befriending and convincing those not yet converted to become Christians. (The chapel was moved to Vernon in 1842 by Unitarians, and has served as the Town Hall since 1892).

Whites were rapidly settling Madison and Oneida Counties in the 1820s. The Federal government responded to a study of Reverend Jedidiah Morse (father of inventor Samuel F.B. Morse), which suggested that the Oneidas be moved west to Green Bay and the Fox River in Wisconsin. President Monroe and Secretary John C. Calhoun asked for Williams's help in leading an Oneida delegation to persuade the western Indians to cede land to them, which they did in 1822. Most of the Oneidas, the Brotherton, and the Stockbridge Indians jointly bought a large tract from the Menominees and were given the joint use of their other land as well.

MISSION CHURCH OF THE ONEIDAS BUILT BY REV. ELEAZER WILLIAMS 1818 MOVED IN 1842 FROM ONEIDA CASTLE BY UNITARIANS. VERNON TOWN HALL SINCE 1892.

Oneida County, 96
Seneca Ave. Between Verona and
Sconondaga St. in Vernon

When Williams married a Menominee girl, her tribe ceded him five thousand acres on the Fox River as her dowry. A few Oneidas remained on their drastically reduced reservation in New York and, except for a small number, gradually became absorbed in the local community.

A few years later, the controversy over the fate of the lost dauphin, son of Louis XVI and Marie Antoinette, recurred. Some claimed that the young prince was taken from his cruel jailor and a dying child substituted in his place. Numerous imposters began to appear in this country and in Europe. John James Audubon, the avian artist, was thought to be the dauphin, and others in a position to know, had no doubt that Williams, by reason of age, coincident events, and appearance, was the royal son.

Williams' sudden appearance in Massachusetts fit with what little is known to have happened to the little boy left imprisoned and abused in the Temple tower, ante chamber to the scaffold in Paris, after his parents were guillotined. Members of the House of Bourbon took Williams for one of their own. His mannerisms and physical features, including unusual scars matching those of the dauphin, gave credence to his claim. Other circumstances and claimants were considered to refute it, and the debate raged on.

When Williams died in 1858 at his final parish in Hogansberg, N.Y. near Akwasasne, the St. Regis Indian reservation, nothing had been settled, and historians generally ignored the Lost Dauphin Theory. However, even as I write this, the two hundred year-old mystery has been solved. In April of 2000, scientists examined a certified lock of Marie Antoinette's hair and compared its DNA to that of the preserved heart of the ten-year old boy who died in the Temple. They found that the DNA of the two tissue samples matched and there is no longer any doubt that the boy who died in his prison was the dauphin.

The land company, Watkins and Flint, acquired title to land south of the Military Tract and west of the Boston Ten Towns, and offered sections in the Watkins Glen and Painted Post area gradually to avoid flooding the market and suffering low prices. But land was quickly becoming available in the Ohio and Mississippi valleys, depressing the central New York market so that even Robert Morris became bankrupt and a resident of debtor's prison in 1797 for most of his few remaining years.

Sure Signs: Stories Behind the Historical Markers of Central New York

A note in the February 28th, 1795 issue of the Family Almanac and Franklin Calendar stated: "It was estimated that twelve hundred sleighs freighted with men, women, children, and furniture passed through Albany in three days from the east to settle in the Genesee country—the treaty with Great Britain and the Six Nations having dispelled every apprehension of danger."

The Holland Land Company hoped to sell large tracts of its land in the western part of the state to wealthy speculators and developers, but this did not happen. The company then made small tracts directly available to settlers and set a land office in Batavia. With so much land coming on the market in the Ohio and Mississippi valleys, business was disappointing. What sales did occur had to be financed on very favorable terms, with very little down payment. As late as 1822, only about half the land had been sold. This left the stockholders with only one practical option; the Company sold the remaining, mostly small, parcels to other small land companies in the area.

CHAPTER TEN

One of the first cash crops the settler had to sell was potash, made from the ashes of trees he was clearing off his land. Chopping the trees down was hard enough, but rolling the logs into piles to concentrate the heat for a complete burn was a colossal undertaking, involving the help of neighbors and their teams of oxen. The common effort was called logrolling, a term later picked up by legislators when trading votes with each other to pass pet bills.

After the burn, the ashes were collected, mixed with water, and converted to crude potash or "black salts". This "cake" was further refined into "pearl ash" which fetched a higher price than black salts. It was used primarily to make soap, glass, paper, in dyes, for tanning, for scouring raw wool, and later, for fertilizer. Early on, fertilizer was not needed because of the natural wealth of millennia of leaf mold composted in the soil, together with any unrecovered potash. Nor did the farmer have to do much hoeing as weeds were practically nonexistent in the deeply shaded virgin forest soil.

Making potash was hard work, but cash or credit was needed at the local general store. Ten acres of hardwood trees, such as maple or elm made into ash, would net two hundred dollars, or more likely two hundred dollars worth of credit, a lot of money at that time. A farmer could sell his product outright or barter for anything, from trace chains to a plethora of grindstones, calico, scythes, candy, fish hooks, hay rakes, sewing needles, boots, and anything else for which there was a demand. At the store he might also hash over local and national problems with his neighbors, or hear the latest gossip and jokes.

Another source of needed cash, provided by the maple tree, was syrup, but it could only be made in late winter when frosty nights, followed by warming days, invite the sap to rise in the tree. The trees were tapped, a hollow reed inserted to catch the flow, and the sap buckets collected for boiling down. Stocking the fire required many cords of wood, but when the farmer finished, he had a gallon of sweet syrup for each 35 to 40 gallons of sap. This was the only sweetening he had for years unless he was fortunate enough to have a nearby bee tree or hive.

The typical residence for most settlers on the frontier was the log cabin, evolved by the Swedes with their ample supply of timber, and brought to this country at their early settlements on the lower

Sure Signs: Stories Behind the Historical Markers of Central New York

Delaware River. Its main virtue was that it could be built with only an axe, a saw, and an auger; the building material was readily at hand. After cutting seventy or eighty ten or twelve-inch logs with an axe, and peeling their bark to rid them of insects and to retard decay, the settler would invite his neighbors to a cabin raising, an intensive work session flavored with food, whiskey, and socializing.

Building the cabin required several skills: careful axe work in notching the logs at the corners so that they anchored themselves in place and so that rain drained away from the joint to reduce rot; splitting cedar log sections into shingles for the roof, and building the fireplace and chimney so that the fire had a good draft to burn well. In the absence of easily split cedar, one could apply sections of girdled bark to roof the place. Three days of combined effort were necessary to roll the logs in place, shingle the roof, and to cut the window and door openings.

The doors were made entirely of wood, including the hinges, latch, and crossbar to prevent forceful entry. The auger was used to drill holes for the pegs or treenails of dry wood that swelled tight when in place and moistened, which served as fasteners. (Ships were put together the same way). Slide shutters closed the windows which were sometimes covered with an oiled skin to let in light; whitewashing the inside walls also helped brighten up the place. Window glass was a rarity, but became more available in 1810, when the Ontario Glass Factory was founded in Geneva. (The amber-hued windows in Geneva Trinity Church were made there.) The gap between the wall logs was chinked with mud and moss to keep out the cold, but this caulking was removed in summer to provide cross ventilation and some relief from the heat. A cabin with puncheons (split logs embedded in the dirt, flat and planed side up) for flooring was considered luxurious.

GLASS FACTORY
BAY
1810-1850
ONTARIO GLASS MANUFACTORY
BLOWERS OF WINDOW GLASS
VILLAGE OF 500 INHABITANTS

Ontario County, 9*
NY 14 1½ miles S. of Geneva

As at a logrolling, everyone had a good time at a cabin raising since it was a break in a solitary routine, and it favored you when it was your turn. When the cabin was completed, tradition required the placing of a small tree atop the ridge pole to bring good fortune to the new residents.

This was as good a time for the housewife to plant seeds at the dooryard: basil, rosemary, oregano, parsley and thyme for flavoring food; chicory to extend the coffee; dandelions, purslane, and nasturtiums for salads; native Oswego Tea to make a refreshing beverage, soapwort to work up a lather, tansy to prevent ants, and all to make a pleasant bouquet. If later she wished to add to her garden, she could buy seed packets at the general store. The Shakers of New Lebanon and Watervliet started the first commercial seed company in 1789, delivering to frontier stores early on.

Furniture was crude except for what was brought from their former home. As fortune improved, and carpenters and cabinet makers arrived, houses and furnishings became more refined. Cooking was done at the fireplace whether in a mansion or humble cabin. The "kitchen" was the only room of the early cabins, but even when the cabin had been enlarged, it was where home life centered; where, in the long winter months especially, harnesses were repaired, shoes made or mended, or a rocking chair, loom or spinning wheel crafted. Reading by the dim light of the fire or an oil lamp was rewarding as bread baked in the Dutch oven and children played with their toys.

FURNACE SITE OF LITCHFIELD IRON MFG. CO. INCORPORATED 1813 MAKERS OF PIG IRON AND VARIOUS KINDS OF IRON HOLLOW WARE

Herkimer County, 18
CR, 2 miles south of Gulph

They set the table with wooden trenchers except when heirloom pewter plates were placed for special occasions. A mortar and pestle, carved out of solid hardwood, for grinding coffee and mustard seeds, sat on the shelf by the drinking cups made of pewter, copper, or the horns sawn off a butchered cow. Kitchen utensils were usually limited to a bake kettle, a metal pot, a large long-handled skillet with legs, a gridiron, a ladle, and assorted forks, spoons, bowls and cups. The absence of closets and cabinets required utensils to be shelved or hung from wooden pegs driven into the overhead beams.

As iron heating and cook stoves arrived from upstate foundries in the 1820s and 30s, people were quick to make use of them and abandon the outdated and inconvenient ways, just as later generations made use of the "ice box", the gas range, and central heating. Wood stoves, such as the one which had been designed by the versatile Benjamin Franklin, reduced the amount of wood otherwise consumed in a fireplace by two-thirds, significantly reducing the farmer's workload.

Lighting became better when the family traded tallow candles for whale oil lamps and, in turn, in the 1850s, upgraded to coal oil (kerosene) which cast more light and didn't crust the wick. Up to that time, the small amounts of oil skimmed off oil springs were sold as cure-all elixirs by charlatans who took their cue from the Senecas who thought the viscous stuff did have magical powers. The term "snake oil" derives from Seneca Oil. Supply of kerosene increased and prices diminished shortly after Dr. Edwin L. Drake first pumped some of that Seneca oil from seventy feet underground in northwestern Pennsylvania in 1859. The tinderbox with flint and steel was replaced (but not discarded) with lucifer matches in the 1830s, by those who would bear the expense. To light their way into the next world, the family Bible, ponderous in both heft and message and carefully hand-inscribed with birth and death dates of the family lineage, could be counted on for guidance.

What meat they didn't put in a pot, they soaked in a barrel of vinegar or brine; salt being available from Syracuse or the salt springs at Montezuma. Lacking these, they could preserve meat by smoking it over corncobs or hickory logs in the smoke shed, or cut it into strips of jerky for drying by a fire. Game was not that plentiful; then as now, hunting was a sport which, if successful, could vary the menu. They raised most of their meat, and knew the value of storable high-protein beans to supplement the larder.

Howard S. Ford

SALT SPRINGS CHIEF SUPPLY FOR INDIANS. LATER EXTENSIVELY DEVELOPED BY EARLY SETTLERS PRIVATELY AND WITH STATE AID

Cayuga County, 99
At Montezuma on old canal by NY 50

For storing vegetables, a room or cave was dug underground, usually a shaded and north slope for cooler ground. These root cellars kept the produce cool in the summer and from freezing in winter, the temperature usually varying no more than about ten or fifteen degrees Fahrenheit.

The cooper was essential to make barrels for pork, flour, and apples, tubs for meat and washing, pails for water and milking, sap buckets, butter churns, and firkins, with one splat extended to serve as a handle, for storing the butter. Absent a cooper, the cabin owner could make a barrel out of a large upended log section, the same way Indians made dugout canoes—by alternately burning and scraping with axe, knife, and scraper. It was called a gum, since gumwood logs were preferred. Cradles were similarly made from a half section of a small log with rockers fashioned for the ends.

Spinning wheels were a prized tool, often possessed by the family for many generations. The smaller wheel, for putting the twist in flax fiber for making linen yarn, was worked by a treadle while sitting, but the larger wheel for wool required a standing-step motion to prod the spokes by the spinster, often a daughter still residing at home. The strong fiber from the flax plant was separated from the stalk and cleaned; wool had to be sheared, cleaned, and carded into strands with the use of special wire brushes, all laborious procedures, so that each could be spun into yarn on the wheel.

For strength and durability, wool cloth was often woven with a linen warp and was called linsey-woolsey. The poorest grade of linen was made into sackcloth, the middle grade into work clothes, and the best into go-to-meeting attire. In 1813, in Madison County alone, 1500 home looms produced over 240,000 yards of woolen and linen cloth to be made into suits, table cloths, dresses, and bed linen for home use. By 1835, there were forty-five woolen mills in central New York.

At home, small sampler blanks of open-weave linen were embroidered with verse or the alphabet by young ladies to prove their skill, a diploma of sorts for the age of homespun. By the time of the Civil War, the flax wheel had been consigned to the attic, and a generation later, the large wheel followed.

SPRING MILLS
ERECTED 1839-40 BY
GEORGE HOWLAND
STONE MILL THIRD BUILT
ON SAME SITE
SECOND WAS WOOLEN MILL

Cayuga County, 150*
At pond, Union Springs

In England, the term "corn" meant wheat; in Scotland it meant oats. But here, corn was called "Injun" corn to avoid confusion, incidentally crediting the Indians who introduced this excellent food to the whites. It became the basic fare for men and beasts. Its simplest, and perhaps tastiest form, was "on the cob", when sweet corn evolved to appear shortly after the close of the Revolution. As the kernel hardened in storage, it was grated off the cob and made into hominy by first soaking the kernels in lye to remove the hull. A large wooden pestle, fastened overhead to a limber sapling to serve as a spring pole and ease the effort, was used to crush the kernels in a scraped-out concavity on top of a handy stump or short up-ended log. Or, the hard corn could be ground by the local water-powered grist mill, if one didn't object to the tenth bushel going to the miller.

In the early years settlers often had to haul their grain as far as twenty miles to a mill. There, they might enjoy the slow water-turned booming rumble of the overshot wheel, as the authoritative Jared van Wagenan called it, "the earliest mechanical music of the wilderness". A hand mill, or quern, could also serve, but it was very tiring to turn for any length of time. It worked on the same principle as the grist mill: two heavy circular stones, the top "runner" rotating on the lower fixed "bedder", grinding the kernels in between.

The runner had a funnel shaped hole through the center into which the grain was poured, and another straight hole in the top surface to fit a handle for turning. The mating surfaces of the stones were dressed with sharp grooves to shear the grain and channel the meal out from between the stones. It was then sifted, and re-ground as necessary for the desired fineness.

OLD MILL
PARTLY BUILT BY CHARLES KELLOGG IN 1823. SOLD TO HORACE ROUNDS IN 1851, TO HIS SON EUGENE ROUNDS 1865, TO W.E. ROUNDS & A RYAN 1919

Cayuga County, 111
NY 41A, just north of New Hope

By 1845, records show there were 10,000 water mills in the entire state. An overshot grist mill can still be seen operating today at New Hope on route 41A. Unlike modern steel rollers which turn at such high revolutions that many of the nutrients heat up, become volatile, and evaporate, the stones grind slowly, with little heat, and all the nutriment remains in the flour.

By boiling, the ground meal became corn mush and was served with milk, maple syrup made from the family's own sugar bush, or sorghum molasses. Or, it was made into batter and cooked into a corn pone, johnny cake (from journey cake), or fried into corn dodgers. The excess corn crop was sent to market as is, or as whiskey to make it more concentrated and easier to ship.

`Corn husking bees were another social and practical event. Friendly team competition to strip the husks off the most ears, often assisted with distilled corn spirits, could, and was expected to, result in a few fist fights. But when the huge piles of corn had been husked, the barn floor was cleared for dancing, and later, all sat down to dinner.

Squash, beans, pumpkins, tobacco, and hard-shelled gourds were also crops introduced to the settlers by the Indians. With potatoes, turnips, carrots, beets, cabbage, flax, some medicinal herbs, and an orchard, the settler's garden was complete. The apple, peach, plum, pear, and cherry were unknown to the Indians until they began dealing with British traders. But their skill in growing these fruits was noted by botanist John Bartram, when he visited the southern shore of Lake Ontario, and later by Sullivan's men in the Seneca villages. The honeybee, new to the western hemisphere, came with the orchards (for pollination) and was called "the white man's stinging fly". Before acquiring fruit trees, Indians dreaded the presence of the honey-bee before the ring of the axe because it presaged the white invader. Honey bees kept about a hundred miles ahead of the frontier as it advanced all the way to the Rockies.

Hogs, sheep, cattle, or poultry, all ran free to feed on acorn and beech mast in the woods in the early days. As such, they were subject to bear, panther, fox and wolf predations, and attractive cash bounties were offered for any of these pests. Deadfalls and pitfalls were used to save time and ammunition in killing predators or taking game. A deadfall consisted of a log or logs perched in such a way that any nudging of the bait would trigger their fall on the prey. Pitfalls were deep holes dug in the ground, covered at the surface with a baited and camouflaged panel pivoted on a level pole to spill a wolf or bear when he stepped on it. Wider at the bottom than at the top, the pit secured the animal from escape.

Metal traps made by the local blacksmith were used to trap animals that preyed on chickens and guinea hens foraging in the dooryard or picking pests off the vegetables in the garden, and the farmer's son added to the family income by tending a trap line for pelts which was one of the few items to bring in hard-to-come-by cash. As the farmer gained time, he would fence in his animals and gardens with brush, old stumps, or rails split off the log and laid in a zigzag line, rail upon rail.

Rattlesnakes were the most dangerous of the creatures to the early settlers, since being struck by a rattler was quite often fatal. The more savvy settler kept hogs, not only for bristles and meat, but because hogs loved to eat snakes, poisonous or not. The hogs thick coat of bristles and a heavy layer of fat under their skin rendered them impervious to the snake's fangs. On a trip through uncertain country, the cautious settler would drive hogs ahead of him and so avoid snakes.

Spring and fall migrations covered the sky with ducks and geese for the larder, and a large cloud of passenger pigeons would literally darken the sky as would a stormy day. When settled in the trees nearby, they could easily be taken in large numbers from the roosts by gun, or simply batting them down. The Indians taught that if one waited until the squabs were not quite ready to fly, the nests could be robbed for these delicious young birds. That they were so easy to catch and there was an insatiable market for them, explains why they finally became extinct in the early twentieth century.

Deer, bear, elk, wild turkey, partridge, and migrating geese and ducks could be taken, and small game such as black or gray squirrels, rabbit, and porcupine were also available; as well, possum were then moving in from the South in increasing numbers. Usually following white settlement, aggressive crows intimidated the resident ravens to leave the area in the early 1800s. Racoons were already on the scene and could be counted on to ravish the corn just as it reached peak flavor. Even bison roamed in western New York, though not in large numbers, before they were seen no more after 1800.

Harsh game laws, like those in Europe where all game belonged to royalty and poachers were fined, mutilated, or hanged, did not evolve in the colonies because the British wanted colonials to defend themselves to avoid sending an expensive army over here. (Of course, later they did send expensive armies over here. But then, it was too late to change policy). Anyone could own a gun. Men could acquire military skills at militia meetings—a sobering thought for aspiring tyrants. The right to own a gun was considered a worthy enough idea to be spelled out in the second article of the Bill of Rights.

Quick running cool streams were full of salmon and brook trout, and we are led to believe that, if you didn't "spook" them, trout could be tickled by hand and lifted out of the water. The Big Spring near Caledonia was ideal for trout, with the water temperature never varying more than ten degrees.

Seth Green grew up nearby on the Genesee River where he studied fish first hand to satisfy his fascination, and became a commercial fisherman. To increase his business, he tried raising brook trout by artificial means, and to others' surprise, was successful at it. He became a recognized expert as he set up his fish hatchery by the Big Spring at the finish of the Civil War, growing fish from the eggs which he had stripped from the fish, and shipping the small fry live to many points around the world. In 1875, he sold the operation to the state (and was retained as superintendent), making it the first state-owned fish hatchery. Even Onondaga Lake, now considered one of the filthiest lakes in the country, was stocked with salmon and trout in 1875 when it was still pristine.

BIG SPRINGS
ANCIENT INDIAN CAMPSITE
ON NIAGARA TRAIL
EARLIEST WHITE TOURIST 1615
SCOTTISH SETTLERS 1799
TERMINUS PIONEER R.R. 1838

Livingston County, 7
NY 5, at Caledonia

We have Seth Green to thank for introducing rainbow trout, native to California, to the Finger Lakes in 1878. The rainbows adapted well and fishermen ever since have looked forward to the yearly spring spawning run up Finger Lake streams such as the most famous, Catharine Creek, which drains into the head of Seneca Lake at Watkins Glen.

As the industrial revolution shifted into gear, the number and variety of factories located along the streams proliferated. The outlets of all the Finger Lakes in time became cluttered with mills and factories powered by water. Typical is a description of the Owasco Lake Outlet (Auburn) in 1810: "The outlet is fourteen miles long and on it are the following hydraulic establishments; nine saw mills, two carding machines, two turner's shops, one triphammer and blacksmith shop, two oil mills, five grist mills, three fulling mills, one bark mill, and several tanneries. At the lower falls, Mr. Dill has a furnace in which he uses old iron, there being no iron ore..." Oil mills ground flax seed for linseed oil, and sunflower seed for its oil, which provided smokeless illumination.

As railroads were able to bring in coal from Pennsylvania, coal production and the use of steam engines to power the new plants of the Industrial Revolution relieved this crowding, and factories were no longer inevitably wedded to rivers and streams for power.

Entrepreneurs on the Susquehanna tributaries such as Arkport, Elmira, and Port Watson (named for Elkanah Watson and later incorporated as part of Cortland) did a large business with towns as far south as Baltimore. They built arks or barges to be piled high with bulk items such as lumber, potash, or grain and ran the outlandish looking rafts to markets downstream (especially during high water) where the cargo would be unloaded, and the arks dismantled for their lumber.

Deposit, astride the county line of Broome and Delaware counties, is so named for its part in the early lumbering trade. The first cut of trees was near water so that the felled trees could be skidded directly to the rivers and easily brought to market, but lumbermen had to go deeper in the woods for their next specimens. The trees were cut, but left in place until snow on the ground made it easier to sledge them to a spacious common site along the West Branch of the Delaware River, and there deposited. Then the Spring runoff was employed to raft them to market downstream.

Much depended on the blacksmith shop for the making and repair of tools, wagons and wheels, the shoeing of horses and oxen, the making of nails, and often the repair of guns. The blacksmith's art was seat-of-the-pants metallurgy at his charcoal forge. He was an expert in heating iron to just the right temperature—indicated by the shade of yellow, red or orange metal—so that he could hammer it on his anvil to the shape and degree of hardness desired.

Kibitzers as well as customers hung about his forge-warmed shop which became a social center in the course of business. The smith would also help the wheelwright by measuring off the correct length of wrought iron band, welding the ends together for a circumference, and heating the iron tire red hot to expand it. Then he and his helpers would lift it with tongs and fit it over the wooden wheel, hammering it on since it would be a close fit. Finally they would quench the hot rim with pails of water, shrinking it to compress the whole assembly, so that the hickory spokes would be forced deeper into the sockets of the hub and fellies of the wheel, to make a super tight and durable unit.

BLACKSMITH SHOP BUILT ABOUT 1837. FIRST TRIP HAMMER IN CAYUGA COUNTY AND FIRST ONE USED IN AUBURN PRISON MADE HERE

Cayuga County, 136
Franklin St. Rd., 2 m. east of Auburn

When the sawmills began turning out boards, dusty, laborious pit sawing was no longer necessary. Carpenters used the boards to make frame houses and post and beam barns, but of course, coffins took precedence when called for. The smith and carpenter might also double as coopers to make staves into barrels, casks, and kegs to store or ship dry items. If he was expert, he could make them "tight" to hold liquids.

Starting in the early 1800s, peddlers went from door-to-door selling or trading everything from pots and pans, candy, spectacles, and ribbons, to wooden clocks from Connecticut, (although countrymen were often able to reckon time from the position of the sun). Many successful peddlers later settled down and opened their own store. Tinkers also made their way to farmers' dooryards to repair such items as pans, ladles, kettles, and pewter ware. To repair a piece, he would fashion a temporary clay dam to hold the molten solder in place until it cooled. The clay was then of no value and discarded, and expressions like "not worth a tinker's dam" or "I don't give a dam" came into use.

Peddlers, tinkers, and other itinerant tradesmen passing through, as well as the highly admired stage drivers, were also sources of news of the nation, or gossip of the neighborhood. Newspapers were put in circulation as soon as the presses could be shipped in from eastern cities. In 1798, Mr. R. Delano's "The Levanna Gazette" (later the "Onondaga Advertiser"), was the first newspaper printed in Cayuga County. But not many could afford newspapers, and editor-publishers, in order to finance their papers, supported a political party that provided subscribers and advertisers and awarded printing jobs, such as legal notices. The politicians were always happy to demean and damn the opposition and proud to point out the rectitude and wisdom of their own views, and have these opinions published. Partisanship led to acrimony and often the real issues became obscure. Does that sound familiar?

FIRST NEWSPAPER IN CAYUGA COUNTY PUBLISHED IN 1798 BY R. DELANO CALLED LEVANNA GAZETTE OR ONONDAGA ORGANIZER

Cayuga County, 89
At Lervanna

Political campaigning was largely accomplished in partisan newspapers, rather than by the candidate making speeches to the crowds. When Andrew Jackson made his first presidential attempt in 1824, candidates became vocal and went "on the stump" in the "hustings" to make their harangues.

Taverns were often the predecessors of towns, and early travelers noted in their journals that a high proportion of log cabin owners on the route had the pretense to offer hospitality. They not only provided a forum for a seemingly parched populace of townsmen, but the traveler could get a meal and stay overnight, even if he had to share a bed with several strangers in various degrees of sobriety. Special drover taverns with animal pens for hogs, cattle, goats or poultry were located at more frequent intervals to allow for the slower daily progress of these entourages. They averaged eight miles a day.

Taverns also served as government offices, churches, and even schools until more suitable buildings could be constructed, as numerous historical markers attest. Three years after Colonel John Hardenbergh built his gristmill at the Owasco outlet in 1793, the first schoolhouse was erected nearby.

SITE OF LOG CABIN 1793 OF JOHN L. HARDENBURGH FIRST SETTLER OF AUBURN FIRST AURELIUS TOWN MEETING HELD HERE 1794

Cayuga County, 2
Market St. in front of Fire Department

Taverns evolved into general stores, law offices, and better hotels. Bagg's Tavern opened near old Fort Schuyler none too soon; travelers no longer had to choose between sleeping in the open or staying at Post's, termed by many hapless travelers as the filthiest habitation in the state. In 1797, Utica was given its name at the new tavern which grew into Bagg's Hotel, a landmark, and a business, social, and cultural center for 117 years. The Syracuse House was built in time for the formal opening of the Erie Canal, and for seventy years it was host to such as Henry Clay, Daniel Webster, and Charles Dickens. The Clinton House was built for fine lodging and board in Ithaca in 1832, one of the last of many projects of Simeon DeWitt. It also had an illustrious history, and was considered the finest establishment of its kind west of the Hudson. The building still stands in good repair, thanks to preservationists, and serves Ithaca as an historical museum.

More than a few cobblestone houses (many for schools), were put up between 1830 and 1860, from Cooperstown to the counties near Lake Ontario, where it was not too far for carrying wagon loads of surf-scoured cobbles from the southern shore. The log cabins were gradually relegated to stable or storage service and replaced by simple frame and clapboard houses.

In Chicago in 1833, the "balloon frame" system of building houses with two by four lumber studs as the standard dimension was developed. This idea, combined with improved machines that turned out many thousand nails a day, resulted in a cheaper, stronger house that took less time to erect than the mortice and tenon heavy post and beam structures that went back to medieval times and required highly skilled craftsmen to build. As a consequence, a much higher proportion of people could own their own homes and the peopling of the new nation, city and country proceeded unabated.

FOUNDED 1843
CHURCHVILLE GRADED SCHOOL
OCCUPIED THIS BUILDING
UNTIL 1895. A FINE EXAMPLE
OF THE LOST ART OF BUILDING
WITH COBBLESTONES.

Monroe County, 24
West Buffalo St., Churchville

If a grander house was desired, the owner could look at a pattern book to make his selection of Federal style, Greek Revival, Gothic Revival, Queen Anne, Georgian, Italianate, or simply a New

England colonial like his grandfather had. Also catalogued were various front door entrance ways, flutings, columns, crown moldings, fan windows, and fireplace mantles from the more enterprising millworks. Farmers of New England origin often followed the practice of their fathers and cannily connected the barn to the house with a number of joined out-buildings so that they could get from one to the other comfortably in order to perform inside chores during poor weather.

HOME OF NATHANIEL TOBEY WHO EMIGRATED FROM BRISTOL CO. MASS. BUILT MANY NEW ENGLAND STYLE HOMES HERE, 1810

Tompkins County, 15
NY 79 at Carline

In 1804, the president of Yale College, Timothy Dwight, traveled along the Seneca Turnpike, making notes in his journal as he went. He observed, "In the western part of Marcellus there is a beautiful lake named Skeneateles (sic); commencing in the township of Tully, crossing the corner of Sempronius and reaching through a considerable part of Marcellus. Its length is fifteen miles and its breadth from one to two. At the outlet of this fine piece of water, sprightly and vigorous, running between high and rough banks, and without any of those marshy encumbrances, which spread deformity and disease among the outlet of so many lakes in the region, there is a small settlement which I thought peculiarly pretty. It is built upon the north end of the lake and upon a handsome clean margin. The lake is in full view and interested me more than any other on this road. The shores on both sides are elegant, arched slopes, the eastern already handsomely cultivated. The soil is excellent and the fields were covered with a glowing verdure. At the south end of the lake the prospect is limited by distant mountains; in the region uncommon, and therefore peculiarly gratifying objects." A dam had been constructed at the outlet of the lake in 1796 to raise the water level about four feet, covering the swampy ground there and giving a better head of water for the mills downstream. It should be noted that Dwight retained a much better reputation than did his first cousin, Aaron Burr.

John Maude, one of Dwight's contemporaries and an English traveler in central New York in 1800, noted that a soldier's right to six hundred acres in the Military Tract was worth only $8.00 in 1788. In 1792, it was worth $30 and in 1800 the same land, even unimproved, would command $3 to $5 an acre.

In 1815, the volcano Tambora on the island of Java erupted, killing twelve thousand people there and spewing an estimated thirty to fifty cubic miles of molten lava and ash. The following year, the ash had so circulated and sullied the earth's atmosphere, that 1816 was known as the year without a summer, or "eighteen hundred and froze to death." The sun could not penetrate to the earth with its normal strength, and no summer month in the northeast escaped a frost. At some places the ground was still frozen hard in June.

Wheat was not fit to cut until September, the corn crop was almost entirely lost, and few tender summer crops of any kind were harvested. On August 22nd of that year, a frost damaged crops as far south as North Carolina, causing widespread food shortages.

Central New Yorkers have to contend with the same general weather patterns as the rest of the country except for the peculiar phenomenon known as "lake effect". If the wind is from the west or northwest, particularly with a long fetch over Georgian Bay, lakes Huron and Ontario, and other conditions are right, incredible amounts of snow fall in a short time on the eastern and southeastern shore of Lake Ontario. The snow falls usually in narrow bands reaching as far downwind as Cooperstown, sometimes to Vermont.

It is not uncommon for thirty to forty inches of snow to fall in twelve hours on Oswego, Pulaski, or Watertown. Each year the hamlets of Bennett's Bridge and Barnes Corners on the Tug Hill plateau vie for the "honor" of the highest annual snowfall mounting occasionally to over 400 inches. On either side of the five to twenty-mile wide snow bands, the sun can be shining on bare ground. Visibility in the snow bands can be to about the end of your extended arm, and these "white outs" are terrifying to travelers trying to stay on the road.

Howard S. Ford

The farther west one goes, the less snow, with Syracuse averaging 120 inches annually and Rochester about ninety. In western New York, the same extraordinary snow-falls occur on the windward shore of Lake Erie, dropping an average of ninety-three inches annually in Buffalo, and occasionally reaching across the southern tier counties to Binghamton. The downwind influence of Lakes Ontario and Erie can dampen central New York in other seasons with clouds and rain. This phenomenon seems to make for hardy, industrious souls, a wry sense of humor, and an ever-present realization that Mother Nature is always in control.

The early settlers were subject to a score or more diseases besides accidentally broken bones, gun-shot wounds, burns, snake bites, assorted cuts, scalds, food poisoning, horse kicks, sprains, abrasions, mosquito, midge, and black fly bites, and childbirth. Diphtheria, cholera, small-pox, measles, mumps, consumption (tuberculosis), ague (malaria), scarlet fever, influenza, typhoid, pneumonia, and the common cold were a constant threat with very little going for the victim unless he was lucky enough to have an iron constitution. Infant mortality and maternal death during childbirth were high.

PATRICK TAVERN
ERECTED 1793
EARLY COURT HELD HERE
CAYUGA COUNTY MEDICAL SOCIETY ORGANIZED HERE 1806

Cayuga County, 78
Dublin Hill Rd. and NY 90, Aurora

Doctors were not called in cases of ordinary illness. Instead, Granny was asked to be in attendance to mix her powders and potions, or pour down half a dipper of castor oil, which would teach the patient to not be sick again if he or she could help it. Besides, doctors were scarce, usually distant, and were limited in their effectiveness because little was known about the cause of disease. They attended children first, women, old men, adult males in that order and, last of all, "known hysterics".

Before antisepsis, invasive surgery was limited to life-and-death situations with the outcome in the lap of the gods. Otherwise, doctors confined their surgery to lancing boils and abscesses, amputations, and bleeding the patient. Licensing doctors to practice was abolished by the New York legislature in 1840 because it was said to create an "undemocratic monopoly" for the profession. The doctors of that time had training in medical schools such as Geneva College, but their apprenticeship with a practicing physician was hands-on and more useful. Midwives delivered many of the babies, and were welcomed by the doctors.

The germ theory regarding infection was not known until Louis Pasteur discovered bacteria in 1862. In the 1870's and 1880's, Doctor Robert Koch in Germany was able to determine the specific bacteria agents responsible for common diseases.

Dr. A. BURGOYNE
(1737-1824)
BURIED IN THIS CEMETERY
PHYSICIAN AT SARATOGA UNDER
GEN. BURGOYNE, 1777. LIVED
WITH DAUGHTER IN AUGUSTA

Oneida County, 12
South Street, Knoxboro

"Anaesthesia" was limited to shots of whiskey, opium, or biting down hard on a soft lead bullet to distract the patient from pain. "Sweet oil of vitriol", discovered in 1540 and renamed ether in 1730, had been used medically only to bring up phlegm by the force of its vapor. Dr. William E. Clark, a dentist in Rochester, successfully used it as an anaesthesia in a tooth extraction in 1842. Four years later, a Boston dentist, Dr. William T. G. Morton, used an ether inhaler designed by him to help remove a neck tumor. From then on, surgery was a practical option for a wide variety of medical disorders.

Chloroform was discovered by Doctor Samuel Guthrie of Sackets Harbor in 1831 (he also invented the percussion cap making obsolete the centuries-old flint lock). It became the anaesthetic of choice when Queen Victoria agreed to its use during her lying-in for the birth of Prince Leopold in April of 1853. "The effect was soothing, quieting, and delightful beyond measure", wrote her Majesty. For local surgery, it was found not necessary or desirable to give general anaesthesia. Cocaine extracted from coca leaves was used as the first local anaesthetic and proved less traumatic to the patient.

Anaesthesia rendered operations bearable but they needed to be made safe from infection which often led to gangrene and death. During the second half of the nineteenth century, such items and procedures as surgeons washing their hands, dressing wounds with an antiseptic solution, sterilization of surgical instruments and appliances, the use of face masks, rubber gloves and surgical gowns (rather than performing operations in street clothes) cut the mortality rate drastically. But, in the whole of the 19th century, most operations were performed in the patient's home.

Responding to a call to a patients home, haste was of the essence, particularly to treat the young in whom the progress of a disease seemed to accelerate. Also, as one cynical wit said, "to get there before the patient recovers." During a delivery or other treatment at home, the father or others might be in the way, gawking at the goings on. He was most often asked to boil a tub of water to keep him occupied and out of the way.

There were no malpractice suits in which a doctor was judged by a court of law in those days. He was judged by the community at quilting bees and across the back fence.

Doctors still bled patients with the lancet well into the middle 1800s, just as they did during George Washington's last illness in mid-December of 1799. It is now believed that Washington died of loss of blood, not of the cold he had contracted. Even so, he lived to two months short of attaining age 68, a lifetime that was longer than general life expectancy until 150 years after Washington's death.

When in winter quarters at Morristown, General Washington ordered soldiers and civilians alike to be inoculated to thwart a growing epidemic of smallpox. Washington was able to write that the effort was "attended with amazing success". Three years before Washington died, English Doctor

Edward Jenner was credited with the practical use of a more effective vaccination against smallpox than that which had been introduced to the country seventy-five years earlier. The antiquated treatment had been to scratch the supplicant and anoint the wound with pus from one already infected. This was a slight risk to undergo for immunization to this dread disease and, in most cases, was not difficult or uncomfortable except for the accompanying purges thought necessary. Occasionally, however, the patient suffered pustules all over his body so that no position of rest was comfortable. He might also have a fever, possibly delirium for up to forty-eight hours, but most of even the worst cases survived. Jenner's vaccination was less virulent and based on a "mild" cowpox virus, related to smallpox, as the inoculate. A giant step for mankind.

The discovery that scurvy was a deficiency disease and could be avoided by eating fruits—especially citrus and green vegetables—became more generally known at this time. Whole ships companies had occasionally become so incapacitated by scurvy that there was no one left with enough strength to sail the ship. The British Navy, grateful to learn of scurvy's cause, served rations of lemon or lime juice to its ship's company starting in 1795; from then on, their sailors were routinely called "limeys" by others.

Herbal medicine and home remedies were practiced. Some worked—like Peruvian bark (quinine) and digitalis (foxglove). Willow bark, rich in salicylic acid (the main ingredient in aspirin) was another. And some remedies didn't work. The trick was to know which was which. "Granny" practitioners would apply mold scraped from cheese to a wound or apply wet tea leaves to a burn, and both worked, but they didn't know why. Penicillin from mold is used today effectively, and burn ointment is based on tannic acid, abundant in tea leaves. But in the same era, they would "purify" the blood with sulphur and molasses, or "cure" a cold and other ills by hanging a bag of evil smelling asafetida around the patient's neck—more superstition than science.

People gradually became educated about simple habits of hygiene, such as careful hand washing with soap and water, avoiding spoiled food, thorough cooking, the necessity of quarantines (so-called for the forty day isolation), preventing the contamination of wells, and, as they became available in the late 19th century, using wire window screens to keep out flies and other insects.

Howard S. Ford

The horseless carriage brought its own contaminants but the streets and lanes became clear of horse droppings and attendant flies, and the general health improved. It was also true that as the forest was leveled to farmland, the clearings permitted the sun to shine through and dry damp ground, and the prevalence of ague declined.

Sure Signs: Stories Behind the Historical Markers of Central New York

CHAPTER ELEVEN

Ease of transportation in central New York was a primary concern if the area was to be settled, and the state authorized several roads to be built. In April 1792, "An Act for Laying Out, Repairing, and Improving Certain Public Roads and Highways" was passed dividing the state into four highway districts with three commissioners in each district. Roads were to be built of stone covered by eighteen inches of gravel or pebbles, and at least twenty-five feet wide from the inside of the ditches on each side. This was shortly increased to a minimum of four rods or sixty-six feet.

Since the Indian trails had been widened with increased usage by whites, the state used them for development. The need for roads was so pressing and the new townships had such woefully inadequate financial resources, that the state needed the help of private companies to build roads. Land speculators needed roads to develop and to increase the value of their holdings, and manufacturers, farmers, and merchants wished to expand their markets. So the legislature was petitioned by businessmen to charter turnpike companies that could build roads and charge tolls. Between 1797 and 1807, eighty-eight turnpike and bridge companies had completed 900 miles of turnpikes.

The War of 1812 proved the need for being able to readily supply the military at Oswego, Sodus Bay, Sackets Harbor, Plattsburgh, and Niagara. With peace, vigorous road building resumed, and by 1821 (the peak year), 278 turnpike companies had built 4000 miles of roads statewide

SENECA TURNPIKE
1800
FROM UTICA TO CANANDAIGUA
VIA SKANEATELES CREEK AT END
OF CHERRY TURNPIKE.
MIGRATION ROUTE TO THE WEST

Cayuga County, 129
US 20, One mile east of Auburn

Howard S. Ford

The original Genesee Road, once an Indian trail, (traveled by Colonel Peter Gansevoort at the end of the Sullivan Campaign), was built to specifications by General Wadsworth during 1790 and 1791. Started at Fort Schuyler in Utica, where the Mohawk Turnpike (Route 5) from Albany terminated, it passed through Vernon, Canastota, Chittenango, Canaseraga, (Sullivan) and went west "near Colonel Sage's farm, where were once the remains of a stockade and a large Indian orchard" (possibly the same Indian orchard mentioned by Conrad Weiser fifty years earlier), and crossed into Onondaga County, "a little north of the Deep Spring". The road continued through Manlius (Route 173), the Onondaga Reservation, Onondaga Hill, Marcellus, Willow Glen, and Auburn (Route 175).

From there it ran west through the Cayuga Reservation, crossed Cayuga Lake using John Harris' ferry a mile south of the village of Cayuga to the opposite shore near Seneca Falls. Crossing the lake avoided the treacheries of Montezuma Swamp immediately north of the lake at the outlet. From the west shore of Cayuga Lake, the road extended "in a line as nearly straight as the situation of the country will admit" to Waterloo, Geneva, Canandaigua, and to Canawaugus (Avon) (Routes 5 and 20).

DEEP SPRING
TE-UNGH-SAT-AYAGH
450 FEET NORTH ON IROQUOIS TRAIL
FIRST ROAD MADE 1790 BY GEN.
JAMES WADSWORTH, COUNTY
LINE AND SURVEY MARK

Onondaga County, 33
NY 173 at county line

Raising money by using lotteries to build churches, schools, and for other public concerns was common. In 1797, the state used them to raise funds to improve the Genesee Road until private investors put their funds into the project, and with turnstiles limiting access, charged tolls so that it became known as the Seneca Turnpike. At Cayuga, a privately owned 22 foot-wide mile-long toll bridge was built by Comfort Tyler in 1800 (the Cayuga town jail was built under the eastern approach) to span Cayuga Lake, and remained after many repairs and several reconstructions until 1857.

The smooth passage over the bridge was welcome relief to those who had endured the lurches and jolts of ruts and potholes in a stagecoach or wagon. Some travelers even went back over the bridge merely for the pleasure of the comfortable ride. Bridges had an additional benefit over ferries; the ferryman often owned the adjacent tavern, and ferry schedules became severely neglected when passengers were spending money in the taproom.

The Cherry Valley road or Great Western Turnpike was built from Cherry Valley on the Albany Pike in 1800 by way of Sangerfield and Cazenovia, linking up with the Seneca Turnpike at Manlius. A few years later, another section was extended from Cazenovia, through La Fayette, to the foot of Skaneateles Lake, where it joins the New Seneca Turnpike (joining Marcellus and Skaneateles); the whole stretch from Albany to Buffalo now being part of U.S. 20.

SITE OF
CAYUGA LONG BRIDGE
ONE MILE LONG. 1800-57
CARRIED GREAT STREAM OF
WESTERN MIGRATION

Cayuga County, 30
Cayuga at end of Genesee St.

Farther south, the Susquehanna Turnpike or Ithaca Road was cut along the valleys from Kingston through Unadilla, Greene, Richford, Ithaca, Bath, and points west, bringing Yankees from Connecticut to the southern tier. (This road was the foundation of parts of NY 28, NY 206, and NY 79.)

Watertight wagons loaded with gypsum at Onondaga were conveyed to the foot of Cayuga Lake, where the wheels were removed and the wagons then floated south to Ithaca. There the wagon boats would be fitted with wheels again and hauled over the mountain south of Ithaca and down the new turnpike to Owego. Three years was required to build the Ithaca Owego Turnpike (NY 96 south of Ithaca) which opened for business in 1811 and linked up with roads extending to Montrose and Honesdale in Pennsylvania, and Newton, Morristown, and Newark, to New York City. That year, the road from Ithaca to Geneva was completed (NY 96 north of Ithaca).

The Hamilton and Skaneateles Turnpike, open in 1806, is thought to have been primarily for drovers of cattle, sheep, and poultry (note Gooseville Corners en route) whose charges perambulated, optimistically, at the rate of ten miles a day from pens to pens. Stagecoaches traveled the route but followed less frequent schedules than on the Seneca Turnpike. The road was the foundation for much of present NY 80.

The north-south roads did not have to carry as much traffic as the east-west migration routes, but commerce and convenience required the roads now known as New York routes 21, 36, 88, 54, 14, 96, 414, 89, 38, 34, 41, 245, 13, 12, 8, 46, 26, 28, 205, 206, 79, 51, 166, 7, 17, and, of course, US 15, 20, and 11. By 1825, most of the road pattern of the state as we know it, was laid out.

Tolls were collected from stage, mail, and freight wagons, but few turnpike companies made any money for their investors, and by the 1820s, the state began taking over the responsibility of road maintenance from the unhappy stockholders.

Plank roads were tried by a later generation beginning in the mid 1840s, and by 1857, the state had chartered more than 350 companies. In 1845, George Geddes built a plank road from Syracuse to Central Square, which was so popular that plank was laid to Oswego, Elbridge, Fayetteville, Manlius, Jordan, and Skaneateles. Sleepers were put down on either side of the road, and heavy cross planks, four inches thick, were laid on top crosswise, making an eight-foot wide path for the busiest direction, with the other opposing lane usually left unplanked.

Like the bridge across Cayuga Lake, the plank roads gave an uncommonly smooth passage, but they were not prosperous either, and went out of business due to higher than expected maintenance, and the depression of 1857. However, the original plank road to Central Square was rebuilt many times, and used as a bicycle racing strip for awhile. It remained in operation until 1913, and is now part of US 11.

1809 STATE ROAD LATER PLANK ROAD, PASSED THROUGH ROOSEVELT HAMLET, FOUNDED BY NICHOLAS J. ROOSEVELT

Oswego County, 33
NY 49 at Roosevelt's Corners

After the plank road craze faded, the state's highways, which had been dependent upon cash-poor communities for maintenance, were not improved to any degree until the 1880s. The increased use of bicycles by the public caused the formation of the League of American Wheelmen in 1880. This was a group of bicyclists whose intention of getting the roads improved was satisfied in 1887 by the passage of the "Liberty Bill", which gave the bikers the right to use the roads and also provided that bike paths could be authorized by local communities if desired.

By that time, cities had had some streets paved or laid with bricks, cobblestones, or Belgian blocks. The best country roads were macadamized (for the Scot, John L. McAdam) first with a three-inch stone course, then gravel, and on top stone dust compacted for a hard surface, and crowned in the middle and ditched at the sides for quick water run-off. When the automobile was no longer considered a "rich man's toy", after 1900, the insistence for better roads produced asphalt (macadam) road surfaces.

The bridge at Cayuga, however long, was relatively easy to engineer and build because pilings could be driven every few feet into the shallow and soft bottom at the lake's northern end. But wooden bridges over the Susquehanna, the Genesee, the Seneca, the Oswego River, and some lesser streams, all required considerable expertise where the river was so wide and the bottom rocky, that two or more spans required one or more abutments in the river.

Where the crossing was no more than a hundred yards, preferably less, the experts could maneuver prepared beams onto temporary supports in the stream bed. When they drove the wooden treenails into the aligned holes of the opposing beams to be joined, the whole bridge took on its desired shallow arch so that it lifted a little above the supports, which were then removed. More spans were extended the same way. Starting in 1805, some bridges were roofed over and sided to protect the structural members from alternations of wet and dry weather in order to retard decay. The first one built in the country was over the Schuykill River near Philadelphia.

One of the grandest bridges was the wooden railroad trestle carrying the Erie Railroad across the Genesee River at Portageville, finished in 1852. Using over two million feet of timber and costing $175,000, it was 800 feet long and 234 feet high above the river. It carried trains for over twenty years before fire consumed it. By then the industrial age had advanced to the point that the successor bridge could be built of steel, and it still remains in service.

In the winter the roads were made manageable by driven herds of the hamlet's oxen and horses treading down the snow, and later by rollers. Two-horse sleighs could travel twice the speed of a wagon, carry more pay-load, and not be concerned about quagmires or streams.

PORTAGE BRIDGE REPLACES LARGEST WOODEN BRIDGE IN THE WORLD. BUILT IN 1825. 300 ACRES OF TIMBER USED IN CONSTRUCTION BURNED IN 1875

Livingston County, 38
Road to Letchworth Park from south

Covered bridge road surfaces were scattered with snow to make them passable. In other seasons, wagons and carts carried the main flow of migration, and many people were on horseback. For those in wagons and carts on trips to "mill or meeting", the turnpike toll was waived if they could show that they were on the way to the gristmill or church.

The two-wheeled cart was favored by the farmer because of its simplicity in construction, with no stringers connecting fore-and-aft wheels or gear to allow for turning needed. Negotiating only a pair of wheels, rather than two pair when harvesting in a field still cluttered with boulders and stumps, relieved a thrifty farmer's mind. Larger wheels were also preferred since they gave more clearance for obstructions and eased the way over rough roads. Doctor Oliver Wendell Holmes poem, **"The Deacon's Masterpiece, or the Wonderful One-Hoss Shay"** commemorates the agility and versatility of the conveyance when in less demanding usage.

The Conestoga wagon, first built by the Pennsylvania Dutch of the Conestoga Valley near Lancaster, was used to carry heavy merchandise, or a family's entire be longings, on long hauls to settlements, and produce back in return. The sloping front and sides of the wagon box reduced the shifting of cargo while moving over hilly and uneven roads and was continued in the rake of the hoops used to stretch the canvas top. This gave a pleasing appearance together with the color scheme, often a blue body, large and wide vermillion wheels and running gear, topped with the white canvas for the length of the wagon. The Conestoga wagon was the predecessor of the railroad freight car. Bells adorned the hames on the harness and served to alert taverns that a teamster and his vehicle were approaching. Tradition demanded that if a wagon became mired and was pulled out by another, it must surrender its bells to its benefactor; "to be there with bells on" meant that no such mishap marred the journey.

Draft horses were used to pull the wagons and farm machinery such as reapers and cultivators and, off the farm, the great Conestoga wagons, or "prairie schooners", were loaded with family and possessions by those emigrating west. Trotters pulled buggies, carriages, and buckboards and also stepped smartly with cutters and sleighs in season. Saddle horses were ubiquitous as were quarter horses, so named for a quarter-mile straight stretch in colonial Williamsburg where early Virginians gathered to race the swiftest horses from around the colony. Horses got you around, near and far, as walking was to be avoided, especially if you were going more than a hundred yards.

The horse was not only important for transportation and farming, but was an important factor in the economy. Livery stables that stabled, fed, and rented horses, farriers and blacksmiths that kept them shod, the tack makers that made the saddles and harnesses, the teamsters that drove the wagons of commerce, and the wainwrights who made the fire engines, wagons, stagecoaches, carriages, and sleighs, not to forget the horse doctors and, of course, the manure haulers. Alas, for all of these professions, the era of the horse went into sharp decline after it peaked in 1920 with twenty-five million horses and mules across the country.

With horses becoming abundant in the early 1800s, George Washington Loomis enjoyed a mania for fine horse flesh as did his many children and grandchildren whom Loomis and his wife schooled in the criminal arts. They stole horses and other stock, changed identifying marks, and hid the animals in dense Nine-Mile swamp close by their fine Sangerfield stock farm. The Loomis Gang, over time greatly enlarged by outsiders attracted to "easy" money, retained lawyers, friendly judges, and lawmen for legal protection, but wreaked vengeance on persistent prosecutors, plaintiffs, and witnesses by burning a business, barn, or house, rustling more horses, and bringing counter suits. The Gang was put down near the century's end about as easily as fighting a pack of wolves but only in yearly stages after sixty years of spreading terror.

Stagecoaches came into use in the colonies in the early 18th century when urban roads improved. By 1785, the roads were considered good enough for several lines to make regular stagecoach connections between New York and Albany. As roads improved in central New York, the stagecoach was introduced to the region, forcing further highway improvement, but the quality of the roads was to be a debatable subject for some time.

Drawn by four to six horses, the stagecoaches stopped every four or five miles to water the horses, and every fifteen or twenty miles at stage-stop taverns. The stage driver, or his postilion, announced their arrival from a mile away with a blast on his horn so that the stable hands could ready a change of horses, and the kitchen and taproom crew could prepare for hungry, dust-dry patrons. There were two, and sometimes three, taverns per mile on the Seneca Turnpike between Albany and Buffalo to provide lodging, meals, fresh teams of horses, and to fortify passengers against thirst.

At the time, stagecoach travel was the least exhausting way to travel distances fast. One line in the Southern Tier announced a new route leaving Owego at two in the morning for Elmira, Painted Post, Dansville, Geneseo, arriving in Rochester in two days. Beside eight to fourteen passengers and their baggage, the coaches carried the mail and small parcels, and had a schedule which was more honored in the breach.

Metal springs were not used at first on any but the finest vehicles. For everyone else, to reduce the constant jolts of travel, the coach body was suspended from end to end on each side by long thick leather straps, which left much to be desired. (A fourteenth century innovation, thorough-braces originated in Hungary in the town of Kocs from which the word "coach" derives).

Most towns of any size had their own carriage maker. Judging by the many markers citing their presence, there were wainwrights turning out carriages, carts, sleighs, and wagons in almost every hamlet that had a corps of mechanics. Skaneateles had its wainwright—the factory was right across the road from the Sherwood Inn blocking a fine view of the lake. Fortunately, at that site there is now a park with the view down the length of the lake unobstructed.

Abbott and Downing, in Concord, New Hampshire, combined padded seats, paneling, and many coats of rubbed-down paint and varnish in their fine coaches. Most important, they had leaf springs to cushion the ride. Fine as the Concord coaches were, people were glad to finish no more than forty or fifty miles in a days travel.

SITE OF THE OLD SHERWOOD INN BUILT ABOUT 1800

Onondaga County, 79
US 20 at Skaneateles

Isaac Sherwood and his son, Col. John H. Sherwood, ran the Sherwood Inn at Skaneateles, and the stage line between Geneva and Fayetteville, including the line to Elbridge, Camillus, and Marcellus from Skaneateles, using eighty four-horse teams.

John Butterfield had a thriving freight business at Albany but never operated stagecoaches until his close friend, President James Buchanan, favored him with a $600,000 contract to deliver the United States mail. He learned fast: in the next year, he set up 165 stations and blacksmith shops, built and repaired bridges, and acquired 100 stage wagons and coaches, 1800 horses and mules, and employed 750 men.

As business expanded, he drove the first stagecoach from the Mississippi to San Francisco, before becoming a co-owner of the American Express Company. Later he organized the Butterfield

Overland Stage Company, with routes across the southwest to the west coast. In 1865, he retired to become mayor of Utica.

William Fargo, born in Pompey, started out as a post driver locally and became a partner with Butterfield in the American Express Company, and later was mayor of Buffalo from 1862-66. Henry Wells, who had a similar background as freight agent and stage driver, was successfully competing with the U.S. Postal Service when he was asked to join forces with Fargo and Butterfield as president of American Express.

GLEN PARK 1852
HOME OF HENRY WELLS
FOUNDER OF
AMERICAN EXPRESS CO. 1850
WELLS FARGO EXPRESS CO. 1852
WELLS COLLEGE 1868

Cayuga County, 88
In front of campus, Aurora

Wells Fargo was an offshoot in 1852 "to forward Gold Dust, Bullion, Specie, Packages, Parcels, and freight of all kinds to and from New York and San Francisco...and all the principal towns of California and Oregon." Welles' success enabled him to found Wells College for women, in 1868, at Aurora, where he built his home (now the college's administration building). A stammerer, he also opened several schools for those so afflicted.

The great days of the stagecoach in the east were over by the 1840s. But on the short routes not served by the railroads, only the advent of the horseless bus in the 1920s supplanted the stagecoach and what had been known as the station wagon.

Hardenburgh Corners grew around the mill built two miles north of the Owasco outlet by Col. John Hardenbergh, a veteran of the Sullivan campaign and direct descendant of Johannes Hardenbergh, grantee of the colonial downstate Hardenbergh Patent. He surveyed part of the military tract with an eye for a parcel suitable to generate water power on the old Genesee trail, now being widened. His choice had already been bought and sold twice but he bought it for $75 an acre.

WASCO
'THE CROSSING PLACE'
SITE OF A CAYUGA VILLAGE
OCCUPIED BY INDIANS BEFORE
AND AFTER SETTLEMENT OF
HARDENBERGH CORNERS

Cayuga County, 8*
State St. btw prison & outlet, Auburn

Ten years later, in 1803 the residents changed the name to Auburn, "the loveliest village of the Plain", from Goldsmith's poem, **The Deserted Village**. It was anything but deserted as other shops aggregated there later including the Osborne family's scythe plant, which went on to make reapers, threshers, and other farm implements. At the end of the century, the company merged with the International Harvester Company.

Colonel Edwin Metcalf founded the Columbia Rope Company initially to make twine for the reapers, and Fred L. Emerson's factory made Enna Jettick Shoes for eighty-five years. Emerson Park, at the foot of Owasco Lake, is one of the Emerson family's gifts to the city. Auburn also boasted of Auburn Paper Mill, flour mills, carriage works, a glass factory, cabinet shops, and The Empire Wringer Company.

Nearby, William H. Seward began his law practice by joining Judge Elijah Miller's firm. He married the judge's daughter, Frances, and on the judge's insistence, the couple lived in the newly built house now known as the Seward Mansion. With the help of his friend, journalist and political leader Thurlow Weed, Seward prospered in politics and became Governor of New York, then Senator in the U.S. Congress.

Seward helped form the Republican Party in 1854 to unify unaligned factions after the demise of the Whig Party, and insisted that an abolitionist stance be part of the party's platform in the 1860 election. He had expected to be the party's presidential candidate, but lost out to Abraham Lincoln who, when elected president, appointed him Secretary of State. Whenever official business permitted, he returned to Auburn, and his home. The Federal style mansion, which still stands in good repair, replete with period furnishings, was made available to the public by its last occupant, William H. Seward III, when he died in 1951 as a memorial to his grandfather and father.

AUBURN PRISON
CONVICTS MADE SEWING SILK
1841–1846
HERE WAS PRINCIPAL CASH
MARKET IN US FOR
COCCOONS AND RAW SILK

Cayuga County, 25
In front of prison, W.side State St.

Another durable, but grim, building in Auburn is the state Prison. Its cornerstone was laid in 1816, the same year as the Seward Mansion, and cost over $500,000 to complete the original building. In 1822, its convicts were hired out to help build the Erie Canal Aqueduct across the Genesee River at Rochester. Three years later, they were used again to build the famous downstate prison, Sing Sing, at Ossining.

Conditions for the prisoners were harsh: the only concession made to moderation by the first warden, William Britten, was his agreement to abandon "double bunking" for the fifty-three original prisoners in the sixty-one 3½ by 7 foot cells. The silent system, in which the convicts were under severely enforced silence during prolonged working hours, was standard procedure, as was walking in lockstep with fellow prisoners, all garbed in striped uniforms. Certain extreme punishments were practiced at the Auburn prison, such as the "shower bath" in which ice-cold water was poured over the prisoner while he was locked in the stocks. The shower bath was another "concession" to reform: it replaced whipping with the cat-o'-nine-tails in 1849.

Penal experimentation began to be practiced here, curbing brutal methods and setting an example for other state prisons, but it was a long time before meaningful reform. The Auburn Correctional Facility, as it is now called, has the dubious distinction of being the first to use the electric chair to execute a murderer, William Kemmler, on August 6, 1890. Since 1916, all state executions have been at Sing Sing.

In contrast to this so necessary, but repressive, place, Auburn aspired to the benefits of education and by 1816, already had a circulating library with 800 volumes.

Two blocks south of Genesee Street is Fort Hill Cemetery, (site of an ancient Indian hill fort), where Seward and many of Auburn's famous are buried. It is the birthplace, (also claimed by Shamokin, Pennsylvania), of Logan, a Mingo chief, named for William Penn's admired humanitarian secretary, James Logan. Beloved by whites and Indians alike, he was the son of Conrad Weiser's friend, Shikellimy, emissary of the Iroquois. In 1774, white renegades massacred Logan's entire family in cold blood in the Ohio Valley. This brought about Logan's swift retribution and his famous lament, "Who is there to mourn for Logan?" an eloquence admired by Thomas Jefferson and later inscribed on the fifty-six foot obelisk erected over Logan's remains at Fort Hill.

—500 FEET
FORT HILL
PREHISTORIC INDIAN FORT
TRADITIONAL BIRTHPLACE
OF CHIEF LOGAN
NOW A CEMETERY

Cayuga County 5,
Fort and Genesee Sts.

John D. Rockefeller was born not far away in Richford, in 1839, but he grew up near the southern end of Owasco Lake. He began a grain and commodities business in Cleveland but had a sideline in illuminating petroleum which had replaced increasingly expensive whale oil. The company succeeded so well that he began acquiring other oil companies, often using ruthless methods, and in 1870 called it the Standard Oil Company of Ohio. The corporation sold kerosene for the new lamps gaining world-wide popularity, making him extremely wealthy at a time when gasoline, a by-product of refining kerosene, had no commercial value. Of course, the advent of the automobile compounded his wealth immensely. At his age ninety-six, in 1935, an old insurance policy, bought when he was a lad, matured and the richest man in the world collected the death benefit of $1000 because the mortality tables used when the policy was issued assumed everyone in the insured group would be dead by age ninety-six.

In nearby Seneca Falls, Seabury Gould advanced from making pumps of wood to fabricating them out of iron, and Goulds Pumps began to ship its products to burgeoning towns in a nation thirsty for water for the farm, home, and industry. Several other companies began making pumps in Seneca Falls—Downs and Cowing in 1840, Seymour Wheeler, and Rumsey, with Goulds Pumps the survivor of various corporate combinations. It was estimated in its heyday that one fourth of the pumps in the world came from Seneca Falls.

In 1849, Seneca Falls' first hand-pumped fire engine was made by the Silsby Manufacturing Company and, six years later, the company came out with a steam-powered rotary pump designed by Gould's neighbor, Birdsall Holly. They also made oak-tanned leather fire hoses, (Goodyear developed rubber hose in 1839), handsomely painted hose carts, brass speaking trumpets, axes and fire buckets. The pumpers generally had pump handles on either side, each wide enough to accommodate as many as twenty men a side who, because of the strenuous work, had to be "fortified" with beer and relieved (of the work) in teams. They could pump hundreds of gallons per minute several hundred feet, depending on the manpower.

With the advent of the steamer, the firemen, almost always volunteers, no longer had to exhaust themselves. Steam-powered pumps on the fire engines could throw yet a more torrential stream of water higher and deeper into the fire. But the men still insisted on pulling the fire engine (despite the heavier machine and the availability of horses), and on having their ration of beer.

Rivalry between engine houses was widespread. For more years than they would like to admit, to be first reaching a fire and a water source seemed more important to the companies than dousing the blaze. And garnering all the firefighting resources in the field of action, to the exclusion of other companies, was not against the rules. Between fires, the attractively painted wood and brass engines and other equipment were kept shined and in readiness, and all was out on parade on the Fourth of July, Memorial Day, and other holidays. The fire companies were well regarded and proud fraternities, rife with camaraderie, and membership was coveted. They added color and panache to the social life of the community.

Firemen finally gave in to the fact that horses could get them and the new steam engine to the fire faster, and soon other methods of arriving promptly and ready for action were innovated. When the alarm sounded, the chain across the stable opening fell away; the well-trained horses moved in front of the steam engine, and the harness was dropped in place for hitching by the hostler. To save time, men housed upstairs could slide down a smooth brass pole to the ground floor. A small stove in the floor of the station house was always kept lit to preheat the boiler in the fire engine parked over it. As the engine left the station house, gas fire-jets ignited the kindling in the fire box so that a head of steam could be attained by the time the fire was reached.

Horses galloping down the road with the fire engine in tow, belching smoke and clanging for people to clear the way (often preceded by the company's pet dalmatians), always drew an excited crowd to appraise the action of the local station. The steamers not only had more water power, but had a special advantage in winter; embarrassment was avoided because water carried in the cistern rarely froze, unlike the tank in the hand pumper which, like as not, could be solid ice at the moment of truth.

Despite the plethora of companies making fire fighting equipment, Seneca Falls had a conflagration in 1890 that burned down the business district. Geneva and Waterloo responded to the call for help, but the post office, three newspaper offices, and a total of eighty-seven stores, offices, and residences were consumed. Seneca Falls was called the "Fire Engine Capital of the World". As if to prove this, the American Fire Engine Company was incorporated there, combining the cumulative assets and talents of the Button, Silsby, Ahrens and Clapp, and Thomas Manning companies in 1891. Twelve years later, the La France Company in Elmira (founded by Truckson Slocum La France) merged with American to form American LaFrance, a leading manufacturer in the industry. And, yes, a town in central New York that burned to the ground changed its name when rebuilt to - you guessed it - Phoenix.

CHAPTER TWELVE

The Iroquois religion coincided with much of what Christianity teaches, but the Indians wondered that many Christians did not match their conduct to their beliefs. The Indians said Christianity is a religion for white men, and if Indians adopted it, would only cause them harm. Nauwaneu is their Great Good Spirit, the creator of the world and every good thing in it, including inoffensive animals, Indians, to whom he is partial, and life's comforts. In the afterlife, where he also reigns, abundance and pleasant living reward those who are qualified by their good behavior and benign hearts.

There is also a bad spirit, Nauwaneu's less powerful brother, who reigns in an adjacent realm, and who is to blame for all malign conditions such as disease and blights, and bad personal behavior. All those rejected by Nauwaneu are consigned to the evil brother and every misery that he can devise for an eternity. Indians are especially skilled in their knowledge of plants, animals, and the caprices of nature, but they are also credulous, and are guided by the spirits's fanciful use of rocks, trees, animals, and dreams to voice their supernatural benign or malign messages.

Offerings are made to abate evil and to bring favor during five feasts throughout the year. The first is after the sugaring. Thanks are given for the sap harvest; then each chief rises to advise the tribe how they should behave and avoid vice to obtain Nauwaneu's favor, and to deflect the evil efforts of his brother spirit. Next is the feast after planting, then the green corn feast, followed by the corn harvest.

When the year's last hunt is concluded, a feast of six or seven days during the old moon in late January celebrates the events and good times of the year. The pattern of giving gratitude for good fortune and beseeching its continuance was repeated. Amid festive games, men garbed in husk false faces gathered alms and, as well, evil spirits which they "transmitted" unto a sacrificial white dog that was burned, ridding them of sin. The chiefs then reviewed the affairs of the year past and agree on their plans for the coming year. On the last day, the entire tribe gathered for the final ceremonial dinner. At its conclusion they enacted the war dance, the peace dance, and smoked the pipe of peace before they retired, composed for the coming year.

Howard S. Ford

The Revolution and its aftermath brought death, despair, sickness, and starvation to the Iroquois and cut their population in New York to less than half, or about 3800 souls. The whites had coerced them out of most of their land, and their own leaders had obtained favors, personal annuities, or special parcels of land by bribing the treaty negotiators. Whites had persistently fueled this nadir in Iroquois history with copious quantities of alcohol that became the Indian's joy and consolation and, at the same time, their despair, and had lead to their personal and communal ruination.

In 1790-91 when Chief Cornplanter met with Washington in Philadelphia, he asked for and was granted technical aid. The Philadelphia Meeting of Friends also contributed tools and men to teach them husbandry and the mechanical arts. Realizing that the Quakers were not self-serving but altruists and sincere in their desire to help, the Senecas embraced them as did the Oneidas, the Onondagas, Cayugas, and the Stockbridge Indians. The Quakers open conduct and hands-on teaching brought about impressive results in the quality of housing, crops, stock raising, blacksmithing, and other manual arts within a few years.

The Quakers were careful to not interfere with traditional Seneca values, even witchcraft, or where vested Indian interests would be offended. But they fervently urged them to abandon drinking, gambling, social dances, unequal sexual division of labor, and the spending of inordinate amounts on personal ornamentation.

HOME OF
BROTHERTON INDIANS
1783-1850
AMONG WHOM LIVED 1785-1792,
SANSON OCCUM
INDIAN PRESBYTERIAN PREACHER

Oneida County 34,
NY 315, 4 m. NW of Waterville

The ancient religion and traditional seasonal ceremonies still roused and enabled them to confront death, disease, or danger. Rituals such as the Society of Faces and special dances comforted or enlivened emotions at New Years, before going to war, or during Green Corn Days. But now alcohol was used by both men and women, even during these rituals, and robbed them of their virtues and self respect.

Handsome Lake, Chief Cornplanter's half-brother and uncle of Red Jacket, was one so besotted. He had been a warrior in many raids, among them Devil's Hole, Cherry Valley, Wyoming Valley, and Canajoharie, where Cornplanter's white father still lived. He had also been a signatory at the Big Tree Treaty of 1797, but he barely subsisted in an inebriated state on the sliver of land granted to Cornplanter down stream of the Allegany reservation. His later days saw him swill so much that he nearly died every day for five years. He was a distraught drunkard and wanted to die.

From this stunned condition he began having visions in which the Creator advised him on matters of personal and tribal significance, and inspired him with enough self determination to quit the habit of drinking and to develop a religious code for his and his tribe's regeneration.

Starting that year, 1799, Handsome Lake began to integrate Quaker forms of Christianity with traditional native practices regarding family, community, and the importance of a landed culture, but with the most stress on temperance. He committed this to writing along with such Indian concepts as the judging one's actions by its effects for seven generations in the future, and regarding the Earth as one's Mother.

The Code of Handsome Lake appealed to many among the Senecas and to numerous Onondagas, Oneidas, Cayugas and other tribes in New York and the Ohio valley, and served its purpose of generating a renaissance of native Americans.

Dissipated from loose living and frail from old age, Handsome Lake died on a visit at Onondaga in 1815 at age eighty-two. After his death, adherents increased and the Code of Handsome Lake is still widely influential in Iroquois country.

The earliest white religious activity in the region was that of Jemima Wilkinson. It was said that during the Revolution, a British officer jilted her, which so dismayed her that she went into a coma.

When she revived, she thought she had died and that her body had been inhabited by an angel—A Universal Friend of Mankind and Savior of the World—and from then on, she so styled herself.

BUILT ABOUT 1790
FRIEND'S HOME
HERE LIVED
JEMIMA WILKINSON
KNOWN AS
THE UNIVERSAL FRIEND

Yates County, 3
CR, 4 m. N. of Branchport

Poorly educated and ignorant, but with an uncommon memory of Biblical verse, she preached to the countryside in Rhode Island and Connecticut, and even established two churches there. When she advocated celibacy, the pooling of assets, and allowed her disciples to refer to her as the Messiah, neighbors' hostility caused her and her cult to seek haven from neighbor harassment. In the mid 1780s, she engaged three agents to scout out an unsettled place to establish their settlement.

She migrated in 1790 from Philadelphia, when she was 38, with her devoted followers, some of whom were wealthy and bought the land for her "Jerusalem" settlement at Dresden. At her new location, she impressed a following of close to four hundred souls, and, according to land agent Thomas Morris, son of Robert Morris, the financier, they were "orderly, sober, industrious, and some of them a well educated and intelligent set of people, and many of them possessed of handsome properties."

With the arts of grandiloquence and affectation, Wilkinson pretended to have had revelations from Heaven in which she had been directed to devote her labors to the conversion of sinners." Once when she was supposed to demonstrate her ability to walk on the waters of Seneca lake, Wilkinson told the gathering that she could do it if they had faith. She then asked them if they did have faith in her, and when they shouted in the affirmative, she avowed the demonstration of her power was unnecessary as they indeed believed her capable, and she returned to her carriage.

The Universal Friend's following showed great obedience to her whims and dictates, and was willing to suffer punishment for slight deviations from her orders, even banishment. After a while, her demands for gifts and humiliating punishments for infractions of her rules caused dissension. Her remaining years were spent in a luxurious house remote from the others. But the fervor of her disciples was already in decline when she died in 1819, and the sect soon disbanded

HERE WAS BUILT IN 1798 FIRST CHURCH IN CAYUGA COUNTY REFORMED DUTCH CHURCH OF OWASCO

Cayuga County, 115
East Lake Road, NY 38A

Organized religion asserted itself early. Colonel John Hardenbergh held church in his new home at Hardenbergh Corners (Auburn) in 1796 and soon afterward, the Dutch Reformed Church was built at Brinkerhoff Point on Owasco Lake, one of the first churches in the Military Tract.

Every pioneer community had its churches in some state of organization even though the congregation had no more than a cabin, a tavern, a barn, or used another denomination's chapel as its place of worship. Congregationalists, Presbyterians, Methodists, Lutherans, Baptists, Episcopalians, Dutch Reformed Church, and Quakers from New England and New Jersey and Pennsylvania were predominant in the earlier years, shortly followed by small enclaves of Catholics and Jews getting established. The down-to-earth preaching was beneficial for the composure of people who labored hard to build, against formidable odds, something out of nothing, and Sunday meeting and its socializing was a welcome relief to those who were socially isolated.

Itinerant preachers and evangelists made their appearance at camp meetings which were the simplest and the only form of worship available to many. The open air attracted crowds from the sparse population beginning with the revivalist movement in 1799. The meeting were managed by a group of preachers who spelled each other, or for larger congregations, harangued their patrons simultaneously in separate areas of the campgrounds. Attendees brought bedding and were well provisioned for several days. Powerful exhortations brought about conversions amid shouting, shaking, and convolutions by, usually, Methodist, Baptist, or newly divergent pastors from established religions. But this behavior was frowned upon by the more conservative and entrenched in the region.

ROMAN CATHOLIC MISSION CHURCH FIRST IN POMPEY WAS LOCATED HERE, 1857–1866, FATHER JAMES CAHILL FIRST PRIEST

Onondaga County, 74
On town road, at Pompey

De Witt Clinton, when searching out a canal route, wrote of coming upon a camp meeting of Wesley's followers near Lyons in 1810; the Methodists had many such gatherings in the countryside over the next fifty years.

Young Joseph Smith, Jr. attended revival camp meetings held near Phelps and his parent's hardscrabble farm. He disclosed that he had had visions in his teens of the existence of ancient and secret records, and in 1827, the hiding place of the golden tablets was revealed to him by the Angel Moroni as being on a hill south of Palmyra.

Sure Signs: Stories Behind the Historical Markers of Central New York

He declared that the talent and instruments necessary to translate them were made available to him alone, enabling him to read the ancient gospel of the Book of Mormon, and that he and a friend, Oliver Cowdrey, were then ordained as high priests.

They needed funds to publish this revelation so they persuaded Martin Harris, a successful local farmer, to mortgage his farm. Thus was the Church of Jesus Christ of Latter Day Saints (Mormons) founded. It quickly gained followers, notable among them Sidney Rigdon, and Brigham Young, who, as a young carpenter, had a hand in building the mantels of Seward's mansion in Auburn and later owned a chair factory and brick kiln in the town of Mendon where he married his first of many wives.

Two years later, the group went to Kirtland, Ohio, looking for a permanent home, then to Missouri, and Illinois. At Nauvoo, Illinois, as at previous "homes", they were persecuted by the "Gentiles", who feared this rapidly-growing and prosperous close-knit communal society. Surprisingly, they received a state charter there which allowed them to maintain their own militia and courts, and power to pass laws provided they did not counteract state and federal laws.

—

4 MILES SOUTH CUMORAH FAMOUS MORMON HILL AND ANGEL MORONI MONUMENT

Wayne County, 8
NY 21 & 31 in Palmyra

With so many converts flocking there, Nauvoo quickly became the largest town in Illinois in 1842. Neighbor envy and hostility increased so much that in 1844, when Smith announced his candidacy for the U.S. presidency, he and his brother, Hyrum, were arrested and charged with treason and conspiracy that June. Within a few days of their incarceration in Carthage, both were murdered in jail by a mob.

Howard S. Ford

Church fathers then chose Brigham Young as their new leader. To avoid antagonism and conflict, Young led them in 1847 on the hegira to the region of Great Salt Lake, then a barren and uninhabited part of Mexico but reported by John C. Fremont, commander of many recent western exploratory expeditions, as a "bucolic region". Within a year of their arrival, the terms of the Treaty of Guadalupe Hidalgo ending the Mexican War made the region part of the United States. Mormon converts were so resolved to settle there that many hiked as far as a thousand miles pushing handcarts loaded with all their belongings. These determined people dug extensive ditches to tap mountain streams to provide fresh-water irrigation to this desiccated area causing it to thrive into what we know as the state of Utah.

It was there, five years later, that Young announced that polygamy was acceptable to the church (since reversed by church leaders), thus beginning a new chapter in the life of this continually growing modern-day religion.

BRIGHAM YOUNG THE MORMON PROPHET LIVED IN THE HOUSE 100 YARDS EAST OF HERE IN 1831. HE WAS BAPTIZED A MORMON IN 1831 AT MENDON, N.Y.

Cayuga County, 94
Port Byron, in front of hotel

European beliefs were melded with Iroquois traditional principals into the new non-Christian religion, as preached by Handsome Lake. Despite the efforts of some whites to beat the Indians down and confiscate their remaining land, others in good faith continued the attempt to convert them but were resisted by such as the sachem and curmudgeon, Red Jacket, who believed in going back to their old religion. When approached by a missionary, he is reported to have said, "Brother, if you white people murdered the Savior, make it up yourselves. We Indians had nothing to do with it."

Because the religion of John Humphrey Noyes and his followers seemed too radical to the people of Putney, Vermont, Noyes and his coterie moved in 1848 to the settlement of Turkey Street, between Utica and Syracuse on the Seneca Turnpike.

They called themselves Perfectionists because they believed Christ had already arrived the second time: people could no longer sin and then repent; they should stop sinning and strive for perfection. They practiced complex marriage precepts and eugenic mating. Noyes had ideas regarding sexual conduct that was considered heretical. He advanced, and practiced the idea that men and women could have many partners, that love did not have to result in a monogamous state. The male partner was the one to take contraceptive precaution by coitus interruptus, a practice which, judging by the number a children in the community, was not totally accepted or successful.

To avoid selfishness, property was held in common, and child raising was a community effort as were many other endeavors of the tightly-knit organization. Their industry, energy, and innovation helped them to thrive. When neighbor Samuel Newhouse designed and made a small animal trap, they sought and obtained his permission to fabricate and sell it. The Community became better known largely owing to the public's reception to what became known as the famous Newhouse animal trap starting in the early 1850s.

Never more than three hundred, the Community shared all labor between men and women, no matter how menial, including Noyes. The repetitiveness of household work stimulated the men to devise machines for washing clothes and dishes and methods to reduce the tediousness of other chores. Children from infancy to twelve years of age were reared in the "Children's House", a section of the substantial brick Mansion House which is still well maintained. They were well taught and cared for, but they were allowed to see their parents only twice a week. Reading and various kinds of education was encouraged for the entire community, as well as the children, and a weekly newsletter concerning activities and ideas was circulated among the group. Many members fondly recalled happy childhoods.

By 1880, the Community was less tolerated by neighboring towns, and it voted to terminate their social experiment. They also created a stock company called the Oneida Community. They sold the animal trap business, and specialized in making silver tableware, but during World War I, they switched over, temporarily, to making fine surgical instruments. Now traded on the New York Stock Exchange as Oneida Limited, but in the trade called Oneida Silversmiths (many of the employees are descendants of the "community"), the company has broadened the line to include stainless steel flatware and holloware, and silver plating for the electronic industry with factories in Canada, Mexico, and Ireland. The company manufactures the largest amount of the world's output of flatware.

By popular demand, Turkey Street was renamed at the end of the century by petition through the efforts of Congressman James S. Sherman of Utica (later vice president of the U.S., 1901-1912), who was given the privilege of naming the town after his young son, Sherrill.

When John H. Vincent of Camptown, New Jersey, wanted to make it more pleasant for his Sunday school teachers to learn how to conduct classes, he took them out of the classroom to the outdoors. This was so successful that he proposed offering a correspondence course to those too distant to attend.

This too, went so well that a friend, Lewis Miller, suggested he use an idle camp-ground on Chautauqua Lake for his two-week summer classes. In 1874, the first summer school at Camp Chautauqua opened with forty men and women taking their Bible classes in the fresh air during the days, and singing around a campfire in the evening. Bible study expanded to include many cultural courses over a two-month session with the blessing of the Methodist Episcopal authorities. The response was overwhelming and each summer thousands from all over the country came to live in local boarding houses and tents and have an enjoyable time learning in a delightful and congenial atmosphere.

Wit and wisdom as well as politics and philosophy were discussed by novelists and humorists, poets and statesmen, including six presidents of the United States. Newsmen said that Chautauqua was an Indian word that probably meant "talked to death". Even a full symphony orchestra conducted by Walter Damrosch, conductor of the New York Philharmonic Orchestra, gave concerts in the outdoor amphitheater. Cottages were built surrounding the campus grounds of which the Greek-columned Hall of Philosophy was the focal point.

Chautauqua was considered a university, with classes in science, music, literature, philosophy, and, of course, religion. In 1893, the State of New York chartered it to grant academic degrees. By

1900, "Chautauquas" were held in over 200 locations, mostly in the East and Midwest, the first adult education offered on such a scale. Courses backed with access to a circulating library of 700 volumes of instruction could be selected by correspondence students.

The summer assembly continues to be a perennial event there alongside the lake, and many individual study groups, calling themselves by different names and started years ago in towns across the country, carry on still.

CHAPTER THIRTEEN

The Treaty of Paris officially ended the Revolution in 1783, but anti-British feeling smoldered for years. The British finally evacuated the Great Lakes forts in 1796, although they still had a great deal of influence on the western tribes, and were supplying guns and aid to the Indian coalition being formed by the Shawnee chief, Tecumseh. The Indians were subdued by General William Henry Harrison in his victory over them on the Tippecanoe River in northern Indiana in late 1811.

The main irritant was that for twenty years Britain had persisted on interfering with American shipping on the high seas, and impressing Americans (more than 6,000) on their ships claiming that they were British deserters. British sailors, subject to difficult conditions and harsh discipline, were attracted to service on American naval and merchant ships, and many switched over when in port. Often short on crew strength, the British frequently used the excuse of uncertain citizenship to complete their ships's company with Americans. It must be admitted that many Americans were British-born and some had not been in their new country long. The USS Constitution boasted a crew of 419 men of whom, it was claimed, that 149 were British subjects.

The U. S. Congress declared war against Great Britain in June of 1812. The War Hawks faction under Speaker of the House, Henry Clay, hoped not only to redress the British transgressions, but to annex Canada, or at least southern Ontario Province; some preferred to take Florida from Spain. New England was opposed to the war because it had a successful trade with Great Britain, which to the rest of the country's chagrin, it maintained during the war, even supplying British troops in Canada.

The Commander-in-Chief was Major General Henry Dearborn, veteran of the Sullivan-Clinton campaign. His plan for border war was a four-pronged attack on Montreal, Kingston, Niagara, and Detroit. It partially relied on the fact that, of 136,000 Upper Canadian citizens, about eighty percent were of American origin, and only one fourth of these were loyalist related. The assumption (later proved false) was that they would rush to help the mother country in a successful invasion.

The British took the initiative on the Great Lakes, and on July 19, the alarm cannon at Sackets Harbor, and its relay guns, signaled to the militia within earshot that British ships were approaching.

Brigadier General Jacob Jennings Brown, a successful Quaker businessman at Brownsville and agent for the Le Rays, was in charge of the militia whom he had been drilling for some months. They responded to the alarm, and formed behind Lieutenant Melancthon Taylor Woolsey on the plateau where the guns of the brig Oneida had been offloaded and hastily placed for a shore battery.

The British under Commodore Earle, sent a boat ashore expecting American surreder. Woolsey refused. The British then fired a shot, that fell short of the shore. A small fort on the bluff had an old thirty-two pounder cannon, called "Old Sow", which had seen historic service. First shipped over from England in 1689, it was one of the artillery pieces captured at Fort Ticonderoga which, Henry Knox had wrestled to Dorchester Heights to force the British evacuation of Boston.

Since only 24-pound cannon balls were on hand at Sackets, housewives contributed their carpets and rags to serve as wadding to make a tighter fit in the larger cannon barrel. Even so, Old Sow's return fire could not reach the ships. An exchange of artillery fire ensued without much effect from either side until the British fired a 32-pounder of their own. One of the balls went past the bluff and was recognized and retrieved by the resourceful militia; Old Sow finally had a ball of the right caliber. It was promptly shot back, severed the mast of the Commodore's flagship, the Royal George, and injured several of the crew. The British sailed back to Kingston, and the North Country was saved from invasion. This was the first battle of the War of 1812. Old Sow is now retired with honors and is alleged to be the cannon that rests on an inconspicuous stone monument in the small town park at nearby Turin.

This promising start of the war was shortly dampened by the inexplicable surrender of Detroit to the British by the aging General William Hull; now the upper lakes were lost to the United States. He was court-martialed, and only his record during the Revolutionary War prevented his execution.

DURING THE WAR OF 1812 BARRACKS WERE ESTABLISHED IN THIS LOCALITY TROOPS PASSING TO AND FROM NIAGARA CAMPED HERE

Cayuga County, 24
North side W. Genesee St., Auburn

Possession of lakes Ontario and Erie was now of the utmost importance. Since the Oneida was the only ship Woolsey had on Lake Ontario, one of his first decisions was to capture smaller British ships to enlarge the fleet. He soon captured a British schooner, the Julia, and bought five other schooners for conversion to war service.

At the same time, the recently appointed Commodore, Isaac Chauncey, was put in charge of the campaign on the lakes except for Champlain. He arranged for ship wrights under master ship builder, Henry Eckford, whose shipyard was near the Brooklyn Navy Yard, to come to Sackets Harbor and apply his innovative design and executive skills to build a Lake Ontario fleet. Local timber was plentiful, but everything else that a ship needed had to be hauled all the way from New York City, with the chance of capture the last thirty miles on Lake Ontario from Oswego to Sackets Harbor, for lack of decent roads.

Eckford needed only forty-five days, from the laying of the oak keel to the finishing of the taffrail, to build the Madison, Chauncey's flagship. His men worked seven days a week felling trees, sawing and adzing them into shape, trenailing planks, and rigging the ships; turning out a ship every forty days at their peak. Made of unseasoned wood, these ships would not resist deterioration and rot for post-war use, but that was of no concern to the immediate need. The growing fleet enabled Chauncey to harass British shipping on Lake Ontario at the same time General Brown was making mischief along the St. Lawrence, and repelling attacks at Ogdensburg.

In the fall, an attempt at invading Canada across from Niagara to placate the War Hawks resulted in the capture of nine hundred Americans, and the resignation of Generals Stephen Van

Rennselaer and Alexander Smyth. This ended fighting on the lake for the year. On the British side, the hero of Upper Canada and victor at Detroit, General Isaac Brock, died of his wounds.

In the early spring of 1813, both sides made forays against each other on the St. Lawrence, and Ogdensburg fell into British hands. Brigadier General Zebulon Pike, celebrated explorer of the Rocky Mountains and southern plains in 1806, was sent to Sackets Harbor that spring to use it as a staging point in a campaign against York (Toronto), capital of Upper Canada and supply depot for British western forces, where it was believed the high number of American immigrants would help an invasion. In late April, Chauncey's fleet sailed up Lake Ontario, and fifteen hundred men made a successful landing. As the British retreated from the beachhead and Pike and his aide, Captain Nicholson, were interrogating a prisoner, a magazine of five hundred barrels of gunpowder blew up causing two hundred and sixty American casualties, among them Pike and Nicholson, who were both killed.

As damaging as this was to the invading Americans, the British did not take advantage of the situation, but continued retreating. The Americans destroyed a warship nearing completion on the stocks and added to their depleted supply of military and naval stores. They evacuated May 2nd, sailing back a captured schooner, the Gloucester, to add to the fleet. Help from the immigrant Americans did not appear.

Chauncey then began to attack Fort George across from Niagara, and with the help of two promising young leaders, Lt. Colonel Winfield Scott and Lieutenant Oliver Hazard Perry, he succeeded. Winning the fort gave the Americans control of the Niagara frontier, paving the way for American naval successes on Lake Erie.

The absence of Chauncey and Pike from the eastern end of Lake Ontario encouraged Sir James Yeo and Sir George Prevost, both high but cautious officers, to make a second attempt on Sackets Harbor. Their main encouragement was the newly completed 637 ton HMS Wolfe with 220 men and 24 guns that could throw a broadside of almost 400 pounds, plus five other ships. When only five miles from Sackets harbor, they came by chance upon nineteen troop transports out of Oswego, and wasted valuable time chasing them, giving the defenders time to prepare for the onslaught, and for General Brown to arrive with six hundred militia. Breastworks were erected at the only possible landing area, and a shore battery placed on the bluff. The militia broke and ran to the rear when the landing force came ashore. The second line of defense was reinforced by a hundred or so of the militia, but it also retreated to the cover of some log huts, where the group dug in and held off the British advance.

General Brown noticed the rear ranks of the militia were idle and not adding to the defense, for which he shamed them, and led them back into the action on the flank. As a result, Prevost thought they were reinforcements about to encircle them, and immediately withdrew his men back to the ships, even leaving behind his dead and wounded. This opportune exploit of a mistake turned a rout into a victory, and Brown was shortly after appointed Brigadier General in the regular army.

In July, Yeo took a supply depot at Charlotte, at the mouth of the Genesee River, and a few days later, put some sailors ashore at Great Sodus Bay to seize several hundred barrels of flour. Indecisive small battles continued, as did frenzied ship building on both sides, but no confrontation of the fleets occurred until early August, when a storm interfered with what could have been serious action.

WALCOTT FALLS CALLED BY INDIANS 'CANADASGUA', LEAPING WATERS ABOVE THE LAKE SITE OF MELVIN'S MILLS ESTABLISHED 1809

Wayne County, 35
US 104 at Wollcott

In mid September, 1813, Oliver Hazard Perry defeated the British fleet on Lake Erie, ("We have met the enemy and they are ours"), setting the stage for the retaking of Detroit, and later, the important Battle of the Thames. In that battle, Tecumseh, who led the Indian tribes and had allied with the British to strengthen the Indian cause, was killed in the fighting on the upper Thames River, and the resolve of the Indian confederacy dissolved.

An attempt to take Montreal failed that fall, although both sides claimed victory at Chrysler's Farm near Morrisburg on the St. Lawrence. The American forces were called off by General Wade Hampton and sent to French Mills on the Salmon River, near Montreal, where they endured a severe winter.

The British were losing eight to ten men a day in desertions to the Americans, but the American forces at Fort George were reduced by enlistments running out. General George McClure, the commander there, had planned little in the face of this certainty. In December, he was reduced to only sixty-five regulars, when William Henry Harrison and his 1,000 troops had to depart for Sackets Harbor after a temporary stay.

In December, the British were close to taking over Fort George, when McClure blew up the fort, causing only slight damage. He also needlessly burned the Canadian town of Newark (Niagara on the Lake). At least he warned the residents of his intention, but this ill-conceived action was repudiated by authorities in Washington. (It is thought that Britain's burning of Washington a year later was reprisal for this atrocity).

The British then occupied Fort George, and since their other positions were secure, they pressed their advantage, and avenged the burning of Newark by attacking Fort Niagara the night of December 19. Even though this was expected, the commander, Captain Nathaniel Leonard, was at home three miles away the night of the attack. The fort was ineptly defended, and was overwhelmed with high casualties. Lewiston was destroyed the next day. On December 29, a second British force crossed the Niagara River and burned Buffalo and Black Rock to the ground on the thirtieth. The U.S. side of the Niagara frontier was quickly deserted by American civilians fleeing to Batavia and points east.

Napoleon's power was about finished, having lost Spain in the Peninsular War in the late fall of 1813 and being seriously weakened by the Russian disaster; France collapsed the following spring. The British could now send experienced troops in force to the war in Canada, which, up to now, was more of an annoying nuisance and an embarrassment to them.

When the British made a weak third attempt on Sackets Harbor in the spring of 1814, the base was alerted so they aborted the action. Because the British thought Oswego to be weak and poorly manned, an attempt to get at the supplies and stores there was worth a try. General Brown had foreseen this possibility, and had garrisoned Fort Oswego with a 300-man artillery unit and thirty sailors in early spring.

WAR OF 1812
CAPTAIN HENRY CROUCH AND
CAPTAIN BENJAMIN BRANCH
SOLDIERS OF WAR OF 1812
WHO DIED WHEN ENCAMPED
NEAR HERE ARE BURIED ABOVE

Onondaga County, 49
NY 173, ½ m. E. of Onondaga Hill

On May third, Yeo appeared off shore with eight ships and a bevy of troop transports. The fort gave them a hot reception, causing the invaders to retire. The next day they returned, and, first raking the shore with grape shot, began to disembark when again the shore batteries opened up, setting one ship afire. Still, the assault troops came on up the slope, forcing the Americans to withdraw to Oswego Falls (Fulton). The British suffered ninety-five casualties, and fearing there was a larger defending force nearby, withdrew. The British caused hardly any damage and the supplies were safe since they had been safely stored at Oswego Falls.

Determined to accomplish something worthwhile, Yeo then blockaded Sackets Harbor, which proved to be more of an inconvenience to Chauncey, the defending commander, since he was expecting guns and cable for new ships being completed on the ways. These heavy and cumbersome items required lake transport, and, as luck would have it, Captain Woolsey appeared at the appropriate moment, and suggested that nineteen batteaux row the thirty-four guns and ten heavy ship cables from Oswego to Stoney Creek, which was done during the night of May 28.

At sunrise the next day they were off Big Salmon Inlet, eight miles short of Sackets, when the British spotted them. Eighteen boats hid up Big Sandy Creek, but one boat didn't make it to shore, and was captured. Yeo sent 180 men up the creek to capture the rest, but Woolsey had expected them and prepared an ambush, which killed eighteen British tars and wounded fifty. Most of the load was taken the rest of the way by ox carts, except for one cable which had a diameter of seven inches and weighed 9600 pounds requiring many husky men to carry the cable on their shoulders the remaining distance to the ship.

ROPE WALK
HERE ROPE WAS MANUFACTURED IN 500 FOOT LENGHTS. IT WAS USED ON THE ALBANY SCHENECTADY R.R.

Wayne County, 12
County road, ½ m. east of Palmyra

In the early autumn of 1814, General Brown was about to invade Canada through the Niagara Peninsula, while in the east General Prevost was waiting for the right set of circumstances to attempt an invasion down Lake Champlain to take Plattsburg. Brown and Winfield Scott won their initial battle at Chippewa, but because of Chauncey's stubborn refusal of naval support, they lost the bloody battle of Lundy's Lane, where both Brown and Scott were wounded, and the invasion failed.

The Americans fell back to Fort Erie, at the mouth of the Niagara River, and resisted a siege by ever-increasing British forces. Because of their precarious position, authorities in Washington ordered Major General George Izard at Plattsburg to march to their aid. Izard drove his men over four hundred miles of difficult terrain to Batavia in just twenty-nine days. The Americans assessed the situation, evacuated and blew up Fort Erie, and retired to the American side. The confrontation became a stalemate so that there was no chance of pushing the "invasion" of Canada further, and Izard's men spent the winter in Black Rock, Batavia, and Buffalo.

At Lake Champlain, the departure of Izard and his men from Plattsburg triggered the British into action. The 10,000 man army, composed mostly of Wellington's veterans of the Peninsular wars, rapidly moved south into the U.S. Brigadier General Alexander Macomb was left to defend the approaches to Plattsburg with woefully inadequate forces. He had 3000 men, but only 1500 of these were effectives. On the British side, experienced and successful army officers resented General Prevost's insistence on spit-and-polish discipline, to the point that uniforms had to be immaculate, even in the heat of a campaign. Prevost was also overly cautious, as was his colleague, the British naval commander, Captain George Downie. Downie was needed to assist the army in taking Plattsburg, but he needed more time to fully prepare his squadron of four ships, twelve gunboats, and about nine hundred men for a successful move, particularly his brand new flagship, the Confiance.

Captain Thomas Macdonough, American veteran of the naval battles at Tripoli in 1803, commanded from his flagship, the Saratoga, a squadron of almost equal force and firepower, in a favorable position guarding Plattsburg Bay. The British army delayed making its final assault until Downie was finally prepared for action, and four days passed before he was ready September 11th to make his move on Macdonough's ships. The winds were light and variable making it difficult for the opposing ships to get into position to deliver their broadsides. Firing began and Downie was soon killed in the action with confusion on both sides. By anchoring and winching his ship around to the right position, plus a little luck, Macdonough was able to fire a withering broadside at the Confiance so that she struck her colors. He then winched the Saratoga to fire at the brig Linnet, which gave up in fifteen minutes.

On shore the British regulars made their move as soon as Downie acted. They advanced quickly despite the American fire, crossed the Saranac River near it's mouth, and were about to scale the redoubt walls, when the order to withdraw was given by Prevost the moment he realized that the British naval squadron had hauled its colors. The Wellington veterans were disgusted and sick at heart but they fell back. The British invasion of the United States had failed. General Macomb reported that over three hundred British soldiers had deserted when they arrived on American soil. Albany and New York were greatly relieved of this threat from the north.

But two weeks earlier, the British managed to burn the Capitol, the White House, and several other government buildings in Washington, after winning a skirmish at Bladensburg, Maryland, five miles away. They continued to Baltimore and bombarded Fort McHenry and Fort Covington, but abandoned the idea of taking the city, and withdrew September 14. Francis Scott Key, an American lawyer who had gone to a British ship to obtain the release of a doctor captured in Washington, and had been detained overnight, watched the bombardment, and wrote how the "rockets' red glare...gave proof thro' the night that our flag was still there." The words were put to a British drinking song and, within the month, the song was performed at a local theater. It gained in popularity over the years despite rivals "Hail, Columbia" and "America", but it was not until 1931 that "The Star Spangled Banner" was adopted by Congress as our official national anthem.

SITE OF THE FIRST LOG HOUSE IN SCRIBA. BUILT 1804 BY MAJOR HIELSTONE TEMPORARY HOSPITAL FOR WOUNDED SOLDIERS 1814

Oswgo County, 34
US 104 at Scriba

In 1812, when it appeared that war would be declared, it had seemed futile to the Americans to consider any serious naval action on the high seas against the world's most powerful navy. The British had over a hundred frigates and an equal number of ships of the line, compared to the sixteen ships of the U.S. Navy, of which only seven were frigates. Even so, the British were fighting on most of the world's oceans, and delegated only a few ships to the lesser war with America. Their main concern was Napoleon and the survival of Europe, not this second nuisance war away from their home waters.

As small as its navy was, the United States had an enviable shipbuilding tradition and a large merchant fleet of which many were commissioned as privateers. The large number of privateers attacking British ships, and the quality of the naval and privateer ships and their crews startled the British by this vigor so that they had to deploy much more of their resources to the western Atlantic. By early November of 1812, privateers had captured 150 merchant ships in the Gulf of St. Lawrence area alone, and the Governor of Barbados in the Carribean complained of the infestation of privateers and their superior sailing abilities.

Throughout the war, the 500 commissioned privateers took as prizes 1300 ships of all kinds, including frigates. The fledgling U.S. Navy had its victories, too. The London Times reported the USS Constitution victory over the HMS Guerriére won by Captain Isaac Hull, and in the same issue, it reported the American surrender of Detroit by his uncle, General William Hull. At the end of the year, the Constitution, this time under the command of Captain William Bainbridge, a hero in the Tripolitan Wars with Squadron Commander Edward Preble, bested the HMS Java. The frigate United States, under Captain Stephen Decatur, another hero of Tripoli, took on and subdued the frigate Macedonian, resulting in one hundred British casualties compared to only twelve American.

QUALITY HILL GREEN
A COMPANY OF HORSE ARTILLERY DRILLED HERE DURING THE WAR OF 1812

Madison County, 37
NY 5, 2 m. west of Canastota

In early 1813, the Admiralty directed Admiral John Warren to blockade the U S coast, but the many small bays and inlets that Americans had sailed from for years were impossible to cover entirely. Warren was constantly criticized by the Admiralty and the British press with embarrassing stories of noted American navy ships, such as the USS Congress and the USS President, sailing undetected across the Atlantic and taking prizes in British waters. It was so bad that the Admiralty was hoping for a quick, significant battle victory to hush its critics.

They got it when Captain Broke of HMS Shannon, blockading Boston, actually issued a formal challenge to Captain James Lawrence of the frigate Chesapeake to a naval duel. Lawrence eagerly sailed from Boston (unaware of the challenge), and the two ships traded broadsides, causing severe loss of life and ship damage on both sides. Broke's crew boarded and took the Chesapeake even as the mortally wounded Lawrence gave his famous final command, which soon became a naval motto, "Don't give up the ship".

Due to the unexpected superior actions of the U S Navy and the privateers, increasingly more ships were requested of the Admiralty to enforce the blockade. The collapse of France freed up those ships, and made it possible to more fully man with competent sailors ships already on station. Admiral Warren was replaced by the more aggressive Vice Admiral Sir Alexander Cochrane in March 1814. The blockade now became very tight and, by the end of September that year, American exports dropped to $7,000,000, compared to $45,000,000 in 1811. Even small towns in Maine were attacked as far south as the Penobscot River, so that the region north to Canada was under British control. The British had ever in mind boundary changes to be made at the peace table.

In the south, Andrew Jackson had made a name for himself by defeating the Creek Indians, who were being armed by the British. The British wanted to cut off the Ohio and Mississippi River trade by taking New Orleans, thus gaining concessions and territory already being discussed at the peace table in Ghent. Jackson took Pensacola (against President Madison's orders), pleasing the Southern War Hawks who wanted Florida, discouraging British ambitions there. He continued on to New Orleans in December, building defenses to thwart the British forces under Major General Sir Edward Packenham, the Duke of Wellington's brother-in-law.

The final clash began January 8, 1815. The fighting was so close and deadly, both Packenham and his Major General Gibbs were killed, and their forces sustained 2500 casualties compared to seventy-one American. The surviving British commanding officer, General Lambert, opted to cut his losses and make a prudent retreat. A veteran of European fighting, he said the action of the army and the navy had been "arduous beyond anything I have ever witnessed". Lambert was able to complete his withdrawal by January 18th.

Andrew Jackson was the hero of New Orleans even though, unknown to the combatants, the Treaty of Ghent had been signed December 24th. The victory served to smartly end any hesitation by Britain, drained financially and emotionally by seemingly endless years of fighting Napoleon and the Untied States, to ratify the Ghent agreement to end the war.

The victory at New Orleans and the treaty with the most powerful nation in the world gave the neophyte United States confidence and a higher status with other countries. The treaty did not even deal with the original points of contention, impressment and neutral shipping rights. The British had conceded on the rights in 1812, but word had not reached the Americans until war had been declared. Impressment was no longer necessary to the British and was discontinued as a matter of policy after the war. The Indians were on the wrong side again; the settlement and development of central New York and the Northwest Territory continued unabated.

There were some inadvertent benefits of the war. The British coastal blockade prevented the importation of certain manufactured goods from overseas. Entrepreneurs in the United States began to manufacture these goods and so lessened America's dependence on foreign imports. The war also had created a demand for rifles and muskets far above the ability of gunsmiths to supply. Eli Whitney, who had gained his reputation inventing the cotton gin, contracted with the government to devise machines and an assembly line system to make gun parts in lots of ten thousand and so that any component part could fit interchangeably with any of the others and be assembled to make the whole gun - lock, stock, and barrel.

Thus came about the birth of mass production in this country, not merely of guns, but of nails, pins, clocks, pots and pans, farm equipment and the host of inventions that could more easily be manufactured to make life easier.

MCCORMICK REAPER MADE HERE IN 1846. SEYMOUR AND MORGAN BY BUILDING 100 REAPERS FOR CYRUS MCCORMICK BEGAN QUANTITY PRODUCTION OF REAPERS

Monroe County, 41
Market & Park Sts., Brockport

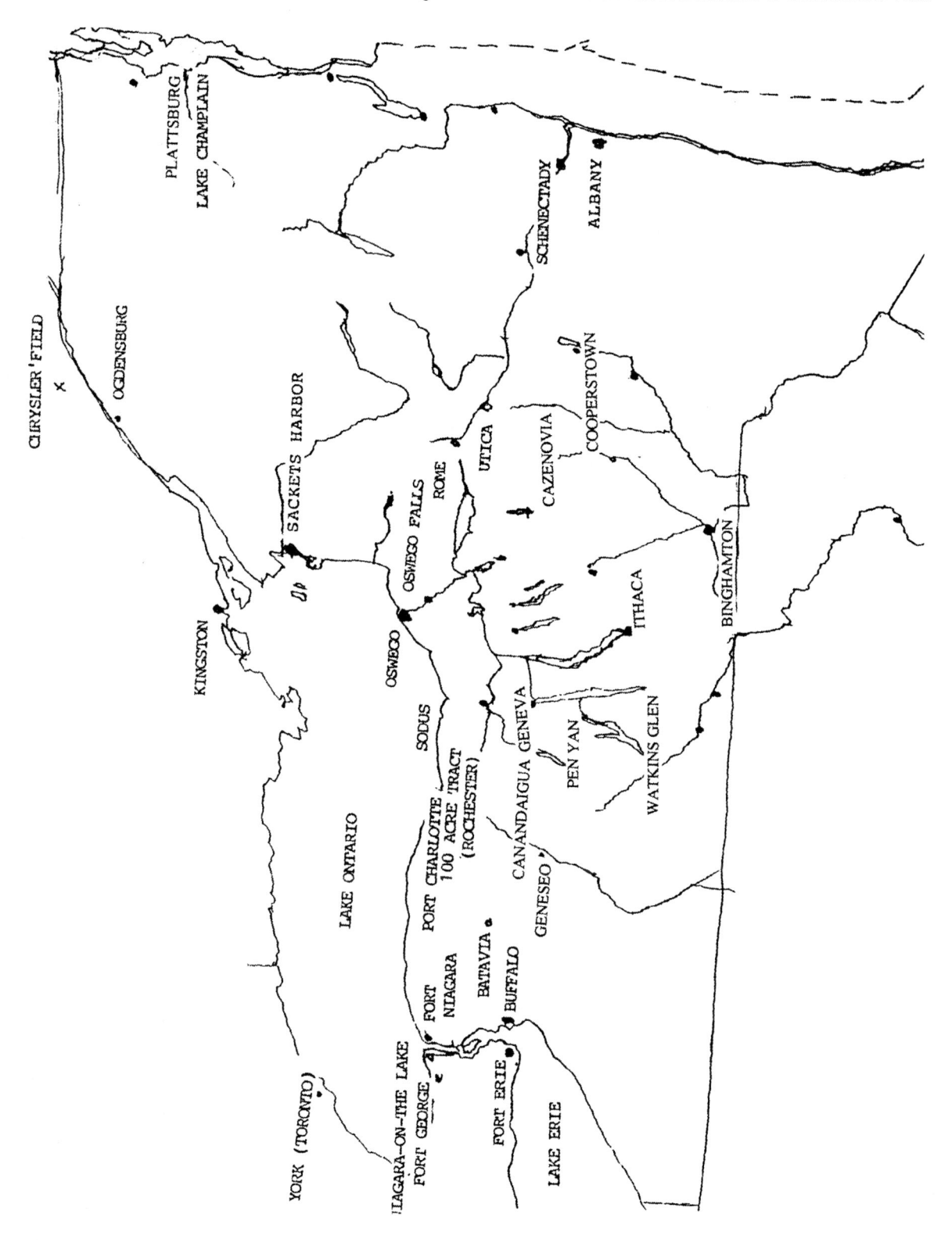

Sure Signs: Stories Behind the Historical Markers of Central New York

THE WAR OF 1812 IN NEW YORK.

CHAPTER FOURTEEN

In 1803, Thomas Jefferson wanted to acquire New Orleans from France as a place to unload goods shipped down the Mississippi for transhipment overseas. When Spain controlled the city, it had at times blocked this right of deposit, causing havoc with the economy west of the Appalachians. At the same time, black revolutionaries and yellow fever had decimated France's troops on the Caribbean island of Santo Domingo, damning any dreams Napoleon had of North American conquest and draining resources he sorely needed in his quest for empire in Europe.

To obtain funds, Napoleon decided to sell not merely the city of New Orleans but the entire territory of Louisiana which reached a thousand miles north, and almost as far west to the Rocky Mountains. The purchase amounted to 828,000 square miles and more than doubled the size of the United States, a bargain at only $15,000,000. Chancellor Robert Livingston was in Paris conducting these negotiations for President Jefferson when he met young and personable Robert Fulton, an expert gunsmith, artist, and inventor. Fulton was the perfect man to help him exploit the steamboat monopoly he had secured five years earlier and Livingston readily agreed to back Fulton in building an efficient and profitable steam-powered boat.

Steam engines, designed by James Watt in England, were becoming known in the United States but they had usually been used to power pumps for draining flooded mines overseas. John Fitch had made trial runs with his steamboat on the Delaware River at Philadelphia during the Constitutional Convention in 1787 and ran a ferry service on the river from Trenton to Burlington during the summer of 1790, but abandoned the project that fall because it didn't pay.

Fulton had made notes of William Symington's steam-powered tug boat in England, and used many of Fitch's ideas, some of James Rumsey's and John Stevens', all of whom were working on a practical steamboat, and he improved on them. He also had available advanced technology and more skillful artisans such as Paul Revere who installed the copper boiler used to power an English steam engine. The boat they completed was named the Clermont after the chancellor's Hudson Valley manor house.

SITE OF
FIRST STEAM
FLOURING MILL
WEST OF HUDSON RIVER
BUILT BY ROSWELL TOWSLEY
1817

Cayuga County, 81
SE. Corner of old stone ware-
House, Lyon property, Aurora

The Clermont was launched at New York with great fanfare and attended by many dignitaries to witness her historic cruise up the Hudson in August of 1807. One hundred fifty feet long, with a beam of 13 feet, she made the trip in 32 hours with the help of large paddle wheels on each side, the brainchild of partner Nicholas Roosevelt. The successful maiden voyage fulfilled the terms of the state-authorized twenty-year monopoly of steam navigation on state waters, but later it was contested on the Hudson by Captain Van Derbilt (sic) of the S.S. Bellona, and in the U.S. Supreme Court by Van Derbilt's employer, who was represented by Daniel Webster. When Chief Justice John Marshall announced the court's decision in Gibbon vs. Ogden in 1824, he held that monopolies are "repugnant to the Constitution and the laws of the United States". Fares were deeply reduced by the ensuing competition.

Flushed with the Clermont's success, Fulton and Livingston directed that Roosevelt move to Pittsburgh in 1809 and build the steamboat "New Orleans" to pioneer steam navigation down the Ohio and Mississippi. This was the same Nicholas Roosevelt, who with his brother, James, had bought, then sold, half of present-day Oswego County to co-owner, George Scriba. Since dabbling in real estate, Roosevelt had become a "mechanician" and engineer, and had worked on steam engines and boats with John Stevens at Hoboken. He also had designed and installed the stationary steam engines to power the pumps at the Philadelphia Waterworks designed by his employer, Benjamin Henry Latrobe, an artist, engineer, one of the country's first professional architects, and father of Latrobe's future fiancé, Lydia.

Howard S. Ford

Two years later, in 1811, Roosevelt, his much younger and pregnant wife, Lydia, and his two-year old daughter with only the crew (the ship was designed for seventy-five passengers) steamed down the mighty Ohio from Pittsburgh that fall on a journey momentous for them personally as well as for the country. To river habitués, canoes, batteaux, and flatboats were common craft. But this much larger boat, belching smoke and ejecting steamy clouds, and sporting large wheels churning the water on both sides and sounding like a Niagara, was a strange sight to red men and white alike.

While stopped at the Falls of the Ohio, (Louisville) waiting for higher water to enable them to run the cataract, their son, Henry Latrobe Roosevelt, was born. They resumed travel and steamed past the mouth of the Wabash unaware that General William Henry Harrison and his men had just won the battle against the Indians at Tippecanoe two hundred miles upstream. Indeed, the Roosevelts had to increase steam to outrun a canoe full of Indians furiously paddling to intercept them.

As they approached the confluence of the Ohio and the Mississippi Rivers, they experienced the most severe earthquake ever to disturb North America in historic times less than fifty miles away from its epicenter downstream at New Madrid, Missouri Territory. (One dislocation of this jarring upheaval is a section of the river blocked off to become Reelfoot Lake, in northwestern Tennessee, now a world-famous bass lake).

Navigating a river full of toppled trees, newly made sandbars, damaged keel boats, and choked and deranged channels during successive after-shocks almost scuttled this historic voyage. But the Roosevelts and crew were determined to succeed and were able to negotiate the massive rafts of flotsam which they didn't outdistance until they had passed Vicksburg, and arrived unscathed at New Orleans in January.

The "New Orleans" couldn't buck the current to return upstream to Pittsburgh, and so stayed in service on the lower Mississippi, as the owners had planned. Steamboats made such a difference in transporting people and goods that demand for them soared and so did improvements in their performance. In 1816, the "Washington" made the round trip between Louisville and New Orleans in thirty-seven days, twenty-five of which were necessary for the upstream passage. By 1840, the upstream trip was shortened to five and a half days.

Sure Signs: Stories Behind the Historical Markers of Central New York

Cornelius Vanderbilt, as a boy of sixteen, started ferrying passengers from Staten Island to Manhattan, and soon afterward, transported stores to the New York harbor forts in the War of 1812. He expanded his enterprise by running a steam packet from New York to New Brunswick for passengers to board the stagecoach for their final destination of Philadelphia. His wife operated Bellona Hall, a small popular tavern at the New Brunswick landing, which provided her a good income, much of which she saved to help her husband increase the number of steamboats in his operation.

After having had a hand in breaking Fulton's monopoly, Vanderbilt eventually controlled the local ferry and freight business, gaining for himself the loosely conferred title, Commodore. He was so successful that the Hudson River Steamboat Association paid him $100,000 and an annual fee of $5,000 to withdraw from the river trade. Years later, he had fleets of steamboats on both sides of the Atlantic and at San Francisco. During the Gold Rush of 1849, Vanderbilt set up a company In Nicaragua to forward freight across the isthmus to cash in on the race to the gold fields.

In 1819, the "Savannah", a combination full-rigged sailing ship and steamboat, crossed the Atlantic from Savannah to Liverpool in twenty-nine and a half days, with three and a half days under steam power. Steamboats were even starting to make regular runs up the Missouri River from St. Louis to the mouth of the Yellowstone River at Fort Benton by 1831. Screw propellers were first used in 1840 and became increasingly popular for their efficiency, except they could not be used on rivers such as the Mississippi and the Missouri where sand bars, sawyers, and snags could be a problem.

The first steamboat on the Finger Lakes was the "Enterprise" on Cayuga Lake in 1819. Skaneateles Lake saw its first steamer, the eighty foot "Independence", financed by Skaneateles Village and suitably launched July 4, 1831. Unfortunately, she and a second steamer on the lake, the forty foot "Highland Chief", also a sidewheeler, were uncomfortable and tippy in rough water. Within three years, both were converted to sailing ships for hauling timber on the lake. Not until 1848 was there another steamer on Skaneateles, a sidewheeler named the "Skaneateles", built to serve the new water cure sanitarium at Glen Haven and the landings and private camps being built.

SITE OF
CLARKTOWN
A NOW EXTINCT HAMLET WITH
WAREHOUSE, STORES, TAVERN
POTTERY, AND FERRY TO
LEVANNA ACROSS THE LAKE

Seneca County, 44
NY 89, 2 m. N of E. Varick

By 1836, three more ships were on Cayuga Lake, carrying passengers and towing barges loaded with lumber, potash, and gypsum. And so it was on all the Finger Lakes.

As roads were built and improved in the lakes region during the balance of the century, steamboat excursions slacked off. The burning of the S.S. Frontenac as it attempted to negotiate fifty-mile an hour winds near Farley's Point on the east shore of Cayuga Lake resulted in eight fatalities in July of 1907, and dampened the popularity of steamboats. This, despite the steamship line's exoneration of any fault; indeed, the personnel were found to be heroes, saving lives under extremely difficult conditions.

The automobile, which offered so many options for a day's outing or a vacation, such as to the Adirondacks, the Catskills, and the Thousand Islands, further eroded the numbers of those who took the fashionable excursions. The era of the commercial steamboat on the Finger Lakes was virtually over by 1915.

END OF TURNPIKE
WEST TO OLD BOAT LANDING
EAST THROUGH LANSING
'ENTERPRISE' FIRST STEAMBOAT
LAUNCHED ON LAKE 1820
ROUND TRIP TWO DAYS

Tompkins County, 59
Aurora & Lincoln Sts., Ithaca

CHAPTER FIFTEEN

The idea of an improved canal from the Hudson to Lake Ontario or Lake Erie gained impetus as the inadequacies of the Inland Navigation Company canals at Herkimer, Little Falls, and Rome became less tolerated. Judge Joshua Foreman and James Geddes of Onondaga, James Ellicott of the Holland Land Company, Robert Troup of Pulteney Associates, General Peter Porter of Black Rock, DeWitt Clinton, and Governeur Morris, distinguished Federalist statesman and first Canal Commission chairman, began to promote a much more substantial project.

The most persistent was DeWitt Clinton. He was the son of General James Clinton of the Sullivan campaign, and the grandson of Charles Clinton who was with John Bradstreet in the raid on Fort Frontenac in 1758. His uncle, George Clinton, also on the Frontenac raid, was the first governor of New York state and vice president under presidents Jefferson and Madison (1805-1812). Clinton was active in politics all his life, and especially interested in engineering and the natural sciences. When he took on a project he was tenacious, like a dog with a bone in its mouth, and not always too careful to avoid making enemies.

Opponents of the canal were generally from New York City and the southern tier who feared the competition for markets. Others felt it should only go as far west as Oswego, Lake Ontario would take people and cargo the rest of the way west, they said. But then it was realized that cargos from the upper lakes would likely gravitate to Montreal rather than Albany and New York if the lake was part of the system. In 1809, James Geddes was commissioned to explore the most level and least expensive route to engineer. His route, which exploited natural contours to minimize construction and operational costs, extended to Lake Erie and was accepted by the commissioners.

The War of 1812 diverted attention for three years, but made clear that exposure on the lake in any future war with Canada should be avoided; an inland route would also avoid the hazards of bad weather on the lake.

State political infighting marred the debate on the route to be followed and the financing. Both Jefferson in 1808, and Madison in 1811, were approached for federal funds: Jefferson thought the idea a hundred years ahead of its time, and Madison approved the idea but put it up to Congress, which because of the likelihood of war, let the proposal die in committee.

SITE OF
HOME OF
JAMES GEDDES. 1798
ERIE CANAL SURVEYOR, 1808
CHIEF ENGINEER 1816–1825

Onondaga County, 1
NY 5, 2 m. W. of Syracuse at Fairmont

Clinton's persistent persuasion began to tell, and the state politicians became so engrossed with the idea of connecting the Hudson with Lake Erie, that they agreed to have the state finance it, and the Canal Act was passed in April of 1817.

The easiest segment to build was from Utica to Montezuma, because it was the most level, would require fewer locks, and so would be the least expensive. It could then be put in operation sooner to generate revenues and build momentum for the completion of the remaining sections. So canal construction began in 1817, on the Fourth of July, as notable functions often did, with great ceremony a few miles west of Rome. Forty feet wide, four feet deep, and twenty-eight feet wide at the bottom, the first section was to be the experimental section where the technology would be learned by doing, there being few in this country possessed of canal engineering experience.

The canal itself proved to be an ad hoc "school" of engineering, turning out "graduates" such as James Geddes, Canvass White, John B. Jervis, Samuel Young, Nathan Roberts, and Benjamin Wright. Wright had the most experience, since he had worked under the English engineer, William Weston, on the Western Inland Lock Navigation Company's project twenty-five years earlier.

Contracts were let all along the line to established farmers or groups of men for sections as short as one-fourth of a mile enabling all to participate in the work. Special machines were contrived: one for pulling out trees by attaching a line near the top of the tree and winching it over and out, roots and all. Another, with a pair of sixteen-foot wheels on the same axle as a two foot drum wound with stout line and chain, and powered by a yoke of oxen, would exert eight-to-one leverage to pry out the larger stumps.

FIRST LIFT LOCK
THE FIRST LIFT LOCK TO BE CONSTRUCTED WEST OF LITTLE FALLS WAS BUILT HERE IN 1809 BY JONAS C. BALDWIN.

Onondaga County 26*
NY 31 & 370 at Baldwinsville

More than fifty contractors, each with their own men and equipment, were involved in the first fifty-eight miles of canal. Just getting the work gangs to their work site was a task, with few roads in the area, and no place to house them. Between 2000 and 3,000 men and 700 horses worked on the middle section during 1818-1819, grubbing, clearing, and excavating. As each contractor finished his section, it was filled with water to test for leaks before he received his final payment.

A blue mud found nearby was used for preventing seepage, and Canvass White, from Whitesboro, found a limestone near Chittenango which could be made into a cement that would cure under water. Early on, they learned that a specially designed root-cutting plow and a large scoop, pulled by many horses, was much more efficient than a spade and a wheelbarrow. Jeremiah Brainerd even improved the wheelbarrow to be lighter, more durable, and easier to dump its load than older models. Canal technology improved, and many reputations were made. The canal was such a technological achievement, that in the 1850s, it was used by Professor Amos Eaton of Rensselaer Polytechnic Institute, founded in 1824, as a training ground for civil engineering students, with a canal boat serving as the classroom.

The first or middle section was completed in 1820, resulting in a navigable stretch of ninety-four miles. Gypsum or grain could now be moved from Ithaca (or Port Byron, Syracuse, Watkins Glen, and Utica) to New York City and beyond, faster and less expensively than before.

Faced with limestone from Medina, the locks were fifteen feet wide by ninety feet long, and cost $1000 per foot of rise. They were essential, since they enabled boats to be raised or lowered as the canal confronted change in working elevation. There were eighty-three of them, climbing a combined rise and fall of 675 feet for the entire canal. Consisting of two pairs of gates ninety feet apart, they were an ingenious, but simple mechanism. The concept was not new, locks having been used in Europe for hundreds of years.

The gates were made of heavy plank, and had a small wicket near the bottom of each side for draining water, and a heavy beam bolted on top extending well over the curbing on either side to give additional leverage to the man pushing them open or closed. When closed, the gates formed an angle with the apex upstream so that the pressure of the higher head of water forced them tightly together allowing little leakage.

When a canal boat was towed into a lock to increase its elevation, the downstream gates were closed behind the boat, forming a compartment, since the upstream gates had already been closed to hold back the canal water. The wickets on the upper gates were then opened to fill the compartment at a controlled rate, and raise the canal boat to the same level as the upper reach of canal. The upper gates would be opened, and the canal boat could continue on its way, towed by the mule team on the tow path. A boat going opposite would then be led into the lock, the gate behind it closed, and the wickets in the downstream gate opened to lower the boat to the lower stretch.

The process took as little as three minutes either way, and it was not unusual for as many as 250 boats to go through a lock in a day. Water in the canal had to be continually replenished by gravity flow from feeder streams and nearby lakes and rivers. The excess was drawn off through waste weirs, and sold to mills nearby to run their equipment. Waste weirs also made it possible to draw down the water to make repairs, and to prevent ice damage in the winter.

With the first section finished and opened, the state authorized completion of the canal from Montezuma west to Buffalo, and from Utica east to Albany, and also the building of the Champlain Canal, from Whitehall on Lake Champlain to Fort Edward on the Hudson. The western section crossed the Seneca River over an aqueduct and passed through Lyons, Palmyra, Newark, and

Fairport. Another aqueduct was to be built to take the canal across the Genesee at Rochester. It consisted of nine masonry fifty-foot span arches over the river and two forty-foot arches over the mill canal, making a total length of 802 feet.

FIRST STEAMBOAT BUILT BY WM. AVERY 1 MILE SOUTH OF ORAN. LAUNCHED IN LIMESTONE CREEK NEAR BUELLVILLE, 1823, LATER FIRST STEAMBOAT USED ON ERIE CANAL

Onondaga County, 65
NY 92, ½ m. NW. of Oran

From there, the canal would follow Geddes' recommendation to parallel the Ridge Road (route 104) for about seventy miles, then turn south through the Tonawanda Swamp, and use Tonawanda Creek as the right-of-way to the Niagara River.

By October of 1822, the mostly Irish work crew had dug through the deathly malarial Montezuma swamps and the embankment above Irondequoit Creek and the relatively easy stretches to Rochester were completed. This made a hundred and eighty miles of operable waterway from Little Falls to Rochester. A year later, completion of the long stone aqueduct over the Genesee was celebrated, where twelve years before only a simple fording place in the wilderness existed.

In the same year, the difficult task of cutting a trench, seven miles long and twenty-seven feet wide for a double flight of five locks topping a sixty foot rise, was begun sixty-five miles west of Rochester. Two miles of this was solid rock which had to be blasted and carted away. They used the much more reliable Dupont's Blasting Powder manufactured by the fifteen year-old company founded by French emigrés. If it rained, blasting had to be delayed while the water was drained away. It was slow going, and while the work was proceeding, the cluster of support buildings grew to be the nucleus of the city of Lockport. In the meantime, the canal had been completed to the

Niagara River, and the western section could be opened as soon as the Lockport locks were installed and in satisfactory operation. They were at the end of June, 1825.

Work on the eighty-six mile eastern section to Albany began with the construction of an 1184 foot stone aqueduct north across the Mohawk to Little Falls, to connect with the important feeder from West Canada Creek there. The main canal led along the Mohawk south bank to the Schenectady-Albany section, where the valley narrows to a gorge with a drop requiring twenty-seven locks in the thirty miles. In addition, at Rexford, a 748 foot aqueduct took the canal north across the river; twelve miles farther east another aqueduct of 1188 feet brought it back again to the south bank.

All this was finished by October of 1823, as was the forty-mile Champlain Canal linking the St. Lawrence River through Lake Champlain with the Hudson. As each section was completed, it was opened to navigation and "ports" along the canal prospered, exceeding the expectations of the visionaries made years earlier. Settlement expanded more than ever, and the economic ripple-effect caused a boom along the new aorta of the state. Villages that had flourished because they were located on the Cherry Valley and Seneca turnpikes, now endured competition from the new towns on the artificial waterway, but, of course, all benefitted.

Political rivalry involving the canal continued, and in their attack on Clinton, his enemies had also attacked the canal, since he was so closely identified with it. When the canal was nearing completion and already producing revenues and increasing trade along its route, it no longer made political sense to be anti-canal. Clinton's rivals then attacked him directly in 1824, and the vote carried in the legislature to remove him from the canal commission.

The public was appalled, and responded the length of the state against the removal and insult to the man who, more than any other, had worked so hard in favor of the waterway now bearing fruit. A groundswell in favor of Clinton in his bid for a third term as governor won the election for him in 1824. Fortunately, it was in time for him to fittingly preside over the festivities and celebration of the completion of the entire canal in late October 1825. Clinton died in office in 1828.

Numerous celebrations had already taken place, usually when a new segment was opened to navigation. The largest to date was in June of 1825, when the Marquis de Lafayette, now sixty-eight, was completing his year-long tour of the country as a guest of the United States. His name was remembered world wide, not only for his heroic role in our Revolution, but because he had invested his fortune and his life in the intervening years fighting oppression in France thus becoming a thorn in the side of kings as well as Napoleon. He came through Buffalo by land until he passed the almost completed locks at Lockport. There, he boarded the elaborately furnished canal boat, "Rochester", and proceeded to that city, enjoying public ovations along the way.

SITE OF OLD HOTEL KEPT BY DR. BILDAS BEACH. GEN. LAFAYETTE STOPPED HERE JUNE 9, 1824.

Onondaga County, 46
NY 175 at Marcellus

Disembarking at Rochester to an elegant reception, he detoured to Canandaigua, Geneva, Auburn, Skaneateles, and Marcellus, returning to the canal at Syracuse. He noted the beautiful teams of horses generously given to the relays pulling his coach. His secretary cited the contributors, particularly Mr. de Zeng of Geneva, and Mr. Sherwood, proprietor of the stagecoaches at Auburn, and owner of a tavern at Skaneateles. The Marquis was celebrated overnight at Syracuse, and departed the next morning by canal boat as he was honored by an artillery salute.

Continuing on to Rome, Utica, Schenectady, and Albany, he was fêted at each location along the canal by approving crowds. Recognition of many of the men he had known almost fifty years earlier enlivened the festivities; there was mutual reminiscence when the Seneca sachem, Red Jacket, appeared on the platform and recalled when they had met at the 1784 Fort Stanwix Treaty. His tour ended at New York to the sound of the guns at the fort, named after him, rendering their final salute.

The celebration of the canal's completion was initiated October 26 at Buffalo with the launching of the canal boat "Seneca Chief", with Clinton and others instrumental in the canal's success on board. At that moment, a cannon at Buffalo was fired, and other cannon, spaced earshot apart along the canal and down the Hudson, were fired in succession. The "Echo Cannonade" took eighty minutes for the final cannon report to reach Sandy Hook, and eighty-one minutes for the acknowledgment to return in the same manner to Buffalo. Many boats, led by the Seneca Chief, stopped at any port where crowds gathered, town officials warmed to making speeches, the militia and band paraded to martial music, and later, a feast was served and long remembered.

Each stop was like a Fourth of July celebration, particularly at Albany where the procession received a twenty-four gun salute (one for each state), and where eight steamboats joined to escort the flotilla down the Hudson. The trip must have been exhausting for those who stayed with it the whole ten days to New York City. The climax of all this was the decanting of a barrel of Lake Erie water into the Atlantic Ocean off Sandy Hook to symbolize the "wedding of the waters". There were probably many other private decanting celebrations.

OLD ERIE CANAL COMPLETED FROM UTICA TO HERE IN 1819. THE 'MONTEZUMA' BUILT HERE WAS THE FIRST BOAT ON THE CANAL. TOOK PASSENGERS TO SYRACUSE 1820

Cayuga County, 98
Seneca River at Montezuma

Packet boat companies began to form, as each section neared completion, to offer quiet and comfortable canal travel to the public. The Erie Canal Navigation Company had the canal boats, "Chief Engineer" and "Montezuma", ready and in the water when the middle section was opened in 1820. Comfort Tyler, active in numerous enterprises in the area, was president of the company, and Simon N. Dexter, treasurer. By 1823, business was so good, that seven more boats were put in service.

To go from Utica to Rochester then took two full days and nights and cost $6.25.

On average, thirty to fifty passengers made the trip. In just one March to December season, one boat costing $1500 furnished made $6000 in earnings—a princely return. Naturally, others became interested and soon two other companies entered the business. To eliminate competition, a merger of the three companies was arranged, and the following year, another rival was bought out.

But monopoly was not to be permitted, and freight canal companies and stagecoach lines got into the canal travel business. By the end of 1824, fares had been cut 70%. In 1827, the fare on a packet boat was about four cents a mile; on a freight boat one and a half cents. Both fares included lodging but not board, compared to stagecoach travel at three-and-a-half cents per mile, which included neither room or board.

The building of canal boats also became one of the new industries, and packet boats and freighters were turned out by six companies in Rochester alone by 1827. The beam was limited to fourteen feet, leaving six inches clearance on each side when the boats went through the locks, and the average length was about eighty feet. Crude at first, the packet boats were increasingly built with comfort and good looks in mind, so that before long, they became "fairy palaces", as a Buffalo editor called them in 1836.

Pride in country gave names such as "Constitution", "Liberty", "Independence", "Tippecanoe" and "Ticonderoga" to the boats. An increasing sense of morality and reform assigned "Enterprise", "Truth", "Temperance", and "Civility" to the name plates for others to contemplate. A few boats had fine private and expensive accommodations; many others hauled freight as well as passengers, with one large cabin serving, as the day progressed, as dining room, lounge, and sleeping parlor, separating men and women by only a curtain to provide barely tolerable privacy. We see glowing accounts of deluxe facilities; others complaining of closeness with fellow passengers, small bunk beds, poor food, and delays.

If the weather permitted, passengers sat on the roof to leisurely enjoy the passing scenery, although when coming to a low bridge, everyone would have to scurry to the lower deck or be swept overboard. Stage lines and canal boat lines had to coordinate their schedules geared to a three to four mile per hour tow horse, and the inevitable waiting one's turn at the basins to move into the locks. But this gave passengers a chance for a welcome stretch and stroll. The age of the packet boat was eclipsed considerably in the early 1840s when the railroads completed track across the state.

However convenient it may have been for the passengers, the main reason for the canal was the cheap and quicker movement of freight. What had cost $100 a ton to ship between Buffalo and Albany now cost $7.00, and it took only seven or eight days to travel the 363 miles. Industry thrived, towns boomed in population, the standard of living increased enormously, and total land values increased by $100,000,000.

In a larger sense, the canal became the conduit for goods and people going to and from the Old Northwest, opening up the territories of western Pennsylvania, Ohio, Indiana, Illinois, Michigan, Wisconsin, Minnesota, and the province of Ontario. The canal was the engine that made New York the Empire State, and New York City the port and metropolis it became.

When construction first started, the Commissioner of Canal Funds floated the first bond issue in what had been a hesitant financial market; two years before, New York had issued its first major loan of $1,500,000 to pay for its expenses in the War of 1812. The canal bonds were to be repaid by tolls, special taxes on the refiners of salt, on steamboat fares, an extra tax on landowners within twenty-five miles of the canal, and other auctions and lotteries. Plans to collect lottery and land taxes were never implemented, and the steamboat taxes were dropped in 1820. Tolls collected from the operation of the first section of the canal far surpassed expectations, and an uncertain investment market became more enthusiastic in subscribing to later canal bond issues.

Tolls were first collected in 1820. They were based mainly on the weight of the boat and the cargo, and the weighlock stations at Albany, Syracuse, West Troy, Utica, Syracuse, and Rochester measured the weight hydraulically. The tolls amounted to $750.000, in 1826 and by 1831, to over $1,000,000 annually. The total cost of the Erie Canal, about $7,000,000, was paid off after eight years of full operation, including the cost of the Champlain Canal, and all the maintenance of both canals. Tolls were reduced several times after that and eventually eliminated.

The Erie Canal was so successful that lateral canals were built to stem the envy of adjacent communities. The canal from Syracuse to Oswego, was completed in 1828 to gratify those who fifteen years before had championed this route. Salt exports made it the most profitable of the laterals. The Chemung Canal, from Seneca Lake south to Elmira, and the canal joining Seneca Lake with Keuka, were completed in 1833. The Chenango Canal was built in two years so that by 1837, Binghamton was linked to Utica by way of New Hartford, Bouckville, Hamilton, Norwich, Greene, and Oxford.

CHENANGO CANAL AUTHORIZED 1833. UTICA TO BINGHAMTON COMPLETED 1836. 72 LOCKS IN 30 MILES ABANDONED 1876

Oneida County, 4
NY 26, Oriskany Falls

In 1829, the non-lateral Delaware and Hudson Canal, running from Honesdale, Pennsylvania, crossing the Delaware, thence to Kingston was completed to haul coal to an energy-hungry market and to placate downstate interests. Many of those engineers who learned their trade working on the Erie were involved. Legislation for the Genesee Valley Canal was passed in 1836, but construction from Rochester stopped at Mount Morris in 1841, and didn't resume to reach Olean and the Allegany River until 1856.

HINMANVILLE LOCK NO. 1 LOCATED NEAR HERE. LOCK TENDER'S HOUSE NEARBY. OLD OSWEGO CANAL COMPLETED 1828 IMPORTANT WATERWAY TO WEST

Oswego County, 32
CR. At Hinmanville

The laterals all added traffic to the main canal, but the increasing trackage of the infant railroads rendered them unprofitable, and they were abandoned, one by one, before the last quarter of the century began. The Black River Canal joined the North Country to Rome not until 1851, but it, too, was abandoned. Portions of it can still be seen along N.Y. routes 46 and 12. One small lateral at DeWitt is still supplied with water although inoperative except for a canoe now and then.

BLACK RIVER CANAL
SITE OF THE ONCE FAMOUS
FIVE COMBINES–WORLD'S RECORD
FOR NUMBER OF CANAL LOCKS
CANAL HAS 109 LOCKS IN 35 MILES
OF WATERWAY

Oneida County, 21
NY 46, at Pixley Falls Park

The success of the Erie Canal caused other states to follow suit, and a lacework of canals connected with and complemented the Erie, binding the northeast not only in trade, but as a national force. The province of Ontario built the Welland canal in 1829, from Lake Ontario to Lake Erie, just west of Buffalo, and far from cutting into traffic on the Erie Canal, it helped funnel traffic to it.

Traffic increased so much that the canal started to became clogged, and construction began anew in 1836 to enlarge the old Erie. The waterway would now have a width of seventy feet and a depth of seven; there would be two locks where one served before, and each lock enlarged to eighteen by a hundred and ten feet. Renovation took place at the same time, but these developments, delayed by business depressions and political wrangling, were not completed until 1863, in the middle of the Civil War. By 1858, the canal had lost much of its freight business to the railroads but continued moving bulky items like lumber, cement, and grain.

To better compete, the Barge Canal was begun in 1905. Not only did this widen the old canal, but the Rome to Montezuma portion was rerouted to cross Oneida Lake, and pass through Three Rivers to the Seneca River. The Erie and the Oswego Canal no longer meet in Syracuse but at

Three Rivers, and obsolete sections of the canals were filled in. What was once part of the "Old Erie", is now part of Syracuse's Erie Boulevard, still bustling, but with trucks, passenger cars, and buses, which do not evoke any degree of the charm we think of for the old canal days.

CAUGHDENOY LOCK CONSTRUCTED BY STATE OF NEW YORK 1841

Onondaga County, 7
CR at Caughdenoy

The Weighlock building is still there at that junction, renovated and serving as a Canal Museum to help us learn how we got to where we are now.

CHAPTER SIXTEEN

With the completion of the Erie Canal, traffic to the west diverted from the National Road, running from Baltimore to Wheeling (much of the same trail the ill-fated Braddock used seventy years earlier), and the leaders in Baltimore decided to build a railroad west to regain that business. The first stone was laid by the sole surviving signer of the Declaration of Independence, 91 year-old Charles Carroll, on July 4, 1828. It was a watershed from an older era to a new period of growth and expansion, as Carroll avowed in his speech to the crowd, and the birth of the Baltimore and Ohio Railroad.

The initial idea was for stagecoaches on flanged wheels to be pulled by horses over wooden rails, much as ore wagons had been used in mines for centuries. But the Baltimore and Ohio had an innovative engineer, Peter Cooper, who put a steam-pump engine, such as those used to pump out flooded mines, on a flat car, with a crank to turn the wheels. He ran this first U.S. built locomotive, the "Tom Thumb", (built by Cooper in his own foundry), over twenty-six miles of track, pulling several cars of journalists and company directors at twelve miles an hour to prove his point, that steam-powered land travel could be fast and practical.

A year earlier, Horatio Allen had brought back from England (where they already had five years of railroad experience) an English locomotive, the "Stourbridge Lion", to run on a rudimentary track at Honesdale, Pa. for the Delaware and Hudson Canal Company. This run was also experimental, the engine proving to be too heavy for the track and terrain. But the genie was out of the bottle, and others became interested in the exciting business of moving people and freight around the country more rapidly and comfortably than ever before.

The first regular paying steam railroad went into service on Christmas Day, 1830, as the South Carolina Canal and Railroad Company, at Charleston. Horatio Allen was hired away from Pennsylvania as chief engineer (he became president of the Erie Railroad years later). The "Best Friend of Charleston" was the name of the engine made at Cold Spring, New York, by the West Point Foundry. "The Best Friend" resembled four wheels supporting a horizontal tank behind an oversized upright wine bottle (the boiler and smoke stack). It pulled five coaches packed with 141 passengers and "flew on the wings of the wind", said the Charleston Courier.

The "Best Friend" blew up in less than a year (because the "annoying" safety valve had been tied down by the fireman) but, undaunted, Allen extended the track to the head of navigation on the Savannah River in order to intercept business from its trans-Atlantic steamship company and the worthy competition there.

LINE OF
ITHACA & OWEGO R.R.
INC. 1828
SECOND CHARTERED IN STATE
OPERATED BY HORSEPOWER
FOR FIRST SIX YEARS

Tioga County, 6
NY 223, village of Candor

In 1830, John Stevens and his son, Robert Livingston Stevens, built a railroad using English-made iron rails and the English locomotive, "John Ball", from Perth Amboy to Trenton which displaced the stagecoach and increased business to their ferry-boat line between New York and New Jersey. By 1870, this rail line, extending from Hoboken to Camden, was leased to the Pennsylvania Railroad.

The section of the Erie Canal between Schenectady and Albany was the most troublesome and time consuming for the passage of passenger and freight because of its many locks. The shrewd leaders in those cities decided to compete with the tediously slow moving traffic of the canal by building the Mohawk and Hudson Railroad from Albany to Schenectady. It was to use steam engines, but the track was laid on fifteen-inch square stone blocks for the purpose of leaving a three-and-a-half-foot path between the rails to enable a horse to pull a car in an emergency.

The first engine, the "DeWitt Clinton", was designed by John Jervis (of Erie Canal fame), and built by West Point Foundry. The large boiler and firebox was horizontal and connected to the thick vertical stack in front. In August of 1831, it pulled a tender and three specially-fitted stagecoaches, crammed full of stockholders and politicians, over the fifteen mile track in less than an hour.

The officers of the line learned that couplings between cars should not be chains because on starting, stopping, or any variation in speed, they jerked the cars, particularly the last one, throwing passengers to the floor. They also found that flame arresters on the chimney should be installed to keep the ladies' parasols and men's beaver hats from catching fire from live cinders, and that the engines should have more power to climb the inclines.

After some minor changes, the management scrapped the "Clinton" entirely and obtained an English locomotive nicknamed the "John Bull" which ran better than the Clinton but had trouble tracking, particularly on curves, causing track damage. Jervis rebuilt the engine and invented a four-wheeled swiveling truck or "bogie" to mount under the front of the engine, and moved the drive wheels back for better balance. This made all the difference in the conformation of the wheels with the track and resulted in a smoother ride.

The inmates at the new Sing Sing prison could not produce enough stone blocks to keep up with the demand, so Jervis substituted wooden cross-ties as a temporary measure. They proved to be much better and were used from then on. The wooden rails had been reinforced on top with an iron strap nine-sixteenths of an inch thick. But the straps had a bothersome habit of coming loose and curving upward to pierce the floor of the passing passenger cars. The strapping was made thicker to eliminate the "snake-heads". This expedient was not satisfactory either, and it was a boon to the adolescent iron industry when the railroads went to all-iron rails a few years later. Robert Livingston Stevens designed the hook-headed spike, still used today, to hold the "T" rails, also his design, to the wooden ties.

Another simple but important innovation came about when a train couldn't get traction because of swarm of grasshoppers made the rails slick. A nameless genius put a container full of sand on top of the boiler with tubes running down either side to a position in front of the drive wheels. Sand could now be tripped onto the track to help climb a steep grade, or whenever more of a grip was needed.

The State of New York, in order to retain toll traffic on its money-making Erie Canal, imposed a tariff on freight carried by the competing railroads equal to the canal toll. The state also mandated that the maximum passenger fare would be four cents a mile. But by 1847, these and other restrictions were removed.

Other lines started up to complete the rails west across the state: the Utica and Schenectady was completed in 1836 and the Syracuse and Utica, connecting those cities, ran its first train down the track in the middle of Washington Street in down-town Syracuse soon afterwards where it remained in operation for almost a hundred years. The Auburn and Syracuse Railroad followed the same year and in 1839 horses were replaced by steam locomotives on that line.

UTICA CLINTON & BINGHAMTON R.R. FORMED 1862. COMPLETED FROM UTICA TO TERMINATE AT THIS SITE 1858 EXTENDED SOUTH 1871

Oneida County, 2
Broad St. Oriskany Falls

Most rail lines paid little attention to conforming track width to a standard gauge, with the result that passengers had to change trains, freight had to be transhipped, and, of course, train schedules did not match up either. It was either luck or cooperative planning that the track gauge on all the contiguous lines across the state was four feet nine inches so that there could be through-trains and inter-company use of equipment. Not until the mid-1880s was a standard gauge of four feet eight-and-a-half inches generally adopted, largely because of the transcontinental railroad specifications that had been ordered by the federal government.

The Tonawanda, the Lockport and Niagara Falls, the Buffalo and Niagara Falls, and the Schenectady and Troy, all began about the same time following the Utica, Syracuse, Auburn, and Rochester lines. They connected to each other, making a road across the state, so that by 1853, it made sense to merge them all into one larger line. Erastus Corning, who had been president of the Utica and Schenectady for twenty years, was elected to head the new company, the New York

Central. The main line was rebuilt from Syracuse to Rochester, bypassing the Auburn section, so that the whole system closely paralleled the Erie Canal.

ITHACA OWEGO R.R.
SECOND CHARTERED IN STATE
INC. JUNE 28, 1828
CROSSED THE VILLAGE PARK
TO TERMINUS ON
SITE OF AHWAGA PARK

Tioga County, 28
NY 17, Owego

Corning and eight other speculators had formed a land company in 1835, to buy 350 acres on the Chemung River to exploit the Chemung Canal spur at the small village there. The town of Corning takes its name from him, even though he visited the place only once, and that was not until twenty years after the investment. (The Corning family over many years has been preeminent in business and politics. Among Corning's descendants was another Erastus Corning, who was mayor of Albany for forty years beginning in the mid-1940s, reprising his ancestor's role a century earlier).

CITY OF CORNING
ERASTUS CORNING AND OTHERS
BEGAN A COMMINITY HERE IN
1835. IT INCORPORATED AS A
VILLAGE IN 1848 AND AS A
CITY IN 1890.

Steuben County

The New York and Erie Railroad was chartered in 1832, and began construction three years later at the official ceremony at Deposit. The road was to extend westward from the lower Hudson

River to Dunkirk on Lake Erie. The construction crew worked its way up the Delaware River shore, blasting cliff faces next to the water to make a footing for their right-of-way after laying track from Piermont to Port Jervis. They continued through Binghamton, Corning, and Hornell, where they located the road's repair and maintenance shops, finally reaching Dunkirk after boom, bust, and politics, in 1851.

Work had been occasionally delayed because of financial as well as engineering problems. When the road wanted to cross the Seneca Reservation, the Indians showed they had learned the white man's ways, and extorted $10,000 from them for the right-of-way privilege.

OWEGO
BIRTHPLACE OF ERIE
HERE WAS HELD CONVENTION
DECEMBER 20, 1831
TO FURTHER THE CHARTER OF
NEW YORK AND ERIE RAILROAD

Tioga County, 30
NY 96, Erie crossing, Owego

Two trains, with 300 notables aboard to celebrate the completion of the line, proceeded from Piermont to run the entire 483 miles of track. President Millard Fillmore, Governor Marcy, and former governors Seward and Fish, were included in the officiating party as was Daniel Webster, who insisted on having his rocking chair strapped to a flat car at the end of the train so he could enjoy the scenery. It reminds one of Frontenac being carried around the Oswego River falls during his last raid.

The Erie served the southern tier as the New York Central served the Mohawk Valley and the central region. The Lehigh Valley Railroad, the Lackawanna, the Syracuse and Binghamton, the Buffalo and Cohocton, (serving Corning to Batavia), the Attica and Hornellsville, the Rome and Watertown, and many smaller lines competed for the connections in between.

The stagecoach type car began to evolve into a form of its own, not unlike present passenger cars, with a center aisle and seats facing forward. Lengthening the cars not only increased the number of passengers they could carry, but the longer wheel-base virtually eliminated the forward pitching and made for a more comfortable ride. An iron wood-burning stove provided heat, making conditions too hot close by and too cold elsewhere, but people's homes at the time had the same limitations. Charles Dickens, commenting on his visit to the United States in 1841 in his **American Notes,** dourly said the passenger cars resembled a "shabby omnibus".

By 1840, 200 companies nationwide had laid over 3000 miles of track. Chicago was connected with the east coast by 1853, and the Mississippi River was crossed three years later. Lawyer Abraham Lincoln, represented the Illinois Central in a case that involved a boating accident at one of the bridge piers, used evidence prepared by engineer Robert E. Lee to successfully support his case that the railroads had the right to bridge rivers. The first fatality occurred in 1833, when an axle broke, killing two people. Ironically, former President John Quincy Adams and Cornelius Vanderbilt were passengers; Adams was not injured but the Commodore was, and he avoided trains for thirty years.

Boilers and steam cylinders were enlarged and more drive wheels were added to increase power and speed. Connecting rods and fascinating linkages tied this burgeoning power together for a smoother ride. By 1850, a cowcatcher that looked like a large mustache was put in front of the engine to deflect wandering animals, and a covered cab was added for the comfort of the engineer. Oil burning glass-enclosed headlights and diamond shaped smokestacks, designed to arrest cinders billowing out the stack from the burning wood, all contributed to the appearance of the powerful behemoth coming to be known as the steam locomotive. Many farmers payed off their mortgages by cutting firewood and cross ties for the railroads and poles for stringing the new telegraph lines.

The engine was topped off with a whistle that echoed across the countryside to catch the attention of anyone within earshot. In the 1850s, ornamentation became popular, as was the case with canal boats, with bright enamels, polished brass, gold leaf, and sporting names like "John Hancock", the "General", or "Empire State".

Mail delivery in the early days was at the expense of the receiver if he chose to pay for the message sent him. When in 1847 the U.S. postal system adopted postage stamps, either adhesive or embossed, the onus was changed and the sender paid for the delivery of his letters. The new arrangement saved officials the expense of sending mail out and back again if rejected by the intended receiver. It also became popular and greatly increased the revenue of the postal service. Contracts to deliver the mail could be quite lucrative, so the use of the trains to transport the mail became an important source of income to the railroads. This same year, 1862, was doubly good for the railroads because President Lincoln signed the bill authorizing a continental link.

When the Union Pacific RR linked up with the Central Pacific RR completing the transcontinental railroad, the country's dinner tables had a more varied menu—such as, but not limited to, fresh vegetables and salad materials in the wintertime, oranges, tangerines, lemons, and grapefruit from California, and salmon from Oregon.

Locomotives grew to behemoths of seventy tons, and between 1867 and 1876, sleeping, dining, and parlor cars designed by George Pullman's company changed rail travel from a tedious chore to a pleasant experience. Because of the heavier trains, steel rails were beginning to be used by 1863 and coal became, more and more, the preferred fuel because of its higher BTU content. Later, engines were known by numbers like old "999", and entire trains were designated with notable titles such as "Twentieth Century", "Commodore Vanderbilt", and the "Broadway Limited".

Every town had its train station, quite often attractive and reminiscent of Swiss chalets with long sloping roofs, and overhangs of as much as ten feet to keep waiting passengers dry. The ticket office also served as a telegraph station for notice of train arrivals, delays, and news of the hour for passengers and hangers-on in the waiting room. Telegraph lines used the railroad's right of way because it made sense, was mutually beneficial, and served to improve safety and later, operate switches, semaphores and other equipment. City depots often varied in design and size, but huge roofs covered many tracks an impressive length, as did Syracuse's Vanderbilt Station.

The Civil War halted track expansion, but the North already had 22,000 miles of track compared to the South's 9,000. Both armies used the trains to move large numbers of men and supplies quickly over long distances, and both did their best to destroy the other's track and rolling stock.

Sherman's army of 100,000 men and 35,000 animals required 16 ten-car trains a day to bring supplies from Louisville to Georgia. The North and its commanding railroad system, and the technology and manufacturing capacity that went with it, contrasted with the predominantly agricultural South. The resulting economic difference between the two regions was a major cause of the Civil War, and, at the same time, one of the main reasons why the Union prevailed.

After the war, car builders agreed to make standardized passenger and freight cars. In 1869, the New York Central merged with the Hudson River Railroad. Cornelius Vanderbilt and his son William had operated that line and others with such startling success that, when the Vanderbilts became associated with a company, the stock soared. Under them, the "Water Level Route" represented the powerful company whose main line of four tracks extended from New York City to Chicago and beyond.

The 1880s saw several improvements in general usage; notably air brakes that had been patented by George Westinghouse in 1872, steam heat using locomotive- heated water to circulate to the passenger cars, and refrigerator cars made more efficient by employing salted ice.

In stagecoach days, the uncertainties of travel made it impossible to know destination time any closer than to the nearest hour. The better railroads could pinpoint their schedule to the nearest minute, and were proud to live up to it. But time across the country was reckoned differently. For example, the Buffalo depot had three clocks: one set to Buffalo time, one for the New York Central set for New York City time, and the third set to Columbus, Ohio time for the Michigan Southern.

Standardization was the only way to avoid chaos, and a system of five time belts, from the Maritime provinces in Canada to the west coast of the United States, was agreed to in 1883. The plan provided that when it was eight in the morning in New York City, it was now eight a.m. everyplace in the eastern time zone, even though the sun was fifty-nine minutes higher in the sky in Eastport, Maine, than it was, say, in Toledo, Ohio, at the western edge of the same zone.

The railroads not only provided transportation, but a diversion to the public as Jay Gould, James Fisk, Daniel Drew, and later, Commodore Vanderbilt, and others fought for control of the New York Central, the Erie, and the Lehigh Valley and other strategically located lines using fair methods and foul.

Sure Signs: Stories Behind the Historical Markers of Central New York

In the spring of 1851, over 2,000 people from the Susquehanna River towns met at Oneonta to organize the Albany and Susquehanna Railroad Company, and bring themselves out of rural isolation. Enthusiasm was such that residents and municipalities alike subscribed to the capital stock of the company. The New York legislature also granted funds. Oneonta, Bainbridge, Unadilla, Sidney, Windsor, Cooperstown, Otego, and Harpursville chipped in and would all benefit. By the summer of 1867, the track had been laid south to Bainbridge, and by Christmas, the railroad was operating west to Harpursville. Completing the remaining line from there to Binghamton, including a 2200-foot tunnel through solid rock, took another year.

Railroad robber barons, James Fisk and Jay Gould, had just nefariously gained control of the Erie, including the road facilities in Binghamton, and were eager to extend the line to Albany. They quickly bought up shares from the towns, claimed majority ownership, and sought legal sanction to operate the road, to the dismay of company management, which also received legal authority to stay in control.

But legal authority seemed insufficient to both sides. The Fisk-Gould forces sent a trainload of toughs north from Binghamton and the company sent a train south from Albany to intercept them. The Fisk locomotive was maliciously derailed when it arrived at the Bainbridge yards that evening, but this did not end the fracas. The next day, the action moved west down river as each side marshaled more men, and their own train for a second confrontation. Both trains drove headlong and collided near the tunnel, where the yelling and cudgel-wielding men spilled out to settle things on a more personal level. Eventually, a regiment of New York State militia arrived to separate them, and the physical clash was over.

Contending in the courts continued for several years, but the company was unyielding. It finally won with J.P. Morgan, a major factor in rail companies, being enlisted by Erie President, Joseph A. Ramsey, to keep Jay Gould from unseating the legitimate directors of the company in a turbulent proxy fight. Management then extended the track to Plattsburgh and Montreal and leased the line to the Delaware & Hudson Canal Company which ran it to become one of the most active freight carriers nationally. The line carried coal from Pennsylvania north to Canada, and heavy rolls of newsprint from Canada and the Adirondacks south to cities in the United States.

On a smaller but more dangerous scale, some individuals saw the trains as a new venue for armed robbery. Jesse James and his gang entranced the nation by robbing the mail and train passengers in the mid-west. But central New York had some excitement of its own in the early 1880s caused by a lone gunman, Oliver Perry, a brakeman for the N.Y. Central. His first robbery attempt downstate was so successful that some speculated that it was pulled off by one of the Dalton, or James gang. His next attempt, six months later, was the stuff on which were based the early train-robbery movie melodramas.

Getting aboard a westbound train at Syracuse, he waited until the train passed Weedsport and the guard was preoccupied before climbing down from the roof on his rope ladder to the door of the express car which he knew was unlocked. Mask in place, he entered the car. As the guard attempted to draw his gun, Perry fired a shot and winged him. The conductor pulled the brake cord for the train to slow, but Perry forced him at gunpoint to wave the engineer to resume speed.

The train halted at the next stop of Port Byron, where the crew saw to the wounded guard but could not find the robber. It stopped again at Lyons, where a trainman became suspicious of a furtive, possibly fugitive, man in the crowd. When questioned, Perry drew his gun and commandeered a nearby freight train that was about to get underway. Menacing the crew to vacate the train, he uncoupled the engine to speed away down one of the four tracks of the Central's main line. The startled trainmen armed themselves, uncoupled the express engine from its cars, and pursued on an adjacent track.

Perry was wily, and soon reversed his locomotive to speed by his pursuers in a quick exchange of shots. Several times he tried this maneuver, but could not shake off the relentless and unencumbered locomotive from closing the gap between them. Soon, he realized that his engine was running out of steam and stopped, hopped out, and made a break for it cross-country. Seeing this, the trainmen returned to Lyons, and arranged for a posse of locals who knew the territory. Before long, they caught up with Perry and brought him to heel. Perry admitted his guilt, and was sent to Auburn prison.

Due to his behavior there, he was considered insane and transferred to Matteawan prison from which he soon escaped with three others. Captured again, this time he intentionally blinded himself in his cell, causing a second transfer to Dannemora, then thought to be the "Siberia" of New York prisons. He led a hunger strike, was force-fed for four years and, in all, spent 49 years in prison where he died in 1930.

In 1893, a few years after Perry's fateful escapade, the brand-new 62 ton number 999 locomotive designed by William Buchanan, Superintendent of Motive Power for the New York Central, was put into service at Albany in hopes of breaking the world speed record. The engine was an enlarged version of the typical American 4-4-0 (four small wheels on the bogie forward, followed by four large drive wheels and no truck wheels aft) of a type in use as recently as the 1930s. It developed 190 pounds per square inch force on the pistons to drive the eighty-six-inch wheels (later reduced for regular service), which the Central was assured would achieve a new speed record, even with four passenger cars and a tender in tow. Testing the engine's power on the run along the Mohawk River before coming into Utica, engineer Charles Hogan was more than satisfied.

When the train approached the long straight stretch west of Batavia and the white ball was displayed high on the pylon signaling a clear track ahead, Hogan again opened up the throttle to "highball it" and fireman Ike O'Dell shoveled frantically to feed the maw of the firebox. In response the locomotive surged. Hogan and O'Dell were able to attain and maintain an authenticated speed of 112.5 miles per hour, almost two miles a minute, more than enough to enable the central to bask in glory against all comers for some time.

The "999" was the first man-made machine to exceed 100 m.p.h. The previous record of 89.5 m.p.h. was made three years before and "999"s achievement was not bettered until 1903, when a German electric-powered locomotive attained 130 m.p.h.

CHAPTER SEVENTEEN

Ebenezer "Indian" Allen had been an officer in the British army dealing with the Indians in the Genesee River area. He was an expert woodsman, a philanderer, an un-convicted murderer, and an all around rogue. When the Revolution was over, he stayed in the region, living with his two squaws along the river at Squawkie Hill near Mount Morris. One winter, when having difficulty with his two wives, he stayed at Gardeau flats with Mary Jemison. In 1786, he built a cabin where the Oatka joins the flow of the Genesee (Scottsville), but three years later sold it to Peter Schaeffer.

FIRST HOUSE
WEST OF GENESEE RIVER
STOOD 1700 FEET DUE SOUTH
'INDIAN' ALLEN, BUILDER, 1786
PETER SCHAEFFER, SETTLER, 1789
FIRST TOWN MEETING 1797

Monroe County, 35
Scottsville-West Henrietta Road

Then land agent Oliver Phelps offered Allen one hundred acres of rattlesnake-infested swampland and river frontage above the upper falls if he would build a saw mill and gristmill for the expected onrush of settlers. Phelps had persuaded the reluctant Senecas to part with an additional tract of 12 by 24 miles on the west side of the lower Genesee, known as the Millyard Tract, by offering to provide the mills for the grinding of their grain and sawing their timber.

Allen built the mills in 1789, but business didn't materialize because prospective settlers were fearful of the Indian problem at that time, so he neglected the mills and finally abandoned them.

Allen's brother-in-law, Christopher Dugan, was custodian of the mills for a short time, followed by the Sprague family, who were succeeded by Colonel Josiah Fish and family. The Fishes were honored by having the first white child born in the area around the turn of the century and by hosting a royal refugee from the French Revolution. Count de Maulevrier, stayed the next night with the

Peter "Sheffers" whose descendants are still there at Scottsville. The Count did not care for the accommodations at either place. Soon afterward, the Fishes succumbed to the bad air (malaria) from the swamps and their survivors moved away.

CASCONCHIAGON INDIAN VILLAGE AT THE FALLS NEARBY. OCCUPIED BY SENECAS UNTIL 1819

Monroe County, 26
Maplewood Park, N. of Driving Park

Zadock Grainger, Gideon King, and Elijah Kent and their families moved from Connecticut, in 1797, after buying from the Phelps-Gorham syndicate 3000 acres the year before on the west side of the Genesee. They sent word back home to relatives and friends, who came to join in the building of King's Landing at the foot of the lower falls where unobstructed access to Lake Ontario offered expectations of a thriving and protected shipping point. Ships and wharves were built with a store on the flat and a road angled into the bluff to the heights above. This hope was nipped in the bud by the same Genesee fever which killed off these enterprising people. In 1809, Frederick Hanford built a tavern there, and now Hanford's Landing thrived for a few years before the competition from Charlotte at the river mouth eclipsed its growth.

On the other side of the river from Hanford's Landing was an equally high bluff, below which extended a level trail alongside the river that was made into a towpath to convey ships to the lake if the wind wasn't right for getting under way.

This competitive edge gave Carthage's early promoters, headed by Elisha Strong, the idea to press their advantage and build a 712 foot wooden bridge to span the gorge below the lower falls and link up the Ridge road, east and west. The engineering marvel was finished in 1819 and greatly facilitated the increased traffic.

Howard S. Ford

Unfortunately, the construction was faulty. The numerous trusses crashed 190 feet to the river below only fifteen months later, and the heavily mortgaged entrepreneurs crashed with it. It is not known if anyone was on the bridge.

The first bridge over the Genesee was built at Avon, in 1804. The second was built at the 100 Acre Tract in the spring of 1812, just before war was declared. At that time Hamlet Scrantom arrived from the North Country to become the first permanent settler. His earlier years along the Black River must have rendered him immune to the Genesee fever, enabling him to live to 1851, when he died at age seventy-eight.

Finally, the 100 Acre Tract ended up in the ownership of Colonel Nathaniel Rochester, a well-to-do gentleman from Hagerstown, Maryland and partners Charles Carroll and William Fitzhugh, also from the south. They had bought this and other land from Charles Williamson at the turn of the century, attracted by the waterpower potential, but deferred moving there for some time. Then, in 1810, Rochester moved north to property he had bought at Dansville, with his wife and nine children and his slaves and other possessions. Rochester was fifty-eight at the time, but confident of starting anew in this new opportunity.

His credentials boasted considerable business success, and he even had an English coat of arms going back to 1558, the year Elizabeth I became Queen. One wonders what part his ancestor had, if any, in helping the daughter of Henry the VIII and Ann Boleyn to survive those dangerous years before she could wear the crown.

Rochester moved to the Genesee Valley to bring his many children to a region ripe with opportunity, and to free his slaves and escape the institution of slavery which he hated. One had to move far from slavery in the South to be able to escape the pressure of the "ethic" which condoned it. At Dansville, he developed a farm, a paper mill, freed his slaves and, after five years, moved to another farm near West Bloomfield. Not until 1818, did he move to Rochesterville, incorporated at his urging the year before and named for him by his neighbors. He had overseen the selling of lots on the 100 Acre Tract from Dansville and West Bloomfield, and by the time he moved there, four mills were busy sawing logs and grinding grain. Rochesterville also boasted a tannery, a brickyard, numerous two story homes, and a newspaper read by almost a thousand residents. The first schoolhouse was one room, erected in 1814, initially with fifteen pupils taught by Miss Huldah Strong, sister of Mrs. Abelard Reynolds, wife of one of the first permanent settlers.

PIONEER SCHOOL
FIRST SCHOOLHOUSE IN ROCHESTER
WAS BUILT OF WOOD ON THIS SITE,
1813. IT WAS REPLACED BY A
TWO-STORY STONE BUILDING, 1836,
AND BY THIS STRUCTURE, 1873.

Monroe County, 29
On Fitzhugh Street

When the stone aqueduct carrying the canal over the Genesee was completed in 1823, Rochester grew even more rapidly. The Genesee Valley, blessed with soil and climate ideal for growing wheat, attracted more people to farm there. More mills were built to tap the river's power and grind the ever-growing grain harvest and saw the lumber needed for new homes. The main product of Rochester was carried in quantity to all parts of the northeast by the canal, endowing Rochester as the "Flour City". On the frontier, there was little cash so bartering prevailed. The cash shortage had existed from colonial times when Britain's parliament prohibited exporting gold and silver coin to the colonies, and sales to the mother country gave the seller credit but not cash. What little cash did circulate was Spanish milled dollars known as pieces, or bits of eight (two bits equal a quarter), and a few English pounds, shillings, and pence.

The United States Mint was established in Philadelphia in 1792 and began trying to produce enough coin for the burgeoning economy assisted by the use of the Jefferson's dollar system versus the English pound, a triumph of common sense over tradition. But the shortage of coins continued. Prices were listed in both currencies, and figuring change was a nuisance. The obsolete currencies were devalued, called in, and re-minted into U. S. coins by a federal act, ending the confusion, but not until 1857.

Banks in central New York started up before the building of the canal, and so were in place to serve as depositories for canal tolls and the funds of the local economy. One result of the clash between President Andrew Jackson and the 2nd Bank of the United States in the mid-1830s was that many state banks were given the right to issue their own bank notes for a time, not always with enough backing. And sometimes, the printer was so proud of his work that he kept a few specimens for himself. The wealth that flowed from Rochester's vigorous economy provided the "seed corn" for other ventures, including seed companies and nurseries.

The first nursery was founded by seedsman William A. Reynolds in 1828, the same year his father, Abelard Reynolds, built the first Reynolds Arcade, an early business plaza. Ellwanger and Barry, founded in 1838, was typical of the city nurseries which not only provided plantings of fruit and shade trees, and shrubs and vines to customers in their own backyard, but stocked inventories to new nurseries springing up in the midwest. By 1855, Rochester had approximately 150 nurseries and seed growers, about half that of the state. The tradition of nurseries and seed companies still exists in the region.

One of the founders of the clothing industry in Rochester, and the Jewish community which largely ran it, was Myer Greentree, a peddler who arrived on the scene in the early 1840s. He married Elizabeth Baker, a Gentile who already had a business making children's clothing which he began to help her manage. The Wile brothers joined the firm, newly called Greentree and Wile, and other clothing firms in the area began as other Jewish immigrants, most fleeing from ferment in Germany, arrived.

By 1856, 2,000 clothing workers sewed themselves into Rochester's economy using Elias' Howe's new invention and soon began making uniforms for the Union Army in the Civil War. Mass production, distribution, and competition made fine suits available to the average man. Fashion Park, Timely Clothes, and Bond Stores began here in the 1890s serving middle-class clothing needs. But fine hand tailoring fell to the pressure of price which forced some old firms to succumb. Michel Stern & Co., founded in 1849, still survives, as does Hickey-Freeman Co., started in 1899, the second oldest clothing manufacturer in a city known for its honored position in the industry.

The city fathers were farsighted in setting aside selective acres for public parks and landscaping them to please the eyes of a populace duly proud of their collective achievement. A gift of nineteen acres to the city by Ellwanger and Barry was the beginning of Highland Park and the Rochester Park system.

HIGHLAND PARK
ROCHESTER'S FIRST PARK
OFFERED IN 1883 BY ELLWANGER
AND BARRY AND ACCEPTED JAN.
13, 1888. PARK COMMISSION
WAS FORMED MAY 1, 1888.

Monroe County, 33
Near Pavillion, Highland Park

The Rochester Institute of Technology had several origins: one began as Rochester's first library, founded by Dr. Levi Ward, Jr. because of his love for books, and developed into the Athenaeum. Another was the Franklin Institute, founded in 1826, (two years after the opening of the first Franklin Institute in Philadelphia), to offer a library, a museum, as well as an auditorium. This organization also melded into the Athenaeum. The Mechanics Institute was founded by Henry Lomb (the cabinet maker half of Bausch and Lomb) when he returned from the Civil War, and by professor Samuel Lattimore. This, too, merged with the enlarged Athenaeum to form a yet larger institution called the Rochester Athenaeum and Mechanics Institute. The final name change came in 1936.

The University of Rochester began in the upper floor of a downtown hotel where it stayed for eleven years until it could make use of eight acres of land on Prince Street given to it by Azariah Boody in 1853. In 1893, the university became coeducational, and ten years later, it received the first of many endowments from George Eastman. The Brockport Academy opened its doors in 1834 and by 1856, had evolved into Brockport Collegiate Institute. The institute became one of the state's Normal schools for the training of teachers eleven years later. Today, as the College of Arts and Sciences, it is part of the SUNY system.

In the 1850s, the wheat midge began to have devastating effects on the local crop. As the Midwest grew and the thick prairie sods were plowed for the growing of wheat, oats, corn, and rye, the mills followed, leaving the flourishing nursery industry to come into prominence causing Rochester now to be called the "Flower City".

SITE OF FIRST
QUAKER MEETING HOUSE
TOWN OF WHEATLAND
FRAME BUILDING 1827
USED UNTIL 1854
BY HICKSITES

Monroe County, 45
Burrell Road S. of Scottsville

Samuel F.B. Morse was a fine portrait artist and teacher of sculpture and painting at New York University. He also dabbled in the popular sciences, most notably the new daguerreotype from France for the fixing of images on a silvered copper plate, and electromagnetism for the transmitting of messages over a wire. In 1843, he transmitted, by a code of his own devising, the message, "What hath God wrought?" over a telegraph line, financed by Congress, from Washington to Baltimore. This capped eleven years of experiment, planning, and using the talents of other men in the technological, financial, managerial, and political fields. With this backing, he successfully defended his patent from many other contenders who were hoping to cash in. In 1865, he helped found Vassar College and Douglas College in 1871.

Small telegraph companies began forming, setting up poles, and stringing lines (many along railroad rights-of-way) and, inevitably, the strong and aggressive started buying up the weak. Hiram Sibley had some capital resulting from several successful ventures in nearby Mendon, and with this stake he accumulated a number of telegraph companies, and was well on the way toward his next financial conquest.

He made a bid to acquire those telegraph companies that had been put together by Ezra Cornell who rejected the offer at first. But the two finally reconciled their differences to form the Western Union Telegraph Company, which had its first main office in the Reynolds Arcade in Rochester. By 1861, Sibley had extended his telegraph line to connect the Atlantic with the Pacific, eclipsing the eighteen-month old Pony Express, which with relays of horses and riders (such as fifteen-year old William F. Cody, later known as Buffalo Bill), had braved hostile Indians, bad weather, and rough country from Saint Joseph, Missouri, to Sacramento, California. A message that had taken eight days to deliver across 2,000 miles by the Pony Express was now instantaneous.

For Hiram Sibley, the new world to conquer was the idea of stretching a line to London, not across 3,000 miles of the Atlantic, but by way of Bering Strait and Russia. When Sibley conferred with Prince Gorchakov, the Russian Chancellor, about securing rights to put a telegraph line across Russia's North American territory, the Prince asked Sibley the cost of building the line, and was told, "five million dollars". The prince gravely replied that Russia would gladly sell all its American territory for that amount.

The incredulous Sibley passed this information on to Washington which had its hands full with a Civil War that was supposed to be "over by Christmas". But in March of 1867, Secretary of State William H. Seward closed on the purchase of Alaska for $7,200,000, his crowning achievement of a life in distinguished government service.

As for Sibley, he had erected poles and strung lines well into the new territory, when the announcement was made that a cable had successfully been laid across the Atlantic that same year (1866) by a syndicate headed by Cyrus Fields. (Fields had succeeded before on his sixth try, in 1858, but after three weeks the cable failed). The forest of poles on which Sibley had spent $3,000,000 was now obsolete.

One of the first automobiles, if not the first, was developed in Rochester in the 1870s by George B. Selden, a patent attorney. Its main component was a light-weight internal combustion engine that ran on gasoline, a derivative of oil when distilled into kerosene, that had, as yet, no practical use. However, it was this petroleum-based fuel which made the automobile possible. The engine also relied on the concurrent development by his friend, Matthew Ewing, of a lubricating oil that would not break down under high heat and pressure.

Ewing had hit on the idea of using a vacuum to distill crude oil, and was joined in the venture by Hiram Everett who had made some money in three businesses, even though all three had failed. They called it the Vacuum Oil Company. Everett later sold 75% of his interest to John D. Rockefeller in exchange for stock in what became the Standard Oil Company of New York, later named Socony Vacuum Oil Company, and finally the Mobil Oil Corporation.

Selden was a visionary who realized the importance of delaying the issuance of his patent for the generic automobile until the time was ripe. It was in 1895 when models from Benz, Daimler, Henry Ford, and the Duryea brothers had materialized and he could begin to claim patent royalties for the full seventeen years. He was able to receive royalties totaling several hundred thousand dollars from auto manufacturers until challenged by Henry Ford in a suit that dragged on for six years.

Selden won the suit but Ford appealed and convinced the court over the next fifteen months that Selden's patent should apply only to the particular car shown in Selden's drawings. The publicity regarding the trial served to advertise Ford and his cars as nothing else could and Selden had to content himself with the result. Bausch and Lomb (optical equipment), Ritter (dental chairs and equipment.), Pfaudler (vacuum process for making beer), the maker of Cutler mail chutes, and the company that turned out the ubiquitous Rochester Lamp were part of the core of corporations in the mid-nineteenth century that gave impetus to lasting growth in Rochester.

Leonard Jerome, publisher, financier and sportsman, whose career was developed during this period in Skaneateles, Auburn and Rochester, became better known in history as the father of the mother of Winston Churchill, Jennie Jerome. Another notable to titillate the city was "Buffalo Bill" Cody, now a sometime army scout who had attained his sobriquet by shooting as many buffalo as he could to provide meat for the hands building the Kansas Pacific Railroad. About to launch a stage career by starring in **The Scouts of the Plains**, written by his friend and author of trashy dime novels, Ned Buntline, he had been in Rochester twice before and liked the surroundings enough to move there for two years with his family, in 1874. He interrupted his residence there only long enough to accept a scouting assignment from his friends in the U.S. 5th Cavalry and enhance his wild west reputation by slaying Chief Yellow Hand in a skirmish against the Cheyenne.

Though surrounded by water, the hamlet that became Syracuse was not settled for water power but because of the presence of its salt springs. Ephraim Webster, veteran of the Revolution under General Philip Schuyler, came to the shores of Onondaga Lake in 1786 because of the alluring stories of easily available salt related to him by the Oneidas at his trading post in their region. He set up shop where Onondaga Creek flows into the lake, and prospered with the Onondagas, as he did with the Oneidas, because of his fair-mindedness.

SALT MAKING
MANUFACTURE OF SALT WAS
BEGUN HERE IN LIVERPOOL
BY JOHN DANFORTH, BROTHER
OF ASA DANFORTH, 1794

Onondaga County, 78
NY 57 & 370 at Liverpool

In time he induced his new friends, Asa Danforth and Comfort Tyler, to move to the region by reason of the fertile soil and the salt, which could be had for the boiling and for which there was a demanding market. The spring was so saline that fifty-five gallons of water from the Onondaga Salt springs would make seventy-five pounds of salt compared to 360 gallons of seawater required to make the same amount.

When not making salt, Danforth built a sawmill near Jamesville. Tyler surveyed part of the new Genesee Road, became active in politics and on the road built a tavern, which briefly served as the court house. The Cayuga bridge was his creation, too.

In 1788, thirty of the thirty-three residents were sick and in the care of the other three, and friendly Onondaga Indians near by also tended the sick and provided food. The next year, the population increased to sixty-six but twenty-three died. Even so, the new community attracted such men as James Geddes who further exploited the salt deposits with heavy equipment for the purpose.

GEDDES
TOWN NAMED FOR JAMES GEDDES 1763-1838, ENGINEER OF STATE CANALS FOR N.Y. WAS FIRST TO MAKE SALT HERE. SURVEYED SITE OF SYRACUSE, 1804

Onondaga County, 80*
NY 48 & Hiawatha Blvd., Syracuse

Wells were sunk to pump the brine up through wooden pipe casing, increasing production. The low swampy ground around the lake made it difficult for oxen to haul the salt to market and Geddes had sufficient political clout to convince the governor to sell state land in the area to finance the building of a road from Dewitt to the salt springs. The road became Genesee Street. Abraham Walton from Albany bought land (the Walton Tract) by Onondaga Creek and built a long-needed grist mill, the "Old Red Mill", which became the nucleus of the new community and eventually its downtown. The mill pond was at the present Armory site. In 1848, it was filled in using fill from Prospect Hill, and named Jefferson Park.

As the marker below attests, Geddes built his home at Fairmount on a slight rise (corner of Milton and Genesee streets) to avoid the miasma of the swamp as did most people at that time. One of the liveliest of town building entrepreneurs was lawyer Joshua Forman who came to town in 1800. Quickly becoming a member of the state assembly, he introduced and got passed the bill to survey the possibilities of building a canal from the Hudson to Lake Erie. Geddes became the surveyor.

In 1819, Forman moved to the Walton Tract from Onondaga Hill and built his home (corner of Clinton and Water streets) at what was then Cossitt's Corners, in spite of warnings from neighbors that living near the swamp was unhealthy. The canny investor and promoter saw to it that the swamp was drained by clearing obstructions in the lake's outlet so that the level of Onondaga Lake was lowered several feet. This increased the desirability and value of the crossroads property there, already enhanced by the completion of the Erie Canal through the village in 1820.

SITE OF
HOME OF
JAMES GEDDES, 1798
ERIE CANAL SURVEYOR, 1808
CHIEF ENGINEER 1816-1825

Onondaga County, 1
NY 5, 2 miles West of Syracuse
at Fairmont Corners

At that time, people were unhappy with the name of Cossitt's Corners. They had previously called it Bogardus' Corners (after an early tavern), then Milan, then Salina, and none satisfied. Judge Forman's new law clerk from Skaneateles, John Wilkinson, solved the problem to the majority's satisfaction with the distinctive name, Syracuse, because of the similarity of natural features to Syracuse, Sicily, (which also had a nearby lake and salt marshes). Perhaps we could call that season, Appellation Spring. Wilkinson later became president of the Syracuse and Utica Railroad whose main track coursed through downtown for the better part of a hundred years.

The demand for salt had so increased by 1821 that a "new" process was developed using the sun's rays to evaporate the brine in 10,000 shallow vats that could quickly be covered should the weather turn wet. Syracuse was the only city in North America making salt in such quantity then, and the monopoly gradually increased its production. By 1834, the vats for solar evaporation covered 110 acres and annually produced almost 164,000 bushels of coarse salt. In addition, that year 1,674,816 bushels of fine salt were boiled down using well over forty-four thousand cords of wood. But by 1863, production peaked out at nine million bushels and then steadily declined in the face of competition from newly-found sources in the west.

The salt deposit was laid down by an ancient ocean that covered central New York over 300 million years ago. When other localities such as Cuylerville and Dresden began mining this deposit deep in the earth rather than pumping salt water for evaporation, Syracuse's monopoly ended. Nor did Syracuse have a competitive edge, and, in 1907, the area comprising the salt springs was sold to the state for $15,000.

ONONDAGA BRICK
THOMAS MARVIN, SOLDIER IN WARS OF 1776 AND 1812, SETTLED HERE 1811 (CAZENOVIA 1800). MADE FIRST BRICK HERE FROM NATIVE CLAY TROD BY OXEN.

Onondaga County, 81
CR ½ m. east of Warners

The salt industry spawned other industries that had enabled the area to grow: barrels had to be made in the hundreds of thousands; boats built to carry salt on the canals; and trees cut to fuel the furnaces and stoves as well as build the boats, houses and business buildings. Engineers were needed to drive, and mechanics to maintain the track and the trains; farmers to produce the grain, the fruit, the meat, and the milk to feed the participants - and artisans and labor to quarry and fashion the stone and bricks and apply the mortar—each economic ripple engendering another.

Seven years after General Clinton's men destroyed the Indian village of Ochenang, which they preferred to call Chenango, Robert Hooper, James Wilson, and William Bingham bought 30,000 acres on either side of the Susquehanna. Bingham, a land speculator and wealthy Philadelphia merchant, also had large land investments in other states (two million acres of virgin timber in Maine), and was so involved in business and politics that he never saw his allotted acres in upstate New York. In 1800, he appointed Joshua Whitney, one of the settlers there, as commission agent to handle sales and development. Whitney, a natural promoter, realized Chenango was actually on adjacent Boston Purchase land, not Bingham's, and persuaded the residents to relocate to the junction of the two rivers. (Whitney's brother, Tom, insisted to the US Post Office that his own upriver settlement be called Whitney's Point).

In 1802, the turnpike from Kingston to Owego was opened, ending Chenango Point's dependency for transportation solely on the Susquehanna River. Fourteen years later, stagecoach service on the pike brought New Englanders and people from down state to town. Growth paralleled that of most other cities in central New York not located on the canal, so that shortly before the Chenango Canal was built and when Chenango was incorporated as Binghamton in 1834, its population was 1500.

INDIAN CASTLE
LOCATED NEAR JUNCTION OF
CASTLE CREEK WITH CHENANGO
RIVER, CALLED OTSININGO.
DESTROYED AUG. 18, 1779
DURING SULLIVAN CAMPAIGN

Broome County, 1
US 11 & NY 12, 3 m. north
of Binghamton

Growth began to increase when the Chenango Canal joining Utica and Binghamton was completed three years later. But not until 1848, when the Erie railroad tied Binghamton, population 5000, to New York City, did Binghamton really thrive. The Syracuse, Binghamton, and New York RR (later acquired by the Delaware, Lackawanna, and Western), gave Binghamton and Syracuse access to the Pennsylvania coal fields in 1854, an industrial shot in the arm, and encouraged the founding of iron foundries, a bonus. Fifteen years later, the completion of the Albany and Susquehanna RR gave Binghamton access to the northeast, but rendered the Chenango Canal obsolete, and it was abandoned in 1875.

Tobacco was grown locally, and the first of more than thirty cigar-making factories in the city was started in the late 1850s. Cigars were rolled by hand and, at the peak thirty years later, five thousand workers were required to make Binghamton's production second in the nation. The factories became worked with many laborers from Europe who were glad to leave the over-crowded tenements of the beachhead they had established in Manhattan.

The Delaware, Lackawanna, and Western Railroad opened its road from Binghamton to Buffalo, in 1882, carrying only coal until 1900. George Scranton, president of the Lackawanna, and for whom that city is named, then hired Ernest Elmo Calkins, advertising guru of the time, to publicize the newly opened passenger service to reassure passengers of clean trains. He launched the successful Phoebe Snow ads which depicted a beautiful young woman dressed in white with the caption: "Says Phoebe Snow/ about to go/ upon a trip to Buffalo/ my gown stays white/ from morn to night/ on the Road to Anthracite."

The making of shoes by a single craftsman in his shop began to fade out when sewing machines sturdy enough to sew the uppers to sole leather were used instead of wooden shoe pegs. In 1854, the Lester brothers began Binghamton's shoe making industry which was to have profound effects on the area and industry in general. In 1889, G. Harry Lester, who had inherited the business, gave his chief foreman, George F. Johnson, free leeway to carry out Johnson's idea to build a new factory two miles down river where the employees could buy houses close by. Lestershire was the name given the small community. The plan worked well, except that Lester insisted on selling the homes at a profit; Johnson would have let the employees buy at cost.

Henry B. Endicott, a leather jobber from Boston, became treasurer of the company, and in a few years, gained control of the business from the Lesters. Endicott appointed Johnson manager because he wanted his worker incentive plan to increase profits. Johnson paid the employees on a piecework basis which resulted in a decent wage, and gave them a share of the profits besides. The novel plan more than justified their expectations, and Johnson was able to buy half the business, giving Endicott his note for the entire purchase price.

In 1900, Johnson proposed the building of a different kind of company town, to be laid out on 200 acres six miles to the west. Surrounding the new factory, he built attractive homes the employees could buy at cost on the installment plan. The new town was named Endicott.

The idea was such a success that a new model community was planned nearby on one thousand acres this time, along the same lines but with spacious parks for the employees recreation and hospital and dental facilities nearby. This was Johnson's famous "Square Deal" which gained national fame. In honor of the boss, Lestershire was renamed Johnson City.

This experiment worked to the benefit of the stockholders and management, as well as the employees, and all were happy. It was difficult, if not impossible, for a labor union to get a foothold at the Endicott-Johnson Shoe Company and the incentive plan there became a pattern for other enlightened businessmen to emulate.

The energetic and long-lived Elkanah Watson finally settled down to be a gentleman farmer in western Massachusetts in 1810. He had pretty much exhausted his interest in canals, but got the itch to promote county and state fairs. Watson acquired some merino sheep which he wanted to show off in the common of Pittsfield. Enthusiasm ensued as did correspondence with other gentlemen farmers, and before long, Watson found himself invited by many local granges to speak before them on organizing agricultural shows. Interest grew to the point that he and James LeRay de Chaumont, of Jefferson County, whom he had known in France over fifty years earlier through Benjamin Franklin, co-founded the New York Agricultural Society in 1832, (when Watson was seventy-four and Le Ray seventy-two). Nine years later, the first state agricultural fair was held in Syracuse.

THE FIRST
CAST IRON PLOW
IN THE WORLD WAS MADE BY
JETHRO WOOD
AT FOOT OF FALLS
1819

Cayuga County, 102
NY 38A by bridge, Montville

Other cities in New York coveted the honor of being fair host so that the fair had no permanent location until induced to return for good to Syracuse in 1890, using the facilities the city made for it on the west shore of Onondaga Lake.

Aside from the amusements and games, the county and state fairs brought improvements to the attention of the farming industry. From Moravia, Jethro Wood's cast iron plow, with three interchangeable parts, substantially increased crop production around the world and gained the approbation (upon receiving models), of the Czar of Russia and Thomas Jefferson, who himself had designed a furrow-turning moldboard.

No doubt Eliphalet Remington's firearms, made in his gun shop on Steele's Creek near Ilion, raised a deal of interest at the fair, boosting his prospects to be a leader in the industry. His company in Ilion later supplied rifles to the U.S. Army for the war with Mexico and the Civil War. In 1856, it began manufacturing farm machinery, and after the Civil War, branched into making sewing machines and typewriters.

OLD REMINGTON HOMESTEAD BUILT IN 1799 BY ELIPHALET REMINGTON WHO FORGED THE FIRST REMINGTON GUN; BIRTHPLACE OF PHILO REMINGTON

Herkimer County, 9*
CR, 4 m. SW of Ilion

The simple tentative step of changing the agricultural industry's motive power from oxen to horses also improved the pace of farm production. John Johnston, neighbor to the Rose Mansion in Geneva, showed a method of improving soil productivity by laying clay drainage tile, a practice used first in England. Johnston was also one of the first in the country to advocate improving the soil by the spread of lime, gypsum, and manure, and the cultivation of hay.

Cyrus McCormick's invention of the reaper in 1819, followed by the threshing machine and cultivator, caught on to ease the farmer's main chores and further increase the amount of acreage he could manage. Years later, Lincoln's Secretary of War, Edwin Stanton, said that without

McCormick's reaper, the North couldn't have won the Civil War, so many farms had been denuded of men to work them. The reaper and one man could do the work of ten.

APPROACHING
THE FARM OF
JOHN JOHNSTON
1791–1880
FATHER OF TILE DRAINING
IN AMERICA

Seneca County, 17
NY 96 A, 4 m. NW of Fayette

The State Agricultural Experiment Station, established in 1881, and managed by the Cornell Agricultural College is, ironically, located at the exact spot as Kanadesaga, the Senecas' proud hub of husbandry. It is especially fitting then that the station directs its efforts to improve strains of fruit, vegetables, cereal grains, and other crops at that location. Better tasting and disease-resistant apples, berries, grapes, corn, and increased dairy production have been the rewards of its work, benefitting the country and the region rich in vineyards, orchards, field crops, and dairy farms.

For over two centuries the Peruvian potato, said to have been introduced to England by Sir Walter Raleigh, provided a near perfect food in Europe. So good was it that it was by far the major crop in Ireland. In 1845, widespread crop failures in western Europe were followed by potato blight which was particularly devastating in Ireland where so much depended on the tuber. Famine ensued, and the poverty-ridden populace considered this the last straw in a long list of economic, political, and social insults, mostly English-made. In the next five years, a million Irish died of starvation and disease, and the British land-lords evicted over 500,000 from their homes for lack of rent payment.

After wrenching decisions which separated family members from each other, they moved in large numbers to other countries, especially the United States where Irishmen individually and in small groups had migrated over the decades to build the canals and railroads, and help the Army fight the Indians. "American wakes" were held for those about to depart, convinced that "going west" was tantamount to dying, since they likely would never see their loved ones again.

At the same time, political upheavals in Europe convinced many French, Prussians, and others to seek refuge from the ancient and callous conventions of the old world for a better future here. Agents for the Erie Canal, and later for the railroads and other projects throughout the country were contracted in Europe to sell or cajole large groups to come to the United States to provide an adequate labor supply which also served to keep wages in line. Central New York received a good share of this influx and benefitted from this transfusion of talents, ideas, and new energy, as did the conscripts.

The process repeated when Italians were induced to come across the Atlantic to help build the West Shore Railroad paralleling the New York Central along the Hudson and west along the Mohawk, in the early 1880s. When construction finished, some moved to Canastota, Syracuse, Oswego, and points west to start truck farms. Others brought their masonry skills and started in the construction of brick and stone buildings, bridges and roads. The Syracuse Saving Bank Building and the Gridley Building, both built at the beginning of the fourth quarter of the nineteenth century, are examples. Poles and Ukrainians also came for the industrial jobs in the cities, and established their own enclaves for mutual support and to retain their ethnic identity, just as the Irish and Italians did before them. They were late comers and followed the usual pattern of starting at the bottom of the economic scale, but they had a better future than back home. As with earlier immigrants, a single member of the family often came first to scout the situation, obtain employment, send money home, and eventually finance the voyage here of the rest of the family.

Many persons from the northeastern states had been emigrating to the West lured by cheap land and the hope of benefitting their condition. In 1836, Marcus Whitman, born at Federal Hollow (later Rushville) sold his country medical practice and, with his bride, Narcissa Prentiss Whitman, and Henry Harding Spalding, and his wife, left to help the condition of others as missionaries sponsored by a joint Presbyterian-Congregationalist board. He and his wife founded a mission at present Walla Walla, Washington to convert the skeptical Cayuse Indians.

Doctor Whitman became a great enthusiast of the Oregon region and returned east to lead back a wagon train which was the beginning of the "great emigration" over the Oregon Trail in 1843. In 1847, he and his wife and their helpers were killed in a massacre by the Cayuse Indians brought about by the same ancient Indian fear that the Jesuits suffered: that their ministrations were the cause of, not the cure, of fatal disease to members of the tribe. News of the massacre back east had much to do with the passing of a bill making Oregon a U.S. territory. In early 1848, gold was found in central California, immensely increasing the number of hopefuls leaving central New York and the east for California and Oregon.

OLD INN SITE
DR. MARCUS WHITMAN, REV.
AND MRS. H.H. SPAULDING
MET HERE FEB. 14, 1836
AND DECIDED TO GO
TOGETHER TO OREGON

Steuben County, 8
NY 70, at Howard

The only blemish in the relations between Canada and the United States since the war of 1812, occurred in 1838 when a group of sympathizers from New York state began to arm themselves to help a budding rebellion across the St. Lawrence against British rule, known as the Patriot's War. General Winfield Scott, under the direction of President Van Buren, was disarming volunteers on this side of the river but other sympathizers got carried away and made a raid on Prescott, across the river from Ogdensburg. They were promptly rounded up by the British authorities and the ringleaders, some of whom were from Onondaga County, were hung and others imprisoned.

BATTERY B
FIRST N.Y. LIGHT ARTILLERY DRILLED NEAR THIS POINT UNDER THEIR ORGANIZER, CAPT. RUFUS D. PETTIT, IN THE SUMMER OF 1861

Onondaga County, 30
NY 370 & Doyle Rd., 3 m. SE of
Baldwinsville

The firing on Fort Sumter, in April 1861, induced many young men to form companies, elect their officers, and entrain to the newly-built recruiting and training station at Elmira. Telegraph offices all over the country reported the disaster of the first battle of Bull Run which tempered Northern Hawks, who had thought the fighting would be over by Christmas; but Union forces were routed and one third of the casualties were from New York. Among other bloody battles, Second Bull Run, the Peninsular Campaign, Antietam, Shiloh, Gettysburg, Vicksburg, Atlanta, Sherman's march across Georgia, Petersburg, and finally, Appomattox all took their toll. The North gained ground while the resources of the South, both men and materiel, were diminishing.

By 1864, Elmira's army base was no longer needed for recruits but as a prisoner of war camp for the sons of the Confederacy where 9,000 were held to the end of the war, and 3,000 of them died.

The North's jubilation when the end of the war was agreed to at Appomattox Court House was dampened in less than a week when the sobering news of Lincoln's assassination was telegraphed to the nation. Two weeks later, his funeral cortege, dedicated to a special train, glumly chugged westward to Springfield, Illinois along the New York Central tracks through Utica, Syracuse, and Rochester. Crowds waited at Syracuse's Vanderbilt Depot to say goodby to the man who had carried the hapless burden of prosecuting the war, albeit to a successful conclusion, but was cheated of his devout wish of reuniting North and South with malice toward none.

Many towns lost a generation of young men as the local companies, in which they had joined for the adventure and to save the Union, were wiped out in fierce combat. Waterloo was overwhelmed with sorrow by its loss of sons, brothers, fathers, and friends in the war, as were other communities.

Town elders decided to dedicate the entire day of May 5, 1866 to honor those who "gave the last full measure of devotion".

APPROACHING
CIVIL WAR
PARADE GROUND
1861-1865

Livingston County, 40
NY 245 & bridge road
Letchworth Park

They closed businesses for the day, draped black bunting, flew flags at half mast, and marched to the grievous cadence of mournful, martial music on the way to village cemeteries. Waterloo has observed this sentiment for veterans of our wars annually ever since. But the day of commemoration was moved to May 30th. In 1873, New York became the first state to proclaim Decoration Day as an official holiday—now celebrated nationally as Memorial Day.

An important and cherished part of the lamentations of Memorial day is the playing of a bugle call which also had its genesis in the Civil War. After the battle of Gaines Mills (near Richmond), in 1862, Major General Daniel Adams Butterfield from Utica brooded over the casualties sustained. With the help of his bugler, twenty-two year old Oliver Norton, Butterfield composed the haunting bugle call known as "Taps" in commemoration of fallen comrades. Taps has been played ever since for its gentle and profound solace. For similar reasons, it is also the last bugle call of the day at military establishments (and boy's camps), signaling lights out.

CARDIFF GIANT
DISINTERRED NEAR THIS
VILLAGE ON OCT. 16, 1869.
REPRESENTED AS A PETRIFIED
PREHISTORIC MAN, IT WAS
SUBSEQUENTLY PROVED A HOAX

Onondaga County, 23, NY 20 at Cardiff

In 1869, a farmer in Cardiff dug up a 3000-pound fossilized giant of a "man". Some declared nationwide that this discovery was an advance in anthropology, until it was proven a hoax. The shrewd and unflappable P.T. Barnum offered $60,000 for merely the rental of the discredited figure. When refused, he had a full-sized model sculptured, and made a fortune displaying the facsimile. This was fortunate, indeed, because Barnum, at that time low in funds, was thereby enabled to reopen his fire-damaged New York city American Museum, and a year later, to put together and inaugurate his circus, the "Greatest Show on Earth". The Cardiff Giant now rests at the Farmer's Museum in Cooperstown.

As the salt industry dwindled, William Cogswell, a chemist from Oswego, wished to exploit a thick layer of salt extending underground eastward from Syracuse in conjunction with a sizeable limestone deposit nearby. The two compounds were doubly valuable when processed together to make soda ash, used in the manufacture of glass, pulp and paper, metallic alloys, baking soda and ceramic ware, to name only a few. Cogswell and Rowland Hazard, a Rhode Island backer, obtained technical backing and a licence to go into production from the Solvay brothers in Belgium, patentees of a soda ash process.

In the early 1880s, many wells were sunk in Syracuse, Cardiff, Jamesville, and finally Tully, before a satisfactory supply of high quality brine could be located and tapped. Then, forty successful wells were drilled to depths of 1200 to 1600 feet to provide the necessary river of brine to flow down the especially built wooden conduit to the Solvay Process plant near the state fairgrounds on the west shore of Onondaga Lake. Close to a thousand tons of limestone was quarried daily at Split Rock, a few miles south of the city at Jamesville, and conveyed to the plant to complete the combination. Prosperity shone on the plant, and the town was renamed Solvay.

Unfortunately, its liquid tailings were allowed to wash into Onondaga Lake, then a pristine body of water, along with the waste from the city of Syracuse, gradually spoiling one of the most valuable of the area's assets, and killing with it, the lakeside resort hotels and amusement parks at the end of the electric trolley line.

Church and Dwight bought soda ash from Solvay Process, its neighbor, processed it, and marketed bicarbonate of soda, used, among other things, in baking powder, and to extinguish fires and stomach aches, under its familiar Arm and Hammer brand, beginning in 1896.

Other industries after the Civil War proliferated: the casting of giant iron salt kettles encouraged the building of steel rolling mills in Syracuse. These mills and those in Elmira, turned out tons of rails for the burgeoning railroads, which by now had spanned the country, coast to coast. In 1876, Sanderson Brothers and Company, of Sheffield, England bought the William Sweet Steel mills in Syracuse. At century's end, the Sanderson Company and twelve other steel manufacturing firms founded Crucible Steel Company of America, makers of special-grade steel where hardness and durability in the face of extreme heat is important, such as for tool fabrication, cutlery and the compounding of other alloys.

In 1876, Adolph Kastor, a German immigrant, opened his cutlery and hardware importing business in New York City. Because of protective tariffs enacted at the end of the century, the resulting higher import prices threatened to put his prosperous firm out of business. Casting about for a new source of supply, he happily came upon a small quality knife factory along the banks of Nine-mile Creek in Camillus. He bought the business and relocated from New York, providing increased employment and growth to the small village. Camillus Cutlery has been there by the creek ever since, weathering the highs and lows of economic activity. It seems the protective tariff served its purpose.

CHAPTER EIGHTEEN

After slavery became an institution in Virginia in 1619, the lure of freedom to blacks was ever-present and many tried to escape their bondage. In the confusion of battle during the Revolution, thousands slipped away to the British who promised them freedom it they would join the British ranks. George Washington lost a few slaves during absences from Mount Vernon, and Jefferson lost twenty-two during the conflict.

In his effort to weaken the South, General Cornwallis had lured five thousand slaves to his side with the promise of freedom by the time of Yorktown. But as the siege played out, he had to force thousands of them to leave the protection of his besieged ramparts as rations ran low. At wars end, Americans insisted that the treaty provide that the British were not "to carry away any Negroes or other property." The Continental Army also used freedom to induce blacks to enlist. It has been estimated that one out of seven rebel soldiers was black, both freemen and slave.

Slavery and growing a cotton crop were beginning to lose their popularity in the South towards the end of the 18th century until Eli Whitney invented the cotton gin (read engine) for easier and rapid separation of the fiber from its seeds. Formerly, it took a slave all day to separate the seeds from one pound of cotton. With the gin, one slave could turn out twenty pounds of cleaned cotton and water power could do fifty. Raising cotton was now much more profitable, especially if one had enough slaves to do the hard work hoeing and picking in the intense heat of the southern sun.

Many who had begun to think of selling or freeing their slaves had second thoughts. Concurrently, a New Orleans Frenchman, Jean Etienne Boré, put together machinery for granulating sugar, and the increased profitability of growing and processing the newly introduced sugar cane contributed to the demand for more slaves in the Deep South.

Colonial Robert Carter, known as "King Carter", owned 600,000 acres of prime Virginia land, a prosperous iron-works near Baltimore, grist mills that turned out 25,000 bushels of flour a year, and six hundred Negro slaves. He was one of the first to see that slavery could not compete efficiently with a system in which the laborers were free. With non-slave labor, a planter had no responsibility to provide shelter, food, clothing, and medical care through sickness, disability, and death as did an owner with slaves. In 1774, Carter began his plan of freeing his slaves. But this resulted in both neighboring slaves and slave owners becoming restive, which discouraged manumission.

The American Colonization Society was founded, in 1817, to buy blacks their freedom and send them to Africa, if they chose. By 1861, no more than 15,000 slaves had been freed by the society to emigrate. But the republic of Liberia came of this in 1857 (the capitol is Monrovia named after president Monroe), with a constitution modeled after that of the United States.

Thomas Jefferson's first draft of the Declaration of Independence included, "He has waged cruel war against human nature itself, violating its most sacred rites of life and liberty in the persons of a distant people who never offended him, captivating and carrying them into slavery in another hemisphere, or to incur miserable death in their transportation thither." This censure of King George III for permitting the slave trade and slavery in the colonies was offensive to the delegates from South Carolina and Georgia who insisted it be deleted. Slavery was a point of political contention early on.

Abolition was proposed by Virginia delegate George Mason, owner of 200 slaves, at the Constitutional Convention, but his idea was anathema to the South and was promptly shot down by his southern colleagues. However, the convention did approve that the slave trade would end in 1808. Then it gave a boon to southern states by providing that three-fifths of a state's slave census would be added to its white numbers to determine its representation in congress. It was agreed at the convention, and later in congress, to have a moratorium on debates on slavery to avoid risking fragmenting the fragile new government struggling to hold together. Though slavery was a forbidden subject in congress, it smouldered and erupted from time to time under the pressure of heated passions.

The 1790 census revealed over 21,000 slaves in New York, 11,400 in New Jersey, 3,700 in Pennsylvania, and even less in all the other states north of the Mason-Dixon line compared to 700,000 in the country. While in the north, slavery could be abolished and owners compensated, in the south the number of slaves would have overwhelmed the ability of even the Federal government to fully compensate owners for their loss.

Great Britain enacted anti-slave trade laws in 1807, 1811, and in 1831 outlawed slavery altogether, as did Canada, in 1833. So had Pennsylvania and New Jersey (slavery had never been profitable in the north), making them havens for slaves who were able to flee servitude and cross the Mason-Dixon line and the Delaware River.

The Northwest Ordinance (1787), which opened up the territory that was to become Ohio, Indiana, Illinois, Michigan, and Wisconsin, also prohibited slavery within its borders but provided for the return of fugitive slaves. Despite these limitations, the slave population, overwhelmingly in the south, grew from an estimated 900,000, in 1790, to over 3,000,000 by 1830, in order to meet the need for the cotton and sugar cane crop and supporting services.

President Andrew Jackson forcibly ejected the Cherokee, Creek, Chickasaw, Choctaw, and Seminole tribes from their lands in the southeast to west of the Mississippi in the second quarter of the century. Few whites objected, what with the land sales helping to fund the new territories and states, (rather than higher taxes), as had happened in establishing the original states. This opened up large tracts to cotton and cane production, requiring more slaves. Cotton production soared from 160 million pounds annually in 1820 to twenty-three billion by 1860.

The growers depended on New York capital, shipping, and manufacturing to get their crop to market, explaining some of the northern sentiment in favor of slavery. Indeed, they bought many of their slaves from New England shipowners who had a tight grip on the colonial seaboard slave markets. The price of a prime young field hand was $500 in 1832 and $1800 by 1860. So slavery required a lot of capital that, in the north, would be free to purchase efficient machinery.

Once entangled in the system of slavery, it was very difficult for planters to disengage because of peer pressure, concern for the slaves, and financial reasons; near half the cotton crop was produced by planters who owned six slaves or less.

As settlement moved west into Louisiana Purchase lands, the politics of slavery became more heated. De facto slavery gave rise to Alabama entering the Union in 1819 as a slave state, making the number of slave and free states equal, but the question of continuing parity remained as other territories sought statehood.

When Missouri qualified for state status in 1820, the balance was satisfied by the Missouri Compromise, which provided for the admission of Maine as a free state and Missouri as slave. But the act provided that future territories south of latitude 36° 30' (Missouri's southern border), would be slave states; all others would be free.

In 1854, the Kansas-Nebraska Act repealed this arrangement, and replaced it with "squatter sovereignty", i.e., each new state would decide its acceptance of slavery. Consequently, factions in both North and South tried to tilt the balance in their favor by fostering emigration to Kansas territory. The area, long considered barren and part of the "Great American Desert" by Major Stephen Long's 1819 Topographical expedition, now began to become populated by zealots, such as John Brown and his Abolitionist Crusaders fighting southern "border ruffians". Such menacing gave the name "bleeding Kansas" and stirred the dissension over the slavery issue to boiling by 1858, when Kansas came into the Union as a free state.

As surely as slaves labored in misery, their outnumbered owners feared the ever-present spectre of slave insurrection. The most notable was that of Nat Turner, who through his mystical and religious charisma and visions, had developed a small following in Virginia in 1831. With a band of seven, Turner attacked and killed his master and five members of his family. Emboldened by this deed of free will, the lawless company grew to seventy and ran amok, killing 57 men, women, and children. The gruesome barbarities perpetrated by both slaves and slave holders were published by the newspapers for both North and South to ponder. In the South, more stringent laws regarding slaves were passed, and manumission societies gradually died out. Now, more than ever, the top-heavy number of slaves in the South never ceased to haunt.

The Abolitionist Movement began shortly after the Turner Revolt with leaders such as William Lloyd Garrison in Massachusetts, and Gerrit Smith in Peterboro, New York, who publicized, through lectures and publications, the evils of the "Peculiar Institution". Those opposed to slavery, many of whom were Quakers, based their position on humanitarian grounds, not economic reform.

In New York, in 1785, the legislature had prohibited the importation of slaves for sale and provided for their manumission by Will or certificate, but laws curbing slavery within the state were incremental. Another law was passed in 1799 mandating that children born of slaves in New York after the Fourth of July that year were freemen, and in 1808, all slaves under the age of sixty-five were declared free. By 1827, the anti-slavery movement had sufficient momentum that slavery in New York was prohibited entirely, and the few remaining slaves were declared free.

Some southern families who had been enticed by Charles Williamson to central New York brought their slaves with them. The Rochesters, Fitzhughs, Dorseys, Roses, and the Nicholas', among others, voluntarily freed their slaves soon after they settled here in the early 1800s. The freed slaves often continued to work for their former masters, other options being limited; of course, they were then paid wages.

The "Underground Railroad", so-called because of its need to be invisible, began to assist slaves in an organized pattern to make their way north from "station to station" with the help of "conductors" along the way. Help, not only in the North but also in the South, was necessary to this effort since the slaves knew little of geography or how to get clear of their own region. Just the same, a slave's decision to escape required great courage; if he attempted to flee with his wife and children or relatives, capture was likely, if he fled without them, success in gaining freedom was still far from sure. And if captured, punishment was swift and often brutal. Harriet Tubman and Frederick Douglass made their own way north, but even so, they had some assistance from sympathetic Southerners.

SALISBURY–PRATT HOMESTEAD USED BEFORE CIVIL WAR AS AN 'UNDERGROUND STATION' WHERE OREN CRAVATH SHELTERED AND AIDED FUGITIVE SLAVES ON THEIR WAY TO CANADA

Cortland County, 19
NY 281, ½ m. s. of Little York

The Fugitive Slave Act was part of the Compromise of 1850 and was signed into law by a son of New York, President Millard Fillmore. Its main provision was that a runaway slave could be caught and sent back to slavery with no right to a trial or a lawyer, nor could he testify or have witnesses in his own behalf. All that was required to send him or her south again was for a federal judge or commissioner to issue an arrest warrant, summarily deciding the fate of the individual. A claimant could present an affidavit which was enough for the official to send out a posse to seize the fugitive. Many free blacks in the North, as well as slaves, were sent south to bondage. Slaves, particularly highly skilled artisans such as blacksmiths, musicians, coopers or cabinet makers, were valuable and could be rented out or sold at will, separating wives from husbands and parents from children. Such valued blacks, free or slave, were avidly sought. The man who caught the "fugitive" received the standard fee of $10.

The new law was so inhuman it was largely flouted in the North even though anyone who hindered the law or was found helping a runaway could be fined $1000 and imprisoned for six months. Many juries in the 1850s legally ignored the judge's instructions and refused to convict those who helped fugitive slaves. Despite possible punishment, the law had the effect of increasing underground activity to move fugitives north to Canada.

Harriet Beecher Stowe, daughter of Dr. Lyman Beecher and interested in social reform, as were all the Beechers, had seen slavery first hand and had helped fugitive slaves in Ohio. She wrote **Uncle Tom's Cabin** which was serialized in an abolitionist paper, the **National Era**, from June of 1851 to the following April before it appeared in book form in 1852. In the first year, it sold over 300,000 copies and was translated into many languages and dramatized on the stage. The book was a catalyst to fan the emotions of both sides of the controversy, although she did not consider herself an abolitionist whom she thought were extremists. She followed up with a second book on slavery, **Dred**, in 1856, which highlighted the U.S. Supreme Court **Dred Scott** test case that was decided unfavorably to the anti-slavery movement.

Philadelphia was a major focus on the east coast for slaves who had crossed the Mason-Dixon line. Under the guidance of William Sills, a black man who operated the station there, the escapees were sent to stations at Harrisburg, then to Williamsport, and on to Elmira. Then they fanned out to Rochester, Sodus or Buffalo by way of Watkins Glen, Geneva, Honeyoye, Naples, Avon, Pittsford,

Canandaigua, and other towns. Or they were directed to Syracuse and Oswego via Binghamton, Ithaca, Dryden, Cortland, Skaneateles, Marcellus, Auburn, and points in between.

KELSEY'S LANDING
FREEDOM WAS ASSURED FOR
ESCAPING SLAVES WHO
BOARDED CANADIAN VESSELS
HERE AT THE END OF THE
UNDERGROUND RAILROAD

Monroe County, 36
Driving Park, W. side of Genesee

Almost any town in the region had people, frequently Quakers, sympathetic to the plight of the fugitive slaves—people who also had a home with a barn, a cellar, or a hidden room or a hidey-hole to conceal "passengers" until they could be shipped in a wagon load of produce, or even a coffin, to the next station or a waiting ship on Lake Ontario. By the beginning of the Civil War, 50,000 blacks had taken refuge in Canada alone, mostly in the province of Ontario. By 1872, many had returned to the United States, leaving only 20,000 still north of the border.

Harriet Tubman was thirty in 1850 when she escaped the cruelty she experienced on the Eastern Shore of Maryland. She had been forced to marry John Tubman, a freedman, but the liaison did not last. When the plantation owner died several years later, she feared being sold and transported to the Deep South, and so planned her escape. A friendly white lady directed her to the first point of departure, and she arrived in Philadelphia weary but unharmed. She immediately joined the underground railroad, working as a cook, to help other fugitives and eventually reached St. Catharines, Canada from which base she worked until 1857.

That year she made her way to Auburn where she met former Governor William H. Seward, leader in the U.S. Senate of the anti-slavery movement. Seward befriended her and sold her some property at the southern edge of town for practically nothing in which she settled her parents whom she had recently rescued. For ten years, she helped over 300 slaves into Canada where the Fugitive Slave Law had no effect. For this, she was called "The Moses of her people".

During the war, she worked as a cook and laundress, and nursed sick blacks at Fort Royal, near the coast of South Carolina, after it was taken by Union forces. She also acted as a spy and actually lead 300 black soldiers to burn of Confederate supplies and buildings, and freed 800 slaves nearby. Her heroic and successful activities resulted in her being honored by Secretary of State Seward, when he recommended her for the post of matron of the Army Hospital at Fortress Monroe, Virginia.

After the war, Harriet Tubman returned to Auburn to provide a haven for poor and sick blacks. She sold produce raised by herself and her "guests". The proceeds went to further her cause. An admirer from Geneva, Mrs. Sarah Bradford, wrote a book, **The Life and Times of Harriet Tubman**, and made the proceeds available to The Harriet Tubman Home for the betterment of indigent blacks in Auburn and in the South.

HOME OF
HARRIET TUBMAN
'THE MOSES OF HER RACE'
UNDERGROUND RAILROAD
STATION IN SLAVERY DAYS

Cayuga County, 18
E. Side South St., city line

Eventually, Tubman acquired the twenty-five acre property next door, and later deeded it to the African Methodist Episcopal Zion Church. Booker T. Washington and other famous people visited her, and Queen Victoria sent her a Diamond Jubilee medal and an invitation to England. When she was 88, she opened a small home for the aged, and cared for as many as 15 people at a time. She died five years later in 1913, honored by her neighbors, and with military honors by the Grand Army of the Republic.

The day after the Nebraska bill was passed, another fugitive slave, Anthony Burns, was spotted by his owner in Boston. He was escorted to the dockside by army and marine units through a congregation of protesters requiring twenty-two companies of state militia to hold the crowd in check. Federal authorities spent $40,000 to return Burns to his master. From these protests, another anti-slavery political party was born in Ripon, Wisconsin on February 28, 1854 and called itself the Republican Party.

Frederick Douglass was a self-educated mulatto slave, who saw much cruelty laid on his fellow slaves, (and experienced them himself when loaned to a neighbor). Though well treated by his master, he decided to gain his freedom in 1838. On his second attempt, a friend loaned him a Navy uniform. In this guise he was able to board a train in Baltimore, and was not even questioned when purchasing his ticket.

Taking the name Douglass from Scott's hero in "The Lady of the Lake", he obtained employment in a New Bedford shipyard and was soon asked to relate his story to a meeting of abolitionists where William Lloyd Garrison was on the program. His natural speaking ability was soon recognized and he became a lecturer for the Massachusetts Anti-Slavery Society, traveling throughout New England and New York.

His first of three autobiographies was widely read, but inflammatory to people in the South. The temper of the times made it advisable for him to flee to England, in 1845, to avoid possible kidnapping. Those who befriended him there were so impressed by his knowledge, wisdom and demeanor, they purchased his freedom for him. Returning to the U.S., Douglass began to write and publish an anti-slavery weekly paper called the **North Star**, which caused a split with his Massachusetts associates.

In 1847, he settled in Rochester, a nucleus of crusading reformers—including Susan B. Anthony and William C. Bloss—and continued to live there for the next twenty-five years. The Fugitive Slave Act nudged him into the Underground Railroad, and, over the next ten years as head of the Rochester station, he conducted almost 500 slaves north to Canada. His efforts brought him into contact with Harriet Tubman and John Brown, but he wisely avoided participating in the ill-fated Harpers Ferry raid.

His two later autobiographies enhanced his fame, and during the Civil War he worked for emancipation and the enlistment of blacks in the Union army. Throughout Reconstruction, he continued his quest for civil rights for black people. He served in many important government capacities in Washington, D.C. and from 1889-91 was U.S. minister to Haiti. In 1884, his wife of over forty years died. Two years later he married his white secretary, Helen, who was the daughter of Gideon Pitts of Honeoye, a station master in earlier days. This caused a stir in white circles to which he replied, "My first wife was the color of my mother. My second wife is the color of my father."

PITTS MANSION
BUILT 1821 BY
GIDEON PITTS
SON OF CAPT. PETER PITTS
PIONEER SETTLER IN 1789

Ontario County, 25
US 20A, at Honeoye

In October of 1851, a mulatto slave who had escaped from a Missouri plantation eight years earlier and was employed making barrels in a cooperage in Syracuse, was clapped in irons by four U.S. Marshals on a trumped-up charge, and hustled to the Clinton Street Bridge police station. Jerry Henry had been educated by his master—who was in fact his father—and given charge of the financial records of the house. But he had wanted to be free and fled north. A crowd of abolitionists quickly gathered and attempted his rescue which failed after a four-block chase along Water Street.

Within twenty-four hours a second attempt in the "Jerry Rescue" was planned by Unitarian Minister Dr. Samuel J. May, Gerrit Smith (then Liberty Party candidate for Congress from Peterboro), and Dr. Hiram Hoyt, who cautioned the crowd against violence. The crowd overwhelmed the police; Jerry was hidden in a wagon and spirited to a nearby home to lay low several days until the authorities gave up the search. He then was disguised as an old man and moved to a station in Mexico, N.Y.

From there, he was taken to Oswego where he was rowed to a schooner about to sail for Kingston, Ontario. This circuitous route was used by Gerrit Smith whose many properties in Oswego came in handy for temporarily housing fugitive slaves until they could be smuggled out by people he could rely on. A Syracuse friend helped set Jerry up in business in a cabinet shop at St. Catharine's, Ontario. But Jerrie's luck ran out—he enjoyed only two years of freedom before he died and was buried in Canada.

Of the fifteen people indicted for interference with the law in the Jerry Rescue, only one was convicted and he died before the appeal was completed. The case against the others was dropped. Mssrs. May, Smith, and Hoyt admitted their complicity in a newspaper column but were never brought to account. Today a statue stands next to the Clinton Exchange Building (until recently, the Syracuse Post Office), in commemoration of the Jerry Rescue and one of Syracuse's finer moments.

John Brown's raid on the U.S. arsenal at Harpers Ferry in the fall of 1859 failed when a detachment of U.S. Marines under Robert E. Lee was sent for to quell the fighting. Brown's plan had been to arm plantation slaves for a massive uprising, and many thought that Gerrit Smith, Frederick Douglass, and other New York abolitionists helped plan and finance the raid. The South was understandably alarmed, and the "irrepressible conflict" (William Seward's term), seemed close at hand.

The following spring, Lincoln won the Republican nomination for presidential candidate on the third ballot by the slimmest of margins over Seward, long a contender for the position. When Lincoln won the presidency in the fall elections, he appointed Seward his Secretary of State, and the South, fearful of the anti-slavery position of these two men, reacted. South Carolina was the first to secede on December 20, 1860. The wiser of the slaveowners feared secession as prelude to a war that would spell the end of slavery. But hotheads on both sides continued to kindle the coming conflagration. By the end of the first week in February, seven southern states had seceded from the Union and the Confederate States of America was formed.

Much of the opposition in the North to the Lincoln administration was because considerable capital was invested in the south by wealthy northerners. As well, laborers in the New York city area, particularly immigrants, feared the competition for jobs from free black labor. The then Democratic Mayor of New York City, Fernando Wood, exploited this situation, and even proposed that the city secede from the Union in the belief that the Union would dissolve, and that a free New York City could maintain trade relations with the South. The idea was firmly trounced by Horace Greeley, John Dix (President Buchanan's Secretary of State), and George Clinton, De Witt Clinton's son.

On April 12, 1861, South Carolina fired on Fort Sumter, at Charleston harbor, four more Southern states seceded, and by July, 47,000 New Yorkers had enlisted in the Union army. Weeks later, the opening battle of the Civil War, the First Battle of Bull Run, called Manassas in the South, occurred thirty miles west of Washington, D.C. and ended in a rout of Union forces; one-third of the casualties were from New York state.

In June of 1862, Congress abolished slavery in the District of Columbia and the territories and, a month later, declared captured blacks forever free and authorized the recruitment of blacks into the Union Army. The pay scale for black privates was set at $7 a month compared to $13 for whites.

After General Robert E. Lee's first attempt to invade the North was blocked at the battle of Antietam in the fall of 1862, Lincoln issued the Emancipation Proclamation, to be effective January 1, 1863. More politically inspired than enforceable, it "freed" only slaves in the combative southern states as Lincoln did not wish to alienate the slave-holding border states. He had hoped that slavery would be renounced by the South, encouraged by federal compensation to slave owners. The western part of Virginia, which only months before seceded from Virginia to become the state of West Virginia, abolished slavery in 1863. The states of Maryland and Missouri did so in 1864, with Tennessee, Delaware and Kentucky the following year, all largely reflecting Union victories

Slavery was abolished by enactment of the Thirteenth Amendment in January of 1865; three months later, the Civil War ended. As important as was the finality of slavery, it became only a step in the fulfillment of its implied promise.

BIRTHPLACE OF
FRANK B. CARPENTER, ARTIST
PAINTED 'LINCOLN AND CABINET'
SON OF ASAPH CARPENTER
WHO SETTLED HERE IN 1800

Cortland County, 18, US 11, 3 m. N. of Homer

CHAPTER NINETEEN

In 1805, the New York Legislature established a permanent fund for the support of elementary education. The initial fund was the proceeds from the sale of 500,000 acres of state land not yet disposed of or set aside. The fund was added to subsequently, but no distribution was to be made until the annual income from the fund attained $50,000. In 1812, additional legislation was passed to create school districts throughout the state, and the income from the school fund was to be apportioned according to child population figures of each district, based on the most recent census.

The town was to match its share from the state fund for the purpose of paying teachers' salaries. All this was put under the watchful eye of a state superintendent over public schools, with provisions for examining and licensing teachers. The school fund generated $50,000 in 1813, and two years later the first payments were made toward providing some semblance of professional standards.

FARM AND GRAVE
JEDIDIAH PECK
1747-1821
FATHER OF THE COMMON
SCHOOL SYSTEM OF THE
STATE OF NEW YORK

Otsego County, 1
CR., 2 ½ m. E. of Burlington

Until the 1860s, most teachers had little, if any, professional training. Anyone who had an education could teach school, it was thought. Textbooks on teaching methods and subject matter were in short supply and not a few were lingering British schoolbooks and, of course, the ever-present **Bible.** The lack of textbooks was so disturbing that Noah Webster, who was teaching in Goshen New York, prepared in his free time **The American Spelling Book, being the First part of a Grammatical Institute of the English Language,** which was published in 1784. It combined spelling, grammar, and moral guidance, and was in tune with the idea of American self-reliance.

A very small example of that which was to be memorized follows:

>Look ere you leap.
>
>Hot love is soon cold.
>
>You have hit the nail on the head.
>
>You must not buy a pig in a poke.
>
>Time and tide wait for no man.
>
>A man may buy gold too dear.
>
>A bird in the hand is worth two in the bush.

Over the next fifty years, a total of over 75,000,000 copies in many editions was printed. Because of the color of its cover it was popularly known as the **Blue Back Speller**.

Webster received less than a cent a copy, but this was enough to support him and his family the twenty years from 1807-1827 while he put together his first and most famous dictionary. Also in circulation was Parson Weems' **The Life and Memorable Actions of George Washington**, in which young Washington was portrayed owning up to his father of being guilty of felling the cherished cherry tree. Another story had him being able to throw a silver dollar across the Rappahannock (at Fredericksburg where the river must be 100 yards across). These stories were frivolous compared to the real deeds and character of the majestic man of paramount prestige. Nevertheless, the book accomplished its purpose. Concurrent with Webster and Weems was Nicholas Pike's **A New and Complete System** (of arithmetic) and **Geography Made Easy** by the Reverend Jedidiah Morse, father of the inventor of the telegraph.

By the Civil War, more sophisticated textbooks on numerous subjects appeared and the **Blue Back Speller** and Parson Weems' fables faded from use.

William Holmes McGuffey's philosophy was that nothing was clearer and easier to comprehend than the steps leading to wisdom. A professor with practical teaching experience, he had published in 1836 the first of his **Eclectic Readers** to be used in school and the home. In addition to the primer, he put out six more volumes, each advancing the student in knowledge, morality, literature,

Howard S. Ford

and other subjects. The one hundred twenty-two million copies published had a profound influence on American perceptions for a century, and on his publisher.

The little one-room schoolhouse persisted for a long time—almost up to the present day in some rural areas. (A neighbor of mine, a retired school teacher, remembers her grammar school days in the 1940s in a one-room school in which only one teacher instructed all grades, one through eight.) The teacher in many cases was not much older than the oldest students, but discipline was kept, the iron stove was stoked, the woodbox filled, the school swept, and the assorted courses were taught.

FIRST SCHOOL BUILT IN PREBLE 1801 RUTH THORPE TEACHER HAD SCHOLARS FROM THE TOWNS OF TULLY AND HOMER

Cortland County, 26
CR, 2 m. east of Preble

Schoolteacher's pay was meager, and as late as the 1870s, the school year was only twenty weeks long to accommodate farm chores in season. The teachers were boarded during the term at a succession of villagers' homes. Some schools offered private courses for a fee for which advanced students could study English composition, geography, grammar, and rhetoric. Geometry, surveying, mathematics, and Latin courses cost a little more.

In 1827, New York became the first state to subsidize private schools for the purpose of training teachers, but this and other legislative efforts was inadequate, and in 1844, the first normal school (from the French *école normale* which provided training of teachers for the lower grades) was opened in Albany to train enough teachers to meet the increasing need.

Answering the demand for a more advanced education, Hartwick Seminary, a Lutheran theological school, was founded in 1797 (in part from the estate of Reverend John Christopher Hartwick with the proceeds from the purchase of Hartwick's Patent paid by neighbor Judge Cooper). Hamilton Institute, a Baptist school, (later named Madison University), first called students to its doors in 1820. The school became nonsectarian, and in 1890, it finally settled on the name Colgate University in honor of benefactor William Colgate, founder of the soap company. Nearby, the forerunner of Cazenovia College opened in 1824 as the Seminary of the Geneva Conference (Methodist). Academies prepared students for the trades and more practical arts.

HARTWICK SEMINARY OLDEST LUTHERAN THEOLOGICAL SCHOOL IN AMERICA, FOUNDED 1797 BY REV. JOHN CHRISTOPHER HARTWICK. LOCATED HERE 1816

Otsego County, 10
NY 28 at Hartwick Seminary

Many of the seminaries (for girls) and academies (for boys) lasted only a short time, and after 1855, the survivors began to diminish in number. Public sentiment was for every child in the state to receive an education through secondary school even if the parents couldn't pay for it. By 1850 the modern public system of grades one through twelve was firmly established throughout the country. The Union Free School Act of 1853 and the Act of 1867 provided that the full expense of the public schools be paid by taxes. Consequently, many private academies and seminaries died out or were bought and converted to public high schools.

Ezra Cornell, from De Ruyter, hiked into Ithaca and began his career by carving a 200-foot tunnel in solid rock so that the millrace of an local mill would be freeze-proof. He sold plows after being laid off during the Panic of 1837, and, in his travels, met Samuel F. B. Morse, who was then perfecting his telegraph apparatus. Having an inventive mind himself, Cornell devised an efficient way of plowing a ditch, laying telegraph line, and backfilling all in one operation.

This put him into the budding telegraph business, and before long, he amassed a fortune and affiliated his company with that of Hiram Sibley, as one of the founders of Western Union. In his opinion, he had more money than his family needed, so he made a gift of a free public library, set up to sustain itself, to the village of Ithaca.

EZRA CORNELL
300 YARDS UP THIS LANE
STOOD HIS BOYHOOD HOME
IN 1828 HE WALKED TO ITHACA
WHERE LATER HE FOUNDED
CORNELL UNIVERSITY

Madison County, 4
CR., 3 ½ m. E. of DeRuyter

In 1862, Congress passed the Morrill Land Grant Act which provided seed money from the sale of federal land for states to establish colleges. Cornell and his close friend, Andrew Dickson White from Syracuse, were both state legislators and wanted to establish a university at Ithaca. Other communities were vigorously contending for these funds when Cornell put up $500,000 of his own money and his 300 acre farm on East Hill, thus securing the land grant money for the new university soon to be named for him.

Some of the land grant dollars went to found Willard State Asylum in Ovid (named for the determined doctor who fell dead while pleading to a state committee for the same funds for the sanitarium). Additional funds went to Genesee College in Lima.

White wrote the University's Plan of Organization, which provided for a general education as well as colleges in engineering, agriculture, and other specialties. Cornell University then opened its doors in 1868. As the first president, White invited famous professors there for brief lecture tours to enhance the Cornell faculty's reputation and to attract students and additional faculty. Numerous workmen were brought in to build endowed Morrill, White, and McGraw Halls, and the Sibley College of Engineering, making the university the largest landowner and industry in Ithaca. Cornell was also the first nonsectarian college in the country, and the first to be coeducational.

In 1892, W. Egbert Grant opened his Conservatory of Music and Affiliated Schools downtown, broadening Ithaca's cultural base. Ithaca College grew out of this.

> **FROM THIS SITE**
> **THE ITHACA CONSERVATORY**
> **OF MUSIC FORMED IN 1892**
> **AND ITS SUCCESSOR ITHACA**
> **COLLEGE CHARTERED IN 1931**
> **OPERATED FROM 1911 TO 1966**
>
> Tompkins County, 61
> Burffalo St bet. Cayuga & Tioga

Genesee Wesleyan Seminary was founded in Lima in 1832, but after thirty-five years, Methodist Church fathers decided the school could benefit from a more urban location. Syracuse businessmen raised funds, as did the City of Syracuse, to attract the school. The Methodist convention, held in Syracuse in 1870, accepted the city's offer, and Syracuse University opened in September 1871 in downtown Syracuse. The Medical College at Geneva, without facilities when its buildings burned in 1870, moved to Syracuse to also become part of the new institution. The University's permanent location was decided in 1873 when the Hall of Languages was built on a nearby hill southeast of the city, and became the nucleus of the quickly expanding campus.

> **GENESEE WESLEYAN SEMINARY**
> **FOUNDED 1832**
> **GENESEE COLLEGE ESTABLISHED**
> **1849 AND ON APRIL 14, 1869**
> **WAS ALLOWED TO REMOVE TO**
> **FORM SYRACUSE UNIVERSITY**
>
> Livingston County, 24
> College Ave. & Genesee, Lima

Determined to have more and better teachers the state opened Oswego Normal in 1861, Geneseo College in 1867, and Cortland Normal School in 1869. Oneonta Normal followed in 1889.

The Geneva Academy, founded in 1796, was merged with Fairfield Theological School in 1822, at the direction of Episcopal Bishop John Henry Hobart to become Geneva College. In 1834, it added the Medical College (which later burned).

School teacher Elizabeth Blackwell applied for admission to the Medical College in 1847; she had already been turned down by seventeen other medical schools simply because she was a woman. The Dean at Geneva was so startled by the novelty of her application, he turned it over to his students for their opinion. In turn, the boys thought it was an outlandish hoax, and called her bluff by granting admission. But it was no joke, and at age thirty-seven, she became a student of medicine, determined to succeed under difficult conditions, mainly imposed by the community of Geneva, morally outraged by the idea of a woman delving into the scientific secrets of the human body!

In 1849, she became the first woman in the country to earn a medical degree, promising at the ceremony "to shed honor on this diploma". But being accepted by the medical world was no easier; no hospital, college, clinic, or surgery would consider her for study or practice. Eight years elapsed when, with her sister and another women, she founded in New York City the New York Infirmary and College for Women that had developed from a clinic she had opened in 1853.

SITE OF GENEVA MEDICAL COLLEGE ELIZ. BLACKWELL RECEIVED HERE IN 1849 THE FIRST DEGREE OF MD EVER CONFERRED UPON A WOMAN

Ontario County, 13
US 29, NY 5 & NY 14 bet
Washington and Hamilton Sts.

She organized women for nursing care during the Civil War, and subsequently established the first school for nurses in the country. When it was unfashionable, she was one of the champions of preventive medicine, teaching hygiene and antisepsis. Moving back to her native England, she continued to shed honor on her diploma for a long time, dying there at the age of ninety-nine in 1910. In the meantime, her alma mater changed its name to Hobart College.

Despite Hobart College's early start, the first "school" there was taught at the mission by Protestant missionary Samuel Kirkland to the Senecas, in 1765, at Kanadesaga. The Senecas liked him, but came to fear his presence because, as with the Jesuits, when he ministered to sick Indians, they often died, (low immunity to white men's diseases persisted). Kirkland wisely moved to the Oneidas, and out of this mission evolved his school for Indians and whites, which later became Hamilton College in Clinton. Kirkland is also credited with persuading his close friend, Chief Shenandoah, and his Oneidas to side with the Americans during the Revolution.

HAMILTON COLLEGE
FOUNDED AS HAMILTON-ONEIDA
ACADEMY, 1793 BY THE REV.
SAMUEL KIRKLAND. CHARTERED
AS HAMILTON COLLEGE
MAY 26, 1812

Oneida County, 30
Hamilton College, Clinton

First chartered in 1852, Elmira College was re-chartered in 1855 as Elmira Female College, with a gift from Simeon Benjamin to become the first women's college in the country to award degrees in science and the arts equivalent to those given in men's colleges. Jointly with a local hospital, it continues to operate a school of nursing.

Making alcoholic beverages, including rum, wine, and applejack brandy from cider, for home use was a common practice in the eighteenth and nineteenth centuries. Occasions of every kind called for toasts in civilian life and in the army. During the Revolution it was common for the officers of the army to drink thirteen toasts in a row—one for each state of the new country. Militia meetings seemed more a pretext for tapping a cask and hoisting a drink with friends than military training. And after delivering lengthy sermons, men of the cloth often joined their flocks at the local tavern for a sociable evening of drinking and to better know their congregation. Each city, and occasionally, small towns, had several distilleries and breweries to satisfy the demand.

The use of alcohol got so out of hand, particularly in the army, that in 1777, member of Continental Congress and the army's surgeon general, Dr. Benjamin Rush, made a plea for temperance, not prohibition, but moderation. Dr. Rush was not against beer and wine which he thought were useful and nourishing. He wrote a pamphlet to the army warning of the debility and low resistance to disease caused by frequent use of rum and whiskey so lavishly supplied to the officers and men by the government.

In 1785, his essay, **The Effects of Ardent Spirits on the Human Body and Mind,** was distributed to religious societies and general assemblies. Leading personages ardently argued for temperance before congregations of every denomination but much of the preaching fell on deaf ears. Even so, in 1808, in Saratoga, New York, the first temperance society was formed. A generation later, Presbyterian Reverend Doctor Lyman Beecher was persuaded by Rush's essay and wrote six temperance essays of his own which were distributed widely.

Central New York was ripe ground for cultivation of reform such as temperance, abolition of slavery, and women's rights, and many of the reformers were interested in all three. Elizabeth Cady Stanton was one such, a woman of education who was determined to achieve reform and she early agitated for equal pay for women teachers.

She and her husband, a journalist and abolitionist sympathizer, were attending an anti-slavery conference in London in 1846, when the women delegates were turned away at the door. This affront channeled her attention more to women's rights. With Lucretia Mott and others, she organized in 1848 the first women's convention in the United States at Seneca Falls, attended by both women and men, and startled the other attendees when she demanded that a woman's right to vote be a part of the conference platform. Frederick Douglass seconded the resolution.

ON THIS HILL IN THE ORIGINAL HOUSE, 31 WOMEN ORGANIZED THE FEMALE CHARITABLE SOCIETY, SECOND OLDEST WOMEN'S SOCIETY IN THE U.S., JULY 27, 1817.

Onondaga County, 28
NY 31, Baldwinsville

FIRST CONVENTION FOR WOMEN'S RIGHTS WAS HELD ON THIS CORNER

Seneca County, 29
US 20 & 5, Seneca Falls

When New York became a state in 1777, its first constitution required the ownership of a twenty-pound freehold, or payment of annual rent of forty shillings to qualify one to vote for assemblymen, and evidence of more worth to vote for senators and governors. By the end of the first few decades of the nineteenth century, Yankees from New England had arrived in New York and demanded more democratic voting rules. The New York Constitutional Convention of 1821 provided universal suffrage for all white males, although property qualifications still applied to free black men. By contrast, women in New Jersey could vote if they could meet the high property qualifications, and free Negroes there had the same voting privileges as white men.

In 1852, at a temperance meeting, Mrs. Stanton met Susan B. Anthony, a Quaker from Rochester, and the two became lifelong friends and co-leaders for women's rights. Concurrently, another Seneca Falls colleague, Amelia Jenks Bloomer, editor of the local suffragette and temperance paper, the **Lilly**, publicized a new type of ballooning "skirt" worn by her friends, Mrs. Stanton and Mrs. Elizabeth Miller (Gerrit Smith's daughter and a second cousin of Mrs. Stanton's), and bloomers became a new fashion paired with the women's movement and part of history.

Howard S. Ford

Of course, the ladies at the lectern were heckled but they were able to cope with it. Once, a woman in the crowd jeered, "What do you do with your children when your out making speeches?" Mrs. Stanton quickly replied, "Ladies, it takes me no longer to speak than for you to listen. What have you done with your children during the two hours you've been sitting here?"

ELIZABETH CADY STANTON PROMOTER OF THE FIRST WOMEN'S RIGHTS CONVENTION LIVED HERE. CONVENTION WAS HELD ACROSS THE RIVER

Seneca County, 34
Washington St. Seneca Falls

New York law still provided that a woman's earnings were subject to her husbands control, as was her inheritance. She also had few rights of control over her children and, of course, women chafed under these restrictions. Fortunately, the New York legislature consisted of men of wisdom and responded to the ladies' overtures so that these wrongs were righted in the Earnings Bill of 1860.

Activist women deferred their cause in favor of serving the Civil War effort, but after the war they worked hard for suffrage for blacks and white women. When the Fifteenth Amendment giving blacks the right to vote was passed in 1870, suffragists resented that women were ignored despite their solicitation for the rights of both groups. To lobby congress and sway public opinion, Miss Anthony and Mrs. Stanton formed the National Woman Suffrage Association to seek an amendment to the Constitution, and Lucy Stone formed the American Woman Suffrage Association to influence state legislatures.

In the 1872 Presidential election, Miss Anthony, her mother, and others voted, to test the constitutionality of the issue, and were arrested for their efforts. Anthony insisted on being handcuffed by a U. S. Marshall. She was defended by Henry Selden, a Rochester attorney (father of patent attorney George B. Selden), and tried by a Federal judge before an all-male jury in Canandaigua. She could not be a witness on her own behalf, was deemed guilty, and directed to pay a $100 fine and court costs. A legal technicality blocked her appeal, but she never paid the fine. Ironically, the publicity of the trial worked in her favor and encouraged other women to form suffrage chapters.

HENRY R. SELDEN
1805–1885
LIEUT. GOV. AND JUDGE LIVED
HERE. GEORGE B. SELDEN
INVENTOR OF 'SELDEN PATENT' FOR
AUTOMOBILE WAS BORN HERE

Monroe County, 3
NY 104 at Clarkson

The rigors and realities of frontier life proved a wife's importance and right to equality, so must have felt the men of the Territory of Wyoming; in 1869, it was the first political entity to grant women unqualified voting rights.

Frances Elizabeth Willard, from Churchville, was active academically, and particularly interested in temperance reform. She helped found the Woman's Christian Temperance Union in 1874, and five years later, became its president. The WCTU was also active in pressing for the right to vote, reasoning that women in the voting booth would be a force benefitting the temperance cause. The possibility of prohibition frightened the liquor industry, and it campaigned viciously against women's suffrage. So did other businesses because they feared they would have to improve working conditions for women should they get the vote.

SUSAN B. ANTHONY OUTSTANDING LEADER IN WOMAN'S RIGHTS MOVEMENT MADE HER HOME HERE WITH HER SISTER, MARY 1866-1906

Monroe County, 38
On Madison St.

In 1902, Elizabeth Cady Stanton died. Susan B. Anthony followed in 1906. But twentieth century women were up to the task, thanks to the legacy of the preceding generation. Harriet Black, Anna Howard Shaw, Lucy Burns, Alice Paul, and Carrie Chapman Catt and many others carried on with their own effective combination of strategies, taking the advice of Miss Anthony, "The only fear you need have is not standing by your cause." With the endorsement by such men as Theodore Roosevelt, they had won women's suffrage in twelve states by 1913.

In a two month period, 8,000 women were recruited by Alice Paul and Lucy Burns to organize a Woman's Pageant demanding a constitutional amendment. It was held the day before Woodrow Wilson's inaugural in Washington, with a parade and floats to publicize their determination. Many men participated in the pageant but male hecklers became mean and a riot ensued. Yet no heckler-rioters were arrested.

A "Susan B. Anthony" Amendment was proposed in Congress but it was defeated in 1915. All was not lost though, for two years later, Jeanette Rankin of Montana became the first woman to be elected to Congress.

When the country entered World War I, suffragette policy was to continue their campaign, but patriotic war work and help in the soldier's canteens took precedence, as it had in the Civil War. But the ladies staged a six-day-a-week dignified picket of President Wilson's White House, protesting his stand against a national women's rights amendment even though he did favor state-by-state choice. Soon, daily riots occurred; police protection wasn't provided and police began arresting the pickets, not the rioters. The protesting women were sent to prison for "obstructing traffic". In all, 168 were jailed and after five months, the guards began harassing the women prisoners, feeding them spoiled food and committing other indignities. This brought about public support for the incarcerated and the women's movement in general, and embarrassed Wilson. His administration finally capitulated and released all the women.

Within a short time, the New York legislature voted women the right to vote, in November of 1917. The House of Representatives scheduled a vote on the amendment for January 18th, and Wilson declared he was in favor of it. It barely passed in the House, with only one more vote than the necessary two-thirds majority. On June 4, 1919, the amendment was passed in the Senate.

By August of 1920, the long sought-after amendment had been ratified by all but one of the required number of states, and the nation held its collective breath waiting for the vote result in the Tennessee State House. Fortunately, legislator Harry Burns had listened to his mother who had written to him to "do the right thing".

He did. Ratification was complete and the Twentieth Amendment giving women the right to vote became the law of the land.

Though not as lofty as obtaining the right to vote, some inventions of the second half of the nineteenth century were of direct importance to women everywhere. They not only lightened their burdens but helped simplify numerous menial chores so that the time saved could be put to the practical use of self education and other personal amenities. Better designed and more-efficient cook stoves, ice boxes for food storage, factory processed canned food, better lighting everywhere, (including the kitchen), dish washers and clothes washers, (yes, even over a hundred years ago, but rudimentary and hand powered), carpet sweepers, sewing machines, and the simple expedient of having a pump or faucet next to the kitchen sink, all contributed to easing women's chores and bettering the work parity between the sexes.

Meanwhile, the temperance movement had been so successful that, by 1913, more than half the country's population was subject to local prohibition. Since liquor taxes had formerly brought in as much as two-thirds of the federal government's revenue, the country was beginning to face shortfalls in operating income. Only during the severely high expenses of the Civil War had there been a tax imposed on citizen's income. But the foreseeable fiscal future of diminishing liquor taxes convinced

Congress to take drastic action. In 1913, the 16th amendment to the Constitution providing for a Federal Income Tax was proposed, passed, and ratified. With national revenue no longer dependent on liquor sales, Congress saw fit to pass, and the country agreed by ratifying, the 18th amendment providing for nationwide prohibition to begin the following year, in 1920.

CHAPTER TWENTY

The Union Glass Company began in Somerville, Massachusetts, where founder Amory Houghton, had just terminated a previous business. He soon moved the firm to Brooklyn, New York, in 1864. There, his company changed its name to The Brooklyn Flint Glass Company to reflect its location and the quality of its product. Four years later, the company found its final home at Corning, and the residents soon came daily to watch the fascinating operations through the big windows in front of the shop.

Inside the gaffers picked up globs of molten glass from the white hot "glory hole" of the furnace with a blowpipe. Blowing, then twirling, blowing again, and then more closely working the piece by rolling it on a flat with special shaping tools, the artisans delighted the crowds as they turned out vases, bowls, bottles and other objects.

So many people were entranced by the craftmen's magic that the company had to limit the number of observers to those with passes. Quickly filling its niche in the Corning economy, the popular company changed its name again, in 1875, to the Corning Glass Works, and made a block of forty percent of its common stock available to the local residents who bought it up with optimistic fervor.

Years later, the glass company's Corning Glass Center evolved as a major attraction in central New York for people from all the states and many foreign countries. Glass technology, which had its beginnings 3500 years ago in Egypt, had vastly expanded over the millennia, from the early making of goblets to the manufacture of everything from whiskey bottles, to windows, intriguingly beautiful paper weights, eyeglasses, medical syringes, the 200-inch glass mirror for the reflecting telescope at Mt. Palomar, microscopes, light bulbs, vacuum tubes, fiberglass, glass fiber optics, and 65,000 other products.

Elsewhere, Charles Flint had a knack for sizing up poorly managed companies with inherent potential that could be combined with other firms and eventually sold for sizeable capital gains. He had put together the combinations that formed the United States Rubber Company and American

Chicle for substantial fees, and later sold both companies for significant profits. He didn't manage the enterprises himself but knew how to acquire capable men who did.

At the turn of the century, he began a new combination with International Time Recording Company of New York, (Endicott), a leader in its field of time clocks, including a devise for metering long distance phone calls, as the core company. Flint soon merged it with The Computing Scale Company. At this point, Flint met Herman Hollerith, inventor of a programmable tabulating device using notched cards (do not fold, spindle, or mutilate), who had won a government contract to tabulate data for the 1890 census. Hollerith's company was named, naturally enough, The Tabulating Machine Company. Flint bought this enterprise, too, and from the three companies, he formed the Computing-Tabulating-Recording Company.

A number of years later, after indifferent results, Flint hired Thomas J. Watson, to head CTR. A son of a southern-tier lumberman who had aspirations for his son to become a lawyer, Watson attended nearby Addison Academy but left when he was seventeen to enroll at Elmira School of Commerce. He later clerked in a Painted Post store, from which he was lured into the romance of selling.

Twenty years of gaining the practical experience to be a professional salesman at various companies followed, most notably under the tutelage of the autocratic John Patterson, president of National Cash Register and developer of the first known canned sales talk and other innovations. Watson became a protégé of Patterson's, but lost this status when the two had a disagreement and he was fired. This seeming stumble in his career placed him into an exclusive "club" of discharged NCR executives who later became famous in their own right when out from under Patterson's shadow.

At CTR Watson improved the sales force (partly with others pirated from NCR) and invested in research to improve their products, particularly tabulating. The sale of punch cards (which were devoured in the millions for the programming of the tabulating machines), and leasing the tabulating and other machines, rather than selling them, provided a steadily increasing stream of reliable income. The early days of the company's existence were still difficult and, sometimes, employees and suppliers had to be paid in company stock, to their and their heirs' lasting gratitude. In 1924, the company changed its name from CTR to International Business Machines.

The earlier and comparatively cumbrous mechanical technology evolved into the electronic computer industry. IBM channeled a good part of its earnings into research and development and in training its personnel, and, taking a leaf from George Johnson nearby, provided generous incentives to the employees to get the desired results. You know the rest.

In 1842, Edward Anthony got in on the ground floor of the new industry just coming into existence and started a daguerreotype supply shop, in New York. Later, he merged his business with Scovill Manufacturing Company, which made cameras. Just after the turn of the century, he moved his firm to Binghamton, and shortened the name to ANSCO to become a serious competitor of the Eastman Kodak Co.

George Eastman's father was enterprising and continually busy, commuting to the business school he ran in Rochester from Waterville, where he also had a thirty-acre nursery, and where George was born in 1854. His father died when George was eight, requiring his mother to move to Rochester to manage the school and young George to get a job by becoming a bank clerk to augment the family income.

BIRTHPLACE OF GEORGE EASTMAN INVENTOR OF KODAK BORN JULY 12, 1854. DIED IN ROCHESTER MARCH 14, 1932.

Oneida County, 66
NY 12 in Waterville

But the new science of photography caught his attention and became his main interest. Photography was then primarily limited to portrait studios and dauntless early professional photographers, such as William Henry Jackson and Matthew Brady, who became famous lugging cumbersome equipment to capture images of the Civil War and the exciting West. The procedure of exposing and developing pictures was unwieldy and complex, involving wet glass plates, dark tents, and other paraphernalia, and prompt attention to detail which cramped the public's enthusiasm for picture taking. Eastman's inventive genius evolved the simpler dry plate when he formed the Eastman Dry Plate Co. in 1880 (renamed three times), and a few years later, nitro-cellulose paper-backed film that could be loaded on a spool in a handy box camera. At first the film, still inside the camera, was sent to Eastman for processing; the developed pictures and camera were returned with a new roll of film installed, ready to go. "You press the button, we do the rest", was the advertisement that helped it catch on. The camera with film cost $25 and the processing $10 for 100 snapshots.

As he recognized the value of inventions and techniques to bring photography to the attention of the public, Eastman created and copyrighted the word "Kodak", in 1888, to apply to his cameras. The word that meant nothing at all, now had meaning for millions of people. With no prior meaning, he reasoned, the word can only be identified with his product. He made the word short for simplicity, and started and ended the word with 'k's be-cause they are strong letters. Time has proven him right in his further assertion that Kodak was not likely to be misspelled or forgotten. Xerox Corporation, a twentieth century copy-machine phenomenon, also based in Rochester, must have copied the idea.

The spool of flexible film was also the answer to Thomas Edison who had been studying moving images and how to show them to audiences. The moving picture camera and projector were developed as a result of Edison meeting with Eastman, and the motion picture industry soon began delighting millions in their new-found leisure time.

Eastman kept his company, now the Eastman Kodak Co. (1892), in Rochester, which gave the city a continuing unique identity and provided worthy employment and investment returns in excess of anyone's dreams. Eastman also proved to be a pioneer in modern business management, reinvesting earnings in research and training, and providing incentive through good pay, pension and profit-sharing plans, and health insurance, enabling him to secure and hold highly qualified personnel.

A bachelor, he made careful and selective charitable gifts to the University of Rochester, the Massachusetts Institute of Technology, and the Tuskegee and Hampton Institutes. He established the Eastman School of Music, the Rochester Dental Dispensary, and the beautiful Eastman Theater, all in Rochester, and gave to several other causes that he favored. It is estimated that his philanthropy exceeded $100,000,000.

"All I had in mind was to make enough money so my mother would never have to work again", Eastman said.

Orchards had been started early in Monroe County and by 1800, two notable apples, the Early Joe and Northern Spy were produced on a farm just across the county line at East Bloomfield. Aggressive nursery and seedsmen exploited the regions need for fruit farms and the beautification of homes so that by 1855, Monroe County had 150, or about half the nurseries in New York. The Flower City also grew, partially, through its nurseries and seedsmen who stocked the new nurseries as western territories were being settled and to help rebuild the South after the Civil War. Ellwanger and Berry, perhaps the leading nursery and known for its wide range of varieties and success in packing bare-root specimens for the distance, shipped to as far away as Tokyo, Korea, and Australia.

As the population grew forty per cent in the seventies and fifty per cent in the eighties, Rochester annexed land sufficient to double its area and city nurseries sub-divided their highly desirable and appreciated property, and moved their nursery equipment to the outskirts. The city finally accepted the gift of the land for Highland Park from Ellwanger and Berry in 1888 and Eastman Kodak acquired what had been originally Hanford's Landing Nursery, renamed Lake Avenue Commercial Nurseries, for its Kodak Park. Crosman Seeds and Joseph Harris' Seed Company still endure today.

Judge Cooper's son, James Fenimore Cooper, dropped out of Yale University, and after a brief career in the Navy, became the first important American novelist, romanticizing the region and its frontier history in the **Pathfinder, The Last of the Mohicans, The Deerslayer**, collectively known as the **Leatherstocking Tales** and giving the name Leatherstocking to the Otsego Lake region. He lived in Europe several years, but was not favored there because he bragged about his country so much, and was shunned at home because his writings found so much fault with it. Returning to

Cooperstown, he adopted the harsh and aristocratic airs of some of the Hudson River landowners, and was unlamented by the townspeople when he died in 1851.

Years after Cooper's death, Mark Twain took literary pot shots at him for what Twain thought were improbable situations and absurd dialogue in the same novels for which Cooper is famous. Despite Twain's censure of Cooper, Cooperstown is proud to have Cooper as a native son.

SUNKEN ISLAND
HOME OF TOM HUTTER
'DEERSLAYER'

Otsego County, 22
NY 80, 5m. N. of Cooperstown

'NATTIE BUMPO'
LEATHERSTOCKING RESCUED
CHINGACHGOOK FROM FLAMES
CHINGACH DYING IN HIS CARE
PIONEER

Otsego County 21,
CR. E. side Otsego Lake
3 m. N. of Cooperstown

Isaac Singer, who spent his childhood in Oswego, developed a practical sewing machine that could be used both commercially and by the housewife. Elias Howe successfully sued him for infringing on his patent, but Singer filed twenty other patents on features of the machine, and by combining these in the finished product and using various manufacturers, he overcame the effects of the lawsuit and prospered.

Singer's friend and legal counsel for the company, Edward Clark, became a partner in the firm. Clark met a Cooperstown girl, Caroline Jordan, married her and fell in love with her town, as well. They bought a summer home by Otsego Lake in 1854 and built a small replica of an 11th century castle on a point on the eastern shore of the lake twenty-five years later and called it "Kingfisher Castle".

Their grandson, Stephen Carlton Clark, was a lawyer and businessman, and as a collector of art, a humanist, and philanthropist, suggested to the trustees of the New York State Historical Association that they move their headquarters to Cooperstown, which they did in 1939. Mr. Clark also gave financial support to the Association, and together with the Scriven Foundation, endowed Cooperstown with several buildings, including Fenimore House, the Association's headquarters and museum. These charming buildings and exhibits enable visitors to learn about early settlement life and the culture that developed in rural central New York.

Rounding out these exhibits, The Farmers' Museum and its Village Crossroads is a collection of homes, barns, a drug store, a doctor's office, a blacksmith's shop, livestock, farm implements and tools of the first half of the nineteenth century, with explanations of the culture, when agriculture was growing into an industry from subsistence farming. The Carriage and Harness Museum has on display a collection of carts, coaches, and phaetons, and a panoply of livery and harness, demonstrating the wheelwright's, the carriage builder's, and tack maker's art.

Baseball was allegedly invented by Abner Doubleday, a Civil War General, and played here first, according to a report made in 1907 by a commission headed by A.G. Mills to study the question. Doubters say the inventor was not Doubleday, nor did the game start here. Outside of that, there is no question in the mind of the fans that Cooperstown does replicate the era and ambience that gave birth to baseball, so it is a good place to have the Baseball Hall of Fame, a museum of the "national game".

In 1839, the rail line went through Rome, even if the Erie canal had not, and five years later, the canal relocated through it also. Rome was established as a hub of transportation when it became the terminus of both the Watertown and Rome Railroad and the Black River Canal in 1851. After the Civil War, two iron mills were founded, soon followed by a shoe and boot factory, a canning plant, and a locomotive works.

The Rome Iron works changed to making brass in 1878 when iron rails for the railroads were made obsolete by rails of steel to carry heavier locomotives and the larger freight cargoes that ensued. By 1890, the Rome Brass and Copper Company became one of the largest in the business, with brass sales amounting to three and a half million pounds, and over a million pounds of copper. We know it now as Revere Copper and Brass, Inc.

NORTHWEST 35 RODS
JESSE WILLIAMS
IN 1851 INAUGERATED THE
CHEESE FACTORY
SYSTEM
THUS REVOLUTIONIZING DAIRYING

Oneida County, 48
NY 46, 2m. N. of Rome

Farmer Jesse Williams began the cheese factory movement in 1851, near Rome and Herkimer, where he collected milk from his neighbors for making cheese. His newly developed equipment eliminated the hard work of hand churning and pressing, and he developed a market for the product made better by improved breeds of cows, better strains of meadow grass, and techniques from county agricultural societies. Soon, Herkimer County supplied one-fourth of the state's cheese production. Area producers organized their marketing, which succeeded and led to the formation of the state Dairymen's Board of Trade.

Utica grew to be the hub of four railroads, and the location of one of the largest freight yards east of the Mississippi. In contrast to this massive amount of big capital equipment, Frank Woolworth opened a small store in Utica specializing in low priced everyday items for sale in 1879. The store failed, but Woolworth's next attempt succeeded at Lancaster, Pennsylvania. it was a new idea in retailing and the beginning of a chain of successful five-and-ten-cent stores across the country. The new style of merchandising was so accepted by the public that it culminated in 1913 with the completion of the Gothic Woolworth Building in downtown New York. For sixteen years it was the highest building in the world with fifty-five floors, yet it was built with nickels and dimes. The first successful Woolworths store still in operation is in Watertown.

Sure Signs: Stories Behind the Historical Markers of Central New York

In the last years of the nineteenth century, two graduates of the engineering college at Cornell, Charles E. Lipe and John Wilkinson (grandson of Syracuse's nomenclator), met with Herbert H. Franklin, and a central New York institution was born. Lipe had invented the two-speed gear for bicycles which later served as a model for automobile transmissions, Franklin was a die-cast specialist, and Wilkinson had invented an air-cooled internal combustion engine.

The three created the Franklin motorcar, made in Syracuse for thirty years, which seventy years after production ceased, is still commemorated by autophiles congregating every summer at Cazenovia. With Alexander Brown and H. Winfield Chapin, Lipe formed a company to make drive train equipment. Brown worked in this partnership for a while, but left to develop the L.C. Smith typewriter, later made in Cortland, Groton, and Syracuse for many years. The firm he left, Brown-Lipe-Chapin was eventually bought out by General Motors.

The telegraph made it possible to send messages anywhere the line went, any time of day, and in any kind of weather. The device had been immediately and immensely successful. But since, after twenty-five years, only one message could be sent on a line at a time, the telegraph poles were festooned with many lines (also unsightly) and were still insufficient to the demand. Western Union was so successful even with the one line-one message system that it became the largest corporation in the country. The need to send many messages on the same line simultaneously and Alexander Graham Bell's efforts to improve the transmission of sound to the deaf drove the research that resulted in the invention of the telephone in 1876. Bell organized the Bell Telephone Company the following year.

Syracuse was introduced to the telephone at a demonstration at the Wieting Opera House in 1878. A year later the first exchange was established in the newly-built Gridley Building to serve sixteen initial subscribers. Within twenty years over 12,000 local lines handled an average of 21,000 calls a day.

Electricity was also introduced in the region in 1878. In eight years, incandescent electric lights replaced the thirty-seven year old gas lights on city streets. Electric trolleys replaced horse cars after ten years and extended the reaches of the city. Soon, a web of trolley tracks and overhead wires joined most of the cities in the northeast. It was said about the inter-urban trolley lines that If one planned in advance, he probably could have peregrinated a peripatetic path from New York to Chicago on the trolleys.

This also made it possible for the average person to widen his work opportunities and choice of home location in his community, rather than being limited to employment within walking distance of home. Real estate prices reacted to this change, as did employers. By means of trolleys, one could make a day's outing to an amusement park such as Roseland at Canandaigua, Suburban Park in Manlius, or Lakeland at the northern end of Onondaga Lake near Syracuse. Indeed, the parks were developed by the trolley companies to extend the line to garner more passengers.

Sparks scratched from the overhead wires by the trolley's pantograph and those from poorly insulated switches and wiring devices frightened people from using electricity in their homes. To sell the safety of electric service, Alfred P. Seymour, of Syracuse Light and Power, consulted James S. Pass, of Onondaga Pottery, makers of ceramic dinnerware, mostly institutional, for answers. The result was not only a safe porcelain insulator, but the beginning of Pass and Seymour, manufacturers of electric switches, spark plugs, electrical fixtures, and, of course, insulators.

The problem of safe electrical connections also brought into being the Crouse Hinds Company in 1897, which by good luck acquired a trolley headlight business as a sideline to their electrical switch and conduit business. The timing was fortuitous; the main product before long became traffic light systems for cities and, later, special lighting systems for airport runways were also made by the company.

When Syracusans dine out during their travels, they cannot resist turning over a cup or saucer to verify the ubiquity of the hometown dinnerware maker's product. Like as not, Onondaga Pottery (now Syracuse China), has put its imprint thereon. Of great interest to housewives (and husbands), was the invention in 1877, by C. A. Dodge, a Vermont farmer, of a machine to wash clothes, the beginning of Easy Washer Company in Syracuse.

Robert Dietz founded the Robert E. Dietz Co. in Brooklyn in 1840 to make lanterns. His lamps lit Mississippi River show boats, Jenny Lind's first American performance, and the important stretch of track in front of railroad locomotives. The company was versatile, making the first kerosene headlamps for early autos. In 1897, the company suffered the loss of its plant downstate and, to stay in business, bought the factory of its major competitor, bringing the company to Syracuse. The ubiquitous Dietz lantern became as well traveled, probably, as Syracuse China's china.

GROVER CLEVELAND PRESIDENT OF UNITED STATES 1884–1888 AND 1892–1896, HIS BOYHOOD HOME IS THE NORTH OF THE CORNER HOUSE

Onondaga County, 36
At NY 5 & NY 92, Fayetteville

Nearby, Grover Cleveland spent nine of his young years in the family home on Genesee Street in Fayetteville under the careful attention of his Presbyterian minister father. He became governor of New York state to the dismay of Tammany Hall which did not share his insistence on integrity. When he ran successfully for the presidency in 1884, his supporters said, "we love him for the enemies he has made."

In 1888, the New Process Raw Hide Company began fabricating boats and canoes of their uniquely hardened leather The firm also fused plies of raw leather into a hard mass from which lamination, gears could be cut for quieter operation in the new electric trolleys. It shifted easily to making steel drive trains for the increasingly popular horseless carriage. The Company retained its novel name, New Process Gear, when it became a subsidiary of the Chrysler Corporation.

Sam Shubert, the new and daring treasurer of the Weiting Opera House in Syracuse, leased the nearby Bastable Theatre in December of 1897. With his two brothers, Lee and Jacob, he opened the first of the Shubert Theaters featuring dramatic stage plays and musical comedy. The chain grew to nine hundred theaters playing to over a million patrons nightly despite opposition of the syndicate which had controlled theaters and artists on Tin Pan Alley. A congerie of their eminent theaters in New York became known as Shubert Alley in the theater district.

First called DeWittsburg, then Newtown Point, Elmira took its final name from an early innkeeper's young daughter. The Chemung River was the villages transportation system in the early days and Elmira area lumbermen used it to ship virgin timber down stream to points as far south as Baltimore. The city envied the prosperity made possible by the Erie Canal and was determined to expand its markets east, west, and north by tying in with this great commercial artery. The Chemung Canal, completed in 1832, gave Elmira and Horseheads access to the canal at Watkins Glen via Seneca Lake and the canal to Cayuga Lake near Montezuma. A year later, the feeder to what was soon to be called Corning was opened. Horseheads, at the junction of the canal and the feeder, grew rapidly and, in 1840, a brickyard began there which was to become one of the largest in the state and the genesis of many buildings in the region, In anticipation of the opening of the Erie Railroad which was to service the southern tier, the Chemung Railroad, connecting Elmira with Watkins Glen, was completed in 1849. Simeon Benjamin, a retired dry goods magnate from New York City who later endowed and promoted Elmira College, was its first president.

Freight and passenger service on the Erie finally commenced in 1851 and at Elmira business expanded handsomely, especially two years later, when the Northern Central Railroad connected the town to Williamsport, Pennsylvania,. The population increased from 8,000 in 1854 to 38,000 at the turn of the century. On the eve of the Civil War, The Empire Steel and Rolling Mills began business turning out miles of railroad track. A shoe and boot factory as well as a woolen mill also inaugurated operations in time to outfit soldiers recruited and trained at the new army center opened in Elmira soon afterward. In 1875, the La France Fire Engine Company, which emanated from the 1834 Button Fire Engine Company in Elmira, produced its first steamer model.

Pioneer penologist Zebulon Brockway was one of the leading organizers of the Elmira State Reformatory, and became its first superintendent in 1876. He believed in separating young criminals from older hard-bitten convicts and providing training and education to rehabilitate and return them to society for a useful life. Good conduct and progress rewarded them privileges and shortened sentences.

Samuel Langhorne Clemens, better known by his pen name, Mark Twain, was introduced to Olivia Langdon from Elmira, by her brother, with whom Clemens had just returned from traveling Europe (and sketching out **Innocents Abroad**). Both were charmed by each other's company and they were soon married. Even though the couple lived in Hartford, Connecticut, they spent most of their summers at their Quarry Farm, just outside of Elmira during the last quarter of the century. Twain wrote **Huckleberry Finn, Tom Sawyer,** and **A Connecticut Yankee in King Arthur's Court** there in his eight-sided study, built for him at the behest of his sister-in-law, in the form of a pilot house reminiscent of his Mississippi River pilot days.

Years after Twain's death, the study was moved from Quarry Farm, and now graces the Elmira College campus where it complements the early college buildings which are also octagonal.

MARK TWAIN STUDY
BUILT ON EAST HILL 1874
GIVEN TO ELMIRA COLLEGE IN
1952. HE WROTE 'TOM SAWYER'
OTHER NOVELS IN THE STUDY
WHEN SUMMERING IN ELMIRA

Chemung County, 19
Edge of Park Place, Elmira

Mark Twain wrote of his readers, "To simply amuse them would have satisfied my dearest ambition." He is buried in Woodlawn National Cemetery nearby family members, and where also are buried many sons of the Confederacy who died at the notorious prisoner of war camp (the former recruiting center) during the Civil War. Union soldiers and veterans of our other wars are buried there as well.

Gail Borden was born in Norwich when the village was in its infancy. He grew up there and, after a surveying sojourn in Texas with Stephen Austin and laying out the plan for Galveston, he returned home to perform experiments with the preservation of food in mind. Canning had by then progressed from the brittle-bottle stage to the period of laboriously hand-made metal cans, and into the industry of rapid machine-made food containers.

Borden came up with evaporated milk just in time to sell a lot of it to the Union Army for the troops in the Civil War. The first Borden Company plant was located in Norwich, by then served by not only the Chenango Canal, but as well by the Delaware, Lackawanna, and Western Railroad and the short-lived New York and Oswego Midland RR.

Norwich was primarily a dairy market town with several mills, but boasted a piano factory and was also known for Boyce and De Lima quality violins until cheaper machine-made instruments put the company out of business. The violin shop then became the location for the Norwich Pharmacal Company, makers of patent medicines including the ubiquitous Unguentine for burns and abrasions.

Oswego was a port of entry into the United States with its fine seawall-protected harbor and lighthouse. At first shipbuilding, and the shipping of lumber and grain were very important, until grain shipments fell off as the granaries moved west to the Great Plains. But Pennsylvania coal was shipped through the port to the extent that 60% of Canada's imported coal cleared from Oswego.

Oswego (and Fulton) became a papermaking center, including the manufacture of a special felt used in the paper-making process. It also boasted an important manufacturer of shade cloth. Once important in historic power struggles, Oswego again provides power of a different kind since the Oswego River was harnessed to generate electricity for an economy that uses huge charges of it.

Baldwinsville and Port Byron were in the boat building business for the Erie Canal that coursed through both towns. To the south, Cortland had factories making such diverse products as wire screens (a significant step towards good health), corsets, and skirts. The Brockway Company there made wooden spoked wheels for wagons, carts, and coaches and, as the age of horses wound down, was agile enough to switch to making trucks and fire engines in the next century.

Edward Noyes Westcott was a successful banker in Syracuse who, when ill with tuberculosis, amused himself by writing **David Harum,** a novel about a shrewd small-town banker. From the start, the book proved to be very popular, mainly because of the homespun situations and that the main character was so engaging as a canny banker and horse trader.

Westcott died shortly before the book was published and did not give a locale for his story. People thought Harum was a real person and that the town of Homer surely fit the scene. To accommodate this thinking, a David Harum Tavern opened on Homer's main street and capitalized on the book's popularity. **David Harum** was eventually made into a play, followed by a movie (starring Will Rogers), which had its national premier at a Cortland theater in 1934.

That the western Finger Lakes area was ideal for growing grapes was discovered in the 1840s by Reverend William Bostwick in Hammondsport. With him it was a hobby, but others started commercial vineyards, and twenty years later, two hundred acres had been planted in grapes for the wine market. In 1860, a French vintner, Charles Champlin, moved to Pleasant Valley, between Hammondsport and Bath, and assayed the soil and climate conditions to be equal to that of the famous vineyard country surrounding Rheims, France.

He wasted no time before he put in vines and formed the Pleasant Valley Wine Company, which was issued the first U.S. bonded winery license. Grape growing became compelling for local farmers and attracted European immigrants familiar with viticulture and enology. By the end of the century, the main industry in the area surrounding Hammondsport, Canandaigua, Naples, Penn Yan, and Geneva became the exacting business of raising grapes (viticulture) and making fine wines (enology).

Even though there is a hint of Old World atmosphere in the region because of the extensive vineyards and wine cellars dug into the steep hillsides, European grapes, (vitus vinifera species), were not grown here. They are susceptible to the indigenous and indomitable aphid-like insect, phyloxxera, which attacks them above and below ground. Mostly Delaware, Catawba, Niagara, and Concord grapes (vitus labrusca species), which are native to the eastern United States were grown in the region.

The Old World grapes grow well in parts of California, and gave that state a domestic natural monopoly in wine made from vinifera varieties. That is, until recently when New York vintners largely overcame this handicap and began growing Old World varieties or hybrids.

The phyloxxera is so destructive that it decimated European vineyards in 1860, causing calamity when it was inadvertently introduced on American vines. Ironically, the French were able to save their valuable wine industry by grafting their susceptible vines on native American rootstock from this area. Vive les Etats Unis!

On his 1743 trip to central New York, plant collector and botanist John Bartram observed the Indians' apple orchards from Fort Oswego westward along the margin of Lake Ontario. A hundred years later, Monroe, Wayne and northern Cayuga county farmers continued to take advantage of the same weather—moderating conditions afforded by the lake. Cold air off the lake in spring delays blossom time to later in the spring, avoiding damage to the apple and cherry blooms due to late frosts. The relatively warm air off the lake in the fall protects the fruit by stemming the frost until after the harvest.

Apples have also been successfully grown along the heights of route 20, west of Lafayette, where the colder air delays bloom both on the northern slopes and in the valleys below near Cardiff where the similar conditions favor the fruit set.

Chenango, Oneida, Madison, and Otsego counties had numerous hop growing farms to supply the many thriving small breweries which prevailed in Utica, Albany, Syracuse, and Rochester during much of the nineteenth century and sixty years into this one. Cabbage was, and still is, grown in Onondaga, Yates and Ontario Counties; hemp in the Genesee Valley and flax in Madison and Chenango counties for upstate ropewalks. Buckwheat is grown in the Penn Yan area (the buckwheat "capital"), potatoes in Savannah and Wayland, and onions and celery in Canastota, Horseheads, and Oswego.

The teasel growing industry was imported by Dr. John Snook when he persuaded friends and relatives from his native Somersetshire, in England, to migrate to Skaneateles in the 1840s. Only the dried seed heads (burrs) of the fuller's teasel, of all the teasels, will serve since their spines end in little hooks. These burrs were mounted on four-foot long, fifteen-inch diameter cylinders which turned against the woolen cloth so that the hooked spines "teased" or raised the nap on the wool. (Teasing a nap on cloth using the peculiar burrs has been practiced since the early Romans).

Woolen mills preferred natural burrs because a snagged spine would break off before it could damage, but a wire one would cause a tear in the material. Burrs were harvested by the thousands, providing additional income for many in the Skaneateles locality. Designers of the wire variety persisted in perfecting their product, and the market for teasels began to collapse in the mid-twenties when manufactured burrs met the necessary requirements and supplanted the natural spines. Tradition dies slowly; not until 1956 was the last commercial crop of teasels in Skaneateles harvested.

500 FEET
GERRIT S. MILLER
HOME OF EARLY IMPORTED
HOLSTEIN CATTLE

Madison County, 42
CR. 2m. NW of Peterborough

The dairy industry has ever prevailed over central New York agriculture. With ample moisture, and sunshine during the growing season, and fertile silt loams, conditions favor pastures, hay and silage crops, and the animals themselves. The Holland Land Company recognized this and introduced Holstein cows to Oneida county before 1800, and shorthorns forty years later. That the entire family could help with the chores and keep costs down is another reason for the profusion of dairy farms. Ice was sawn in blocks and harvested in great quantity off the lakes and ponds, and stored in sawdust or straw-packed ice-houses where it kept remarkably well throughout the summer. This ample resource made it possible to store and ship milk and other perishables, expanding the dairyman's market to the larger cities after the Civil War. The market for dressed beeves, hogs, and poultry also widened. A patent issued in 1849 for a cold-air refrigeration machine had no effect on the increasing value of ice rights on northern ponds until the 1880s when artificial ice began to be used on the new refrigerator railroad cars as well as in commercial and home ice boxes.

Extensive cornfields are associated with the dairy farms mostly because of the huge amount of silage necessary to feed the cows over the winter months. Large amounts of hay are also required, and the many fields in hay, in corn, or in pasturage, as well as the forested hills, the streams, waterfalls, and the lakes in this region continue to give the countryman pleasant vistas through the seasons. Older generations remember fondly the great sentinel American elms which gracefully lined our roads and hedgerows before succumbing to Dutch Elm disease during our lifetimes.

Central New York also abounds in natural springs, some as well endowed with therapeutic minerals as the spas of Europe. Sharon Springs, Richfield Springs, Clifton Springs, Slaterville Springs, the springs of Canawaugus (Avon), and those at Dryden, Lakeville, Watkins Glen, Elmira, and Dansville were all sought out by the Indians, then the settlers, for their invigorating waters. They became popular resorts offering "hydro-therapy" and recreation to upscale society beginning in the early 1800s.

Clara Barton, the Angel of the Battlefield, nursed Union wounded on the front-line, and at the direction of President Lincoln, continued after the war to correspond with the families of missing or dead Union army prisoners regarding their fate and whereabouts. She was able to identify thousands of the Union dead at the notorious Andersonville, Georgia, prison camp from hospital and burial records.

Later, she visited the newly-formed International Red Cross at Geneva, Switzerland, and even went to the front for the German Red Cross in the Franco-Prussian War. When she returned to the U.S. in 1876, fatigued from this effort, she went to the spa in Dansville for "rest, fresh air, exercise, and simple diet" to regain her health. She liked the town that harvested lumber, and sold shade trees from its nurseries at the same time—so much so, that she bought a home there.

Five years later, in 1881, she founded at St. Paul's Lutheran Church in Dansville, the first chapter of the American Red Cross whose headquarters she had organized in Washington, D.C., and of which she was president until 1904. On that same tour to open Red Cross chapters, she opened chapter number three in Syracuse.

IN THIS CHURCH WAS ORGANIZED FIRST LOCAL RED CROSS SOCIETY IN THE UNITED STATES BY CLARA BARTON AUGUST 22, 1881

Livingston County, 31
Exchange & Church Sts.
Dansville

The Dansville spa was owned by Dr. James C. Jackson who had pioneered the "water cure" at Glen Haven at the head of Skaneateles Lake in 1841. Guests of his Glen Haven Water Cure arrived by stage from Homer, or took the train to Skaneateles, and then proceeded by steamboat to the south end of the lake for a regimen of warm and cold baths and showers, together with exercise and a vegetarian diet. The treatment apparently worked, since the 200 guest hotel was full every season until just before World War I when it closed. Dr. Jackson did best of all, living to be 107 years old.

SITE OF GLEN HAVEN HOUSE WHICH IN 1845 WAS CONVERTED INTO GLEN HAVEN SANITARIUM DESTROYED TO PROTECT SYRACUSE WATER SUPPLY

Cayuga County, 127
West Lake Rd. Near head
Of Skaneateles Lake

Most people still lived on farms at the end of the century, and only ten percent of them had indoor plumbing. The lucky few hand-pumped their water from their own well or had a windmill do it, but the pump or spigot was usually only in the kitchen. The majority filled the wooden or tin bathtub with water heated on the wood stove, but for day-to-day, they kept a pitcher and a wash bowl in the bedroom for a daily wash up. Chamber pots were common in the bedrooms and relieved the family at night from tramping out to the outhouse.

Alas, water closets were slow to take hold as were plumbed bathtubs and showers, even when city water pipes and sewers made them possible.

By the nineteenth century's end, central New York could be proud of the infra-structure it had put into place over the hundred years. Not just roads improved by the process perfected by the Scot, John L. McAdam, but canals, railroads, water lines, educational facilities, sewer lines, electricity, trolleys, and the telegraph and telephone all made possible an easier life, and an economic and technological base for further improvement. White occupation had been confined mostly to the

Hudson and lower Mohawk valleys at the century's beginning and much of the wealth was in few hands.

Social conventions changed with the influx of immigrants from New England, New Jersey, Pennsylvania, and the countries of Europe. Ownership of land and the means of generating wealth became more widely distributed, and conditions that gave rise to a growing middle class gave hope to those who were yet less favored, and to future generations.

Women began to move from the home to business, not as menial laborers in a spinning mill as eighty years earlier, but in white-collar jobs made possible by the telephone and typewriter, and even in the professions as their broader education increased their political persuasion and determination. Progress in granting women status and rights was slow but they could see, however dimly at times, that gaining the right to vote was nearer reality than fifty years earlier when they started the movement.

Temperance reform would be successful but it overshot the mark in bringing Prohibition, with unhappy and unexpected results. There has been no strife between United States citizens and Canadians on the Canadian border after the War of 1812, with few exceptions, notably when revenue agents intercepted contraband liquor being smuggled across to the U.S. during the thirteen proscribed years.

Every child could get a free education through high school, and many in the middle class could go on to higher education and professional training, and in their own region if they chose. Town libraries proliferated, thanks to many far-seeing townsmen and philanthropists such as George Eastman, Ezra Cornell, and Andrew Carnegie. Benefactors, like William Pryor Letchworth and Robert Treman, had the vision to save from despoliation scenic areas such as the Genesee Gorge, Mendon Ponds, Taughannock Falls, Highland Forest, and Connecticut Hill, to name but a few.

Syracuse raised the dam at Skaneateles Lake another six feet and tapped the water to flow downgrade to the city's reservoirs in 1894, and pledged to perpetuate the purity of the lake. The power of the Niagara, the Genesee, and the Oswego rivers has also been set to work turning dynamos to generate electricity for home and business. Sanitary sewers became a reality in the scheme of sanitation, and medicine finally had focused its attention on scientifically finding the cause and effective cures of disease, and even on prevention.

Buffalo Bill and his traveling company gave new generations some idea of the conquest of the country, even with the help of Chief Sitting Bull of the Sioux, a member of the troupe for a while, in the 1880s. In the years of the waning century, ragtime suggested a comfortable style of music and living, with better yet to come. Movies such as the "Exploits of Elaine" and other cliff-hangers were not yet made, but the natural beauty of the Ithaca area was certainly noted by those who would soon film them there. Glenn Curtiss soon pioneered technical innovations in aviation and was the first to teach the public and the military to fly; Hammondsport and the world has never been the same. Airplanes and the "newfangled" horseless carriages have not only enabled people to go where they want quickly, but they have changed the entire manner and arrangement of living and doing business, and the landscape of town and country.

People like Nicholas and Lydia Latrobe Roosevelt, who retired to the quiet village of Skaneateles in 1839, lived long enough to see much of the change. When he was born in 1767, the way of living was not that much different from that of Elizabethan times, and when she died in 1878, it had some resemblance to that of the twentieth century to come. The period served as sort of a bridge from renaissance to modern times. The settlement of central New York was accomplished rapidly because it coincided with the industrial and social revolution underway in this country and in Europe. The ensuing migration, together with the forces of education, social reform, technology, and the proliferation of incentives resulted in vast change.

The stories are brought to our attention by these cast iron chronicles.

Howard S. Ford

HISTORICAL MARKERS GUIDE

BROOME COUNTY

TOWN OF CHENANGO

INDIAN CASTLE
LOCATED NEAR JUNCTION OF
CREEK WITH CHENANGO
RIVER, CALLED OTSININGO.
DESTROYED AUG. 18, 1779
DURING SULLIVAN CAMPAIGN.
1
(US 11 & NY 12 3 m.
north of Binghamton)

TOWN OF DICKINSON

FIRST COURT
IN THIS SECTION
WAS HELD HERE IN 1791
UNDER ELM TREE

2
(US 11 & NY 12, 1/2 m
north of Binghamton)

TOWN OF WINDSOR

SAGE CREEK
NAMED FOR SETH PAGE CASTLE
1748-1822, CAPTAIN
IN THE AMERICAN
REVOLUTION

3
(2 m N. of Windsor on
NYS 79)

CAYUGA COUNTY

CITY OF AUBURN

PIONEER ROADS
OLD GENESEE ROAD 1791
NEW GENESEE ROAD 1797
OLD CHENANGO ROAD 1791
LATER KNOWN AS CAYUGA AND
SENECA TURNPIKE 1802
1*
(Marker fastened to east face
of store, NW. corner Genesee &
North Sts., second story)

SITE OF LOG CABIN 1793
OF JOHN L. HARDENBERGH
FIRST SETTLER OF AUBURN
FIRST AURELIUS TOWN
MEETING HELD HERE 1794

2
(On Market Street, in
front of Fire Department)
stone mill recently razed)

SITE OF FIRST LOG
DAM AND MILL
ON OWASCO RIVER BUILT BY
JOHN L. HARDENBERGH 1793
ENLARGED 1802
PRESENT STONE MILL 1824
3 *
(On face of gas station
S. side Genesee at Market.

FORT HILL
OF MOUNDBUILDER ORIGIN
LATER CAYUGA COUNCIL SEAT
AND VILLAGE FORT WASCO
TRADITIONAL BIRTHPLACE
OF CHIEF LOGAN
4*
(At entrance Ft. Hill Cemetery
south side of Fort St.)

___ 500 FEET
FORT HILL
PREHISTORIC INDIAN FORT
TRADITIONAL BIRTHPLACE
OF CHIEF LOGAN
NOW A CEMETERY
5
(SW. corner Fort and
Genesee Sts.)

JOHN HUGGINS
HERE MADE FIRSTSETTLEMENT
ON GENESEE TURNPIKE BETWEEN
ELBRIDGE AND CAYUGA FERRY
IN 1791. HIS SON ZENAS
BUILT THIS TAVERN 1804
6 *
(N. side W. Genesee St., bet.
Crane Brook & city limits)

* indicates marker could not be located.

FIRST TAVERN AND STORE
OPENED IN A LOG CABIN
BUILT BY
SAMUEL BRISTOL
1796
HARDENBERGH CORNERS

7 *
(On face Auburn Trust Co.
Genesee St. side)

WASCO
"THE CROSSING PLACE"
SITE OF A CAYUGA VILLAGE
OCCUPIED BY INDIANS BEFORE
AND AFTER SETTLEMENT OF
LAFAYETTE A GUEST 1825
1793

8 *
(State St.-grass plot between
Prison wall and river)

SITE OF
BOSTWICK'S
TAVERN 1803-1868
REBUILT 1824, RENAMED
WESTERN EXCHANGE HOTEL

9
(On east face Pearson block
cor. Genesee & Exchange)

CENTER HOUSE
TAVERN 1805. LAW OFFICE OF
GOV. ENOS THROOP
FIRST PRES. CHURCH ORG. 1810
1ST WHITE S.S. 1819
REMOVED TO FULTON ST. 1829
10
(Genesee and Market Sts.)

ON THIS SITE THE
BANK OF AUBURN
FIRST BANK IN AUBURN AND
PREDECESSOR OF NAT. BANK
OF AUBURN WAS OPENED 1817
IN DUMAREE'S TAVERN
11 *
(National Hotel wall)

SITE OF
WILLARD TAVERN 1810
REBUILT 1828-1830 AS
AMERICAN HOTEL
BURNED 1879

12 *
(On 2nd story face,

141 Genesee St.)

OSBORNE WORKS
DAVID M. OSBORNE, CYRUS C.
DENNIS AND CHAS. P. WOOD
MASKERS OF KIRBY REAPER
AND OTHER FARM MACHINERY
ORIGINAL FACTORY 1858
13 *
(On 2nd story face Osborne bldg
N. side Genesee & Osborne Sts.)

SITE OF FIRST
SCHOOL HOUSE
ESTABLISHED IN AUBURN 1796
BENJAMIN PHELPS
SCHOOLMASTER

14
(on west side North St. in
front Holy Trinity H.S.)

CALVARY PRES. CHURCH
OLDEST CHURCH EDIFACE
IN AUBURN ERECTED 1815-17
AT FRANKLIN AND NORTH STS
AS FIRST PRES. CHURCH
MOVED HERE 1869
15 *
(Cor. Capitol and Franklin
Sts. in front of church)

MILITARY DEPOT CAMP
DURING CIVIL WAR

16
(Cor. of Camp St & Lake Ave.)

CENTER HOUSE
EARLY TAVERN ERECTED 1805
AT GENESEE AND MARKET STS
MOVED HERE 1829

17 *
(2nd story face south side
block Genesee & Market Sts.)

HOME OF
HARRIET TUBMAN
"THE MOSES OF HER RACE"
UNDERGROUND RAILROAD
STATION IN SLAVERY DAYS
18
(East side of South St
at city line)

FRANCIS HUNTER
ERECTED TAVERN HERE 1808
UNDER NEARBY ELM
COUNCILS WERE HELD
BETWEEN WHITE SETTLERS
AND INDIANS
19 *
(North side E. Genesee St.)

FIRST SCHOOL
IN VICINITY OF AUBURN
ERECTED BEFORE 1796
ORIGINALLY ON GENESEE ST
AND DUNNING AVE
MOVED HERE 1818
20
(West side Dunning Ave.)

CAYUGA COUNTY COURTHOUSE
FRAME BUILDING ERECTED
REAR OF THIS LOT 1809
PRESENT BUILDING
ERECTED 1836
RECONSTRUCTED 1922-24
21
(Court House, Genesee St.)

Howard S. Ford

HOUSE BUILT 1802 BY
JEHIEL CLARK WHO HERE
FOUNDED CLARKSVILLE 1795
HIS GRIST, SAW AND
CARDING MILLS WERE NEARBY
ALONG OWASCO RIVER
22
(W. side cor. Aurelius Ave.

NORTH STREET CEMETERY
MOST OF THE SETTLERS OF
HARDENBERGH'S CORNERS
AND EARLY INHABITANTS OF
AUBURN ARE BURIED HERE
MAIN CEMETERY UNTIL 1852
23
(In front of cemetery North St.)

DURING THE
WAR OF 1812
BARRACKS WERE ESTABLISHED
IN THIS LOCALITY
TROOPS PASSING TO AND
FROM NIAGARA CAMPED HERE
24
(North side W. Genesee St.)

AUBURN PRISON
CONVICTS MADE SEWING SILK
1841-1846
HERE WAS PRINCIPAL CASH
MARKET IN U.S. FOR
COCCOONS AND RAW SILK
25
(In front of prison, west
side State St.)

AUBURN PRISON
ERECTION COMMENCED 1816
FIRST PRISONERS 1817
ASSISTED IN CONSTRUCTION
FIRST ELECTROCUTION
IN THE WORLD 1890
26
(In front of prison west
side State St.)

FIRST
FREIGHT DEPOT
AUBURN AND SYRACUSE R.R.
BUILT BY C.W. POMEROY, 1836
BUILDING USED LATER
AS GENESEE OPERA HOUSE
27 *
(2nd story face Schreck Bros.
store, 16 E. Genesee St)

TOWN OF AURELIUS

WM. G. FARGO
MAY 20, 1818-AUG 3, 1881
ORGANIZER OF WELLS-FARGO
EXPRESS COMPANY
SERVED HERE AS
FIRST FREIGHT AGENT

28*
(2nd story face Schreck Bros.
store, 16 E Genesee St.)

SULLIVAN'S CAMPAIGN
ONE MILE WEST
COL. BUTLER CROSSED
CAYUGA LAKE AND DESTROYED
CAYUGA VILLAGE AND TICHERO
EARLY COUNTY JAIL WAS

29
(On NYS 5 & 20, 1 1/2m.
east of bridge)

SITE OF
CAYUGA LONG BRIDGE
ONE MILE LONG, 1800-1857
CARRIED GREAT STREAM OF
WESTERN MIGRATION
UNDER THIS END OF BRIDGE

30
(In Cayuga village on green
at end of Genesee St.)

COL. JOHN HARRIS
FIRST WHITE SETTLER IN
CAYUGA COUNTY BUILT LOG
CABIN HERE 1788
ESTABLISHED HARRIS FERRY
ACROSS CAYUGA LAKE
31
(On county road 1/2 mile south
near entrance to
Cowan's Point settlement)

SITE OF
TREATY FOR PURCHASE
CAYUGA RESERVATION
FROM THE INDIANS
RED JACKET AND FISH CARRIER
SPOKESMEN FOR CAYUGAS
32
(On county road 1/2 m. south
of Cayuga near entrance to
Cowan's Point settlement)

PIONEER ROADS
INDIAN TRAIL AND
EARLIEST ROAD
S.W. TO HARRIS FERRY
GENESEE TURNPIKE TO
CAYUGA BRIDGE BUILT 1800
33
(West Genesee St. State Road
at Lehigh Valley RR.)

TOWN OF BRUTUS

FIRST CAYUGA COUNTY
COURT HELD HERE 1799
REMOVED TO AURORA 1804
AND TO AUBURN 1809

34
(South of Cayuga, east side
on route 90)

1789-1800
OLD GENESEE ROAD
FROM HARDENBERGH CORNERS
TO HARRIS FERRY CROSSED
HERE
35*
(On NY 326, 1 m. north
of Oakwood)

CENTERPORT
SETTLED BY BENJ. HAIKES
1805-06. WAS IMPORTANT
VILLAGE ON OLD ERIE
CANAL IN 1825
36
(Centerport)

TOWN OF BRUTUS
FORMED FROM AURELIUS 1802
FIRST SETTLEMENT IN TOWN
MADE BY AARON FROST 1795
HE BUILT THE FIRST
GRIST MILL
37
(Weedsport)

WEED'S BASIN
NAMED AFTER ELIHU AND EDWARD
WEED WHO CONSTRUCTED A
BASIN ON OLD ERIE CANAL
1821. P.O. ESTABLISHED 1822
WEEDSPORT INC VILLAGE 1831
38
(Just north of Hotel, NY 34)

CAYUGA COUNTY
EARLY IROQUOIS COUNTRY 1768
PART OF MONTGOMERY CO. 1784
PART OF HERKIMER CO. 1791
PART OF ONONDAGA CO. 1794
CAYUGA CO. SET OFF 1799
39*
(NY 5 at Onondaga Co. line)

TOWN OF CATO

OLD MILL
FIRST GRIST MILL IN IRA
BUILT IN 1818. BY JOHN
HOOKER, ASSOCIATE OF
ETHAN ALLEN. MILL WAS OLD
PART OF PRESENT BUILDING
40
(West of Cato, east side of RR)

JAKWAY'S CORNERS
VILLAGE FORMERLY SO CALLED
FROM DR. JOHN JAKWAY
SETTLING 1809, ASSOCIATE
OF ETHAN ALLEN. PLATT
TITUS FIRST SETTLER 1805
41
(Center of Cato village)

1800
FIRST SETTLEMENT
IN THE TOWN OF CATO
MADE BY SAMSON
LAWRENCE

42
(At intersection, 1 m.
north of Seneca R.)

METHODIST
EPISCOPAL
CHURCH
ORGANIZED IN 1820
BRICK EDIFICE BUILT 1828
REMODELED ABOUT 1870
43
(On Brick Church Road)

ABRAMS FERRY
FROM 1805 FOR MANY YEARS
ABRAMS WHO SETTLED IN
THAT YEAR MAINTAINED A
FERRY UNTIL THE TOLL
BRIDGE WAS BUILT
44
(Near bridge over Seneca R.)

CATO FOUR CORNERS
GEO. LOVELACE AND ABEL PASKO
FIRST SETTLERS IN 1804
JESSE ELWELL AND ABNER
HOLLISTER SETTLED IN 1805,
CALLED MERIDIAN SINCE 1849
45
(Meridian)

Howard S. Ford

TOWN OF CONQUEST

CEREMONIAL FIRE
SITE OF PERMANENT VILLAGE
AND PERPETUAL COUNCIL FIRE
OF CAYUGA BRANCH OF THE
IROQUOIS. LAMOKAS, SENECAS
TRAIL TO ONONDAGA FOR SALT
46*
(1 1/2 m. south of Meridian, on

TOWN OF CONQUEST
SET OFF FROM CATO 1821
FIRST SETTLERS 1800
GEO. SNYDER, A SOLDIER
OF THE REVOLUTION AND
ISRAEL WOLVERTON
47
(Conquest village, NY 38)

CONQUEST CENTER
SETTLED 1802 BY JAMES
PERKINS AND SONS, IRA
GILBERT, JEREMIAH, AND
JOHN. JOHN WAS A CAPTAIN
IN THE WAR OF 1812
48
(Conquest village, NY 38)
Weedsport county highway)

TOWN OF FLEMING

PINEVILLE
FORMERLY CO CALLED FROM
THE PINE FORESTS WHICH
COVERED THIS LOCALITY
NAME CHANGED IN 1874
TO SPRING LAKE
49
(At Spring Lake)

"THE PEPPER MILL"
SO CALLED FROM THE FIRST
GRIST MILL IN TOWN BUILT
1810 BY THEOPHILUS EMERSON
WHO WITH HIS BROTHER
CLEMENT SETTLED HERE 1802
50*
(In Emerson)

JOSIAH CHATFIELD
FIRST SETTLER
OF FLEMING VILLAGE 1798
ERECTED HIS HOME ON
THIS SITE

51
(NW. corner, Fleming)

FIRST BAPTIST CHURCH
IN AURELIUS WAS ERECTED
HERE IN 1876
PASTOR DAVID IRISH
FIRST CHURCH IN FLEMING
SECOND IN CAYUGA COUNTY
52
(Bluefield Rd. NW. of Fleming)

GEORGE FLEMING
CAPTAIN IN REVOLUTION
BREV. BRIG. GEN. 1816
BUILT THIS HOME ON HIS
MILITARY BOUNTY LAND
TOWN NAMED AFTER HIM 1823
53
(NY 34B 1/2 m. S. of Mapleton)

SAND BEACH CHURCH
REFORMED PROTESTANT DUTCH
CHURCH AT THE OWASCO OUTLET
ORGANIZED 1807
FIRST BUILDING 1810
PRESENT CHURCH 1855
54
(Sand Beach Rd. W of circle)

TOWN OF GENOA

GREAT
IROQUOIS TRAIL
FROM CAYUGA TO OWASCO LAKES
PART OF THE GREAT TRAIL FROM
NIAGARA TO ALBANY DURING
THE AMERICAN REVOLUTION
55 *
(On NY 34 1/4 m S. LVRR @ school)

HOME OF
HENRY WYCKOFF
BUILT 1835. JACOB BYERS
SETTLED HERE 1790. PLANK
ROAD FROM HERE TO MORAVIA
BUILT IN 1852
56
(W. side NY 38 S. of Auburn)

FORKS
OF THE CREEK
PINE LUMBER WAS SAWED
HERE FOR CONSTRUCTION
OF EARLY FARMHOUSES
IN THIS VICINITY
57*
(E of Five Cor. at the Forks)

PRESBYTERIAN
CHURCH, FIRST IN GENOA
ORGANIZED AUG. 13, 1798
BY EARLIEST SETTLERS IN
REGION, THEN KNOWN
AS THE MILITARY TRACT
57
(front of church, Kings Ferry)

SITE OF
OLD CHURCH
FIRST CONGREGATIONAL IN TOWN
OF MILTON. ORGANIZED 1798
FIRST LOG MEETING HOUSE
BUILT HERE IN 1802
58
(1 m. E. & 1 m. s. Kings Ferry)

SITE OF
LOG MEETING HOUSE
BUILT 1802, BY CONGREGATIONAL
CHURCH OF MILTON, ORGANIZED
IN 1798. SECOND OLDEST
CHURCH IN CAYUGA COUNTY
59
(Correcting above marker)

TOWN OF IRA

TOWN OF GENOA
ORGANIZED AS MILTON 1789
NAME CHANGED TO GENOA 1808
JOHN CLARK WAS THE FIRST
SETTLER IN 1791
60
(Genoa, S. side of church)

FIRST STORE
IN THE TOWN OF GENOA
WAS OPENED HERE BY
ELIHU TALLADAY
PRIOR TO 1800
61
(East Genoa, NY 34)

BURIAL PLACE
OF THE PIONEERS OF THIS
SECTION, INCLUDING SEVERAL
REVOLUTIONARY VETERANS
1809-1860
62
(West of Cato-Meridian HS)

IRA CORNERS
SETTLED IN 1805 BY THOMAS
BARNES, LUTHER SAMUEL AND
SRAEL PHELPS, TWO LATTER
OPENED FIRST STORE, 1813. PHELPS
BUILT HOTEL 1820, WHERE FIRST
TOWN MEETING WAS HELD, 1821
63
(Stands on town line near LVRR)

TOWN OF IRA
SET OFF FROM CATO, 1821.
FIRST SETTLEMENT IN TOWN,
1800, BY DAVID AND ELIZABETH
STOCKWELL, WILLIAM
PATTERSON AND HENRY CONRAD

64
(Center of village)

FOX'S KILN
ANCIENT LIMESTONE QUARRIES
OPENED UP PRIOR TO 1835

65
(3/4 m. west of Ira)

TOWN OF LEDYARD

RESIDENCE OF
MAJOR BENJAMIN LEDYARD
FIRST CLERK OF ONONDAGA
AND CAYUGA COUNTY
TOWN NAMED IN HIS HONOR
WELL KNOWN SCHOOL
66
(South of old academy in Aur-
ora off Main St.)

CAYUGA LAKE
ACADEMY
CHARTERED BY REGENTS 180
FIRST BUILDING 1803
PRESENT STRUCTURE 1835
SULLIVAN-CLINTON CAMPAIGN
67
(In front old brick school
opposite Pres. Church)

FIRST HOME
BUILT BY A WHITE MAN
CAPT. ROSWELL FRANKLIN
IN CAYUGA COUNTY 1789
HE WAS AN OFFICER IN
SULLIVAN-CLINTON CAMPAIGN
68
(Aurora, W. side NY 90)

Howard S. Ford

GRAVE OF
CAPT. ROSWELL FRANKLIN
FIRST SETTLER 1789
DIED 1792

69*
(So. side Paines Creek Gully
1000 ft. E. of bridge)

PIONEER HOUSE
BUILT ABOUT 1799 BY
BENJAMIN HOWLAND
HERE SAME YEAR WAS HELD
FIRST MEETING IN COUNTY
OF SOCIETY OF FRIENDS
CAMPAIGN SEPT. 1779
70
(Chapel Cor., Paines Creek
Rd. to Poplar Ridge)

SITE OF
CHONODOTE
"PEACH TOWN"
CAYUGA VILLAGE DESTROYED
WITH ORCHARD OF 1500
TREES DURING SULLIVAN

71
(North end vill. NY 90)

SCIPIO LODGE
MASONIC CHARTER 1797
BUILDING ERECTED 1806
USED BY THE CRAFT
UNTIL 1819
72
(Main St. Scipio, nr. school)

PAINES CREEK GULLY
"MOONSHINE FALLS"
ONE MILE UPSTREAM
SITE OF EARLY SAW, GRIST
AND WOOLEN MILLS
73 *
(South of Aurora, NY 90)

TO
MOONSHINE FALLS

74*
(NY 90 at Paines Creek Rd)

TO
MOONSHINE FALLS

75*
(Prospect Cor., 1 m. E. NY 90)

UPPER CAYUGA
MARKING THE PROBABLE
FORTIFICATION FOR NEARBY
INDIAN VILLAGES DESTROYED
BY COL. BUTLER'S SOLDIERS
SEPTEMBER 22-23, 1779
76
(Great Gully Fort site.
Accessible only to hikers)

SITE OF
UPPER CAYUGA
VILLAGE
DESTROYED BY COL. BUTLER'S
DETACHMENT OF SULLIVAN'S
ARMY, SET. 22-23, 1779
77
(Side Rd. Young farm
owned by Cayuga Museum)

PATRICK
TAVERN
ERECTED 1793
EARLY COURT HELD HERE
CAYUGA COUNTY MEDICAL
SOCIETY ORGANIZED HERE 1806
78
(Dublin Hill Rd. & NY 90 Aurora)

BUILT 1804
HERE IN 1846 WAS BORN
ELIZA MOSHER
EMINENT WOMAN PHYSICIAN
1875-1928

79
(1 m. west Ridgeway Cemetery)

ISAAC MEKEEL
HERE DEVELOPED
MANUFACTURE OF
AMBER CANE SYRUP
1860-1904

80
(1 m. west Ridgeway Cemetery)

SITE OF
FIRST STEAM
FLOURING MILL
WEST OF HUDSON RIVER
BUILT BY ROSWELL TOWSLEY
1817
81
(SE. cor. Old stone ware-
house, Lyon property Aurora)

BIRTHPLACE OF
THEODORE LEDYARD CUYLER
BORN JAN. 10, 1822
DIED FEB. 26, 1909
PREBYTERIAN CLERGYMAN
AND WRITER

82*
(Aurora, opp. RR station)

OLD ELM TREE
REMAINING FROM
THE PRIMEVAL FOREST

83*
(Aurora-Poplar Ridge Rd.
1/2 m. west of RR)

ALGONKIAN
NAMED FROM BENJ. LEDYARD
CALLED CHAPINS CRS. FROM
P. CHAPIN, SETTLED 1800
AND TALLCOTTS CRS. FROM R.
TALLCOTT, SETTLED 1812
84
(NY 34B, village of Ledyard)

BOUNDARY OF
INDIAN VILLAGE SITE PRIOR
TO IROQUOIS DURING STONE
AGE OCCUPATION ABOUT 1000
A.D. EXCAVATIONS 1932-34
SHOW HEARTHS AND BURIALS
85
(1 mile east of Levanna)

LEDYARD
RESERVATION
SOUTHEAST CORNER OF EAST
CAYUGA RESERVATION. CAYUGAS
RESERVED IT 1789. CEDED TO
N.Y. STATE BY TREATY 1794
86
(Aurora-Sherwood Rd. west of Sherwood)

SEQUOIA
(CALIFORNIA REDWOOD)
PLANTED IN 1826

87*
(NY 90, north end Aurora)

GLEN PARK 1852
HOME OF HENRY WELLS
FOUNDER OF
AMERICAN EXPRESS CO., 1850
WELLS FARGO EXPRESS CO., 1852
WELLS COLLEGE, 1868
88
(Front Wells College, W. side st.)

FIRST NEWSPAPER
IN CAYUGA COUNTY PUBLISHED
IN 1798 BY R. DELANO
CALLED LEVANNA GAZETTE
OR ONONDAGA ADVERTISER

89
(At Levanna)

TOWN OF LOCKE

WELLS COLLEGE
FOUNDED BY HENRY WELLS
1868
ORGANIZER OF AMERICAN AND
WELLS FARGO EXPRESS COMPANIES

90
(Front, Wells College, e. side st.)

HOME OF
JETHRO WOOD
INVENTOR OF CAST IRON
PLOUGH

91
(½ m. west Poplar Ridge)

INDIAN
FORT SITE
THIS VICINITY IS SITE OF
AN INDIAN VILLAGE
PROBABLY FORTIFIED
AND INDIAN BURIAL GROUND
92*
(West of Locke)

TOWN OF MENTZ

TOWN OF LOCKE
SET OFF FROM MILTON NOW
GENOA IN 1802, LOCKE
VILLAGE FORMERLY CALLED
MILAN FIRST SETTLED 1790

93*
(NY 90 & 38 in Locke)

BRIGHAM YOUNG
THE MORMON PROPHET LIVED
IN THE HOUSE 100 YARDS
EAST OF HERE IN 1831. HE
WAS BAPTIZED A MORMON IN
1832 AT MENDON, N.Y.
94
(Port Byron front of hotel)

PORT BYRON
NAMED 1832. INC. 1837
FORMERLY CALLED BUCKSVILLE
FROM AHOLIAB BUCK, SETTLER
IN 1798, ALSO KING'S
SETTLEMENT FROM P. KING 1797
95
(In front of Port Byron Hotel)

Howard S. Ford

TOWN OF MONTEZUMA

HENRY WELLS
FOUNDER OF WELLS FARGO
EXPRESS COMPANY WAS A
SHOEMAKER BY TRADE AND
LIVED IN THIS HOUSE
FROM 1827 TO ABOUT 1830
96*
(NY 31 & 38 in Port Byron)

MONTEZUMA
NAMED FROM THE AZTEC
EMPORERS. TOWN FORMED FROM
MENTZ IN 1859. VILLAGE
INCORPORATED IN 1866

97
(In Montezuma by hotel)

SQUAGONNA
ABORIGINAL NAME FOR
"PARADISE OF MUSQUITES"
THE RIVER WAS TIOHERO
"RIVER OF RUSHES"

98
(E side bridge at Seneca R.)

SALT SPRINGS
CHIEF SUPPLY FOR INDIANS.
LATER EXTENSIVELY DEVELOPED
BY EARLY SETTLERS PRIVATELY
AND WITH STATE AID

99
(On old canal by NY 90)

COL. COMFORT TYLER
1764-1827
REVOLUTIONARY SOLDIER, COL.
IN WAR OF 1812, SURVEYOR,
ENGINEER SALT MAKER,
SETTLED HERE IN 1811
100
(On north corner NY 31)

OLD ERIE CANAL
COMPLETED FROM UTICA TO
HERE 1819. THE "MONTEZUMA"
BUILT HERE WAS THE FIRST
BOAT ON THE CANAL. TOOK
PASSENGERS TO SYRACUSE 1820
101
(On old canal by NY 90)

TOWN OF MORAVIA

THE FIRST
CAST IRON PLOW
IN THE WORLD WAS MADE BY
JETHRO WOOD
AT FOOT OF FALLS
1819
102
(NY 38A by bridge, Montville)

SITE OF
OLD ARSENAL
NEW YORK STATE ARSENAL
NUMBER 68. BUILT IN
1800. STOOD FOR OVER
100 YEARS
103
(Village of Moravia side st.)

OLDEST HOUSE
IN MORAVIA
THE KITCHEN OF THIS HOUSE
IS THE ORIGIAL CABIN BUILT
BY GERSHOM MORSE IN 1794

104
(S Main St., NY 38, in village)

OWASCO FLATS
SITE OF INDIAN VILLAGE
LAND CULTIVATED PRIOR TO
WHITE SETTLEMENTS.
NEIGHBORING SETTLERS CAME
TO HARVEST HAY 1789-90
105
(NY 38 west of village)

JOHN STOYELL
FIRST SETTLER IN MORAVIA
1790. BUILT FIRST HOUSE AT
REAR OF THIS LOT. WAS 1ST
JUSTICE AND SUPERVISOR OF
SEMPRONIUS IN 1798
106
(Corner Main & Cayuga Sts.)

TOWN OF MORAVIA
FORMED FROM SEMPRONIUS IN
1833. VILLAGE OF MORAVIA
INCORPORATED IN 1837
REINCORPORATED IN 1859.

107
(Back of gas station E. Cayuga)

TOWN OF NILES

CADY TAVERN
IN 1801 ZADOC CADY BUILT
A LOG TAVERN HERE. A FEW
YEARS LATER HE BUILT THE
PRESENT BUILDING

108
(South Main St. in village)

OLD SALT ROAD
OVER THIS ROAD
SALT
WAS FORMERLY TRANSPORTED
OVERLAND FROM SYRACUSE TO
PENNSYLVANIA AND NEW YORK
109
(Kelloggsville)

KELLOGGSVILLE
NAMED AFTER JUDGE CHARLES
KELLOGG, WHO OPENED THE
FIRST STORE HERE IN 1804

110
(In front of store)

TOWN OF OWASCO

OLD MILL
PARTLY BUILT BY CHARLES
KELLOGG IN 1823. SOLD TO
HORACE ROUNDS IN 1851, TO
HIS SON EUGENE ROUNDS 1865,
TO W. E. ROUNDS & A RYAN 1919
111
(Just north New Hope NY 41A)

TOWN OF NILES
SET OFF FROM SEMPRONIUS
IN 1833. FIRST SETTLED 1792.
NAMED FROM ELDER ROBT. NILES
A PASTOR OF THE 1ST BAPTIST
CHURCH OF SEMPRONIUS
112
(At Dutch Hollow, NY 38A)

FORD
ACROSS WASCO OUTLET ON
GREAT IROQUOIS TRAIL USED
BY COL. PETER GANSEVOORT
WHO ENCAMPED HERE
SEPT. 21, 1779
113
(By Owasco L. outlet bridge)

WILLOW BROOK
HOME OF ENOS T. THROOP
1784-1874
CONGRESSMAN 1815
CIRCUIT JUDGE 1823
GOVERNOR OF NEW YORK 1829-32
114
(E Lake Rd., NY 38A, foot of L.)

HERE
WAS BUILT IN 1798
FIRST CHURCH
IN CAYUGA COUNTY
REFORMED DUTCH CHURCH
OF OWASCO
115
(E. Lake Rd.38A, Burtis Pt)
NY 38A)

ALGONKIAN
VILLAGE SITE
OF THIRD PERIOD CULTURE
ONE OF LARGEST INDIAN
POTTERY JARS IN STATE
FOUND HERE
116
(In Enna Jettick Park on L.,

TOWN OF SCIPIO

TOWN OF OWASCO
FORMED FROM AURELIUS 1802
FIRST SETTLEMENTS 1792.
REFORMED DUTCH CHURCH OF
OWASCO ORGANIZED 1798
CHURCH BUILT 1815
117
(In Owasco, NY 38A)

CAYUGA CASTLE
STOOD TWO MILES WEST
RAZED BY COL. BUTLER
IN SULLIVAN CAMPAIGN
SEPTEMBER 22-23, 1779
COL. BUTLER IN 1779
118*
(NY 34 B ½ m. s. Rt 1)

INDIAN SITE
REMAINS OF LARGE VILLAGES
FOUND ON FARMS ON
EITHER SIDE OF THIS ROAD.
CAYUGAS DRIVEN OUT BY

119
(NY 34 B, S. of Scipioville)

PIONEER SITE
SETTLED 1794-95 BY
JUDGE SETH SHERWOOD
ERECTED HOUSE WHEREIN
COURT WAS HELD 1804 WHEN
VILLAGE WAS COUNTY SEAT
120
(Sherwood, front of store)

WARING PLACE
BUILT AS A TAVERN 1806
MASONIC LODGE QUARTERS
1811-14, 1922-42
LOWER STORY USED AS
SCHOOL
121
(NY 34, S of Scipio Ctr)

EARLY NEWSPAPER,
THE WESTERN LUMINARY,
SECOND IN THE COUNTY
WAS PUBLISHED IN THIS
HOUSE MARCH 24, 1801

122
(Scipioville, NY 34B)

EMILY HOWLAND
1827-1929
NOTED EDUCATOR
PHILANTHROPIST, FOUNDED
THE SHERWOOD SELECT SCHOOL
1872, LIVED HERE
123
(Sherwood, NY 34B)

TOWN OF SCIPIO
ONE OF THE ORIGINAL
TOWNS OF THE MILITARY TRACT
FORMED IN 1794. NAMED
AFTER THE ROMAN GENERAL
BUILT IN 1825
124
(At Scipio Center)

#1 - THE SQUARE
SO NAMED BECAUSE OF BEING
ON LOT ONE OF THE TOWN
OF SCIPIO. THIS
PRESBYTERIAN CHURCH WAS

125
(NY 34B & old Ridge Rd.)

OLD SALT ROAD
OVER THIS ROAD
SALT
WAS FORMERLY TRANSPORTED
OVERLAND FROM SYRACUSE TO
PENNSYLVANIA AND NEW YORK
126
Dresserville on CR 1/2 m.
west of NY 41A)

SITE OF
GLEN HAVEN HOUSE WHICH IN
1845 WAS CONVERTED INTO
GLEN HAVEN SANITARIUM
DESTROYED TO PROTECT
SYRACUSE WATER SUPPLY
127
(W. Lake Rd. near head
of Skaneateles Lake)

SAYLES CORNERS
FIRST SETTLEMENT IN
SEMPRONIUS 1793 BY EZEKIEL
SAYLES, SURVEYOR AND FIRST
TOWN CLERK. HIS LOG HOUSE
STOOD ABOUT HERE
128
(Cty Rd. bet. NY 38A & 41A)

TOWN OF SENNETT

SENECA TURNPIKE
1800
FROM UTICA TO CANANDAIGUA
VIA SKANEATELES CREEK AT END
OF CHERRY VALLEY TURNPIKE.
MIGRATION ROUTE TO THE WEST
129
(US 20 1 m. E of Auburn)

EARLY HOME
BUILT ABOUT 1795 BY
DANIEL SENNETT
SIDE JUDGE OF
CIRCUIT COURT
TOWN NAMED IN HIS HONOR
130
(NY 5 east of Sennett)

FIRST STORE
IN VILLAGE OF SENNETT
OPENED 1795
RUFUS SHELDON AND
CHAUNCEY LATHROP
FIRST POST OFFICE 1806
131
(NE cor in Sennett

THIS HOUSE
ERECTED 1823
DR. SYLVESTER WILLARD

132
(Center of Sennett, old NY 5)

OLDEST CHURCH
IN SENNNETT. BUILT 1820
ORGANIZED 1809 AS
FIRST CONGEGATIONAL
REMODELED 1847
BECAME PRESBYTERIAN 1870

133
(Southwest cor of Sennett)

BLACKSMITH
SHOP
BUILT PRIOR TO 1825
LOCAL METHODIST SOCIETY
HERE ORGANIZED AND PLANNED
ERECTION OF THEIR CHURCH

134
(S. side road E of Sennett)

FIRST TAVERN
IN VILLAGE OF SENNETT
BUILT 1795

135
(Northwest cor of Sennett)

BLACKSMITH SHOP
SHOP
BUILT ABOUT 1837. FIRST
TRIP HAMMER IN CAYUGA
COUNTY AND FIRST ONE USED
IN AUBURN PRISON MADE HERE

136
(Franklin St. Rd. E. Soule Cemtry)

BAPTIST
CHURCH
ORGANIZED 1799
FIRST STONE CHURCH BUILT
ON SITE 1808
PRESENT CHURCH BUILT 1825

137
(East of Sennett)

TOWN OF SPRINGPORT

GREAT GENESEE ROAD
FROM OLD FORT SCHUYLER TO
THE GENESEE RIVER VIA
HARDENBERGH CORNERS AND
CAYUGA BRIDGE. BUILT 1794

138
(Owl's Nest, Franklin St.
Rd. 1 m. E of Soule Cemetery)

EAST CAYUGA-OLD TOWN
INDIAN VILLAGE OF 13 HOUSES
DESTROYED SEPT. 22, 1779
BY COL. WILLIAM BUTLER'S
DETACHMENT OF
SULLIVAN CAMPAIGN

139
(Gully Rd. ½ m. W of NY 34B
town of Springport)

FRONTENAC
ISLAND
ANCIENT ALGONKIAN VILLAGE
SITE. INDIAN BURIAL PLACE
GIVEN TO UNION SPRINGS
BY THE STATE 1856

140
(Island off Union Springs)

___WEST
FRONTENAC
ISLAND
SITE OF ALGONKIAN VILLAGE
DEEDED TO UNION SPRINGS
BY THE STATE FOR USE
AS A PARK 1856
141
(NY 90 & Seminary St
Union Springs)

GE-WAUGA
A SMALL CAYUGA VILLAGE
WHERE COL. BUTLER
CAMPED SEPT. 21, 1779

142*
(In front of old High School
Main St. Union Springs)

CAYUGA CASTLE
"GOI-O-GOUEN"
SITE OF PRINCIPAL
CAYUGA VILLAGE
DESTROYED SEPT.23, 1779
SULLIVAN CAMPAIGN

143
(On Sesqui Monument lot
nr. Gr. Gully Rd. & NY 90)

Howard S. Ford

CAYUGA CASTLE
SITE TWO MILES EAST
CAYUGA VILLAGE DESTROYED
IN SULLIVAN CAMPAIGN
SEPTEMBER 1779

144
(NY 90 & Great Gully Rd.)

UPPER CAYUGA
SITE OF VILLAGE AND FORT
ON OPPOSITE BANK OF
GREAT GULLY
DESTROYED BY COL. BUTLER
IN SULLIVAN CAMPAIGN
145*
(S. side Great Gully Rd.
2 miles east of NY 90)

RESERVATION OF
CAYUGAS
SOLD TO THE STATE 1779
A BODY OF TUSCARORAS WERE
THE LAST OF THE IROQUOIS
TO OCCUPY THIS POINT
146
(On Farley's Point)

FIRST
SCHOOL HOUSE
IN TOWN OF SPRINGPORT
ERECTED ON THIS SITE

147
(NY 90 & Auburn Rd.)

INDIAN MOUND
JUST EAST OF HERE
KNOWN TO BE THE SITE OF
AN EARLY JESUIT MISSION

148
(On Sesqui Mon. lot NY 90)

CAYUGA MINE
RESERVATION
NORTHWEST COR. OF SQ. MILE
RESERVED TO CAYUGAS BY
TREATIES 1789
SOLD TO THE STATE 1799
149*
(Auburn Rd. NY 326, 2 m E NY 90)

SPRING MILLS
ERECTED 1839-40 BY
GEORGE HOWLAND
STONE MILL THIRD BUILT
ON SAME SITE
SECOND WAS WOOLEN MILL
150*
(At pond, Union Springs)

HOME OF
JOHN J. THOMAS 1810-95
PROMINENT AGRICULTURIST
AN EDITOR OF "THE COUNTRY
GENTLEMAN" AND PROMOTER
OF CAYUGA LAKE RR
151
(Union Springs, Homer St.)

FIRST CHURCH
ERECTED IN SPRINGPORT
1816 STOOD ON THIS SITE
USED UNTIL 1840

152
(At cross roads)

TOWN OF STERLING

YAWGER TAVERN
BUILT BY PETER YAWGER, 1810
ON THE JUNCTION OF THE
INDIAN TRAILS WASCO
GEWAUGA AND CHUHARO
TO GOIOGOVEN
153*
(NY 326 & CR 1 m E NY 90)

IROQUOIS TRAIL
FROM CAYUGA TO OWASCO
LAKES, PART OF THE GREAT
TRAIL FROM NIAGARA TO
ALBANY DURING THE
AMERICAN REVOLUTION
154 *
(NY 326 north of Oakwood)

TOWN OF STERLING
NAMED AFTER A REVOLUTIONARY
OFFICER, LORD WM. ALEXANDER
STERLING. SET OFF FROM CATO
1812. FIRST GRIST AND SAW
MILL BUILT HERE IN 1813
155
(Sterling Ctr. on NY 104A)

STERLING VALLEY
FIRST SETTLEMENT MADE HERE
1805 BY PETER DUMAS, A
SOLDIER WITH LAFAYETTE.
EARLIER CALLED COOPERS
MILLS AFTER JOHN COOPER 1819
156
(At Sterling Valley, NY 104A)

FAIR HAVEN
LITTLE SODUS
SETTLED PRIOR TO 1811
FIRST HOTEL, ABIJAH HUNT, 1825
FIRST STORE, G. TAYLOR, 1825

157
(Fair Haven, NY 104A)

MARTVILLE
CHAUNCEY HICKOCK AND
TIMOTHY AUSTIN SETTLED 1823,
BUILT FIRST MILLS. ROBT.
LAY BUILT FIRST STORE 1825

158
(Martville on NY 104)

TOWN OF SUMMERHILL

MILLARD FILLMORE
13TH PRESIDENT OF
THE UNITED STATES, WAS BORN
IN A LOG CABIN IN
THE ADJACENT FIELD
JANUARY 7, 1800
159
(Country rd ½ m NW CR 135)

OLD SALT ROAD
OVER THIS ROAD
SALT
WAS FORMERLY TRANSPORTED
OVERLAND FROM SYRACUSE TO
PENNSYLVANIA AND NEW YORK
160
(In Summerhill, NY 90)

OLD SALT ROAD
OVER THIS ROAD
SALT
WAS FORMERLY TRANSPORTED
OVERLAND FROM SYRACUSE TO
PENNSYLVANIA AND NEW YORK
161
(W side rd. at Sherman Gulf)

TOWN OF THROOP

SUMMERHILL
FORMED FROM LOCKE AS PLATO
1831, NAME CHANGED 1832.
FIRST SETTLEMENT MADE BY
HEZEKIAH MIX IN 1797
ONE MILE WEST OF HERE
162
(In Summerhill, NY 90)

HOME OF
GEN. JOHN S. CLARK
BORN 1823. DIED 1912
CIVIL ENGINEER, HISTORIAN,
CIVIL WAR OFFICER AND
FIRST SUPERVISOR OF THROOP
163
(CR #1148 1 ½ m NW Throopville)

WARDS SETTLEMENT
NAMED FROM JONAS WARD AND
SON, CALEB, WHO SETTLED HERE
IN 1796, FIRST SETTLEMENT IN
THROOP MADE NEAR HERE IN 1790
BY EZEKIAL CRANE
164
(Near. Townline Rd from
Throopsville to Montezuma)

TOWN OF VENICE

TOWN OF THROOP
FORMED 1859 FROM PORTIONS
OF ARELIUS, MENTZ, AND
SENNETT. NAMED AFTER FORMER
GOVERNOR ENOS T. THROOP
OF AUBURN
165
(Throopsville)

THROOPSVILLE
FIRST SETTLED BY CHRISTOPHER
JEFFRIES, HOTEL KEEPER, IN
1799. REV JOHN JEFFRIES
FIRST BAPTIST PASTOR
MENTZ ORGANIZED 1803
166
(Throopsville)
Stewarts Corners)

HOME OF
DANIEL HOLLEY
SETTLED HERE, 1797. THE
FRAME HOUSE BUILT SOON
AFTER IS PART OF BARN
167
(1 m S & ½ m E of

BAPTIST
CHURCH
FOUNDED JUNE 9, 1795 BY
ELDER DAVID IRISH
PRESENT CHURCH ERECTED
1812-14
168
(Stewarts Corners)

SITE OF
FIRST STORE
BUILT ABOUT 1800 BY
JETHRO WOOD, INVENTOR
PRESENT STORE BUILT FROM
SOME OF ORIGINAL TIMBERS
169
(Poplar Ridge)

INDIAN FIELDS
FARMS OF THE CAYUGAS
BEFORE REVOLUTION
HERE WHITE SETTLERS FOUND
CLEARED AND CULTIVATED
FIELDS, VILLAGES AND FORTS
170
(NY 34 south of Venice Center)

INDIAN FIELDS
FARMS OF THE CAYUGAS
BEFORE REVOLUTION
HERE WHITE SETTLERS FOUND
CLEARED AND CULTIVATED
FIELDS, VILLAGES AND FORTS
171
(On NY 34 north of town line)

TOWN OF VENICE
SET OFF FROM SCIPIO 1823
SETTLED AS EARLY AS 1790
JOSHUA MURDOCK CAME HERE
IN 1800 AND BUILT A
HOMESTEAD IN 1816
172
(Venice Center)

TOWN OF VICTORY

TOWN OF VICTORY
SET OFF FROM CATO 1821
FIRST SETTLEMENTS 1800 BY
JOHN MCNEAL AND JOHN
MARTIN. VILLAGE SETTLED
BY JAMES GREGORY IN 1806
173
(In Victory)

NORTH VICTORY
FIRST SETTLEMENT BY CONRAD
PHROZINE IN 1812. HERE IS
THE SITE OF THE MILL HE
BUILT

174
(Intersection Rts 104 & 38)

WESTBURY
FIRST SETTLED IN 1806 BY
WILLIAM AND JACOB
BURGHDUFF. M.E. CHURCH
ORGANIZED 1816, BUILT 1838

175
(1½ m. northwest of Victory)

CHEMUNG COUNTY

TOWN OF ASHLAND

NEWTOWN
SO NAMED BY GENERAL SULLIVAN
OCCUPIED BY BRITISH
AND INDIANS
DESTROYED BY GENERAL
SULLIVAN, AUGUST 30, 1779
1*
(NY 17 1 m. W of Lowman)

THIS RIDGE
FORTIFIED BY THE BRITISH
FORMED THE SOUTH LINE
OF DEFENCE
AUGUST 29, 1779

2
(NY 367 south of Lowman)

LINE OCCUPIED
RIFLE CORPS
UNDER GENERAL HAND
AT OPENING OF BATTLE
AUGUST 29, 1779

3*
(On NY 17 at Lowman)

TOWN OF BIG FLATS

LINE OF RUDE
BREASTWORKS
WHERE BRITISH AND INDIANS
DISPUTED ADVANCE OF
SULLIVAN"S ARMY
AUGUST 29, 1779
4
(Intersection of NY 17 & 367)

FIRST SETTLER
CHRISTIAN MYNEER BUILT
FIRST LOG CABIN 1787 AND
FIRST FRAME HOUSE AND
PLANTED FIRST ORCHARD IN
TOWN OF BIG FLATS
5*
(On 17E 1½ m. W of Elmira)

RUNONVEA
INDIAN VILLAGE
DESTROYED BY GENERAL SULLIVAN
AUGUST 13, 1779

6
(NY 17 at Big Flats)

TOWN OF CHEMUNG

MILITARY ROUTE
OF THE SULLIVAN CLINTON
ARMY ON ITS CAMPAIGN
AGAINST THE BRITISH
AND INDIANS OF WESTERN
NEW YORK IN 1779

7
(NY 17 nr. Chemung-Tioga Co. line)

CHEMUNG RIVER
DERIVED ITS NAME FROM
"BIG HORN" OR TUSK OF
MAMMOTH FOUND IN
RIVER BEFORE 1757

8
(NY 17 3 m. W of Chemung)

CAMP OF
GEN. MAXWELL'S
BRIGADE
SULLIVAN-CLINTON CAMPAIGN
AUGUST 28, 1779

9
(NY 17 2 m. W of Chemung)

MILITARY ROUTE
OF THE SULLIVAN-CLINTON
ARMY ON THE CAMPAIGN
AGAINST THE BRITISH
AND INDIANS OF WESTERN

10
(NY 17 at Chemung)

CAMP OF
GEN. CLINTON'S
BRIGADE
SULLIVAN-CLINTON CAMPAIGN
AUGUST 28, 1779

11
(NY 17 2 m. W of Chemung)

SULLIVAN-CLINTON CAMPAIGN
ARMY CAMP
ON RIVER FLATS TO SOUTH
AUGUST 27, 1779

12
(NY 17, ½ m. W of Chemung)

CITY OF ELMIRA

SULLIVAN ROAD
OVER NARROWS MOUNTAIN
BUILT FOR USE OF
SULLIVAN'S ARMY
EXPEDITION AGAINST INDIANS
1779

13
(NY 17, 1½ m. W of Chemung)

OLD CHEMUNG
INDIAN VILLAGE
DESTROYED BY GEN. SULLIVAN
AUGUST 13, 1779

14
(On NY 17 at Chemung)

DEWITTSBURGH
NEWTOWN POINT
BOUNDARY ABOUT 1790
VILLAGE NAMED AFTER
MOSES DEWITT

15
(On E. Water St. in Elmira)

OLD FERRY
OPERATED FROM ABOUT
1800 TO 1824
PRECEEDED FIRST BRIDGE
Set. 24-29, 1779

16*
(In Brand Park, Elmira)

ENCAMPMENT
SULLIVAN'S ARMY
ON RETURN FROM EXPEDITION
AGAINST THE INDIANS
REVOLUTIONARY WAR, WAR OF 1812
AND THE UNION ARMY

17
(On East Water St. Elmira)

OLD SECOND
STREET CEMETERY
1838-1919, HERE ARE BURIED
PIONEERS, AND SOLDIERS OF THE

18
(NW cr College Ave & W.
2nd St. in Elmira)

CITY OF ELMIRA

MARK TWAIN STUDY
BUILT ON EAST HILL 1874
GIVEN TO ELMIRA COLLEGE IN
1952. HE WROTE "TOM SAWYER",
OTHER NOVELS IN THE STUDY
WHEN SUMMERING IN ELMIRA
19
(Edge of Park Place, Elmira)

TOWN OF ELMIRA

MILITARY ROUTE
OF THE SULLIVAN-CLINTON
ARMY ON ITS CAMPAIGN
AGAINST THE BRITISH
AND INDIANS OF WESTERN
NEW YORK IN 1779
20
(NY 17 Entrance to New-
town Battlefield State Pk)

MILITARY ROUTE
OF THE SULLIVAN-CLINTON
ARMY ON ITS CAMPAIGN
AGAINST THE BRITISH
AND INDIANS OF WESTERN
NEW YORK IN 1779
21
(NY 13 & 17, Elmira Heights)

TOWN OF HORSEHEADS

MILITARY ROUTE
OF THE SULLIVAN-CLINTON
ARMY ON ITS CAMPAIGN
AGAINST THE BRITISH
AND INDIANS OF WESTERN
NEW YORK IN 1779
22
(NY 14 1 m. N of Horseheads)

TOWN OF SOUTHPORT

FITZSIMMONS
CEMETERY
CONTAINS REMAINS OF MANY
PIONEERS AND MEMBERS OF
SULLIVAN-CLINTON CAMPAIGN
NEW YORK IN 1779
23
(NY 427 S of Elmira)

TOWN OF VETERAN

MILITARY ROUTE
OF THE SULLIVAN-CLINTON
ARMY ON ITS CAMPAIGN
AGAINST THE BRITISH
AND INDIANS OF WESTERN

24
(NY 14 at Millport)

GREEN BENTLY
1741-1821
SERVED IN SULLIVAN-CLINTON
CAMPAIGN AND WAS A PIONEER
IN MILLPORT. DEDICATED BY
BOY SCOUTS OF MILLPORT
25
(NY 14 at Millport)

CHENANGO COUNTY

TOWN OF AFTON
MORMON HOUSE
JOSEPH SMITH, FOUNDER
OF THE MORMON CHURCH
WAS MARRIED IN THIS HOUSE
JANUARY 18, 1827
TO EMILY HALE

1
(On NY 41 at Afton)

TOWN OF BAINBRIDGE
FIRST TOLL GATE
ON THE
SUSQUEHANNA-BATH
TURNPIKE
WAS NEAR THIS POINT
INDIANS AND TORIES

2
(NY 206 3 m. NW of Bainbridge)

TOWN OF COLUMBUS

1/4 MILE
TO HISTORIC
CARR FARM
MEETING PLACE OF BRANT'S

1770-1778
3
(NY 8, 6 m. north of New Berlin)

TOWN OF GREENE

WILCOX HOMESTEAD
FIRST TAVERN IN THE TOWN
OF GREENE ERECTED ON THIS
SITE BY CONRAD SHARP, IN 1794.
FIRST TOWN MEETING
HELD HERE IN 1798
4*
(NY 12 2 m. north of Greene)

GO-WON-KO
MOHAWK
AN INDIAN PRINCESS
LIVED IN THIS HOUSE

5*
(NY 12 at Greene)

FIRST HOTEL
IN GREENE
ERECTED ON THIS SITE
IN 1803 BY THOMAS
WATTLES

6*
(NY 41 at Greene)

FIRST CHURCH
IN VILLAGE OF GREENE
THIS CONGREGATIONAL CHURCH
WAS ORGANIZED IN 1811
THE FIRST PASTOR WAS
REV. JOHN B. HOYT.
7
(NY 12 at Greene)

FIRST
BAPTIST CHURCH
IN CHENANGO COUNTY
ORGANIZED ON THIS SITE
BY ELDER NATHANIEL KELLOG
IN 1795
8
(NY 12 4 m. NE of Greene)

GREENE
SETTLED IN 1792
BY STEPHEN KETCHUM;
ALSO BY FRENCH REFUGEES.
TALLEYRAND VISITED HIS
COMPATRIOTS HERE IN 1795.
9*
(NY 12 at Greene)

NEAR THIS SITE
STEPHEN KETCHUM
THE FIRST SETTLER IN
TOWN OF GREENE, BUILT
HIS LOG CABIN IN 1792

10*
(NY 12 at Greene)

FIRST BRIDGE
ACROSS THE CHENANGO RIVER
WAS BUILT ON THIS SITE IN
1807. SUSQUEHANNA AND BATH
TURNPIKE CROSSED HERE

11
(NY 41 at Greene)

GREENE
VILLAGE LAID OUT IN 1806
BY ELISHA SMITH. WAS FIRST
CALLED HORNBY. LATER NAMED
FOR GEN. NATHANIEL GREENE
INCORPORATED 1842

12*
(NY 12 at Greene)

Howard S. Ford

TOWN OF LINCKLAEN

TOWN OF MC DONOUGH

JOHN B. FINCH
GREAT TEMPERANCE ORATOR,
BORN HERE MARCH 17, 1852.
RIGHT WORTHY GRAND TEMPLAR
OF THE WORLD-WIDE ORDER OF
GOOD TEMPLARS, 1884-87
13
(CR 1½ m. N of Lincklaen)

TOWN OF
MC DONOUGH
SET OFF FROM TOWN OF PRESTON
APRIL 17, 1816. NAMED FOR
COMMODORE THOMAS
MAC DONOUGH, 1783-1825
14
(NY 220 at Mc Donough)

SETTLERS OF
MC DONOUGH
FIRST PERMANENT SETTLERS:
SYLVANUS MOORE, NEH. DUNBAR
BENJ. KETCHAM, BENJ. KENYON
HENRY LUDLOW, EPH. FISH
15
(CR at Mc Donough)

TOWN OF NEW BERLIN

DEACON TOWNE
CAME WITH PIONEERS FROM NEW
ENGLAND AND HELD FIRST
RELIGIOUS
SERVICES HERE IN LOG CABINS.
BURIED ON FORMER MICHAEL AND
DANIEL PIKE FARM, SOUTH OF FENCE
16
(On town road 2 m. NE MC Donough)

JOHN P. USHER
SECRETARY OF THE INTERIOR
UNDER ABRAHAM LINCOLN
PRACTISED LAW ON THIS SITE
IN COMPANY WITH JOHN HYDE
1837-1839

17
(NY 8 at New Berlin)

NEW BERLIN
FIRST SETTLED ABOUT 1790
ANSON BURLINGAME BORN HERE
NOVEMBER 14, 1820
U.S. MINISTER TO CHINA
UNDER PRESIDENT LINCOLN

18
(NY 8 at New Berlin)

TOWN OF NORTH NORWICH

SITE OF
DANIEL SCRIBNER'S HOME
BUILT 1790, FIRST HOUSE IN
16 TH TOWNSHIP. LARGE, LOG
BUILDING USED AS TRADING
POST AND FOR TOWN MEETINGS
19
(NY 8 2 m. S of New Berlin)

UNADILLA RIVER
LANDS WEST OF RIVER CEDED
TO N. Y. STATE INDIANS IN
A TREATY MADE BY GOV. GEORGE
CLINTON AT FORT SCHUYLER,
SEPTEMBER 22, 1788
20
(NY 8 2 m. S of New Berlin)

ON THIS SITE
IN 1798 STOOD THE HOME
OF OBADIAH GERMAN, MILITIA
GENERAL, LAND AGENT, STATE
ASSEMBLYMAN, UNITED STATES
SENATOR 1809-1815
21
(CR at North Norwich)

TOWN OF NORWICH

WHITE STORE CHURCH
BUILT 1820 BY
BAPTISTS, METHODISTS, AND
UNIVERSALISTS. CHURCH IN
ORIGINAL FORM EXCEPT
PULPIT LOWERED 1863
22
(NY 8 at White Store)

1789
CAPT. JOHN HARRIS, SEAMAN
AND PIONEER, BOUGHT LAND
FROM BROAD STREET TO RIVER.
FIRST NORWICH TOWN MEETING
HELD IN HIS HOME
23
(NY 12 at Norwich)

1/4 MILE WEST
"THE CASTLE"
ONEIDA INDIAN FORT.
COUNCILS HELD THERE
UP TO 1790

24
(On CR ½ m. S Polkville)

TOWN OF OXFORD

FIRST LOG CABIN
IN NORWICH WAS BUILT ON
THIS SITE ABOUT 1790 BY
COLONEL WILLIAM MONROE
"DRUMMER BOY OF THE
REVOLUTIONARY WAR"
25
(Grounds of C. Courthouse)

AVERY POWER
FIRST SETTLER IN TOWN
OF NORWICH 1788; OWNED
ADJOINING RIVER FLAT.
LUCY POWER, FIRST WHITE
NATIVE OF CHENANGO VALLEY
26
(NY 12 ½ m. south of Norwich)

OXFORD
NAMED BY BENJAMIN HOVEY
AFTER HIS NATIVE TOWN,
OXFORD, MASSACHUSETTS

27
(NY 220 at Oxford)

OXFORD
FIRST TOWN MEETING
HELD IN APRIL 1794
INCORPORATED AS VILLAGE
APRIL 6, 1806.
28
(On former NY 12 at Oxford)

BLACKMAN FARM
SETTLED BY ELIJAH BLACKMAN
1788; THE FIRST SETTLER
IN THE TOWN OF OXFORD

29
(On NY 12 1 m. NE Oxford)

FORT HILL MILL
BUILT IN 1794 BY THEODORE
BURR AND JONATHON BALDWIN

30
(On NY 12 at Oxford)

LAKE WARN
ACCORDING TO TRADITION BURIAL
PLACE OF THICK NECK, GIANT
CHIEF OF THE ANTONES, A TRIBE
OF THE TUSCARORAS. KILLED
BY THE ONEIDAS.
31
(On NY 12 4 m. SW Oxford)

SITE OF
LOG HOUSE BUILT BY
BENJAMIN HOVEY, 1790,
WHO SERVED IN THE
REVOLUTION AND WAS KNOWN
AS "FATHER OF THE SETTLEMENT"
32
(In park in front of Oxford)

JUNCTION OF
ITHACA-CATSKILL TURNPIKE
AND THE UTICA-BINGHAMTON
LINE OF POST-COACHES.
STAGE ROUTE AND MAIL
LINE FORMED IN 1822.
33
(On Washington Ave. Oxford)

HOUSE BUILT BY
JONATHAN BALDWIN IN 1794.
BUILDER OF MANY OF THE FIRST
HOUSES, FIRST SCHOOL HOUSES
AND SECOND RIVER BRIDGE IN
OXFORD

34
(On State St. Oxford)

SITE OF
ST. PAUL'S EPISCOPAL CHURCH
ERECTED IN 1816. THE
FIRST CHURCH
EDIFICE IN THE

VILLAGE OF OXFORD
35
(In park in front of Oxford
High School)

CONGREGATIONAL CHURCH
OLDEST CHURCH EDIFICE STANDING
IN THE VILLAGE OF OXFORD
DEDICATED JULY 31, 1823

36
(On NY 220 at Oxford)

Howard S. Ford

TOWN OF SHERBURNE

FIRST SITE OF
OXFORD ACADEMY
CHARTER GRANTED, 1794.
URI TRACY, FIRST PRINCIPAL.
ONE OF THE FIRST FOUR CHARTERS
GRANTED WEST OF HUDSON RIVER
37
(On NY 220 at Oxford)

SITE OF ANCIENT
INDIAN FORT
IN 1791 EARLY SETTLERS
FOUND EVIDENCE OF THIS
FORT HAVING BEEN IN USE
FOR MANY YEARS
38
(Park, front of Oxford HS)

"WESTERN ORACLE"
FIRST NEWSPAPER IN CHENANGO
CO. WAS PUBLISHED ON THIS
SITE IN 1803 BY ABRAHAM
AND NICHOLAS REMEYN

39
(CR at Sherburne Four Corners)

TOWN OF SMYRNA

WEST HILL – 1802
COLONEL WILLIAM S. SMITH,
AID TO WASHINGTON, OWNED
150,000 ACRES HERABOUT IN
1791; MARRIED ABIGAIL ADAMS.
BURIED AT REAR, DUE NORTH
40
(NY 80 2 m. NW Sherburne)

ALBANY-ITHACA TURNPIKE
A STAKE DRIVEN HERE
MARKED 100 MILES WEST
FROM ALBANY ON THE
ALBANY-ITHACA TURNPIKE
BUILT 1805
41
(NY 80 1 m. E of Sherburne)

ALBANY-ITHACA TURNPIKE
A STAKE DRIVEN HERE
MARKED 100 MILES WEST
FROM ALBANY ON THE
ALBANY-ITHACA TURNPIKE
BUILT 1805
42*
(NY 80, Sherburne)

CORTLAND COUNTY

TOWN OF CORTLANDVILLE

JOHN MILLER
BUILT LOG CABIN HERE
IN 1792. THIS HOUSE
BUILT BY HIS SON
GENERAL DANIEL MILLER

1
(NY 13 nr Homer-Cortland line)

HEADWATERS OF
THE TIOUGHNIOGA RIVER
SITE OF A LARGE INDIAN
VILLAGE. A FAVORITE
STOPPING PLACE OF
EARLY PIONEERS
2
(Clinton Ave. Cortland)

LAMONT MEMORIAL
LIBRARY-BOYHOOD HOME OF
DANIEL S. LAMONT
PRIVATE SECRETARY TO PRESIDENT
CLEVELAND 1885-89 – SECRETARY
OF WAR 1893-97
3
(McGraw cr. Main & Church St.)

TOWN OF CUYLER

PORT WATSON
NAMED AFTER ELKANAH WATSON
BUSY RIVER PORT 1800–1850
SITE SHIP YARDS, ROPE WALK,
FACTORIES. "ARKS" CARRIED
CARGOES TO PENNSYLVANIA
4
(Cortland bridge at Port Watson St)

PIONEER CHURCH
FIRST CHURCH SERVICES
HELD IN A BARN
ON THIS SITE IN 1808
BY BENONI HARRIS
5
(TR rd. 2½ m. N Cuyler)

GATES CABIN
ZEBIDIAH GATES SETTLED
HERE IN 1807
CAME FROM MASSACHUSETTS

6
(CR 1 m. SE Cuyler)

BROWN CABIN
BENJAMIN BROWN FROM
CONNECTICUT SETTLED HERE
IN 1795. FIRST ASSESSOR
AND SECOND TOWN CLERK
IN FABIUS
7
(CR ½ m south of Keeney)

SITE OF CABIN
JOB WHITMARSH FROM
VERMONT SETTLED HERE
IN 1796
PROPERTY STILL IN
POSSESSION OF FAMILY
8
CR ¾ m south of Keeney)

FOX CABIN
SAMUEL FOX SETTLED HERE
IN 1795 FROM CONNECTICUT
THIS HOUSE ERECTED
ABOUT 1821

9
(TR, ½ m. east of Keeney)

KEENEY CABIN
THOMAS KEENEY
SETTLED HERE IN 1796
BUILT THIS HOUSE 1810
PROPERTY STILL IN
FAMILY POSSESSION
10
(Town rd. 1 m. N of Cuyler)

SITE OF CABIN
DAVID MOSS SETTLED HERE
IN 1792 FROM NEW JERSEY
ON LAND GRANTED FROM
GOVERNMENT. STILL IN
FAMILY POSSESSION
11
(Town rd., Cuyler)

SITE OF CABIN
PIONEER HOME OF WANTON
COREY, WHOSE MARRIAGE TO
DEBORAH MOSS IN 1806
WAS FIRST IN TOWN

12
(Lincklaen St., Cuyler)

PIONEER HOME
OF JAMES LOCKWOOD
BUILT ON 100 ACRES OF
LAND GIVEN HIM BY
DAVID MOSS

13
(On town rd. near Cuyler)

CAMPFIRE SITE
HERE DAVID MOSS AND
JAMES LOCKWOOD MADE
FIRST CAMPFIRE APRIL 1792
AND MADE FRIENDS WITH
INDIANS
14
(On town rd. near Cuyler)

LEE HOMESTEAD
BENJAMIN LEE
SETTLED HERE ABOUT 1796
BUILT THIS HOUSE
1810

15
(Town rd. 2 m. N Cuyler)

Howard S. Ford

TOWN OF HOMER

SITE OF
POTTER CABIN
NATHANIEL POTTER
SETTLED HERE IN 1792

16
(On town rd.1½ m. SW Cuyler)

GRISWOLD CABIN
ERECTED PRIOR TO 1825
PAINTED "LINCOLN AND CABINET"
SON OF ASAPH CARPENTER

17
(Town rd. 3.m. NW Cuyler)

BIRTHPLACE OF
FRANK B. CARPENTER, ARTIST
WHO SETTLED HERE IN 1800

18
(US 11, 3 m. N of Homer)

SALISBURY–PRATT HOMESTEAD
USED BEFORE CIVIL WAR AS
AN "UNDERGROUND STATION"
WHERE OREN CRAVATH
SHELTERED & AIDED FUGITIVE
SLAVES ON WAY TO CANADA
19
(NY 281, ½ m. S Little York)

EARLY SETTLER
THOMAS GOULD ALVORD, SR.
BUILT HIS CABIN HERE IN
1794 ON LAND GRANTED FOR
SERVICES IN
REVOLUTIONARY WAR
20
(NY 41 & 41A)

ELI DE VOE
BORN HERE IN LOG CABIN
MEMBER OF U.S. SECRET SERVICE
DETECTED AND FRUSTRATED
A PLOT TO KILL LINCOLN

21
(NY 41 & 41A)

TOWN OF PREBLE

JOHN ALBRIGHT
REVOLUTIONARY SOLDIER
BUILT THIS HOUSE IN 1827
FOR HIS DAUGHTER, MRS.
NANCY GRIFFITH
22
(On NY 13, East Homer)

SITE OF THE
FIRST LOG CABIN
SCHOOLHOUSE
OF DISTRICT NO. 8
1828–1838
23
(NY 41 2 m. west of Homer)

FIRST CHURCH
IN TOWN OF PREBLE
STOOD HERE. BUILT 1804
REMOVED TO VILLAGE 1859

24
(US 11 2 m. NE Preble)

SLAB CITY
SITE OF SAW MILL 1800
GRIST MILL 1806
SCHOOL DISTRICT NO. 4
ORGANIZED 1813
PRESENT SCHOOL BUILT 1843

25
(US 11 2½m. SE Preble)

FIRST SCHOOL
BUILT IN PREBLE 1801
RUTH THORP TEACHER
HAD SCHOLARS FROM THE
TOWNS OF TULLY AND HOMER.

26
(CR 2 m. E Preble)

SITE OF
OLD LOG CHURCH
M.E. CHURCH ORGANIZED 1814
LOG CHURCH BUILT SAME YEAR
ON GOSPEL AND SCHOOL ACRE
AND USED UNTIL THE NEW
CHURCH WAS BUILT IN 1824
27
(Town rd. Preble)

BALTIMORE
TANNERY AND SHOE SHOP. 1810
POST OFFICE 1812-1832
HOTELS 1814-24; 1830-56
SCHOOL 1801 ON EAST HILL
ROAD ¬ MILE E. BRICK
YARD 1812. STORE 1810
28
(US 11 ½ m. east of Preble)

WILLIAM VAN DENBURG
ERECTED LOG CABIN 1802
FIRST FRAME HOUSE BUILT
1806 AND USED AS HOTEL

29
(NY 281, Preble)

PRESBYTERIAN CHURCH
ORGANIZED AS CONGREGATIONAL
1804 REORGANIZED PRESBYTERIAN
1810; MOVED TO ITS PRESENT
SITE 1859

30
(CR ¼ m. east of Preble)

TOWN OF VIRGIL

METHODIST
EPISCOPAL CHURCH
ORGANIZED 1814
CHURCH ERECTED 1824

31
(CR at Preble)

FIRST
STATE ROAD
IN TOWN OF VIRGIL
BUILT 1793-94 BETWEEN
OXFORD AND CAYUGA
BY JOSEPH CHAPLIN

32
(NY 392 in Virgil)

FIRST
SCHOOL HOUSE
IN TOWN OF VIRGIL
WAS ERECTED ON THIS SITE
1799

33
(CR 1¼ m. SW of Virgil)

NATHAN BOUGHTON
1802 - 1876
WHO WROTE AND PUBLISHED
A HISTORY OF THE
TOWN OF VIRGIL
WAS BORN ON THIS FARM
34
(CR 2 1/2 m. SW of Virgil)

HERKIMER COUNTY

TOWN OF COLUMBIA

ORENDORF BARN
FIRST BUILDING WHERE
RELIGIOUS SERVICE WAS HELD
BODIES WERE BURIED UNTIL
1803 AT NORTHEAST CORNER

1
(NY 28, ½ m. N Orendorf Corners)

PETRIE'S CORNERS
ON ROUTE OF SCOUT ADAM F.
HELMER'S FAMOUS RUN TO WARN
SETTLERS OF GERMAN FLATS OF
APPROACH OF BRANT'S INDIANS
SEPTEMBER 17, 1778

2
(Columbia Center)

REFORMED PROTESTANT DUTCH
CHURCH. ORGANIZED JULY 8,
1798. CEMETERY DEDICATED
1803. HAS 20 REVOLUTIONARY
VETERANS AND 22
SOLDIERS OF WAR OF 1812

3
(1 m. west of Orendorf Cors)

Howard S. Ford

| SITE OF
FIRST STORE
AND HOUSE BUILT BY DAVID
V.W. GOLDEN BEFORE 1798,
WHO WAS FIRST JUDGE OF
COURT HELD AT WHITESTOWN.
4
(CR about 1½ m. west of
Orendorf Corners) | MASONIC LODGE
BUILT BY D.V.M. GOLDEN 1812
FOR WARREN LODGE NO. 155
ORGANIZED MARCH 4, 1807
CEASED PAYING DUES 1818.
5
(CR about 2 m. west of
Orendorf Corners) | PIONEER HOME
OF COL. JACOB D. PETRIE
WHO WITH SIX SONS
FOUNDED PETRIE'S CORNERS
6
(Intersection of Co. roads
at Columbia Center) |

TOWN OF DANUBE   TOWN OF FRANKFORT

| SITE OF
PIONEER HOME
OF ANDREW MILLER AND 6 SONS
WHO FOUNDED MILLER'S MILLS
ABOUT 1790. BUILT
SAMILL AND GRISTMILL.
7
(On town rd. at Millers Mills) | FT. HENDRICK
1754-1760
BRITISH POST GUARDING
MOHAWK CASTLE. NAMED FOR
KING HENDRICK KILLED
AT LAKE GEORGE, SEPT 1755
8
(On NY 5S at Indian Castle) | OLD REMINGTON HOMESTEAD
BUILT IN 1799 BY ELIPHALET
REMINGTON WHO FORGED THE
FIRST REMINGTON GUN;
BIRTHPLACE OF PHILO
REMINGTON
9*
(On CR 4 m. SW of Ilion) |

TOWN OF GERMAN FLATS

| FOLTS HOMESTEAD ERECTED
1796 BY MAJOR WARNER FOLTS
WHO SERVED IN WAR OF 1812 AT
SACKETS HARBOR; MEMBER OF
ASSEMBLY 1823-24 HOUSE
OCCUPIED
SINCE BY HIS DESCENDANTS
10
(NY 5S at Ilion) | TRAIL OF SCOUT
ADAM F. HELMER
ENTERING MOHAWK VALLEY TO
WARN GERMAN FLATS OF APPROACH
OF BRANT'S INDIANS, SEPT. 17
1778
11
(NY 5S at Mohawk) | MOHAWK'S FIRST
PUBLIC SCHOOL
BUILT IN 1809 ON THIS SITE USED
AS A SCHOOL UNTIL 1853. SERVED
AS A CHURCH FOR FIVE YEARS
HOUSE NOW STANDS IN REAR
12
(NY 28 at Mohawk) |

TOWN OF LITCHFIELD

| SHOEMAKER TAVERN
BUILT BEFORE THE REVOLUTION
GEN. WASHINGTON HAD DINNER
HERE
UNDER TREE ON HIS VALLEY TOUR IN
1783. WALTER BUTLER CAPTURED
HERE; LATER ESCAPED ALBANY JAIL
13*
(On NY 5S at Mohawk) | F. E. SPINNER HOME
HERKIMER CO. SHERRIF 1834
MEMBER OF CONGRESS 1854-1860
APPOINTED TREASURER OF THE
UNITED STATES BY LINCOLN
SERVED 1861-1875
14
(NY 5S & NY 28 at Mohawk) | SITE OF
AVERY HOMESTEAD
PURCHASED IN 1819 BY
JOHN STANTON AVERY, ONE OF
THE EARLIER SETTLERS IN
LITCHFIELD
HOME DESTROYED
BY FIRE IN 1934.
15
(CR 4 m. SW Ilion) |

JERUSALEM
HILL CEMETERY
OLDEST BURIAL GROUND
TOWN OF LITCHFIELD
FIRST INTERMENT IN 1791

16
(town road at Jerusalem Hill)

BIRTHPLACE OF
JOHN CURTIS UNDERWOOD
1809-1873
U.S. DISTRICT JUDGE
OF VIRGINIA. APPOINTED
BY PRES. LINCOLN 1863

17
(town road at Jerusalem Hill)

FURNACE SITE
OF LITCHFIELD IRON MFG. CO.
INCORPORATED 1813
MAKERS OF PIG IRON AND
VARIOUS KINDS OF
IRON HOLLOW WARE

18
(CR 2 m. S of Gulph)

SITE OF HOME OF
NATHANIEL BALL
WHERE THE FIRST BAPTIST
CHURCH IN LITCHFIELD
WAS ORGANIZED
MARCH 15, 1795

19
(CR about 2 m. S of Gulph)

BIRTHPLACE OF
CHARLES F. WHEELOCK
1849-1928
SCHOOL TEACHER AND
EDUCATOR FOR HALF CENTURY

20
(½ m. N of Cranes Corners)

OLIVE BRANCH LODGE
NO. 40, F. AND A.M.
FIRST MEETING OM THIS SITE
JULY 16, 1812. DEWITT CLINTON
WAS GRAND MASTER AT THE TIME

21
(CR at Cranes Corners)

TOWN OF NORWAY

HOME SITE OF
ELIJAH SNOW
WHO SETTLED HERE IN 1786
LOCALITY THEN CALLED
SNOW'S BUSH
NOW LITCHFIELD

22
(TR rd. 1 m. N Cranes Corners)

A RAIDING FORCE LED BY
MAJOR ROSS AND WALTER
BUTLER WAS HERE ATTACKED
BY COL. MARINUS WILLET'S
PATRIOT SOLDIERS
OCTOBER 30, 1781

23
(CR 3 m. SE of Gray)

IN THIS CEMETERY ARE THE
GRAVES OF SOLDIERS OF THE
FOUR WARS
FRENCH-INDIAN, REVOLUTION,
WAR OF 1812, CIVIL WAR

24
(CR at Norway)

TOWN OF OHIO

TOWN OF POLAND

WOOD HOME
WHEELOCK WOOD (1794-1887)
AND
WIFE, HANNAH SOUTHWICK
COMSTOCK
(1797-1892) OF MASS. LOCATED
HERE IN
1829 AND BUILT THIS HOUSE.

25
(CR 4 m. east of Gray)

OCTAGONAL HOUSE
BUILT ABOUT 1850 BY
LINUS YALE
INVENTOR OF THE
YALE LOCK

26
(NY 28 at Newport)

THE YALE LOCK
WAS FIRST MADE BY
LINUS YALE
IN A SHOP ON THIS SITE
1847

27
(NY 28 at Newport)

Howard S. Ford

TOWN OF SCHUYLER

NEW PETERSBURGH
FORT
A STOCKADE BUILT AND USED
BY THE PIONEERS OF SCHUYLER
PRIOR TO AND DURING
THE AMERICAN REVOLUTION

28
(NY 5 3 m. west of N. Ilion)

SITE OF HOME
HEINRICH STARING
B. 1730 – D. 1808
CAPTAIN 4TH REGIMENT TRYON
COUNTY MILITIA AND FIRST JUDGE
OF COURT OF COMMON PLEAS
OF HERKIMER COUNTY

29
(NY 5 4 m. E of W. Schuyler)

FIRST CHURCH
SCHOOL HOUSE
IN TOWN OF SCHUYLER
BUILT HERE IN 1809

30
(CR 3 m. NE. Schuyler)

TOWN OF WARREN

FIRST PUBLIC
BURYING GROUND
1766-1840
IN THE TOWN OF SCHUYLER
WAS LOCATED ON THIS FLAT

31
(CR 2½ m. N of East Schuyler)

EAST OF THIS POINT
ON BRIDENBECKER CREEK
JOHN FINSTER BUILT THE
FIRST SAWMILL
OPERATED SUCCESSFULLY
IN TOWN OF SCHUYLER

32
(CR 2 m. N of East Schuyler)

MARSHALL CEMETERY
_____ 1/2 MILE
JOHN MARSHALL, 1764-1863
REVOLUTIONARY SOLDIER; WITH
WASHINGTON AT YORKTOWN WITNESSED
SURRENDER OF
CORNWALLIS
33
(US 20 At Warren)

JOHN TUNNICLIFF, JR.
B. 1751, DERBY, ENGLAND, CAME
TO AMERICA 1772; REVOLUTIONARY
SOLDIER; SETTLED HERE 1793;
DIED 1814; BURIED ONE MILE
SOUTH, TUNNICLIFF CEMETERY
35
(US 20 at Warren)

SITE OF
PAUL CRIM HOUSE
PAUL CRIM CAME FROM GERMANY
ABOUT 1757. ONE OF FOUNDERS
OF ANDRUSTOWN. HOUSE BURNED
AT ANDRUSTOWN MASSACRE
36
(CR 2 m. S of Henderson)

SITE OF HOME OF FREDERICK
BELL, FREDERICK, JR.
AND WIFE DOROTHY CRIM
FATHER AND SON MASSACRED
FREDERICK BELL III STOLEN
BY INDIANS—JULY 18, 1778
37
(TR ½ m. N Cranes Corners)

HENDERSON HOUSE
FORMER CRUGER MANSION
GRANT 1739
FRAME HOUSE BUILT 1787
STONE HOUSE BUILT 1832
38
(CR 4 m. N of Jordanville)

LIVINGSTON COUNTY

TOWN OF CALEDONIAN

JOHN HUGH
MAC NAUGHTON
1826-1891
LIVED HERE 20 YEARS
FAMOUS POET AND SONGWRITER

1
(NY 5 4 m. SE of Caledonia)

ERECTED 1826
BY MAJOR GAD BLAKSLEE
EARLY POST OFFICE
FIRST BANK
APOTHECARY SHOP
NOW CALEDONIA LIBRARY

2
(NY 5 at Caledonia)

CALEDONIA
ORGANIZED 1803 AS TOWN OF
SOUTHAMPTON; NAME CHANGED
TO CALEDONIA 1806; SCOTTISH
EMMIGRANTS SETTLED 1799
VILLAGE INCORPORATED 1891

3
(NY 5 west side Caledonia)

CALEDONIA
ORGANIZED 1803 AS TOWN OF
SOUTHAMPTON; NAME CHANGED
TO CALEDONIA 1806; SCOTTISH
EMMIGRANTS SETTLED 1799
VILLAGE INCORPORATED 1891

4
(NY 36 north end of Caledonia)

CALEDONIA
ORGANIZED 1803 AS TOWN OF
SOUTHAMPTON; NAME CHANGED
TO CALEDONIA 1806; SCOTTISH
EMMIGRANTS SETTLED 1799
VILLAGE INCORPORATED 1891

5
(NY 5 south end of Caledonia)

ERECTED 1827
BY JAMES R. CLARK
EARLY TAVERN, POST OFFICE
EARLY BANK, LIBRARY
CERTIFIED BY HISTORIC
AMERICAN BUILDING SURVEY

6
(NY 5 at Caledonia)

TOWN OF CONESUS

BIG SPRINGS
ANCIENT INDIAN CAMP SITE
ON NIAGARA TRAIL
EARLIEST WHITE TOURIST 1615
SCOTTISH SETTLERS 1799
TERMINUS PIONEER R.R. 1838

7
(NY 5 at Caledonia)

MILITARY ROUTE
OF THE SULLIVAN CAMPAIGN
ARMY ON ITS CAMPAIGN
AGAINST THE BRITISH
AND INDIANS OF WESTERN
NEW YORK IN 1799

8
(US 15 at Foots Corners)

MILITARY ROUTE
OF THE SULLIVAN-CLINTON
ARMY ON ITS CAMPAIGN
AGAINST THE BRITISH
AND INDIANS OF WESTERN
NEW YORK IN 1779

9
(NY 256 1 m. S Maple Beach)

TOWN OF GENESEO

TOWN OF GROVELAND

UNION CEMETERY
HERE IS BURIED
CAPTAIN DANIEL SHAYS
1747-1825
SERVED IN THE REVOLUTION
LEADER OF SHAY'S REBELLION

10
(NY 256 1 m. N of Scottsburg)

ABOUT 1/4 MILE WEST
TREATY OF
BIG TREE
SITE OF MEMORABLE TREATY
RELEASING SENECA TITLE TO
3,600,000 ACRES OF LAND
SEPTEMBER 15, 1797

11
(NY 63 at Geneseo) *

SITE OF
WILLIAMSBURG
FIRST SETTLEMENT IN COUNTY
ESTABLISHED 1792 BY
CHARLES WILLIAMSON

12 *
(NY 63 3. m. south of Geneseo)

Howard S. Ford

MILITARY ROUTE
OF THE SULLIVAN-CLINTON
ARMY ON ITS CAMPAIGN
AGAINST THE BRITISH
AND INDIANS OF WESTERN
NEW YORK IN 1779

13
(NY 63 1¼ m. S Hampton Corners)

1 MILE
GROVELAND HILL
TORY-INDIAN AMBUSH
SULLIVAN EXPEDITION
1779
FIFTEEN SCOUTS KILLED
BOYD AND PARKER CAPTURED
14
(NY 256 at Maple Beach)

GROVELAND HILL
TORY-INDIAN AMBUSH
SULLIVAN EXPEDITION
1779
FIFTEEN SCOUTS KILLED
BOYD AND PARKER CAPTURED
15
(TR 1m. W Maple Beach)

TOWN OF LEICESTER

SITE OF
DE-YU-IT-GA-OH
(VALLEY BEGINS TO WIDEN)
SENECA INDIAN VILLAGE
THE SPRING USED BY
MARY JEMISON IS NEARBY
*
(On Squawkie Hill Rd. about
2 miles south of Leicester)
16

THIS
LOG HOUSE
ERECTED AND OCCUPIED
BY THOMAS JEMISON
(BUFFALO TOM)
GRANDSON OF MARY JEMISON
*
(On Squawkie Hill Rd. about
1 ½ miles south of Leicester)
17

SITE OF
A-ON-DO-WA-NUH
(BIG TREE)
SENECA INDIAN VILLAGE

(TR 1½ m. S Leicester)

18

TOWN OF LIMA

BOYD-PARKER
TORTURE TREE AND BURIAL
MOUND. WESTERN LIMIT
SULLIVAN'S EXPEDITION
1779. SENECA VILLAGE
LITTLE BEARD'S TOWN

19*
(On US 20 & NY 39 about ½ m.
east of Cuylerville)

2 MILES ____
BOYD-PARKER
TORTURE TREE AND BURIAL
MOUND. WESTERN LIMIT
SULLIVAN'S EXPEDITION
1779. SENECA VILLAGE
LITTLE BEARD'S TOWN

20*
(At intersection US 20A &
NY 36 at Leicester)

SITE OF
SKA-HASE-GA-O
(WAS-A-LONG-CREEK)
A POPULACE MODERN
SENECA INDIAN VILLAGE

21
(US 20 & NY 5 at Lima)

WARNER HOUSE
BUILT BY ASHAHEL WARNER, 1810
WHO WAS PIONEER IN 1795
USED BY TRINITY MARK MASONIC
LODGE NO. 59, 1810
UNION LODGE NO. 59 1810
22
(US 20 & NY 5 at Lima)

GANDICHIRAGOU
"AT THE FORKS OF THE TRAIL"
NAME RECORDED 1634. DESTROYED
BY DENONVILLE'S FRENCH ARMY
1687. SITE ALSO OF FATHER
GARNIER'S CHAPEL OF ST. JEAN
23
(Intersection US 20 & NY 5 at Lima)

GENESEE WESLEYAN SEMINARY
FOUNDED 1832
GENESEE COLLEGE ESTABLISHED
1849 AND ON APRIL 14, 1869
WAS ALLOWED TO REMOVE TO
FORM SYRACUSE UNIVERSITY
24
(College Ave & Genesee, Lima)

TOWN OF LIVONIA

1/3 MILE EAST SITE OF HOME SOLOMON WOODRUFF FIRST SETTLER OF LIVONIA, 1789	JACKSONVILLE FOUNDED 1830 BY ANDREW HOLDE COMPRISED 130 HOUSES, 10 MILLS, BRICKYARD, 2 DISTILLERIES	MILITARY ROUTE OF SULLIVAN-CLINTON ARMY ON ITS CAMPAIGN AGAINST THE BRITISH AND INDIANS OF WESTERN NEW YORK IN 1779
25 (CR 3/4 m. S Livonia Center)	26 (TR 1 m. NE of Hemlock)	27 (NY 15A 1 m. S of Hemlock)

TOWN OF MOUNT MORRIS

		TOWN OF NORTH DANSVILLE
BIRTHPLACE OF FRANCIS BELLAMY 1855-1931 AUTHOR OF "THE PLEDGE OF ALLEGIANCE TO THE FLAG"	FRANCIS BELLAMY MEMORIAL PARK NAMED IN HONOR OF FRANCIS BELLAMY, 1855-1931, AUTHOR OF "THE PLEDGE OF ALLEGIANCE TO THE FLAG"	SITE OF THE FIRST CHURCH IN DANSVILLE GERMAN EVANGELICAL LUTHERAN CHURCH 1826-1918
28 (On NY 36 at Mount Morris)	29 (On NY 36 at Mount Morris)	30 (On Main St. Dansville)

TOWN OF OSSIAN

IN THIS CHURCH WAS ORGANIZED FIRST LOCAL RED CROSS SOCIETY IN THE UNITED STATES BY CLARA BARTON AUGUST 22, 1881	SITE OF FIRST HOUSE IN DANSVILLE, BUILT IN 1795 BY CORNELIUS MCCOY WHO CAME TO AMERICA FROM IRELAND IN 1788	OSSIAN CENTER SETTLED IN 1804 BY JUDGE RICHARD AND JAMES PORTER. THEY WITH THEIR BROTHER, NATHANIEL, WERE FIRST SETTLERS IN THE TOWN
31 (Exchange and Church Sts.	32 (NY 36 at Dansville)	33 (cross roads at Ossian in Dansville)
HOME – 1850 OF LUTHER BISBEE II AND HIS WIFE, ELIZA WEST, DESCENDANTS OF THOMAS BESBIDGE AND FRANCIS WEST, FREEMEN OF PLYMOUTH COLONY, MASSACHUSETS	TELEGRAPH ROAD ROUTE OF NEW YORK AND ERIE TELEGRAPH LINE CONSTRUCTED IN 1848 UNDER THE SUPERVISION OF EZRA CORNELL FOUNDER OF CORNELL UNIVERSITY	BISBEETOWN SETTLED 1819 BY LUTHER BISBEE BORN 1762-DIED 1856 SOLDIER OF THE AMEICAN REVOLUTION FROM MASSACHUSETTS SITE OF FIRST HOUSE 1 MILE SOUTH
34 (RT 436 4 m. east of Nunda)	35* (TR ¼ m. E of Westview)	36 (RT 436 4. m. east of Nunda)

Howard S. Ford

TOWN OF PORTAGE

INDIAN CABIN
NEARBY IS THE SITE OF
LAST CABIN IN THIS TOWN,
OCCUPIED BY THE SENECAS,
BEFORE THEIR REMOVAL TO THE
BUFFALO RESERVATION, 1826.
37
(RT 436 4 m. west of Nunda)

APPROACHING
CIVIL WAR
PARADE GROUND
1862-1865

40
(NY 245 and bridge road)

PORTAGE BRIDGE
REPLACES LARGEST WOODEN
BRIDGE IN THE WORLD. BUILT
IN 1852. 300 ACRES OF
TIMBER USED IN CONSTRUCTION
BURNED IN 1875
38
(Rd. to Letchworth Pk. fr south)

APPROACHING
CIVIL WAR
PARADE GROUND
1862-1865

41
(Portage end of bridge road)

CIVIL WAR
PARADE GROUND
1862-1865
130TH N.Y. RET., LATER 1ST
N.Y. DRAGOONS AND 136TH N.Y.
REGT. OF INFANTRY, 1862
39*
(Road near Erie RR. bridge)

KISH-A-WA
FIRST SETTLERS IN 1816
ONLY VILLAGE IN 15 MILES;
HOME OF MANY FAMOUS PEOPLE:
PATH OF "OLD INDIAN TRAIL"
42
(CR at Hunt's Hollow)

TOWN OF YORK

SCHOOL SITE
FRAME BUILDING, ABOUT 1819;
ABANDONED FOR ONE OF TWO
ROOMS AS NUMBER OF PUPILS
GREW. SAMUEL HUNT BROTHER
OF GOVERNOR HUNT, TAUGHT HERE.
43
(On CR ½ m. W of Hunts Hollow)

SITE OF
O-HA-GI
(CROWDING THE BANK)
TUSCARORA INDIAN VILLAGE
ONLY ONE IN THE COUNTY

44*
(town rd. ½ m. S Piffard)

BRICK SCHOOL
DISTRICT NO. 8; BUILT
1825. PRESIDENT CHESTER
A. ARTHUR ATTENDING THIS
SCHOOL 1837 TO 1842

45
(On NY 36 at York)

MADISON COUNTY

TOWN OF CAZENOVIA

FIRST COUNTY SEAT
THIS BUILDING ERECTED FOR
COURT HOUSE 1810, COURTS
HELD 1812-17. SOLD TO
METHODISTS 1818. CONFERENCE
SEMINARY ESTABLISHED 1824.
1
(Seminary St between Sullivan & Lincklaen Sts.)

BAPTIST CHURCH
FIRST IN TOWN OF CAZENOVIA.
UNBROKEN SERVICE SINCE
ORGANIZATION JULY 17, 1801
THIS BUILDING ERECTED 1815.

2
(NY 13 AT New Woodstock)

TOWN OF DE RUYTER

MULLER HILL
ESTATE OF LOUIS A MULLER
WHO LOCATED HERE ON 1808.

3
(CR about 5 m. E of De Ruyter)

TOWN OF EATON

EZRA CORNELL
300 YARDS UP THIS LANE
STOOD HIS BOYHOOD HOME
IN 1828 HE WALKED TO ITHACA
WHERE LATER HE FOUNDED
CORNELL UNIVERSITY

4
(CR 3 ½ m. east of De Ruyter)

———
3 1/2 MILES
SITE OF BOYHOOD HOME
EZRA CORNELL
FOUNDER OF
CORNELL UNIVERSITY

5
(NY 13 at De Ruyter)

SITE OF HOME
1793, COL. JOSHUA LELAND
FIRST SETTLED IN THIS VALLEY
HE BUILT FIRST GRIST MILL
ON STREAM BETWEEN THESE PONDS.

6
(NY 26 2 m. NE of Eaton)

TOLL GATE NO. 1
PECK'S PORT, EATON AND
GEORGETOWN PLANK ROAD, 1849
SAWEN MORSE, 1ST WHITE CHILD
BORN IN EATON WAS 1ST
KEEPER OF THIS GATE

7
(NY 26 1 m. NE of Eaton)

SITE OF LOG HOUSE
OF LEVI BONNEY, BORN 1775,
MARRIED RHODA PRATT. CAME
FROM CORNWALL, CONN., 1795
FIRST TO COME AND REMAIN IN
THIS VALLEY

8
(NY 26 ½ m. NE of Eaton)

HOME OF
CYRUS AND ELIZABETH
HEMINWAY FINNEY. MARRIED
MARRIED JULY 25, 1797. CAME
FROM NEW ENGLAND AND
SETTLED HERE 1797.

9
(NY 26 at Eaton)

SITE OF FARM
BOUGHT IN 1799 BY CALEB
DUNBAR, BORN BRIDGEWATER,
MASS., 1760. MARRIED
HANNAH DRAKE, BORN
EATON, MASS. 1762.

10
(town rd. ¼ m. N. of Eaton)

BAPTIST CHURCH
ORGANIZED 1816. ERECTED
REPAIRED AND IMPROVED 1856.
REV. J. COLLEY, 1ST MINISTER.
REV. NATHANIEL KENDRICK,
PASTOR 1817–1833

11
(On NY 26 at Eaton)

SAGE TAVERN IN LOG CITY.
BUILT AND RUN BY ISAAC
SAGE 1802. OLDEST HOUSE
IN VILLAGE OF EATON.

12
(On NY 26 at Eaton)

TOWN OF EATON

TOLL GATE NO. 2
PECK'S PORT, EATON
GEORGETOWN PLANK ROAD, 1849

13
(NY 26 ½ m. west of Eaton)

FANNY FORESTER
AUTHOR OF "ALDERBROOK TALES",
BORN EMILY CHUBBECK AUG. 22,
1817; MARRIED DR. A. JUDSON;
HER HOME "UNDERHILL COTTAGE"
STOOD ABOUT ON THIS SITE.

14
(NY 26 ½ m. west of Eaton)

MORSE MILL DAM
DEVELOPMENT OF EATON BROOK
WATER POWER BEGUN BY
JOSEPH MORSE 1796 CREATED
COUNTY INDUSTRIAL CENTER
LASTING A CENTURY TO 1896

15
(On NY 26 at Eaton)

Howard S. Ford

DR. JAMES PRATT FIRST PHYSICIAN IN TOWN OF EATON, 1797, TAUGHT FIRST SCHOOL IN HOMES OF JOSEPH MORSE COL. LELAND AND THOMAS MORRIS ALTERNATELY. 16 (On NY 26 at Eaton)	MORSE HOUSE JOSEPH MORSE, EUNICE BIGELOW FROM SHERBURNE, MASS. 1796 FOUNDED "LOG CITY" 1800 LATER NAMED EATON 1807 BUILT THIS HOUSE 1802 17 (On NY 26 at Eaton)	SITE OF CHAMPLAIN BATTLE 1615 ------------------ NICHOL'S POND PARK, AN ONEIDA INDIAN VILLAGE SITE 10 MILES NORTH 18 (On US 20 at Morrisville)

TOWN OF FENNER

N.Y. STATE SCHOOL OF AGRICULTURE MORRISVILLE, N.Y. ESTABLISHED 1908 FIRST DIRECTOR, F.G. HELYAR APRIL 1, 1910–NOVEMBER 15, 1917 19 (On US 20 at Morrisville)	N.Y. STATE SCHOOL OF AGRICULTURE MORRISVILLE, N.Y. ESTABLISHED 1908 FIRST DIRECTOR, F.G. HELYAR APRIL 1, 1910–NOVEMBER 15, 1917 20 (On US 20 at Morrisville)	SITE OF CHAMPLAIN BATTLE HERE CHAMPLAIN AIDED BY HURON INDIANS ATTACKED THE STOCKADED ONEIDA VILLAGE OCT. 10-16, 1615 21* (Strip Rd. 6 m. S Canastota)
ONEIDA STONE OF 1615 ONEIDA MEANS PEOPLE OF THE STANDING STONE. IN EACH VILLAGE WAS SUCH AN ALTAR AND COUNCIL PLACE 22* (On Strip Rd. 6 m. south of Canastota via Oxbow Rd.)	GRAIN PITTS THESE PITTS ARE REMAINS OF COMMUNITY STORAGE CELLARS FOR CORN, BEANS AND SQUASH. USED BY THE IROQUOIS INDIANS 23* (ON Strip Rd. 6 m. south Canastota via Oxbow Rd.)	INDIAN SPRING THIS WAS OUTSIDE THE AREA OF THE FORT AND NOT PROTECTED BY THE PALISADES 24* (On Strip Rd. 6 m. south Canastota via Oxbow Rd.)

TOWN OF GEORGETOWN   TOWN OF HAMILTON

MULLER HILL ESTATE OF LOUIS A. MULLER DISTINGUISHED FRENCH REFUGEE WHO LOCATED HERE IN 1808. DOUBTLESS NOBLEMAN FLEEING FROM VENGEANCE OF NAPOLEON 25 (Town rd. 1 ½ m. W Georgetown)	---------- MUULER HILL ESTATE OF LOUIS A. MULLER 26 (NY 80 at Georgetown)	MADISON STREET CEMETERY ESTABLISHED ABOUT 1830 ELISHA PAYNE FOUNDER OF THE VILLAGE OF HAMILTON IS BURIED HERE 27 (On Madison St. at Hamilton)

TOWN OF LEBANON

1/4 MILE LEFT
STOOD THE HOME OF
COL. WM.S. SMITH AIDE
TO WASHINGTON AND
ABIGAIL ADAMS SMITH
SEE MARKER AHEAD
28
(NY 12B 4 ¼ miles south of Hamilton)

1/4 MILE RIGHT
STOOD THE HOME OF
COL. WM. S. SMITH AIDE
TO WASHINGTON AND
ABIGAIL ADAMS SMITH
SEE MARKER AHEAD
29
(NY 12B 3 ¾ miles south of Hamilton)

SMITH'S VALLEY
COL. W. S. SMITH & FAMILY
EARLY SETTLERS AND OWNERS
OF GREAT TRACTS OF LAND
IN THIS SECTION

30
(CR at Randallsville)

HOUSE BUILT BY
ENOCH STOWELL, JR.
EARLY SETTLER. HOME OF
HORACE STOWELL, PROMINENT
ABOLUTIONIST. STATION OF
UNDERGROUND RAILROAD
31
(CR 2 miles south of Eaton)

HERE IN 1778 STOOD
THE BARK HUT
OF BATES, STOWELL AND
SALISBURY, FIRST SETTLERS
OF WHAT IS NOW
MADISON COUNTY
32
(CR 2 miles south of Eaton)

SITE OF
MESSINGER HOTEL
ERECTED IN 1814
BY GEORGE MESSINGER

33
(NY 31 at Messinger Bay)

HOME OF
THOMAS BARLOW
HISTORIAN, COUNTY JUDGE
IN 1843, MEMBER OF THE
NEW YORK STATE SENATE,
1844-1847
6 MILES SOUTH
34
(Main St. Canastota)

HOME OF
MILTON DELANO
CLERK OF TOWN OF OLD
LENOX. TWICE ELECTED
SHERIFF OF MADISON COUNT
MEMBER OF CONGRESS, 1888-1892

35
(NY 13 & Rasbach St. Canastota)

SITE OF
CHAMPLAIN BATTLE
1615

NICHOLS POND PARK
AN ONEIDA VILLAGE SITE

36*
(NY 5 at Canastota)

TOWN OF LINCOLN
QUALITY HILL
GREEN
A COMPANY OF HORSE
ARTILLERY DRILLED HERE
DURING THE WAR OF 1812

37
(NY 5 2 m. west of Canastota)

TOWN OF NELSON
TO SITE OF
CHAMPLAIN BATTLE
1615

38
(On town rd. at Clockville)

WELSH CHURCH
ONE MILE_____
WELSH CONGREGATIONAL
SOCIETY FOUNDED JUNE 22, 1850
PRESENT CHURCH BUILDING
ERECTED 1876
39*
(US 20 1 mile east of Nelson)

Howard S. Ford

TOWN OF SMITHFIELD

| TO SITE OF
CHAMPLAIN BATTLE
1615

40
(CR at Peterborough) | TO SITE OF
CHAMPLAIN BATTLE
1615

41
(On Mile Strip Rd.
6 miles S Canastota) | ---------
500 FEET
GERRIT S. MILLER
HOME OF EARLY IMPORTED
HOLSTEIN CATTLE
42
(CR 2 m. NW of Peterborough) |

TOWN OF STOCKBRIDGE

BIRTHPLACE
W. DEMPSTER HOARD, BORN
OCT. 10, 1836. GOVERNOR
OF WISCONSIN 1889-90
FOUNDER HOARD'S DAIRYMAN

43
(NY 46 1 m. south of Munnsville)

MONROE COUNTY

TOWN OF BRIGHTON		TOWN OF CLARKSON
IRONDEQUOIT SITE OF A LARGE ALGONKIN TOWN THE SENECAS LINGERED HERE UNTIL 1845 1 (Blossom Rd. east of Landing Rd. North)	CITY OF TRYON FIRST WHITE SETTLEMENT WEST OF CANANDAIGUA FOUNDED 1797, ABANDONED 1818. JOHN LUSK WAS THE FIRST SETTLER 1789 2 (East side Landing Rd. near Blossom Rd.)	HENRY R. SELDEN 1805-1885 LIEUT. GOV. AND JUDGE LIVED HERE. GEORGE B. SELDEN INVENTOR OF "SELDEN PATENT" FOR AUTOMOBILES WAS BORN HERE 3 (NY 104 at Clarkson)
HOME OF SIMEON B. JEWWETT 1801-1869 POLITICAL LEADER, JURIST, PARTNER OF HENRY R. SELDEN, U.S. MARSHALL, NORTHERN N.Y. UNDER PRES. BUCHANAN 4 (On NY 19 at Clarkson)	HOUSTON TAVERN A POPULAR STOPPING PLACE IN STAGE COACH DAYS. BUILT SOON AFTER 1825 FOR ISAAC HOUSTON WHO WAS THE SOLE PROPRIETOR FOR MANY YEARS 5 (NY 104 1 m. east of Gerland)	PHILIP BOSS ARTIST AND CABINET MAKER LIVED HERE FROM 1820 TO 1830 MOVING TO ROCHESTER, THEN, HE ACHIEVED GREAT POPULARITY AS A PAINTER OF PORTRAITS 6 (On NY 104 at Clarkson)

TOWN OF IRONDEQUOIT

FORT SITE
HERE DENONVILLE'S FRENCH ARMY
LANDED TO INVADE THE SENECA
COUNTRY; JULY 12, 1687, 400
MEN WERE LEFT TO BUILD FORT;
BATTLE AT VICTOR. JULY 13, 1687

7
(Sea Breeze bluff, L. Ontario)

FORT DES SABLES
A FRENCH TRADING POST
BUILT BY JONCAIRE NEAR
THIS SITE IN 1717 AS A
SENECA LINK TO NEW FRANCE
AROUSED BRITISH IRE

8
(Sea Breeze bluff, L. Ontario)

TOWN OF MENDON

CAMP SITE
OF PRIMITIVE ALGONKINS
WHO FISHED HERE AGES AGO
DRIVEN OUT BY THE IROQUOIS
WHO OCCUPIED THIS REGION

9*
(Canfield Rd. Mendon Ponds Park)

TOWN OF OGDEN

TOTIAKTON
SENECA TOWN OF 120 CABINS
WAS LOCATED HERE
BURNED BY DENONVILLE, 1687
JESUIT MISSION, 1668-1683

10
(East side Plain Rd. south of
Rochester Junction)

WAR SITE
DENONVILLE'S ARMY OF 3000
FRENCH AND INDIAN ALLIES
CAMPED HERE 23 JULY 1687
RETURNING TO IRONDEQUOIT
AFTER RAZING SENECA TOWNS

11*
(Mendon Ponds Park)

BIRTHPLACE OF
JOHN T. TROWBRIDGE
1827-1916
POET; AUTHOR OF "DARIUS
GREEN AND HIS FLYING
MACHINE" AND OTHER STORIES

12
(Nichols St 2 m. SE of
Spencerport)

TOWN OF PARMA

INDIAN HILL
INDIAN ENCAMPMENT WHEN WHITES
ENTERED REGION
GRANDPARENTS OF FRANCIS E
WILLARD
SETTLED HERE IN 1816
AS PIONEERS ON THIS LAND

13
(On Bangs Rd. 2 miles north
of Churchville)

METHODIST CHURCH
OLDEST WEST OF THE GENESEE
FIRST SERMON PREACHED 1804
CLASS ORGANIZED 1811

CHURCH BUILT 1830

14
(On NY 259 at Parma Center)

TOWN OF PERINTON

LA SALLE ROAD
ROUTE USED BY THE FRENCH
ARMY OF DENONVILLE TO
DESTROY SENECA INDIANS AT

TOWN SOUTH OF VICTOR, N.Y.
JULY 13, 1687

15
(On NY 96 ¬ mile east of
Bushnell Basin)

Howard S. Ford

TOWN OF PITTSFORD

SENECA TRAIL
CROSSING THE IRONDEQUOIT
THICKLY WOODED, PERILOUS
DEFILE WHERE DENONVILLE
EXPECTED AN AMBUSCADE ON
JOURNEY TO GANNOGARO, 1687
16
(On NY 96 1 ½ miles east of
Pittsford Village)

DENONVILLE
WITH ARMY OF 3000
FRENCH AND INDIANS
CROSSED THESE GROUNDS
TWICE IN JULY 1687

17
(On golf course, Oak Hill
Country Club)

FIRST LIBRARY
IN THE GENESEE COUNTRY
NORTHFIELD LIBRARY CO., 1803
1808, KEPT ITS BOOKS AT THE
FARM OF EZRA PATTERSON,
FIRST LIBRARIAN
18
(Mendon Ctr. Rd. about 1 mile
southeast of Pittsford)

THE FIRST HOUSE
IN PITTSFORD VILLAGE
WAS ERECTED ON THIS
SPOT BY ISRAEL STONE

19
(NY 31 at Pittsford)

ON THIS SPOT
STOOD THE FIRST SCHOOL
HOUSE IN MONROE COUNTRY
ERECTED 1794; FIRST
TEACHER, JOHN BARROWS
20
(NY 64 1 mile S Pittsford)

PITTSFORD VILLAGE
FOUNDED AUGUST 1789
BY CAPTAIN SIMON STONE
AND LIEUTENANT ISRAEL STONE

21
(NY 96 & 31 at Pittsford)

OLD TAVERN
BUILT BY J. THOMSON, 1808
FIRST FRAME HOUSE AND FIRST
POST OFFICE IN TOWN OF RIGA
THOMAS ADAMS HOMESTEAD.

22
(Riga-Mumford Rd at Riga Ctr.)

RIGA ACADEMY
A FLOURISHING SCHOOL FOR
BOARDING AND DAY PUPILS
WAS ORGANIZED HERE IN 1846.
THE BUILDING WAS EARLIER
KNOWN AS THONSON'S TAVERN
23
(Riga-Mumford Rd. at Riga Ctr.)

FOUNDED 1843
CHURCHVILLE GRADED SCHOOL
OCCUPIED THIS BUILDING
UNTIL 1895. A FINE EXAMPLE
OF THE LOST ART OF BUILDING
WITH COBBLESTONES.
24
(West Buffalo St. Churchville)

CITY OF ROCHESTER

FRANCIS E, WILLARD
GREAT TEMPERANCE LEADER
WAS BORN IN HOUSE.
STANDING ON THIS SITE SEPT. 28, 1839
THE WILLARDS LEFT THIS HOME FOR
OHIO TWO YEARS LATER
25
(On Main St. Churchville)

CASCONCHIAGON
INDIAN VILLAGE AT THE
FALLS NEARBY. OCCUPIED
BY SENECAS UNTIL 1819

26
(Maplewood Park, north of
Driving Park)

SITE OF
INDIAN FORT
BUILT BY EARLY ALGONKINS
IN FORM OF A SEMICIRCLE
EARTHEN EMBANKMENT
WITH THREE ENTRANCES
27
(West bank Genesee R, east
of N.end of River St.)

INDIAN TOWN
IN PRIMITIVE WILDERNESS
HERE WAS A LARGE ALGONKIN
VILLAGE WHOSE BARK CABINS
AND TILLED FIELDS COVERED
NINE ACRES
28
(E. side River Blvd. near
Elmwood Ave.)

PIONEER SCHOOL
FIRST SCHOOLHOUSE IN ROCHESTER
WAS BUILT OF WOOD ON THIS SITE,
1813. IT WAS REPLACED BY A
TWO-STORY STONE BUILDING, 1836,
AND BY THIS STRUCTURE, 1873.
29
(On Fitzhugh St.)

LEWIS HENRY
MORGAN'S HOME
1855-1881. HERE HE WROTE
HIS GREAT BOOKS: "THE AMERICAN
BEAVER", "THE HUMAN FAMILY"
"ANCIENT SOCIETY".
30
(Intersection of Fitzhugh
and Troup Streets)

JONATHAN CHILD
FIRST MAYOR OF ROCHESTER
1834-1835, BUILT THE HOUSE
IN 1838 AND LIVED HERE WITH
HIS WIFE, SOPHIA ELIZA ROCHESTER
CHILD, UNTIL 1850
31
(At Fourth Church of
Christ Scientist)

OLD HIGH SCHOOL
BUILT ON THIS SITE, 1827
BY BRIGHTON DISTRICTS 4 AND 14
NAMED ROCHESTER COLLEGIATE
INSTITUTE 1839. DR. CHESTER
DEWEY WAS PRINCIPAL 1836-52.
32
(1st Unitarian Church on
Cortland St.)

HIGHLAND PARK
ROCHESTER'S FIRST PARK
OFFERED IN 1883 BY ELLWANGER
AND BARRY AND ACCEPTED JAN.
13, 1888. PARK COMMISSION
WAS FORMED MAY 1, 1888.
33
(Near Pavilion, Highland Park)

SITE OF
EARLY SCHOOL
QUAKERS MET HERE
1824-1827

34
(Burrell Rd. South of Scottsville)

FIRST HOUSE
WEST OF GENESEE RIVER
STOOD 1700 FEET DUE SOUTH
"INDIAN" ALLEN, BUILDER, 1786
PETER SCHAEFFER, SETTLER, 1789
FIRST TOWN MEETING 1797
35
(Scottsville-West Henrietta Road
Scottsville)

KELSEY'S LANDING
FREEDOM WAS ASSURED FOR
ESCAPING SLAVES WHO
BOARDED CANADIAN VESSELS
HERE AT THE END OF THE
UNDERGROUND RAILROAD
36
(Driving Park, West Side of
Genesee River)

TOWN OF RUSH

INDIAN SPRING
ATTRACTED INDIANS HERE;
SUPPLIED GOOD WATER TO
ROCHESTER'S FIRST SETTLERS
FOR A DECADE AFTER 1812;
GAVE NAME TO SPRING STREET.
37
(Spring and Washington St.)

SUSAN B. ANTHONY
OUTSTANDING LEADER IN
WOMAN'S RIGHTS MOVEMENT
MADE HER HOME HERE
WITH HER SISTER, MARY
1866-1906
38
(On Madison St.)

SITE OF A SETTLEMENT OF
TUSCARORAS
6TH NATION OF IROQUOIS
LEAGUE. DRIVEN FROM
CAROLINAS BY BRITISH
1714-1722
39
(Avon Rd. Monroe Co. line)

Howard S. Ford

TOWN OF SWEDEN

TOWN OF WHEATLAND

HONEOYE
VALLEY
THREE INDIAN TRIBES
HAVE HUNTED, FISHED
AND TILLED THE SOIL HERE
FOR THOUSANDS OF YEARS
40
(E. River Rd. W. Rush)

MCCORMICK REAPER
MADE HERE IN 1846. SEYMOUR
AND MORGAN BY BUILDING 100
REAPERS FOR CYRUS MCCORMICK
BEGAN QUANTITY PRODUCTION
OF REAPERS
41
(Market & Park Sts. Brockport)

NORTHAMPTON
FIRST TOWN WEST OF GENESEE
RIVER ORGANZIED HERE 1797
EBENEZER ALLEN HOME 1786
PETER SCHAEFER FARM 1789
TERMINUS PIONEER R.R. 1888
42
(Main St., Scottsville)

BURIAL SITE
QUAKER CEMETERY
BOUGHT 1833
FROM DARIUS SHADBOLT

43
(Burrell Rd. S. of Scottsville)

ERECTED 1854
BY ORTHODOX QUAKERS
USED THIRTY YEARS

44
(South Rd. S. of Scottsville)

SITE OF FIRST
QUAKER MEETING HOUSE
TOWN OF WHEATLAND
FRAME BUILDING 1827
USED UNTIL 1854
BY HICKSITES
45
(Burrell Rd S. of Scottsville)

ONEIDA COUNTY

TOWN OF AUGUSTA

"STONE CHURCH"
BUILT 1834 BY THE
CONGREGATIONAL SOCIETY
DEDICATION SERMON BY REV.
O. BATHOLOMEW, EARLY PASTOR
REV. JOHN CROSS
1
(NY 12B at Oriskany Falls)

UTICA CLINTON &
BINGHAMPTON R.R.
FORMED 1862. COMPLETED
FROM UTICA TO TERMINATE
AT THIS SITE 1858
EXTENDED SOUTH 1871
2
(Broad St. Oriskany Falls)

CASSETY HOLLOW
SETTLED IN 1794 BY COL.
THOMAS CASSETY, WHO
ERECTED A GRIST MILL
HERE. LATER RENAMED
ORISKANY FALLS
3
(NY 12B & 26 Oriskany Falls)

CHENANGO CANAL
AUTHORIZED 1833. UTICA TO
BINGHAMTON. COMPLETED 1836.
72 LOCKS IN 30 MILES
ABANDONED 1876

4
(NY 26, Oriskany Falls)

SITE OF
THE GUNN HOUSE
ABOUT 500 FEET FROM HERE
BUILT IN 1793. FIRST HOUSE
IN THE TOWN OF AUGUSTA BUILT
BY A WHITE SETTLER

5
(College St. Road, ½ mile
north of Oriskany Falls)

AUGUSTA ACADEMY
FOUNDED 1834. SEMICIRCULAR
STONE BUILDING USED UNTIL
1878. ITS UNIQUE DESIGN
WAS A CURIOSITY. FIRST
TEACHER MELVILLE ADAMS
6
(NY 26, Augusta)

AUGUSTA CHURCH ORGANIZED 1797 BY CONGREGATIONAL SOCIETY FORMED FROM THE 7 (NY 26 in Augusta)	AUGUSTA ONEIDA COUNTY MARCH 15, 1798 SAVED GENERAL LAFAYETTE"S LIFE. TOWN OF WHITESTOWN 8 (NY 26 in Augusta)	AMOS PARKER (1762-1842) TALLEST MAN IN AMERICAN ARMY. PRESENT AT THE SURRENDER OF CORNWALLIS. BURIED HERE 9 (Sallsville—Augusta County Rd)
SITE OF LOG SCHOOL FIRST IN AUGUSTA, BUILT 1797 AUGUSTA THEN KNOWN AS BARTLETT'S CORNER. USED AS CHURCH AND MEETING HOUSE 10 (Sallsville–Augusta Co. Rd. (1 ½ miles S. of Augusta)	UNION CHURCH BUILT 1849 BY METHODISTS AND PRESBYTERIANS. LUMBER HAULED FROM OLD CHURCH BUILT ABOUT 1800 ON EAST HILLS. CONVERTED TO SCHOOL 1873. 11 (South & East St., Knoxboro)	DR. A. BURGOYNE (1737-1824) BURIED IN THIS CEMETERY PHYSICIAN AT SARATOGA UNDER GEN. BURGOYNE, 1777. LIVED WITH DAUGHTER IN AUGUSTA. 12 (South St. in Knoxboro)
KNOX HOUSE BUILT 1820 BY GEB. J.J. KNOX PIONEER SETTLER, 1791-1876. VILLAGE OF KNOXBORO NAMED IN HIS HONOR 13 (South St. in Knoxboro)	INDIAN TRAIL USED BY ONEIDA, TUSCARORA BROTHERTON AND STOCKBRIDGE INDIANS AS A CHANNEL OF COMMERCE ABOUT 1700. MADE HIGHWAY SOON AFTER 1800 14 (West St. in Knoxboro)	SITE OF LOCK COMPANY ORGANIZED 1861 BY J. C. KNOX. HIGH GRADE LOCKS WERE MANUFACTURED HERE FOR A NUMBER OF YEARS 15 (West St. in Knoxboro)

TOWN OF BOONVILLE

OLD FRENCH ROAD BUILT BY FRENCH COLONISTS, 1790 ON WAY TO SETTLE CASTORLAND; FIRST ROAD TO NORTH COUNTRY FOLLOWING AN IROQUOIS WAR TRAIL 16 (NY 12 1 m. SE of Boonville)	FIRST PRESBYTERIAN CHURCH SOCIETY ORGANIZED 1805 PRESENT EDIFICE BUILT 1855-56 REDEDICATION 1955 17 (James St., Boonville)	POST HOUSE, 1817 FIRST USED AS A SCHOOL LATER BOUGHT WITH LARGE TRACT OF LAND BY JOHN G. POST PASSED FROM FAMILY IN 1905 18 (Post St., Boonville)

Howard S. Ford

BOONVILLE
SETTLED 1795; NAMED FOR
GERRIT BOON: NATIVE OF LEYDEN,
HOLLAND, AGENT OF HOLLAND
LAND
CO; TOWN FORMED 1805; VILLAGE
INCORPORATED 1855

19
(NY 12D in Boonville)

BLACK RIVER CANAL
SITE OF LOCK 71 SUMMIT
LEVEL; 710 FEET ABOVE ROME
FROM HERE WATER FLOWED
NORTH TO ST. LAWRENCE
SOUTH TO MOHAWK

20
(NY 12 in Boonville)

BLACK RIVER CANAL
SITE OF THE ONCE FAMOUS
FIVE COMBINES-WORLD'S RECORD
FOR NUMBER OF CANAL LOCKS
CANAL HAS 109 LOCKS IN 35
MILES
OF WATERWAY

21
(NY 46 entrance to Pixley Falls Pk)

TOWN OF BRIDGEWATER

TOWN OF DEERFIELD

BIRTHPLACE OF
DR STEPHEN MOULTON BABCOCK
INVENTOR OF BABCOCK MILK TEST
SCIENTIST, EDUCATOR, FRIEND
BENEFACTOR OF AGRICULTURE
1843-1931

22
(Town Rd. at Babcock Hill)

BRIDGEWATER
ONEIDA COUNTY
MARCH 24, 1797
TRANSFERRED FROM
CHENANGO COUNTY
APRIL 4TH 1804

23
(US 20, Bridgewater)

DEERFIELD
ONEIDA COUNTY
MARCH 15, 1798
FORMED FROM THE
TOWN OF SCHUYLER
HERKIMER COUNTY

24
(NY 8, 2 m. N of NY 5 & 12)

TOWN OF FLOYD

TOWN OF FORESTPORT

-----
17 MILES
TOMB OF
BARON STEUBEN
IN STATE MEMORIAL PARK
NEAR REMSEN
25
(NY 12 1 m. N. of NY 5)

FLOYD
MARCH 4TH 1796
NAMED IN HONOR OF
WILLIAM FLOYD, 1734-1821
A SIGNER OF THE
DECLARATION OF INDEPENDENCE
26
(NY 46 in Floyd)

FORESTPORT
TOWN-1869. VILLAGE-1903.
FIRST SETTLEMENT 1795
IN 1777 ST. LEGER'S INDIANS
RETREATED THROUGH HERE
ORISKANY TO CROWN POINT.
27
(River & White Lake Sts. in Forestport)

TOWN OF KIRKLAND

ST, LEGER'S HILL
1777
EASTERLY OVER THIS ROUTE
450 OF ST. LEGER'S INDIANS
RETREATED FROM ORISKANY
TO CROWN POINT
28
(N. Lake Rd. 5 m. E Forestport)

FIRST GRIST MILL
NEAR THIS SPOT FIRST GRIST
MILL WAS BUILT IN WINTER
OF 1787, BEFORE THIS EARLY
SETTLERS HAD TO CARRY GRIST
TO WHITESTOWN
29
(NY 412 in Clinton)

HAMILTON COLLEGE
FOUNDED AS HAMILTON-ONEIDA
ACADEMY, 1793 BY THE REV.
SAMUEL KIRKLAND. CHARTERED
AS HAMILTON COLLEGE
MAY 26, 1812.
30
(Hamilton College, Clinton)

HAMILTON COLLEGE CHAPEL
1827
AN UNUSUAL AND DISTINCTIVE
THREE STORY CHURCH
DESIGNED BY PHILIP HOOKER
OF ALBANY
31
(Hamilton College, Clinton)

ELIHU ROOT
SECRETARY OF WAR
SECRETARY OF STATE
UNITED STATES SENATOR
WAS BORN IN THIS BUILDING
FEBRUARY 15, 1845
32
(Hamilton College, Clinton)

WASHINGTON TRACT
THESE LANDS ARE PART OF
PARCEL OF GROUND DEEDED
TO NATHANIEL GRIFFIN BY
GEORGE WASHINGTON AND
DEWITT CLINTON IN 1790
33
(NY 233 1½ m S. of Kirkland)

TOWN OF MARSHALL

HOME OF
BROTHERTON INDIANS
1783-1850
AMONG WHOM LIVED, 1785-1792,
SAMSON OCCOM
INDIAN PRESBYTERIAN PREACHER
34
(NY 315 4 m. NW. of Waterville)

TOWN OF MARCY

___17 MILES ___
TOMB OF
BARON STEUBEN
IN STATE MEMORIAL PARK
NEAR REMSEN

35
(NY 49 & 12C)

TOWN OF NEW HARTFORD

A GRIST MILL
WAS BUILT 350 FEET EAST OF
HERE IN 1790 BY JEDEDIAH SANGER
FIRST SETTLER AND FOUNDER OF
NEW HARTFORD

36
(Oxford PL.& Mill St.,
New Hartford)

TOWN OF PARIS

JEDEDIAH SANGER
FOUNDED NEW HARTFORD IN
1788 BY PURCHASING 1000
ACRES OF LAND AND SETTLING
HERE WITH HIS FAMILY

37
(NY 5 and 12, New Hartford)

1ST RELIGIOUS
SOCIETY
OF THE TOWN OF WHITESTOWN
ORGANIZED 1791
CHURCH DEDICATED
NOV. 29, 1797
38
(NY 5 and 12, New Hartford)

_____
7/8 MILE
BIRTHPLACE OF
DR. ASA GRAY
WORLD FAMOUS BOTANIST

39
(NY 8, Pinnacle Rd., Sauquoit)

TOWN OF REMSEN

BIRTHPLACE OF
____ DR ASA GRAY
BORN NOVEMBER 18, 1810
DIED JANUARY 30, 1888
WORLD FAMOUS BOTANIST

40
(Pinnacle Road, Saquoit)

METHODIST CHURCH
FIRST SERMON PREACHED IN
NORTHERN NEW YORK 1788
BY ELDER FREEBORN GARRETSON
WITHIN WHITESTOWN
SAUQUOIT SOCIETY FORMED 1788
41
(Mohawk St.& Pinnacle Rd

_____
4 MILES
TOMB OF
BARON STEUBEN
IN STATE MEMORIAL PARK
NEAR REMSEN

42
(NY 12 & 12 B, Remsen)

Howard S. Ford

REMSEN

NEXT TURN RIGHT TO
TOMB OF
BARON STEUBEN
IN STATE MEMORIAL PARK

43
(NY 12 B in Remsen)

ONEIDA COUNTY
MARCH 15, 1798
FORMED FROM THE TOWN OF
NORWAY, HERKIMER COUNTY

44
(NY 12 B, in Remsen)

1 MILE EAST
COLONEL MARINUS WILLETT ROUTED
BRITISH-TORY FORCE OCT. 3, 1783
ALONG WEST CANADA CREEK
WALTER BUTLER, TORY LEADER
WAS KILLED BY AN ONEIDA

45
(Fairchild Rd., north of
Hinckley Reservoir)

TOWN OF ROME

ORISKANY
BATTLEFIELD
1777
PUBLIC WELCOME
IN STATE MEMORIAL PARK

46
(NY 69 at Oriskany Battlefield)

20 MILES
TOMB OF
BARON STEUBEN
SYSTEM
NEAR REMSEN

47
(NY 46 north to Rome)

NORTHWEST 35 RODS
JESSE WILLIAMS
IN 1851 INAUGERATED THE
CHEESE FACTORY
THUS REVOLUTIONIZING
DAIRYING

48
(NY 46, 2 m. N. of Rome)

CITY OF ROME

LOWER LANDING
AND
ORISKANY
BATTLEFIELD
49
(Mill and Martin Sts.)

FORT STANWIX
AND
REVOLUTIONARY
SKIRMISHES
50
(Mill and Whitesboro Sts.)

FORT CRAVEN
DESTROYED IN
BRITISH PANIC
BEFORE COMPLETION
AUG. 31, 1756
51*
(E. Whitesboro St. between
Bouck and Mill Sts.)

1755-1756
FORT WILLIAMS
GUARDED
UPPER MOHAWK LANDING
BURNED IN A PANIC
BY BRITISH GEN. WEBB
52*
(Bouck St. between E. Whitesboro
and E. Dominick Sts.)

REVOLUTIONARY
BATTLEFIELDS
AND
COLONIAL
FORT SITES
53
(E. Dominick & Bouck Sts)

INLAND CANAL
BEGUN 1792
AND SECOND
ERIE CANAL
COMPLETED 1844

54*
(S. James & E. Whitesboro Sts.)

OLD BLACK RIVER CANAL
BUILDING 1836-1855; CONNECTED
MOHAWK VALLEY WITH BLACK RIVER
COUNTRY; OPENING UP 90 MILES
NAVIGABLE WATERWAY; JOINED
ERIE CANAL HERE

55
(Black R. Blvd. & E. Whitesboro St.)

HISTORIC ELM
THIS ELM WAS A SAPLING
GROWING ON THE SOUTHWEST
BASTION
IN 1804

56*
(E. Dominick St. between
James and Spring Sts.)

HERE PASSED
FROM EAST TO WEST
ANCIENT CARRY
FROM THE MOHAWK TO
WOOD CREEK

57*
(George and Liberty Sts.)

HERE THE
ANCIENT CARRY
PASSED SOUTHWARD TO
FORT NEWPORT AND
WOOD CREEK

58*
(West Dominick & Jay Sts.)

SITE OF
U.S. ARSENAL
MAINTAINED DURING
WAR OF 1812 AND
SUBSEQUENTLY

59
(W. Dominick ST. between
Arsenal & Jay Sts.)

ONE BLOCK
TO SITE OF
FORT NEWPORT
AND WOOD CREEK
LANDING

60*
(W. Dominick & Arsenal Sts.)

FORT NEWPORT
A SMALL COLONIAL POST
WHICH GUARDED
UPPER WOOD CREEK
LANDING PLACE
61
(Calvert St. bet. Arsenal St.
and Brewer Alley)

ROME
MARCH 4TH 1796
FORMED FROM
THE TOWN OF
STEUBEN
62
(N. James St. & W. Park Sts.)

DURING SIEGE OF
FORT STANWIX AUG. 1777
MAIN BRITISH CAMP
WAS BETWEEN THIS POINT
AND THE BLUFF TO SOUTH
63
(E Bloomfield St. &
Roosevelt Ave.)

TOWN OF SANGERFIELD

THE CENTRAL N. Y.
SCHOOL
FOR THE DEAF
FOUNDED JAN. 27, 1875 BY
ALPHONSO JOHNSON, THOMAS
GALLAUDET AND ROME CITIZENS
64
(On NY 26)

PROPERTY LINE
WESTERN BOUNDARY OF
CIVILIZATION FIXED BY
FORT STANWIX TREATY
NOV. 5, 1768. WITNESSED
BY SIR WILLIAM JOHNSON
65*
(NY 12 north of Waterville)

BIRTHPLACE OF
GEORGE EASTMAN
INVENTOR OF KODAK
BORN JULY 12, 1854.
DIED IN ROCHESTER
MARCH 14, 1932.
66
(NY 12 in Waterville)

Howard S. Ford

TOWN OF STEUBEN

SANGERFIELD
ONEIDA COUNTY
MARCH 15, 1795
TRANSFERRED FROM
CHENANGO COUNTY
APRIL 4TH 1804
67
(NY 12 at town line)

WELSH IMMIGRANTS
BEGINNING 1795 CLEARED AND
SETTLED GREATER PART OF
STEUBEN GRANT. BUILT
FIRST CHURCH HERE 1804.

68
(CR ½ mile W. of Remsen)

300 FEET WEST
SITE OF HOME
ROBERT EVERETT (1791–1875)
ANTI-SLAVERY REFORMER
MINISTER CHAPEL UCHA 37 YEARS
EDITOR "CENHADWR" (WELSH) 35 YEARS
69
(CR 1 mile W. of Remsen)

EBENEZER WEEKS
SETTLED HERE 1791
BURIED IN ADJOINING MEADOW
BUILT BAKE OVEN AND DID
COOPERING FOR BARON STEUBEN
70
(Co.Rd. ½ m. W. of Remsen)

THIS PARK
WAS CREATED IN MEMORY
OF FRIEDRICH WILHELM BARON
STEUBEN, MAJOR GENERAL IN
THE WAR FOR INDEPENDECE
71
(At Baron Steuben Memorial)

STEUBEN PARK
MEMORIAL PARK
DEDICATED SEPTEMBER 12, 1931
BY FRANKLIN D. ROOSEVELT,
GOVERNOR OF NEW YORK
72
(Baron Steuben Memorial)

BARON STEUBEN
INSPECTOR GENERAL OF ARMY
MAJOR GENERAL IN REVOLUTION
CITIZEN OF UNITED STATES
AND NEW YORK STATE

73
(Baron Steuben Memorial)

STEUBEN STATE
MEMORIAL PARK
INCLUDES 50 ACRES GIVEN
IN 1804 BY COL. BENJ. WALKER,
FRIEND AND AID OF STEUBEN
TO SECOND BAPTIST CHURCH
74
(Baron Steuben Memorial)

SACRED GROVE
IS THE NAME GIVEN IN 1804
TO THESE WOODS HALLOWED
BY ASSOCIATION WITH
BARON STEUBEN, THE
AMERICAN PATRIOT
75
(Baron Steuben Memorial)

THIS MONUMENT
COVERS THE REMAINS
OF BARON STEUBEN
GOVERNOR HORATIO SEYMOUR
LAID CORNERSTONE JUNE 1, 1870
ERECTION COMPLETED 1872
76
(Baron Steuben Memorial)

FRIEDRICH WILHELM
BARON VON STEUBEN
BORN SEPTEMBER 17, 1730
MAGDEBURG, GERMANY. DIED
DIED HERE NOVEMBER 28, 1794

77
(Baron Steuben Memorial)

GERMAN-AMERICAN
ORGANIZATIONS ASSISTED BY
STATE OF NEW YORK ERECTED
THIS TOMB IN HONOR OF THEIR
GREAT FELLOW COUNTRYMAN

78
(Baron Steuben Memorial)

STEUBEN GRANT
OF 16,000 ACRES BY THE
STATE OF NEW YORK, JUNE 27, 1786
FOR SERVICE IN THE REVOLUTION
HE CLEANED 60 ACRES NEAR HERE
FOR HOME SITE (1788–1793)
79
(CR W. of Steuben Memorial)

FIRST GRAVE
OF BARON STEUBEN NEAR THIS SPOT
BY HIS OWN WISH HE WAS BURIED
WRAPPED IN HIS MILITARY CLOAK
IN AN UNMARKED GRAVE

80
(CR W. of Steuben Memorial)

STARR HILL
NAMED FOR DAVID STARR
CAPTAIN IN CONTINENTAL ARMY
FRIEND AND NEIGHBOR OF
BARON STEUBEN
SETTLED HERE 1791
81
(CR 1 m. W. of Memorial)

TOWN OF STEUBEN
FORMED APRIL 10, 1792
NAMED IN HONOR OF
BARON STEUBEN
ORIGINALLY EXTENDED TO
NORTH BOUNDS OF THE STATE
82
(NY 46 A in Steuben)

-----
2 MILES
TOMB OF
BARON STEUBEN
IN STATE MEMORIAL PARK

83
(CT. from Steuben & Remsen)

SAMUEL SIZER
FIRST SETTLER ON STEUBEN
GRANT, 1787. FARM
MANAGER FOR BARON STEUBEN
BURIAL PLACE IN MEADOW 80
RODS NORTH OF THIS MARKER
84
(CR. 2 m. E. of Steuben)

SAW MILL
OF BARON STEUBEN
BUILT 1790 NEAR THIS SPOT
REMAINS OF DAM VISIBLE

85
(Nr. creek N. of Fuller Rd.)

BURIAL PLACE
OF SAMUEL SISER, ABIGAIL
SISER, ASA SISER, AND
ABIGAIL TYLER MITCHELL, THE
MOTHER OF ABIGAIL SISER

86
(In field ¼ m. N. of CR.,
2 m. E. of Steuben)

CAPEL ISAF OR
SECOND BAPTIST CHURCH
ONCE LOCATED HERE
CARED FOR THE GRAVE
OF BARON STEUBEN FOR
NINETY-FIVE YEARS
(1804-1899)
87
(CR 1 m. W. of Remsen)

TOWN OF TRENTON

FULLER FARM
ACQUIRED 1793 FROM BARON
STEUBEN BY CAPT. SIMEON
FULLER, B. 1761 D. 1852
HELD BY HIM AND HIS
DESCENDANTS TO THE PRESENT DAY
88
(CR. 1 m. W. of Remsen)

CAPT. SIMEIN WOODRUFF
CIRCUMNAVIGATED GLOBE WITH
CAPTAIN COOK. LEASED THIS
FARM MAY 26, 1791
FROM BARON STEUBEN
BURIED CAPEL UCHA CEMETERY
89
(CR ½ m. W. of Remsen)

TRENTON
ONEIDA COUNTY
MARCH 24, 1797
FORMED FROM THE
TOWN OF SCHUYLER,
HERKIMER COUNTY
90
(NY 12 in Barneveld)

CINCINNATI CREEK
NAMED BY BARON STEUBEN
TO COMMEMORATE THE SOCIETY
OF THE CINCINNATI WHICH
HE HELPED TO FOUND IN 1783

91
(NY 28, 2 m. SE. of Trenton)

BAGG'S TAVERN
ORIGINALLY A LOG HOUSE
FOUNDED 1794 BY MOSES BAGG
WASHINGTON, LA FAYETTE
HENRY CLAY & GEN. GRANT
WERE GUESTS HERE
92
(Genesee and Main Sts.)

------
21 MILES
TOMB OF
BARON STEUBEN
IN STATE MEMORIAL PARK
NEAR REMSEN
93
(Oneida St. between Geer
and Ferris Ave.)

Howard S. Ford

TOWN OF VERNON

___17 MILES___
TOMB OF
BARON STEUBEN
IN STATE MEMORIAL PARK
NEAR REMSEN

94
(NY 5, E. of NY 8 & 12)

ONEIDA CASTLE
CHIEF VILLAGE OF ONEIDA
TRIBE OF INDIANS
MEMBERS OF
IROQUOIS CONFEDERACY

95
(NY 5 in Oneida Castle)

MISSION CHURCH
OF THE ONEIDAS BUILT BY
REV. ELEAZER WILLIAMS 1818
MOVED IN 1842 FROM ONEIDA
CASTLE BY UNITARIANS,
VERNON TOWN HALL SINCE 1892.

96
(Seneca Ave. between Verona
Sconondaga St. in Vernon)

TOWN OF VERONA

STARK'S LANDING
JABEZ HOUGH STARK, PIONEER
BUILT FIRST PRESBYTERIAN
CHURCH, SENECA FALLS 1807.
CAME HERE 1821; BUILT
HOUSE ACROSS CANAL 1823-
97
(NY 46 in Higginsville)

ROYAL
BLOCKHOUSE
60 RODS EAST OF
THIS POINT STOOD
FORT ERECTED BY
BRITISH IN 1759
98
(NY 13 in Sylvan Beach)

TOWN OF WESTERN

----
11 MILES
TOMB OF
BARON STEUBEN
IN STATE MEMORIAL PARK
NEAR REMSEN
99
(NY 46 & 46A in Frenchville)

TOWN OF WESTMORELAND

TOWN OF WHITESTOWN

WESTERN
ONEIDA COUNTY
MARCH 10, 1797
FORMED FROM THE
TOWN OF STEUBEN

100
(NY 46 nr. school in
Westernville)

BIRTHPLACE OF
SAMUEL EELLS
1810-1842
WHO IN 1842 FOUNDED THE
ALPHA DELTA PHI FRATERNITY
AT HAMILTON COLLEGE
101
(CR. in Westmoreland)

ENGLISH HOME
BUILT 1792. BIRTHPLACE OF
HENRY INMAN, 1801-46
ARTIST WHO EXCELLED IN
PORTRAITS, LANDSCAPES
AND MINIATURES
102
(NY 69 in Yorkville)

WHITESTOWN
MARCH 7TH 1788
NAMED IN HONOR OF
JUDGE HUGH WHITE
A FIRST SETTLER
MAY 1784.
103
(Main St. & Victor Parkway
Whitesboro)

1ST PRESBYTERIAN
CHURCH OF WHITESBORO
ORGANIZED APRIL 1, 1793
BETHUEL DODD, 1ST PASTOR

104
(Elm & Main Sts.,Whitesboro)

TOWN HALL
ERECTED 1807
EARLY CO. COURT HOUSE
PRESENTED TO WHITESTOWN
BY HON. PHILO WHITE
1860
105
(In front ot Town Hall
Whitesboro)

SITE OF
WOOLEN MILL
ERECTED IN 1810
BELIEVED TO BE THE 1ST
IN AMERICA TO MANUFACTURE
FABRICS FROM RAW MATERIAL
106
(NY 69 in Oriskany)

HERE STOOD THE HOME OF
COLONEL GERRIT G. LANSING
OFFICER IN CONTINENTAL ARMY
WHO PURCHASED LAND WHEREON
ORISKANY WAS FOUNDED 1802

107
(Dexter Ave. between Graham and
Utica Sts. in Oriskany)

ONONDAGA COUNTY

TOWN OF CAMILLUS

TOWN OF CICERO

SITE OF
HOME OF
JAMES GEDDES, 1798
ERIE CANAL SURVEYOR, 1808
CHIEF ENGINEER 1816-1825
1
(NY 5 2 m. W of Syracuse
at Fairmont Corners)

SITE OF INDIAN VILLAGE
TECHIROGUEN
VISITED BY LE MOYNE 1654
AND BY LA SALLE 1673

2*
(On US 11 at Brewerton)

TOLL-GATE HOUSE
BUILT AT SOUTH END
OF FIRST HIGHWAY BRIDGE
1824 AT BREWERTON. MOVED
TO THIS SITE ABOUT 1850.
3
(On Bennett St. at Brewerton)

LANDING PLACE
NEAR THIS POINT
VAN SCHAICK EXPEDITION
AGAINST ONONDAGAS LANDED
APRIL 20, 1779
4*
(US 11 at Brewerton)

EARLY SCHOOL
HERE STOOD SCHOOLHOUSE;
DISTRICT NO. 1, BUILT 1824,
FIRST DISTRICT SCHOOL IN
TOWN OF CICERO
5
(CR. ½ m. S. of Brewerton)

JOHN LEACH
MADE FIRST SETTLEMENT
AT CICERO CORNERS IN
1802. KEPT A TAVERN
IN LOG HOUSE
6
(US 11 at Cicero)

TOWN OF CLAY

CAUGHDENOY
LOCK
CONSTRUCTED BY
STATE OF NEW YORK
1841.

7
(CR at Caughdenoy)

OAK ORCHARD
LOCK
CONSTRUCTED BY
STATE OF NEW YORK
1840.

8
(CR ½ m. N. of Euclid)

SITE OF
MC GEE'S INN
(ACCORDING TO TRADITION)
PATRICK MC GEE, FIRST SETTLER
TOWN OF CLAY 1793, IN 1791
KEPT FIRST INN AT BREWERTON
9*
(S. bk Barge Canal, Three Rivers)

Howard S. Ford

TOWN OF DEWITT

ONONDAGA NATION
OF INDIANS SETTLED HEREABOUTS
ACCORDING TO TRADITION
SEVERAL CENTURIES BEFORE
DISCOVERY OF AMERICA
BY COLUMBUS, 1492

10*
(NY 57 1 m. S. Three Rivers)

JOHN YOUNG
1752-1834
REVOLUTIONARY SOLDIER
FIRST SETTLER HERE IN
1791
VILLAGE FIRST CALLED
YOUNGSVILLE

11*
(NY 5 & 92 at Dewitt)

MOREHOUSE FLATS
BENJ. MOREHOUSE SETTLED HERE 1789
HIS LOG TAVERN OPENED 1790
MEXICO TOWN ORGANIZED HERE 1791
MEETING HERE PROPOSED FORMATION
OF ONONDAGA COUNTY.
DEC. 23, 1793

12*
(NY 173, 1½ m. E. of Jamesville)

TOWN OF ELBRIDGE

UNION
CONGREGATIONAL
CHURCH
BUILDING ERECTED 1808
SOCIETY MOVED TO JAMESVILLE
1828

13*
(NY 173 ½ m. E. of Jamesville)

DANFORTH MILLS
ON THIS SIDE OF THE CREEK
SAW MILL BUILT 1792
GRIST MILL 1793
STATE SUPERINTENDENT OF

14*
(CR ½ m. N. of Jamesville)

THIS LOT
WAS PART OF MILITARY TRACT
OF CAPT. WM. STEVENS, MEMBER
MASS. SOCIETY CINCINNATI:
SALT INDUSTRY.

15
(On NY 5 at Elbridge)

TOWN OF FABIUS

BUILT ABOUT 1820
HOME OF COL. JOHN STEVENS,
ONONDAGA COUNTY MILITIA,
WAR OF 1812

16
(NY 5 at Elbridge)

BAPTIST CHURCH
FIRST IN TOWN OF FABIUS
UNBROKEN SERVICE SINCE
ITS ORGANIZATION ON
AUG. 24, 1803. THIS
BUILDING ERECTED 1818.

17
(NY 80 at Fabius)

SITE OF
WOODRUF CABIN
PIONEER HOME OF
GURDON WOODRUF
BUILT ABOUT 1795

18
(CR. 2 ½ m. S. of Fabius)

ANDREWS CABIN
BUILT BY
WILLIAM ANDREWS
ABOUT 1821
BIRTHPLACE OF SON JOHN

19
(CR 2 ½ m. S. of Fabius)

SITE OF
KEENEY CABIN
INHABITED 1795 BY
SIMON KEENEY, JR.
IN THIS VALLEY
FIRST WHITE CHILD
BORN IN THIS VALLEY 1797

20
(CR 2 ½ m. S. of Fabius)

WEBSTER CABIN
BUILT ABOUT 1820 BY
ELI WEBSTER
FIRST FRAME HOUSE

21
(CR 3 m. S. of Fabius)

Sure Signs: Stories Behind the Historical Markers of Central New York

TOWN OF LAFAYETTE

FIRST CHURCH
IN THE VALLEY
ORGANIZED HERE 1803
FIRST BAPTIST CHURCH
OF FABIUS

22
(CR 3 m. S. of Fabius)

CARDIFF GIANT
DISINTERRED NEAR THIS
VILLAGE ON OCT. 16, 1869.
REPRESENTED AS A PETRIFIED
PREHISTORIC MAN, IT WAS
SUBSEQUENTLY PROVED A HOAX

23
(NY 20 at Cardiff)

NEAR HERE WAS THE HOME OF
MOSES DEWITT
PIONEER SETTLER, SURVEYOR
MAJOR OF MILITIA AND
JUDGE OF THE COUNTY COURT

24*
(NY 91 at Jamesville)

TOWN OF LYSANDER

_____ 600 FEET
SITE OF INDIAN TOWN
ONONDAGA
1684-1696
DESTROYED AT TIME OF
FRONTENAC'S INVASION 1696
25*
(NY 91 1 ½ m. S. Jamesville)

FIRST LIFT LOCK
THE FIRST LIFT LOCK TO BE
CONSTRUCTED WEST OF LITTLE
FALLS WAS BUILT HERE IN
1809 BY JONAS C. BALDWIN.

26*
(NY 31 & 370 at Baldwinsville)

LOG CABIN SITE
JONAS C. BALDWIN, FOUNDER
OF BALDWINSVILLE, BUILT
THE FIRST LOG CABIN
ON THE NORTH SIDE OF THE
RIVER NEAR THIS SPOT IN 1807
27
(NY 31 & 370 at Baldwinsville)

ON THIS HILL
IN THE ORIGINAL HOUSE, 31
WOMEN ORGANIZED THE FEMALE
CHARITABLE SOCIETY, SECOND
OLDEST WOMEN'S SOCIETY IN
THE U.S., JULY 27, 1817.
28*
(On NY 31 at Baldwinsville)

FIRST SETTLER
THE HOME OF THE FIRST WHITE
SETTLER IN THE TOWNSHIP OF
LYSANDER, JONATHAN PALMER,
REVOLUTIONARY SOLDIER
WAS BUILT ON THIS SITE, 1793
29*
(On CR at Jacksonville)

BATTERY B
FIRST N.Y. LIGHT ARTILLERY DRILLED
NEAR THIS POINT UNDER THEIR
ORGANIZER, CAPT. RUFUS D. PETTIT,
IN THE SUMMER OF 1861

30
(NY 370 & Doyle Rd 3 m. SE.
of Baldwinsville)

TOWN OF MANLIUS

GRACE CHURCH
THIS EPISCOPAL CHURCH WAS
THE FIRST CHURCH IN THE

UNITED STATES, ACCORDING TO
TRADITION, TO BE LIGHTED
BY ELECTRICITY

31
(Elizabeth St., Baldwinsville)

SITE OF
HALFWAY TAVERN
1814-34

STOPPING PLACE FOR STAGE
AND FOR OUNDIAGA, INDIAN
RUNNER, FIRST MAIL CARRIER
BETWEEN SYRACUSE AND OSWEGO
32
(NY 48 3 1/4 m. N. Baldwinsville)

DEEP SPRING
TE-UNGH-SAT-AYAGH
450 FEET NORTH ON IROQUOIS
TRAIL
FIRST ROAD MADE 1790 BY GEN.
JAMES WADSWORTH, COUNTY
LINE AND SURVEY MARK

33
(NY 173 at county line)

THIS WELL
DUG IN 1795 BY
JOSEPH WILLIANS
SOLDIER OF THE REVOLUTION
WHOSE LOG HOUSE STOOD
ABOUT 50 FEET NORTH
34
(Town Rd. 1 m. E. Manlius)

CHRIST CHURCH
OLDEST CHURCH EDIFICE AND
OLDEST EPISCOPAL PARISH IN
ONONDAGA COUNTY, INC. 1804,
1811; BUILT 1813; REMOVED
TO THIS SITE, 1832
35
(On NY 173 at Manlius)

GROVER CLEVELAND
PRESIDENT OF UNITED STATES
1884-1888 AND 1892-1896,
HIS BOYHOOD HOME IS THE
NORTH OF THE CORNER HOUSE
36
(NY 5 & 92 at Fayetteville)

FAYETTEVILLE
FIRST CALLED "MANLIUS FOUR
CORNERS". SETTLED IN 1791
BY ORIGEN EATON AND JOSHUA
KNOWLTON. BOYHOOD HOME OF
GROVER CLEVELAND
37*
(NY 5 & 92, Fayetteville)

FAYETTEVILLE
FIRST CALLED "MANLIUS FOUR
CORNERS". SETTLED IN 1791
BY ORIGEN EATON AND JOSHUA
KNOWLTON. BOYHOOD HOME OF
GROVER CLEVELAND
38*
(On NY 5 at Fayetteville)

GEN. JOHN J. PECK
BORN HERE JAN. 4, 1821; WON
PROMOTION FOR GALLANTRY
MEXICAN WAR; MADE MAJ. GEN.
1862; DEFENDED SUFFOLK, VA.:
DIED SYRACUSE, APRIL 21, 1878.
39
(On NY 173 at Manlius)

CHERRY VALLEY TURNPIKE
TERMINATED HERE
COMPLETED ABOUT 1809, JOINING
THE SENECA TURNPIKE HERE

40*
(On Academy St. at Manlius)

THE FIRST
SCHOOLHOUSE
IN THE TOWN OF MANLIUS
WAS BUILT OF LOGS AND
STOOD NEAR HERE IN 1798.

41
(On NY 92 at Manlius)

THE MANLIUS SCHOOL
FOUNDED 1869

42
(On NY 92 at Manlius)

TOWN OF MARCELLUS

THE MANLIUS SCHOOL
FOUNDED 1869
AS ST. JOHN'S SCHOOL
OLDEST BOY'S PRIVATE
PREPARATORY SCHOOL
IN CENTRAL NEW YORK
43
(NY 92, ¼ m. S. of Manlius)

SITE OF
FIRST CHURCH EDIFICE
IN ONONDAGA COUNTY,
COMPLETED 1803; PRESENT
CHURCH BUILT 1851

44
(On NY 175 at Marcellus)

SITE OF
TAVERN KEPT BY DEACON
SAMUEL RICE 1800
FIRST CHURCH SERVICES
WERE HELD HERE, ALSO
TOWN MEETINGS
45
(On NY 175 at Marcellus)

SITE OF
OLD HOTEL KEPT BY DR.
BILDAS BEACH. GEN.
LAFAYETTE STOPPED HERE
JUNE 9, 1824.

46
(NY 175 at Marcellus)

SITE OF
FIRST FRAME HOUSE IN TOWN
OF MARCELLUS. BUILT BY DR.
ELNATHAN BEACH, WHO SERVED IN
AMERICAN REVOLUTION: SHERIFF OF
COUNTY FROM 1799 TO 1801
47
(On NY 175 at Marcellus)

FIRST SAWMILL
IN TOWN OF MARCELLUS
BUILT 1796 BY DEACON
SAMUEL RICE AND JUDGE
DAN BRADLEY

48
(NY 175 at Marcellus)

TOWN OF ONONDAGA

WAR OF 1812
CAPTAIN HENRY CROUCH AND
CAPTAIN BENJAMIN BRANCH
SOLDIERS OF WAR OF 1812
WHO DIED WHILE ENCAMPED
NEAR HERE ARE BURIED ABOVE
49
(NY 173, ½ m. E. Onondaga Hill)

SITE OF
FIRST COURT HOUSE
ERECTED IN 1802 ON LAND
DONATED TO ONONDAGA COUNTY
BY GEORGE HALL
AND THADDEUS WOOD
50
(On NY 175 at Onondaga Hill)

FRANCIS ASBURY
FIRST BISHOP OF THE
METHODIST EPISCOPAL CHURCH
PREACHED JUNE 26, 1807,
IN ONONDAGA COURT HOUSE
THEN STANDING ON THIS SITE
51*
(On NY 175 at Onondaga Hill)

MORAVIANS
BISHOP SPANGENBERG AND DAVID
ZEISBERGER AS MISSIONARIES
CAME TO ONONDAGA INDIANS
NEAR HERE IN 1745. DAVID
RETURNED '50, '52, 53, 54, 56
52*
(NY 11A 1 m. S. of Syracuse)

SENTINEL HEIGHTS
PIONEER CEMETERY
ANDREW SHARE, 1763-1847, REV.
SOLDIER WHO GAVE LAND FOR
CEMETERY, SCHOOLHOUSE, AND
METHODIST CHURCH, BURIED HERE
53
(Bull Hill Rd. 4 m. SE.
of Syracuse)

ONONDAGA RESERVATION
ESTABLISHED IN 1788,
THE ONONDAGA INDIAN NATION
FOUNDED THE IROQUOIS LEAGUE.

54*
(NY 11A 1 m. S. of Syracuse)

TOWN OF POMPEY

FIRST SCHOOL
ERECTED IN TOWN OF POMPEY
1797 AND USED UNTIL 1810
HEPSABAH BEEBE—TEACHER
CEMETERY ADJOINED SCHOOL
GROUNDS, LATER REMOVED
55
(On NY 91 at Pompey)

BIRTHPLACE OF
GOV. HORATIO SEYMOUR, 1811
TWICE GOVERNOR OF NEW
YORK STATE. DEMOCRATIC
CANDIDATE FOR PRESIDENT
AGAINST GRANT
56
(NY 91 & US 20 at Pompey)

PRATT'S FALLS
FIRST MILLS IN ONON. CO.
BUILT BY MANOAH PRATT, SR.
AND ABRAHAM SMITH IN 1796
FIRST A SAW MILL AND THEN
A FLOUR MILL IN 1798.
57
(CR. at Pratt's Falls Park)

LOG HOUSE
ERECTED 1791 BY EBENEZER
BUTLER, JR. FIRST WHITE
SETTLER ON POMPEY HILL
A REV. WAR SOLDIER
58
(US. 20 at Pompey)

CONGREGATIONAL CHURCH
ORGANIZED OCT. 19, 1796
BY AMENI R. ROBINSON
CHURCH BUILT 1817-18.
NOW POMPEY PRESBYTERIAN
59
(On county rd. at Pompey)

OLDEST FRAME HOUSE
IN TOWN OF POMPEY
BUILT BY EBENEZER
HANDY, 1806

60
(US 20 at Pompey)

Howard S. Ford

HANDY'S TAVERN
1797 FIRST FRAME BUILDING
ERECTED BY E. BUTLER, JR.
AND RUN AS A TAVERN BY HIM.
THE ORIGINAL FRAME IS
STILL IN THE HOUSE.
61
(On NY 91 at Pompey)

ATWELL'S CORNERS
JOSEPH ATWELL, 1754-1834
REVOLUTIONARY SOLDIER
SETTLED HERE 1792. OVERSEER
OF POMPEY HIGHWAYS 1794
OWNED LOT IN MILITARY TRACT
62
(CR at co. line, 4 m. south of Oran)

DROVER'S TAVERN, 1820
BUILT OF MATERIALS TAKEN FROM
PREMISES; DESIGN OF MAIN HOUSE
ON FILE LIBRARY OF CONGRESS;
LAST REMAINING TAVERN
FOR DROVERS
63
(NY 92 1 m. SE. of Oran)

FIRST MASS
IN NEW YORK STATE
WAS OFFERED ABOUT 300 FEET
NORTH
OF THIS MARKER BY REV. J. M.
CHAUMONT, 1655, IN BARK CHAPEL
64
(At Indian Hill on town rd. southwest of Oran)

FIRST STEAMBOAT
BUILT BY WM. AVERY 1 MILE
SOUTH OF ORAN. LAUNCHED
IN LIMESTONE CREEK NEAR
BUELLVILLE, 1823, LATER FIRST
STEAMBOAT USED ON ERIE CANAL
65
(NY 92, ½ m. NW. of Oran)

INDIAN HILL
WAS THE HOME OF THE ONONDAGA
INDIANS. LARGE POPULATION
LIVED HERE IN 1655.
66
(At Indian Hill on town rd. southwest of Oran)

INDIAN WAR STONE
GRINDSTONE OF THE ONONDAGA
INDIANS. USED TO SHARPEN
ARROWS AND SPEARS AT INDIAN
HILL UNTIL 1666. MOVED TO
LEMOYNE PARK, POMPEY, 1905.
67
(County rd. at Pompey)

CAPE COD COTTAGE
BUILT 1795
SLAVE RUNNING STATION
FOR SHELTERING SLAVES
DURING CIVIL WAR.
.
68
(County rd. 1 m. SE. of Oran)

SITE OF
FIRST SCHOOL
BUILT HERE ABOUT 1800
GEORGE CLARK, FIRST TEACHER
AND AFTERWARDS THE FIRST
MERCHANT IN ORAN
69
(On county road at Oran)

BAPTIST CHURCH
BUILT 1820 BY N. STERLING.
FREDERICK FREEMAN FIRST
PASTOR. ABANDONED IN 1834.
ROMAN CATHOLIC CHURCH
1866-92. NOW LEMOYNE HALL.
70
(On county rd. at Pompey)

SITE OF
GREEN'S HOUSE
BUILT OF LOGS IN 1796 BY
DAVID GREEN. THE SETTLEMENT
WAS KNOWN FOR YEARS AS
GREEN'S CORNERS
71
(US 20 at Pompey Center)

BIRTHPLACE OF
CHARLES MASON
BORN HERE IN LOG HOUSE 1804
GRADUATE WEST POINT 1829
CHIEF JUSTICE IOWA 1838-42
U.S. COMM'R. PATENTS 1853-57.
72
(US 20 3 m. NE of Pompey)

SITE OF
POMPEY ACADEMY
1810-1834
ORIGINAL ACADEMY WAS 40 BY 50
FEET FRAME BUILDINGS, TWO
STORIES,
GABLE END FACING SOUTH.
73
(On town rd. at Pompey)

ROMAN CATHOLIC
MISSION CHURCH
FIRST IN POMPEY WAS
LOCATED HERE, 1857-1866,
FATHER JAMES CAHILL,
FIRST PRIEST
74
(On town rd. at Pompey)

SITE OF
LOG CITY
RIVAL OF POMPEY WITH A
STORE, ASHERY, TANNERY,
SHOE, AND CARPENTER SHOPS,
AND A SCHOOLHOUSE.
75
(NY 91 1 ¼ m. N. of Pompey)

TOWN OF SALINA

ORAN
SETTLED IN 1793 BY THE
BARNES BROTHERS, ASA
ROSWELL, AND PHINEAS.
CAME HERE WITH THEIR
FAMILIES FROM MASSACHUSETTS
76
(NY 92 at Oran)

FIRST TAVERN
1796-1808
BUILT AND KEPT BY JOB
BARTHOLOMEW. BURNED 1808.
ANOTHER BUILT ON SAME SITE
IN 1809 KEPT BY WM. SCOVILLE
77
(NY 92 at Oran)

SALT MAKING
MANUFACTURE OF SALT WAS
BEGUN HERE IN LIVERPOOL
BY JOHN DANFORTH, BROTHER
OF ASA DANFORTH, 1794
78
(NY 57 & 370 at Liverpool)

TOWN OF SKANEATELES

SITE OF AN UNDERGROUND RAILROAD STATION
JAMES CANNINGS FULLER HOME
NOTED ABOLITIONIST 1834-1861
HE GAVE TO THE CAUSE OF
FREEDOM FOR SLAVES
79
(US 20, ½ m. W. of Skaneateles)

SITE OF THE OLD SHERWOOD INN
BUILT ABOUT 1800

80
(US 20 at Skaneateles)

SAINT JOHN'S BEACH
BISHOP FREDERIC CAMMERHOFF
AND DAVID ZEISBERGER,
MORAVIAN MISSIONARIES,
BUILT THE FIRST SKANEATELES
SHELTER ON THIS SITE 1750
81
(US 20, ¼ m. E. of Skaneateles)

SITE OF ONONDAGA STREET PRIMARY
THE HILLTOP SCHOOL
FIRST PUBLIC ELEMENTARY
SCHOOL IN THE VILLAGE
IN USE FROM 1804-1910

82
(State and Academy Streets)

SITE OF THE ACADEMY
PRIVATE SCHOOL 1829
UNION FREE SCHOOL 1854
SKANEATELES HIGH SCHOOL
1910
NOW TWO RESIDENCES
83
(East & Onondaga Streets)

SITE OF THE SKANEATELES RAILROAD PASSENGER STATION
1867-1947
SERVICE UNTIL 1932
TO SKANEATELES JUNCTION

84
Near corner Fennell & Jordan Sts.

SITE OF

THE GREAT FIRE
SEPTEMBER 28, 1835
THIRTEEN LAKESIDE BUILDINGS
WERE DESTROYED COMMENCING
IN PARSONS CABINET SHOP

85
US 20, opposite library

CITY OF SYRACUSE

GEDDES
TOWN NAMED FOR JAMES GEDDES
1763-1838, ENGINEER OF STATE
CANALS FOR N. Y. WAS FIRST
TO MAKE SALT HERE. SURVEYED
SITE OF SYRACUSE, 1804
84*
(NY 48 & Hiawatha Blvd. Syracuse)

TOWN OF VAN BUREN

ONONDAGA BRICK
THOMAS MARVIN, SOLDIER IN
WARS OF 1776 AND 1812,
SETTLED HERE 1811 (CAZENOVIA
1800). MADE FIRST BRICK HERE FROM
NATIVE CLAY TROD BY OXEN
85
(CR ½ m. E. of Warners)

Howard S. Ford

ONTARIO COUNTY

TOWN OF BRISTOL

BURNING SPRINGS
CHARTED ON EARLIEST MAPS
OF NORTH AMERICA AFTER
LA SALLE'S VISIT AUGUST 1669
CAUSED BY ESCAPING NATURAL
GAS. ONCE MYSTERY TO VISITORS

1
(Case rd. 1 m. NW. Bristol Ctr.)

GRANGER HOMESTEAD
HOME OF GIDEON GRAINGER
POSTMASTER GEN. IN CABINETS
OF JEFFERSON AND MADISON
RESIDENT HERE 1814-1822

4
(NY 332 between Granger and
Chapel Sts.)

TOWN OF CANANDAIGUA

------
8 MILES NORTH, ROUTE 21
CUMORAH
FAMOUS MORMON HILL
AND
ANGEL MORONI MONUMENT

2
(NY 21 & 332 intersection
N. Main & Gibson Sts.)

CANANDAIGUA ACADEMY
INCORPORATED 1795
FIRST ACADEMY ON
PHELPS AND GORHAM TRACT

5
(NY 332 between Fort
Hill Ave. and Granger St.)

SITE OF
PIONEER HOME
CAPT. JASPER PARRISH
SETTLED HERE IN 1792
INDIAN CAPTIVE SIX YEARS LATER
GOVT. INTERPRETER LATER
DIED IN 1826

3
(US 20 & NY 5 intersection
S. Main & Parrish Sts.)

PHELPS-GORHAM PURCHASE
PIONEER LAND OFFICE IN
WESTERN N.Y. ESTA. HERE
1789
HOME SITE OLIVER PHELPS
1ST JUDGE OF CO. 1789-93

6
(US 20, NY 5 & 21 between
Niagara & Ontario Sts.)

TOWN OF FARMINGTON

HERENDEEN HOMESTEAD
BUILT BY JAMES HERENDEEN
1832. ENTRANCE PORCH ADDED BY
JOSEPHEEN HERENDEEN
1932

7
(CR. 2 ½ m. S. of Farmington)

GANECHSTAGE
SITE OF SENECA VILLAGE
AND JESUIT MISSION
FOR THE INDIANS
ESTABLISHED 1687
10*
(White Spring Rd. at
western limits of city)

TOWN OF GENEVA

SITE OF KANADESAGA
CHIEF CASTLE OF
THE SENECA NATION
DESTROYED SEPT. 7, 1779
IN GEN. JOHN SULLIVAN'S
RAID

8
(CR. to Seneca Castle ¼ m.
west of Geneva)

SMITH
OBSERVATORY
WORLD FAMOUS FOR THE
DISCOVERIES OF DIRECTOR
DR. WILLIAM R. BROOKS

11
(Castle St. between
Hillcrest & Highland Ave.)

GLASS FACTORY
BAY
1810 – 1850
ONTARIO GLASS MANUFACTORY
BLOWERS OF WINDOW GLASS
VILLAGE OF 500 INHABITANTS
9*
(NY 14 1 ½ m. S. of Geneva)

SITE OF LOG HOUSE
ERECTED 1787 LATER
KNOWN AS
ELARK JENNINGS TAVERN

12
(S. Exchange St. south
of Washington St.)

SITE OF GENEVA
MEDICAL COLLEGE
ELIZ. BLACKWELL RECEIVED
HERE IN 1849 THE FIRST
DEGREE OF MD EVER
CONFERRED UPON A WOMAN
13
(US 29, NY 5 & NY 14 between
Washington and Hamilton Sts.)

PREEMPTION LINE
BOUNDARY DRWN BETWEEN
MASSACHUSETTS AND NEW YORK
DECEMBER 16, 1786
CAUSE OF LONG CONTROVERSY
IN WESTERN NEW YORK
14
(US 20 & NY 5 at western
edge of the city)

SITE OF
GENEVA HOTEL
ERECTED 1796
BY
CAPT. CHARLES WILLIAMSON

15
(Washington St. between
Pulteney and Main Sts.)

TOWN OF GORHAM

TOWN OF MANCHESTER

TORY QUARTERS
SITE OF MILITARY DEPOT
UNDER COMMAND OF
COL. JOHN BUTLER
DESTROYED SEPT. 1779 IN
SULLIVAN EXPEDITION
16*
(US 20 & NY 5, Seneca Lake)

MARCUS WHITMAN
PIONEER MISSIONARY PATRIOT
COLONIZER IN OREGON TER.
BORN HERE SEPT. 4, 1802

17
(On NY 245 at Rushville)

-----
2 MILES NORTH
CUMORAH
FAMOUS MORMON HILL
AND
ANGEL MORONI MONUMENT
18
(NY 21 & 96 at Manchester)

TOWN OF NAPLES

HILL CUMORAH
THE MORMONS BELIEVE THAT
HERE IN 1827 JOSEPH SMITH
RECEIVED THE BOOK OF MORMON

19
(NY 21 2.m. W. of Manchester)

FOSSIL TREE
ONE MILE WEST OF THIS SPOT
WAS DISCOVERED THE FOSSIL
DEVONIAN TREE TRUNK IN THE
BED OF GRIMES CREEK. IT IS
NOW IN THE STATE MUSEUM
20*
(NY 21 & 245 at Naples)

FIRST CHURCH
ON THIS SITE WAS ORGANIZED
THE "FIRST RELIGIOUS COMPACT
OF MIDDLETOWN 1800" THE
CHURCH WAS BUILT IN 1824

21
(In village park, Naples)

TOWN OF RICHMOND

NAPLES
FOUNDED 1789 ON THE OLD
SENECA VILLAGE OF NUNDAWAO;
FIRST KNOWN AS WATKINSTOWN;
IN 1796 CALLED MIDDLETOWN;
ON APRIL 6, 1808, NAMED NAPLES
22
(On NY 21 & 245 at Naples)

NAPLES
KNOWN AS WATKINSTOWN 1789;
NAMED MIDDLETOWN 1796,
MIDWAY BETWEEN CANANDAIGUA
AND BATH; NAPLES APRIL 6, 1808

23
(On NY 21 & 245 at Naples)

OLD REED
HOMESTEAD
FIRST BRICK HOUSE
IN TOWN OF RICHMOND
BUILT 1803 BY
PHILIP REED

24
(Red Rd. ½ m. S.
of Richmond Hills)

Howard S. Ford

PITTS MANSION
BUILT 1821 BY
GIDEON PITTS
SON OF CAPT. PETER PITTS
PIONEER SETTLER IN 1789

25
(on US 20A at Honeoye)

NEARBY IS THE SITE OF
PIONEER HOME
CAPT. PETER PITTS
FIRST SETTLER IN TOWN
OF RICHMOND
NEW YORK IN 1779
26
(US 20A ½ m. E. of Honeoye)

MILITARY ROUTE
OF THE SULLIVAN-CLINTON
ARMY ON ITS CAMPAIGN
AGAINST THE BRITISH
AND INDIANS OF WESTERN

27
(US 20A 1 ½ m. E. of Honeoye)

TOWN OF VICTOR

EZRA WILMARTH
OPENED STAGECOACH INN HERE
DEC. 25, 1815. ORIGINAL
INN SIGN HAD MASONIC EMBLEM.
SOLDIERS OF WAR OF 1812
GATHERED ON THIS SITE
28
(CR 1 m. S. of Victor)

PARK PLACE
BUILT BY SIMEON PARK
APRIL 13, WHO CLEARED
A LARGE TRACT OF LAND.
FAMOUS PLANK ROAD WENT
BY HERE
29
(TR 1 ¼ m. E. of Fishers)

FISHER HOMESTEAD
OLDEST HOUSE HERE, BUILT
BY CHAS. FISHER 1811. FISHERS
NAMED FOR HIM. POST OFFICE
1850. HOME Of HENRY PARDEE,
ASSEMBLYMAN, 1840.
30
(On County rd., Fishers)

SENECA TRAIL
TRAVERSED BY FRENCH ARMY
OF DENONVILLE, 1687. HERE
WERE SENECA LODGES WHERE
FRIENDLY INDIAN FOLLOWERS
OF TRAIL WERE WELLCOMED
31
(TR. 3 m. NW. of Victor)

OSWEGO COUNTY

TOWN OF CONSTANTIA

FIRST SETTLER
NEAR THIS SPOT
CHRISTOPHER MARTIN
MADE FIRST SETTLEMENT
IN CLEVELAND
1821
1
(NY 49 at Cleveland)

KEMPWYK
HOME OF
FRANCIS ADRIAN
VAN DER KAMP
1793

2
(NY 49 1 m. W. of Cleveland)

FIRST SETTLER
NEAR THIS SPOT
JOHN BERNHARD
MADE FIRST SETTLEMENT
IN BERNHARD'S BAY
1795
3
NY 49, Bernhard's Bay)

TOWN OF HASTINGS

FRENCHMAN'S
ISLAND
CAMPSITE OF VAN SCHAICK'S
EXPEDITION ON RETURN
FROM ATTACK ON ONONDAGA
APRIL 22, 1779
4
(NY 49 ½ m. E. of Constantia)

TRINITY
EPISCOPAL CHURCH
ERECTED 1831, 24 ACRES
AND BUILDING DONATED BY
FREDERICK W. SCRIBA

5
(NY 49 at Constantia)

FORT BREWERTON
ORIGINAL EARTHWORK
OF FORT ERECTED BY
BRITISH IN 1759

6
(US 11 at Brewerton)

FIRST SETTLER
NEAR THIS SPOT
OLIVER STEVENS
MADE FIRST SETTLEMENT
IN BREWERTON AND
OSWEGO COUNTY, 1789
7
(US 11 at Brewerton)

NEAR THIS SPOT
SAMUEL DE CHAMPLAIN
ON OCTOBER 9, 1615
CROSSED THE RIVER
AND DISCOVERED
ONEIDA LAKE
8
(US 11 at Brewerton)

OVER THIS WATER ROUTE
ST. LEGER'S
ARMY
PASSED TO INVEST
FT. STANWIX
JULY 29, 1777
9
(US 11 at Brewerton)

A FEW RODS SOUTH
OLIVER STEVENS
1ST SETTLER IN BREWERTON
ERECTED A BLOCKHOUSE
1794
10
(US 11 at Brewerton)

FIRST SETTLER
NEAR THIS SPOT
MYRON STEVENS
MADE FIRST SETTLEMENT
IN CAUGHDENOY
1797
11
(At CR. at Caughdenoy)

INDIAN FISHERY
T'KAH-KOON-GOON-DA-NAH-YEA
WAS LOCATED
NEAR THIS SPOT
1753

12
(At CR. at Caughdenoy)

TOWN OF MEXICO

CITY OF OSWEGO

SILAS TOWNE
REVOLUTIONARY HERO
HERE OVERHEARD PLANS OF
ST. LEGER'S ARMY WHEREBY
PATRIOTS SAVED FORT STANWIX
13
(CR. on shore of Lake Ontario
4 miles north of Mexico)

SPY ISLAND
AND THE GRAVE OF
SILAS TOWNE

14*
(CR 3 m. N. of Mexico)

FIRST
COURT HOUSE
ERECTED 1822 ON PRESENT SITE
REMOVED 1859 AND SINCE USED
FOR CHURCH PURPOSES
15
(E. Oneida & E. Second St.)

Howard S. Ford

TOWN OF REDFIELD

THIS WAS THE FIRST BUILDING IN OSWEGO TO BE USED AS A SCHOOL HOUSE, CHURCH AND PUBLIC HALL ERECTED ABOUT 1806	HERE WAS THE OLD CABLE FERRY BY WHICH THE RIVER WAS CROSSED 1803	CAPTAIN NATHAN SAGE OF CONN. MADE THE FIRST SETTLEMENT IN TOWN OF REDFIELD NEARBY ABOUT 1795
16*	17*	18
((W. Seneca & W. First St.)	(W. Seneca & W. First St.)	(CR. at Redfield)

TOWN OF RICHLAND   TOWN OF SCHROEPPEL

SAMUEL DE CHAMPLAIN HERE ON LAKE SHORE CHAMPLAIN WITH FRENCH AND HURONS LANDED, OCT. 1615 ON HIS EXPEDITION AGAINST IROQUOIS	KUH-NA-TA-HA INDIAN FISHING VILLAGE 1654 KNOWN TO THE INDIANS AS "PLACE OF TALL PINES" DISCOVERED BY FATHER LE MOYNE	TREASURE ISLAND FRENCH COLONISTS CAMPED ON WEST ISLAND IN ESCAPING FROM ONONDAGA INDIANS IN 1658. SAID TO HAVE LIGHTENED THEIR WAR CHESTS AND DEPOSITED CANNON AND GOLD HERE
19	20	21
(On US 11 at Pulaski)	(On NY 57 at Phoenix)	(On NY 57 at Phoenix)

SITE OF FIRST LOG CABIN APRAM PADDOCK KNOWN TO INDIANS AS "BEAR HUNTER PADDOCK", FIRST WHITE SETTLER IN SCHROEPPEL BUILT HIS CABIN HERE 1801	TOWN MEETING FIRST TOWN MEETING IN SCHROEPPEL WAS HELD HERE AT HOME OF JAMES B. RICHARDSON IN 1833	SITE OF TOLL GATE PLANK ROAD BUILT 1855 CONNECTED PHOENIX WITH PENNELVILLE. ROAD FIVE MILES IN LENGTH
22	23	24*
(State & Culvert St. Phoenix)	(On NY 57 at Phoenix)	(NY 264 1 m. N. of Phoenix)

FENNELL SAW MILL BUILT HERE BY DR. RICHARD FENNELL IN 1833	BURIAL PLACE GEORGE CASPER SCHROEPPEL FOUNDER OF TOWN OF SCHROEPPEL, OWNER OF TWENTY THOUSAND ACRES DIED 1825	SITE OF SALT WELL WELL SUNK 340 FEET IN 1864 BY CAPT. E.S. COOK RESULTED IN STRONG SALT BRINE. SIX KETTLES WERE BUILT INTO AN ARCH FOR MANUFACTURING SALT
25	26	27
(CR. in Pennellville)	(CR. at Pennellville)	(TR. at Gilbert's Mills)

GRIST MILL
FIRST IN TOWN OF SCHROEPPEL
BUILT HERE AT GILBERT'S
MILLS BY ANDRUS AND HIRAM
GILBERT IN 1819

28
(TR. at Gilbert's Mills)

SITE OF
BRITISH CAMP
SIR JEFFERY AMHERST WITH
TEN THOUSAND TROOPS WAS
HERE 1760 ENROUTE TO
CANADA TO CRUSH FRENCH
POWER IN AMERICA
29
(NY 57 at Three Rivers)

SITE OF
STOCKADED FORT
1758-1759
ABOUT 60 FEET SQUARE
CONTAINING 3 STORHOUSES
BUILT BY COLONY OF N.Y.

30
(NY 57 at Three Rivers)

SCHROEPPEL
HOMESTEAD
FIRST FRAME HOUSE BUILT
IN SCHROEPPEL TOWN 1818 BY
GEORGE CASPER SCHROEPPEL

31
(TR. at Schroeppel's Bridge)

HINMANVILLE
LOCK NO. 1
LOCATED NEAR HERE. LOCK
TENDER'S HOUSE NEARBY. OLD
OSWEGO CANAL COMPLETED 1828.
IMPORTANT WATERWAY TO WEST
32
(CR. at Hinmanville)

1809 STATE ROAD
LATER PLANK ROAD. PASSED
THROUGH ROOSEVELT HAMLET,
FOUNDED BY NICHOLAS J.
ROOSEVELT

33
(NY 49 at Roosevelt's Corners)

TOWN OF SCRIBA
SITE OF THE FIRST
LOG HOUSE
IN SCRIBA. BUILT 1804
BY MAJOR HIEL STONE
TEMPORARY HOSPITAL FOR
WOUNDED SOLDIERS 1814
34
(On US 104 at Scriba)

TOWN OF WILLIAMSTOWN
JEROME I. CASE
1819-1891
BORN NEAR HERE
PIONEER BUILDER OF
POWER FARM MACHINERY

35
(NY 13 at Willaimstown)

OTSEGO COUNTY

TOWN OF BURLINGTON
FARM AND GRAVE
JEDIDIAH PECK
1747-1821
FATHER OF THE COMMON
SCHOOL SYSTEM OF THE
STATE OF NEW YORK

1
(CR. 2 ½ m. E of Burlington)

TOWN OF CHERRY VALLEY
-----
2 MILES NORTH TO
WORMUTH ROCK
MARKING SPOT WHERE
LIEUT. WORMUTH FELL 1778
SHOT BY JOSEPH BRANT
FIRST LEFT, THEN RIGHT FORK
2*
(On US 20 at Cherry Valley)

CHERRY VALLEY
MASSACRE 1778
MONUMENT 1/5 MILE SOUTH

3*
(US 20 at Cherry Valley)

Howard S. Ford

TOWN OF EXETER

1/2 MILES NORTH TO SITE
FORTIFIED
HOME
OF COL. SAMUEL CAMPBELL
1778

4*
(US 20 at Cherry Valley)

2/5 MILES WEST TO SITE
DUNLAP HOME
DESTROYED AT TIME OF
CHERRY VALLEY MASSACRE
NOVEMBER 11, 1778

5*
(US 20 at Cherry Valley)

SITE OF
HERKIMER FARM
ORIGINAL HERKIMER HOMESTEAD
IN EXETER, THEN TRYON COUNTY.
SETTLED BY HENDRICK HERKIMER
PRIOR TO REVOLUTION

6
(NY 28 at Schuyler Lake)

SITE OF
HERKIMER CEMETERY
HENDRICK HERKIMER, BROTHER
OF GEN. NICHOLAS HERKIMER,
HIS SONS GEORGE AND ABRAHAM,
WHO SERVED IN AMERICAN
REVOLUTION ARE BURIED HERE

7
(NY 28 at Schuyler Lake)

OLD STONE CHURCH
BUILT 1839-40
BY GEORGE HERKIMER
NOW USED AS A
UNIVERSALIST CHURCH

8
(NY 28, Schuyler lake)

TUNNICLIFF-1755
HOMESTEAD OF JOHN TUNNICLIFF,
SR.
EARLY COLONIZER OF NEW YORK
ALSO HIS SON, MAJOR JOSEPH
TUNNICLIFF, SOLDIER IN
WAR OF 1812

9
(CR. 3 m. SW of Schuyler Lake)

TOWN OF HARTWICK

HARTWICK SEMINARY
OLDEST LUTHERAN
THEOLOGICAL SCHOOL IN
AMERICA, FOUNDED 1797
BY REV. JOHN CHRISTOPHER
HARTWICK. LOCATED HERE 1816
10
(NY 28 at Hartwick Seminary)

HOME OF
MARCUS WELLS
1815-1895
WROTE WORLD FAMOUS HYMN
"HOLY SPIRIT, FAITHFUL GUIDE"

11
(NY 205 at Hartwick)

BAPTIST CHURCH
FIRST CHURCH IN
TOWN OF HARTWICK
ORGANIZED AUGUST 1795
WITH 12 CHARTER MEMBERS
THIS BUILDING BUILT 1854
12
(E. Main St. at Hartwick)

SOUTH HARTWICK
CEMETERY 1812
REV. EBENEZER WHITE, 1770-1813
NOTED METHODIST ITINERANT
MINISTER IS BURIED HERE

13
(CR. at South Hartwick)

ABNER ADAMS
1745-1825
REVOLUTIONARY SOLDIER;
ONE OF ISRAEL PUTNAM'S
RANGERS; IS BURIED
IN THIS CEMETERY
14
(TR. 1 ½ m. NE. of S. Hartwick)

HARTWICK COLLEGE
FOUNDED AS HARTWICK SEMINARY
1797
CHARTERED AS HARTWICK COLLEGE
FEBRUARY 17, 1928

15
(Campus, Clinton & West Sts.)

TOWN OF MORRIS

BUTTERNUT VALLEY
NAMED FOR THREE BUTTERNUT
TREES GROWING FROM ONE
STUMP, THE ORIGINAL CORNER
OF HILLINGTON, WELLS AND
OTEGO PATENTS 1170' DUE S.E.
16
(NY 51 2 m. NE. of Morris)

COUNCIL ROCK
FAMOUS MEETING PLACE
OF THE INDIANS

19
(Lake St. Cooperstown)

TOWN OF OTEGO

**REVOLUTIONARY
ARMY CAMP**
SULLIVAN-CLINTON FORCES
CAMPED NEAR THIS SPOT
AUGUST 11, 1779

17
(NY 7, 2 m. NE. of Otego)

CLINTON'S DAM
DAM OPENED AUGUST 9, 1779
2000 MEN AND 200 BATEAUX
WENT DOWN THE SUSQUEHANNA

20
(On Lake St. Cooperstown)

TOWN OF OTSEGO

GEORGE CROGAN
INDIAN AGENT – LAND SPECULATOR
LIVED IN PIONEER LOG HOUSE
LOCATED HERE 1769-1770.
GENERAL JAMES CLINTON'S
HEADQUARTERS HERE 1779.
18
(On Main St., Cooperstown)

"NATTY BUMPO"
LEATHERSTOCKING RESCUED
CHINGACHGOOK FROM FLAMES
CHINGACH DYING IN HIS CARE
"PIONEER"
21
(CR E. side Otsego Lake about
3 m. North of Cooperstown)

TOWN OF RICHFIELD

SUNKEN ISLAND
HOME OF TOM HUTTER
"DEERSLAYER"

22
(NY 80 5 m. N. Cooperstown)

FEDERAL CORNERS
FORMER HOME OF LEMUEL
VIBBER, OWNER OF TWELVE-
FORGE BLACKSMITH SHOP.

HOUSE ERECTED 1798

25
(TR 1 m. SE Richfield Springs)

HUTTER'S POINT
WHERE HETTIE SAVED HER
FATHER, TOM HUTTER
AND HURRY HARRY
FROM THE HURON
"DEERSLAYER"
23
(NY 80 4 ½ m. N. Cooperstown)

FEDERAL CORNERS
ONCE A BUSY HAMLET, SITE OF
AVERILL INN, VIBBER'S TWELVE-
FORGE SHOP, STORE, TANNERY HOME

SCHOOL OF DR. JAS. L. PALMER
PHYSICIAN AND TEACHER
26
(TR 1 m. SE Richfield Springs)

FRENCH WAR-1757
HERE ENGLISH TROOPS
GUIDED BY INDIANS
SOUGHT SULPHER DEPOSIT
SITE GREAT SULPHER SPRING
OPENED TO PUBLIC 1820
24
(US 20 at Richfield Springs)

RICHFIELD HOTEL
OLDEST TAVERN IN RICHFIELD BUILT
BY NATHAN DOW IN 1816, WHO WAS
WITH ETHAN ALLEN AT
TICONDEROGA
FIRST SUMMER GUESTS, 1821, WHEN
BOARD WAS $1.25 PER WEEK
27
(US 20 at Richfield Springs)

ST. LUKES
EPISCOPAL CHURCH
ORGANIZED MAY 20, 1799
FATHER NASH, FIRST RECTOR
NOTED MISSIONARY, MENTIONED
IN COOPER'S "THE PIONEERS"

28
(County Rd. at Richfield)

SITE OF
BEARDSLEY HOME
BUILT 1790 IN FOREST BY
OBADIAH BEARDSLEY AND FAMILY,
FIRST SETTLERS IN RICHFIELD.
ST. LUKE'S CHURCH, A LIBRARY AND
SCHOOL WERE FOUNDED SOON AFTER

29
(CR ½ m. NW. of Richfield)

BUTTERNUT ROAD
INDIAN TRAIL FROM FORT
PLAIN TO UNADILLA; ON
MAP BY BRITISH OFFICER,
1757, DURING FRENCH
AND INDIAN WAR

30
(TR ½ m. E. Richfield Springs)

TOWN OF SPRINGFIELD

MONTICELLO
SITE OF BAPTIST CHURCH
BUILT 1824, RAZED 1920,
NEARLY OPPOSITE SITE OF
UNIVERSALIST CHURCH
BUILT 1880, RAZED 1921
31
(On county rd. Richfield)

CONTINENTAL SCHOOL
LOG SCHOOLHOUSE
ON THIS SITE IN 1797
FIRST SUNDAY SCHOOL IN
TOWN ORGANIZED HERE 1819

32
(Town rd. 2 m. South of
Middle Springfield)

ONE OF THE EARLY
TOLL GATES
ON THE THIRD DIVISION
OF THE WESTERN TURNPIKE
COMPLETED IN 1808

33
(US 20 at East Springfield)

SPALSBERRY
CENTER
AN EARLY SETTLEMENT HERE
BURNED BY INDIANS UNDER
JOSEPH BRANT
JUNE 18, 1778
34
(CR. 1½ m. north of East
Springfield)

FIRST CHURCH
IN SPRINGFIELD, AND FIRST
BAPTIST CHURCH WEST OF
HUDSON VALLEY 1787. USED
BY ALL DENOMINATIONS AND
FOR TOWN MEETINGS
35
(US 20 at Middle Springfield)

NEAR HERE STOOD THE
LOG SCHOOL
HOUSE, PROBABLY FIRST IN
THE TOWN. BUILT BEFORE
ORGANIZATION OF SPRING-
FIELD IN 1797
36
(CR. ½ m. north of East
Springfield)

TOWN OF WORCESTER

CLINTON CAMP
OCCUPIED BY 4TH PENNSYLVANIA
REGIMENT WHO SERVED AS GUARD
FOR SUPPLY WAGONS
1779
37
(US 20 at Middle Springfield)

CAMP AND FORT
AT HYDE BAY, OTSEGO LAKE
2 1/2 MILES SOUTH, OCCUPIED
BY 4TH MASSACHUSETTS REGIMENT
1779
38
(US 20 at Middle Springfield)

GARFIELD FARM
SITE OF HOME OF SOLOMON
GARFIELD AND SON THOMAS.
ABRAM GARFIELD, FATHER OF
PRESIDENT JAMES A. GARFIELD
LIVED HERE PRIOR TO 1827
39
(On NY 7 at Worcester)

FIRST CHURCH
IN VILLAGE OF WORCESTER
ORGANIZED 1792 AS
CONGREGATIONAL
BECAME PRESBYTERIAN 1917
PRESENT EDIFICE ERECTED 1892
40
(On NY 7 at Worcester)

MURPHY HOME
TIMOTHY MURPHY, FAMOUS
REVOLUTIONARY SOLDIER
LIVED ON THIS FARM
1812-1817

41
(CR. 1 m. W. of S. Worcester)

SCHUYLER COUNTY

TOWN OF CATHARINE
CATHARINE M.E. CHURCH
ON SITE OF EARLIER EDIFICE
WHICH WAS THE
FIRST CHURCH
BUILDING IN COUNTY
ERECTED IN 1807
1
(On CR. in Catharine)

TOWN OF DIX
JAMES A. DELANO
FOUNDER AMERICAN RED CROSS
NURSING SERVICE 1909
BORN IN TOWNSEND
MARCH 12, 1862

2
(front of Grange Hall, Townsend)

TOWN OF HECTOR
FERRY
ESTABLISHED 1805 BETWEEN
THIS POINT AND STARKY
BY JOHN GOODWIN
CHARTERED BY STATE, 1820
FRANK WOOD, PILOT, 1867-97
3
(Lake shore at Valois)

CON-DAW-HAW
SITE OF IROQUOIS VILLAGE
CONSISTING OF CORNFIELDS
LONGHOUSES AND CABINS
DESTROYED SEPT. 4, 1779 BY
GEN. SULLIVAN'S TROOPS
4
(On NY 414 at Valois)

EARLY SETTLER
STATES SURVEY 1790
LOCATED HERE CABIN ONE
MASTERS
WITH TWENTY ACRES
CLEARED LAND
5
(NY 414 north of Hector)

CAMP SITE
GEN. POOR'S
BRIGADE
CAMP, LINE NORTH-SOUTH
SULLIVAN-CLINTON CAMPAIGN
SEPT. 3, 1779
6
(NY 414, ½ m. S. of Hector)

CAMP SITE
GEN. MAXWELL'S BRIGADE
CAMP EXTENDING NORTH HERE
SULLIVAN-CLINTON CAMPAIGN
SEPTEMBER 3, 1779

7
(TR 1 m. south of Hector)

CAMP SITE
GEN. CLINTON'S
BRIGADE
CAMP, LINE EAST-WEST
SULLIVAN-CLINTON CAMPAIGN
SEPTEMBER 3, 1779
8
(TR. 1 m. SW. of Hector)

CAMP SITE
GEN. HANDS
LIGHT CORPS
CAMP. EXTENDING WEST HERE
SULLIVAN-CLINTON CAMPAIGN
SEPTEMBER 3, 1779
9
(On NY 414 at Hector)

SAW MILL CREEK
FIRST SAW MILL IN SECTION
LOCATED HERE, BUILT BY
REUBEN SMITH 1795-6

10
(On NY 414 at Hector)

EPISCOPAL PARISH
CONSECRATED HERE 1830 BY
BISHOP HOBART. CHURCH
BUILDINGS AND SUPPORT OF
RECTOR MADE POSSIBLE TH ROUGH
GIFTS OF ELIZABETH WOODWARD
11
(On NY 414 at Hector)

MILITARY ROUTE
OF THE SULLIVAN-CLINTON
ARMY ON ITS CAMPAIGN
AGAINST THE BRITISH
AND INDIANS OF WESTERN
NEW YORK IN 1779
12
(NY 414, ½ m. S. of Hector)

FIRST PRESBYTERIAN CHURCH
ORGANIZED 1809
PRESENT EDIFICE BUILT 1818
SUNDAY SCHOOL
HELD CONTINUOUSLY
SINCE 1813
13
(On NY 414 at Hector)

PEACH ORCHARD
(GA-DI-ODJI-YA-DA)
SITE OF IROQUOIS VILLAGE
GEN. SULLIVAN CAMPED HERE
SEPTEMBER 3. 1779
14
(On NY 414 at Hector)

SITE OF CABIN OF
WILLIAM WYCKHAM
FIRST SETTLER IN
TOWN OF HECTOR 1791.
DIRECT DESCENDANT OF
EARL OF WYCKHAM
15
(NY 414 2 m. S. of Hector)

WAREHOUSE
ON THIS SITE IN 1823
A VESSEL LOADED 70 TONS
OF WHEAT AND REACHED PORT
OF NEW YORK THROUGH
THE ERIE CANAL
16
(NY 414 3 m. N. of Watkins Glen)

SAMUEL A. SEELEY ERECTED A
WOOLEN MILL
AT THIS PLACE IN 1801
THE FIRST IN
SCHUYLER COUNTY

17
(NY 414 3 m N of Watkins Glen)

SITE OF
OLDEST HOUSE
IN TOWN OF BURDETTE
USED AS A TAVERN, SCHOOL &
MASONIC HALL. CONTAINS
INTERESTING RELICS
18
(NY 227 at Burdette)

TOWN OF MONTOUR

MILITARY ROUTE
OF THE SULLIVAN-CLINTON
ARMY ON ITS CAMPAIGN
AGAINST THE BRITISH
AND INDIANS OF WESTERN
NEW YORK IN 1779
19
(NY 227 at Burdette)

HON. HENRY FISH
HOMESTEAD
BUILT 1815-1820. FIRST
ASSEMBLYMAN FROM SCHUYLER
COUNTY 1858, CHAIRMAN
FIRST BOARD SUPERVISORS
20
(NY 79 at Mecklenburg)

FIRST ROAD
IN SCHUYLER COUNTY
BUILT JUNE, 1799 FROM
PRESENT OWEGA ST. BRIDGE
TO SPENSER. KNOWN AS THE
CATH. SPENSER TURNPIKE
21
(NY 14 at Montour Falls)

MILITARY ROUTE
OF THE SULLIVAN-CLINTON
ARMY ON ITS CAMPAIGN
AGAINST THE BRITISH
AND INDIANS OF WESTERN
NEW YORK IN 1779
22*
(NY 14 just S. of Montour Falls)

CATHARINE'S
LANDING
1ST STORE AND INN IN REGION
LOCATED HERE 1805
AT HEAD OF LAKE NAVIGATION

23
(NY 14 at Montour Falls)

SHE-QUA-GA
"TUMBLING WATERS"
A SKETCH NOW IN THE LOUVRE
MADE ABOUT 1820 BY
LOUIS PHILIPPE
LATER KING OF FRANCE
24
(Genesee St. at Montour)

TOWN OF READING

TOWN OF TYRONE

UNDERGROUND
RAILROAD
LUTHER CLEVELAND AND WIFE
SHELTERED FUGITIVE SLAVES
HERE, AND HELPED THEM ON
THEIR WAY TO CANADA
25
(NY 14 3 m. N. Watkins Glen)

SITE OF
PRE-HISTORIC
INDIAN VILLAGE
OLDEST FOUND IN NEW YORK
ESTIMATED TO DATE
FROM 1000 B.C.
26
(CR. ½ m. west of Weston)

SENECA COUNTY

TOWN OF COVERT

OLD BAPTIST CHURCH
FOUNDED COVERT, N.Y., FEB. 16,
1803. FIRST PASTOR MINOR.
THOMAS
"MOTHER CHURCH" OF SENECA
BAPTIST ASSOCIATION
OLD COVERT CEMETERY NEARBY
1
(NY 96 at Covert)

THE BEEHIVE
TAVERN OF PIONEER DAYS
ERECTED 1824
3RD FLOOR USED FOR
VARIOUS MEETINGS

2
(NY 96 at Interlaken)

OLD SCHOOL HOUSE
THIS BUILDING WAS THE 2D
USED FOR SCHOOL PURPOSES
IN FARMERSVILLE, NEW YORK
IN 1845 WAS KNOWN AS THE
"FARMERSVILLE INSTITUTE"

3
(NY 96A at Interlaken)

Howard S. Ford

TOWN OF FAYETTE

SITE OF
INDIAN VILLAGE
DESTROYED BY TOOPS UNDER
COL. HENRY DEARBORN
SEPT. 21, 1779
4
(TR on Cayuga shore 2 ½ m.
southeast of Canoga)

SITE OF INDIAN VILLAGE DESTROYED BY TROOPS UNDER COL. HENRY DEARBORN SEPT. 21, 1779 5 (TR. lake shore 2 ½ m. SE. Canoga)	SITE OF HOWLAND'S LANDING FORMERLY A LANDING AND WAREHOUSE, SHOWN ON THE DELAFIELD MAP OF 1852 6 (NY 89 3 m. N. E. Varick)	CAYUGA LAKE SITE OF LANDING OF MORAVIAN MISSIONARIES ZEISBERGER AND CAMMERHOFF JUNE 27, 1750 7 (NY 89 3 m. S. of Canoga)
CANOGA GA-NO-GEH OF THE INDIANS INCLUDED IN RESERVATION BY INDIAN SACHEM FISH-CARRIER BY TREATY OF 1795 8 (On NY 89 at Canoga)	CANOGA CREEK SITE OF THE INDIAN VILLAGE OF SKANNAYUTENATE RED JACKET, THE INDIAN ORATOR WAS BORN HERE HUGH MC ALLISTER 9 (NY 89 ½ m. north of Canoga)	FIRST SUNDAY SCHOOL IN FAYETTE, 1819, TAUGHT HERE IN OLD LOG SCHOOL HOUSE BY DEACON 10 (CR. 3 m. W. of Canoga)
CANOGA SPRING REFERRED TO IN THE SURVEY OF SENECA CO. BY JOHN DELAFIELD IN 1850 AS BUBBLING PURE NITROGEN GAS 11 (CR. ¾ m. W. of Canoga)	____ 1 MILE SITE OF INDIAN VILLAGE DESTROYED BY TROOPS UNDER COL. HENRY DEARBORN SEPT. 21, 1779 12 (NY 89 1 ½ m. S. of Canoga)	CANOGA LANDING SITE OF INDIAN VILLAGE DESTROYED DURING SULLIVAN CAMPAIGN, 1779 FRONTENAC IS. JUST EAST & NEARLY ACROSS THE LAKE 13 (L. shore 1½ m. SE of Canoga)
____ 1 MILE INDIAN VILLAGE AT CANOGA LANDING DESTROYED DURING SULLIVAN CAMPAIGN 1779 14 (US 89 ½ m. S. Canoga)	SITE OF TAVERN KEPT BY CAPTAIN NATHAN COOK 1756-1838 HIS GRANDSON, STEPHEN V. HARKNESS LIVED HERE-ONE OF FOUNDERS OF STANDARD OIL COMPANY 15 (CR 1 m. north of MacDougall)	BURROUGHS POINT SITE OF INDIAN VILLAGE DESTROYED DURING SULLIVAN CAMPAIGN, 1779. TROOPS UNDER COL. HENRY DEARBORN ENCAMPED HERE 16 (NY 89 3 m. N. of Canoga)

TOWN OF OVID

APPROACHING
THE FARM OF
JOHN JOHNSTON
1791-1880
FATHER OF TILE-DRAINING
IN AMERICA

17
(NY 96A 4 m. NW of Fayette)

THOMAS R. LOUNSBURY
ILLUSTRIOUS YALE PROFESSOR
BORN HERE 1835. SON OF
REV. THOMAS LOUNSBURY AND
MARY JANETTE WOODWARD.
STUDENT OF OVID ACADEMY

18
(NY 414, village of Ovid)

SULLIVAN TRAIL
BEFORE SETTLEMENT AT
WHITE MEN. COL. HENRY
DEARBORN OF THE SULLIVAN
EXPEDITION VIEWED CAYUGA
LAKE HERE, SEPT. 22, 1779

19
(NY 96 1 ½ m. N of Interlacken)

TOWN OF ROMULUS

WHITNEY'S LANDING
LATER KNOWN AS JACACKS'
LANDING
WAS A PROMINENT LANDING
SHOWN IN
THE DELAFIELD MAP OF 1852

20
(NY 89 6 m. south of E. Varick)

DEGORY PROWTT
DRUMMER BOY, 1776-1783
AT SIEGE OF FORT STANWIX
ON THE SULLIVAN EXPEDITION,
AT SURRENDER OF CORNWALLIS,
LIVED A MILE WEST OF HERE.

21
(NY 89 4 m. south of E. Varick)

DEAN'S COVE
(SWAH-YA-WA-NAH)
INDIAN VILLAGE DESTROYED
BY DETACHMENTS FROM
SULLIVAN'S ARMY
SEPTEMBER 22, 1779

22
(NY 89 2 ½ m. S of E. Varick)

TOWN OF SENECA FALLS

U.S. NAVAL TRAINING
STATION AND CENTER 1942-1946
WORLD WAR 2, 411,429 SAILORS
& WAVES TRAINED HERE, THEN
FOUGHT FOR OUR COUNTRY'S
FREEDOM ALL OVER THE WORLD

23
(NY 96A 6 miles NW of Ovid)

KEN-DAI-A
INDIAN VILLAGE
DESTROYED BY
SULLIVAN'S ARMY
SEPTEMBER 21, 1779

24
(NY 96A 5 m. NW of Ovid)

SITE OF INDIAN VILLAGE
GAR-NON-DE-YO
DESTROYED DURING
SULLIVAN CAMPAIGN
SEPT. 21, 1779

25
(NY 89 1 ½ m. N. of Canoga)

VAN CLEEF LAKE
NAMED FOR GEORGE CUNNINGHAM
VAN CLEEF, ONE OF THE FIRST
WHITE CHILDREN BORN IN
SENECA COUNTY 1797

26
(L. shore, Trinity Lane &
Seneca Falls)

HOME OF
GARY V. SACKETT
1790-1885
JUDGE COURT OF COMMON
PLEAS-PROMOTER OF
CANAL SYSTEM

27
(W. Bayard & Sackett Sts.
Seneca Falls)

MYNDERSE
ACADEMY
NAMED FOR COL. WILHELMUS
MYNDERSE, FOUNDER OF
SENECA FALLS

28
(US 20 & 5, Seneca Falls)

Howard S. Ford

FIRST CONVENTION FOR
WOMEN'S RIGHTS
WAS HELD ON THIS CORNER
1848

29
(US 20 & 5, Seneca Falls)

OLD GENESEE
STAGE ROUTE
CAYUGA LAKE BRIDGE MADE
THIS THE MAIN ROUTE UNTIL
THE ERIE CANAL OF 1822
AND THE RAILWAY OF 1840
30
(CR. ½ m. E. Seneca Falls)

POTTER INN FARM
NATHANIEL J. POTTER, INNKEEPER
BLACKSMITH ON GENESEE ROAD,
1801-1808. HIS SON, HENRY S.
POTTER, LIVED HERE. 1ST PRES.
WESTERN UNION TELEGRAPH, 1851.
31
(CR. ½ m. E. Seneca Falls)

KINGDOM CEMETERY
RESERVED IN DEED TO THOMAS
LAWRENCE. HERE UNTIL 1856
WERE MILLS, DISTILLERIES,
TAVERNS, SCHOOL, JUSTICE CT.,
MASONIC LODGE, RACE TRACK.
32
(US 20 & 5, 1 m. E of Waterloo)

MILITARY ROUTE
OF THE SULLIVAN-CLINTON
ARMY ON ITS CAMPAIGN
AGAINST THE BRITISH
AND INDIANS OF WESTERN
NEW YORK IN 1779
33
(US 20 & 5, E end, Waterloo)

ELIZABETH CADY
STANTON
PROMOTER OF THE FIRST
WOMAN'S RIGHTS CONVENTION
LIVED HERE. CONVENTION
WAS HELD ACROSS THE RIVER
34
(Washington St., Seneca Falls)

KINGDOM CEMETERY
RESERVED IN DEED TO THOMAS
LAWRENCE. HERE UNTIL 1856
WERE MILLS, DISTILLERIES,
TAVERNS, SCHOOL, JUSTICE CT.,
MASONIC LODGE, RACE TRACK.
35
(US 20 & 5, 1 m. E of Waterloo)

MILITARY ROUTE
OF THE SULLIVAN-CLINTON
ARMY ON ITS CAMPAIGN
AGAINST THE BRITISH
AND INDIANS OF WESTERN
NEW YORK IN 1779
36
(US 20 & 5, E end, Waterloo)

ELIZABETH CADY
STANTON
PROMOTER OF THE FIRST
WOMAN'S RIGHTS CONVENTION
LIVED HERE. CONVENTION
WAS HELD ACROSS THE RIVER
37
(Washington St., Seneca Falls)

BRIDGEPORT
FORMERLY CAYUGA FERRY
& WEST CAYUGA TERMINUS OF
STAGE LINE BRIDGE
PROMINENT WHEN AUBURN WAS
"HARDENBERGH'S CORNER"
38
(CR. 2 m. E. Seneca Falls)

ALONG NORTH SIDE OF RIVER
MARCHED SULLIVAN'S FORCES
EXPEDITION COMMANDED BY
COL. PETER GANSEVOORT &
LT. COL. WILLIAM BUTLER
SET. 20-21, 1779
39
(US 20 & 5 1 m. E. Waterloo)

CRUSOE ISLAND
SITE OF CRUSOE POST OFFICE
UNTIL 1852. HOME OF
DAVID EVANS, 1837-1920
STAGE RELAYING BARNS WERE
LOCATED HERE
40
(On NY 414 at Crusoe)

EAST VARICK
ONCE PROMINENT LANDING WITH
HOTEL, WAREHOUSE, STORES,
RESIDENCES. EARLY HOME OF
ROBERTS, PHILLIPS, BURROUGHS,
CHRISTOPHER, BARRICK FAMILIES
41
(NY 89 at East Varick)

SITE OF
FRISBIE'S FERRY
A NOW EXTINCT HAMLET WITH
STORE, MILLS, DISTILLERY,
TAVERN AND FERRY TO
AURORA, 1796.
42
(NY 89 1 ½ m. S of E. Varick)

BIRTHPLACE OF
ISAAC PHILLIPS ROBERTS
JULY 24, 1833
REPRESENTATIVE EXTRA-
ORDINARY OF AMERICAN
FARMER
43
(NY 89 1 m. N of E. Varick)

SITE OF
CLARKTOWN
A NOW EXTINCT HAMLET WITH
WAREHOUSE, STORES, TAVERN,
POTTERY, AND FERRY TO
LEVANNA ACROSS THE LAKE
44
(NY 89, 2 m. N of E. Varic k)

PRESBYTERIAN
CHURCH
ORGANIZED 1796 BY REV.
DANIEL THATCHER OF VIRGINIA
THIS BUILDING ERECTED 1838

45
(NY 96, village of Romulus)

STEUBEN COUNTY

TOWN OF BATH

PULTENEY SQUARE
HERE IN 1793 WAS MADE
THE FIRST CLEARING
IN STEUBEN COUNTY BY
COL. CHARLES WILLIAMSON

1
(On Morris St., Bath)

U.S. VETERANS
ADMINISTRATION FACILITY
SITE OF BATH SOLDIERS' AND
SAILORS' HOME, BUILT IN 1877
THE CIVIL WAR
2
(On US 15 north of Bath)

TOWN OF CAMERON

AVERELL HILL
BIRTHPLACE OF
WILLIAM WOODS AVERELL
MAJOR GENERAL, U.S.A.
NOTED CAVALRY LEADER OF

3
(On CR at West Ameron)

TOWN OF CANISTEO

FRENCH OCCUPATION
HERE IN 1690 SIEUR DE
VILLIERS AND ABBE FENELON
DISCOVERED A SETTLEMENT,
ERECTED A CROSS, AND
PLANTED THE FLAG OF FRANCE
4
(NY, 21 Canisteo village park)

KANESTIO
CASTLE
INDIAN VILLAGE BURNED 1764
BY CAPTAIN ANDREW MONTOUR
AND A PROVINCIAL FORCE

5
(NY 21, Canisteo village park)

TOWN OF HORNELLSVILLE

OLDEST HOUSE
IN STEUBEN COUNTY
ERECTED 1797 BY
COL. JAMES MCBURNEY
A PROBALE STATION OF
UNDERGROUND RAILWAY
6
(NY 21 at town line)

Howard S. Ford

TOWN OF HOWARD

TOWN OF WHEELER

HERE INDIANS AND TORIES
USED PINE TREES TO BUILD
CANOES FOR TRANSPORT TO
WYOMING–WYOMING MASSACRE
JULY 3, 1778

7*
(CR 1 m. N. of Hornell)

OLD INN SITE
DR. MARCUS WHITMAN, REV.
AND MRS. H.H. SPALDING
MET HERE FEB. 14, 1836
AND DECIDED TO GO
TOGETHER TO OREGON
8
(NY 70 at Howard)

HENRY HARMON SPALDING
MISSIONARY TO INDIANS OF NORTH-
WEST TERRITORY AND
PIONEER TO STATE OF IDAHO
BORN HERE, NOV. 26, 1803

9
(NY 53, 2 m. S of Wheeler)

TIOGA COUNTY

TOWN OF BARTON

MAUGHANTOWANO
WHERE IN SPRING OF 1779
ENCAMPED SAWYER AND COWLEY
AMERICAN SOLDIERS
WITH FOUR INDIAN CAPTORS
EN ROUTE TO BRITISH LINES
1
(NY 17 4 ½ m. E. of Waverly)

ELLIS CREEK
NAMED IN HONOR OF
EBENEZER ELLIS
REVOLUTIONARY SOLDIER
PIONEER IN FOREST 1787
THIS COMMUNITY–ELLISTOWN
2
(NY 17 1 ½ m. E. of Waverly)

THE FIRST
GRIST MILL
ON CAYUTA CREEK, BUILT
HERE SOON AFTER 1800 BY
GEORGE WALKER.
WAS ACTIVE FOR A CENTURY
3
(NY 17 & 34 N.end Waverly)

TOWN OF CANDOR

SITE OF
SHEPARD TAVERN
BUILT ABOUT 1816 BY
JOHN SHEPARD AND ENLARGED
BY ISAAC SHEPARD IN 1825
DESTROYED BY FIRE 1853
4
(NY 17 at West Waverly)

CARANTOUAN
SPANISH HILL, 650 FT. SOUTH
WHERE ETIENNE BRULE, SCOUT
OF CHAMPLAIN CAME IN 1615.
THE FIRST WHITE EXPLORER
KNOWN TO REACH THIS REGION
5
(NY 17 west end of Waverly)

LINE OF
ITHACA & OWEGO R.R.
INC. 1828
SECOND CHARTERED IN STATE
OPERATED BY HORSEPOWER
FOR FIRST SIX YEARS
6
(NY 223 Village of Candor)

TOWN OF NEWARK VALLEY

JAMES MCMASTER
PIONEER, REVOLUTIONARY SOLDIER
TO WHOM WAS GRANTED TITLE
"MCMASTER'S HALF TOWNSHIP"
1788
LIES BURIED NEAR HERE
7
(CR north end of Candor)

WADE FARM
PURCHASED 1833 BY LEWIS WADE
1791-1862, MUSICIAN WAR OF 1812
OWNED AND WORKED SUCCESSIVELY
BY LEWIS WADE; WILLIAM WADE;
EDGAR O. WADE' FLOYD E WADE
8
(NY 38 2 m. south Newark Valley)

BY TRADITION THIS
MAPLE TREE
WAS BLAZED IN 1786
SPARED WHEN INDIAN TRAIL
WAS WIDENED
INTO WAGON ROAD
9*
(NY 38, Newark Valley)

TOWN OF NICHOLS

COXE 'S MANOR
31,470 ACRES OF LAND
ALONG THIS SUSQUEHANNA VALLEY
WERE GRANTED TO DANIEL COXE
AND ASSOCIATES BY THE CROWN
OF ENGLAND JANUARY 15, 1775
10
(NY 283, 2 ½ m. W. of Owego)

ASBURY CHURCH
ERECTED 1822-23
SOCIETY FORMED 1818 BY REV.
JOHN GRIFFING WITH MEMBERS
ELIJAH, PHEBE, ANN, MARIAH
AND DANIEL MCD. SHOEMAKER
11
(CR. 5 m. W. of Nichols)

LOUNSBURY
FORMERLY NAMED
CANFIELD CORNERS
BENJAMIN LOUNSBURY
SETTLED HERE 1793. EXRA
CANFIELD FIRST POSTMASTER
12
(NY 283 at Lansbury)

TOWN OF OWEGO

BEFORE 1800 THIS ROAD LED
TO A FERRY ACROSS
THE SUSQUEHANNA RIVER TO
TIOGA CENTER, OPERATED BY
JOHN DECKER AND GIDEON
CORTRIGHT, REV. SOLDIER
13
(NY 283 at Lounsbury)

TAVERN 1831
BUILT BY PIONEER MERCHANT
RANSOM STEELE
THE BARNABY ACADEMY
WAS LOCATED HERE SEVERAL
YEARS DURING THE CIVIL WAR
14
(CR. at Apalachin)

CAMPVILLE
NAMED IN HONOR OF
COL. ASA CAMP
REVOLUTIONARY SOLDIER
WHO SETTLED HERE 1800
& CONDUCTED 1ST TAVERN
15
(NY 17C 6 m. east of Owego)

OWAGEA
AN INDIAN VILLAGE
BURNED AUGUST 19, 1779
GEN. CLINTON'S FORCE
ENROUTE TO JOIN
GENERAL SULLIVAN
16
(NY 17, N end bridge at Owego)

JAS. MCMASTER
WAS GRANTED TITLE TO THE
WEST HALF OF TOWNSHIP
SITE OF PRESENT
VILLAGE OF OWEGO
1788
17
(NY 17 at Owego)

ISAAC HARRIS
WHO SETTLED HERE IN 1786
WAS DELEGATE TO PHILADEL-
PHIA IN 1790 AND SECURED
SQUATTERS RIGHTS FROM THE
PATENTEES OF COXE"S MANOR
18
(Old NY 17 at Apalachin)

Howard S. Ford

1828
OLD ACADEMY BUILDING
ON THE SITE OF THE FIRST
SCHOOLHOUSE
OF OWEGO SETTLEMENT
BUILT OF LOGS ABOUT 1797
19
(On Court St., Owego)

HERE THE
INDIAN TRAIL
FROM CAYUGA LAKE JOINED
THE SUSQUEHANNA TRAIL
TRAVELED PATHS LONG BEFORE
COMING OF THE WHITE MAN
20
(On Front St., Owego)

A LOG HOUSE
FIRST PERMANENT BUILDING
IN THIS PART OF THE VALLEY
BUILT 1785 NEAR HERE BY
JAMES MCMASTER & PARTY

21
(On W. Front ST., Owego)

TURNPIKE
IN 1822 THE SHORTEST ROUTE
FROM OWEGO TO NEW YORK VIA
MONTROSE, DUNDAFF, MILFORD,
NEWTON, MORRISTOWN, NEWARK
NUMEROUS HILLS & TOLLGATES
22
(NY 283, village of Owego)

OWEGO FEMALE SEMINARY
OPENED IN 1828
BY JULIETTE M. CAMP.
OWEGO FEMALE INSTITUTE
IN 1843 HEADED BY
PROF. AND MRS JOSEPH M. ELY
23
(NY 17C, village of Owego)

FIRST TAVERN
IN OWEGO, BUILT BY
CAPTAIN LUKE BATES
IN 1795, STOOD HERE
FIRST TOWN MEETING
HELD IN TAVERN
24
(On Church St., Owego)

OWEGO & ITHACA
TURNPIKE
INCORPORATED 1807
GIVING NORTHERN SETTLEMENT
ACCESS TO MARKETS OF
PENNSYLVANIA AND MARYLAND
25
(NY 96 N. end of Owego)

FIRST SAWMILL
IN OWEGO, BUILT BY
JAMES MCMASTER & AMOS DRAPER
BEFORE 1791, STOOD
JUST ABOVE THIS BRIDGE

26
(NY 17, W. end of Owego)

TOLL BRIDGE
IN 1828, SWEPT AWAY BY
FLOOD OF 1867.
TRESTLE BRIDGE OF 1868,
PURCHASED BY VILLAGE, 1881.
STEEL BRIDGE ERECTED, 1893.
27
(NY 17, south end of bridge
over Susquehanna River)

ITHACA OWEGO R.R.
SECOND CHARTERED IN STATE
INC. JUNE 28, 1828
CROSSED THE VILLAGE PARK
TO TERMINUS ON
SITE OF AHWAGA PARK
28
(NY 17, village of Owego)

KA-NAU-KWIS
KNOWN AS CAPTAIN CORNELIUS
IN TIME OF NEED HERE
SUPPLIED VENISON AND
"CORN FLOUR" TO FAMILY OF
PIONEER BENANUELL DEUEL
29*
(NY 17, village of Owego)

OWEGO
BIRTHPLACE OF ERIE
HERE WAS HELD CONVENTION
DECEMBER 20, 1831
TO FURTHER THE CHARTER OF
NEW YORK AND ERIE RAILROAD
30
(NY 96, Erie RR Xing, Owego)

TOWN OF RICHFORD

NICHOLAS
DELAWARE WARRIOR
SUCCESSFUL FARMER AMONG
THE PIONEERS; WHOSE SQUAW
GAVE NAME TO SQUAW ISLAND,
CLAIMED THIS FLAT
31
(NY 283 ¼ m. W. of Owego)

PUBLIC SQUARE
GRANTED BY DEED TO
TOWN OF RICHFORD
BY THE PIONEERS
EZEKIEL RICH & STEHPEN WELLS
OCTOBER 9,1821
32
(NY 38 & 79, Richford)

EARLY TURNPIKE
COMMISSION OF 1797
"TO LAY OUT THE ROAD LEADING
FROM CATSKILL LANDING
TO CATHERINESTOWN
IN THE COUNTY OF TIOGA."
33
(NY 38 & 79, at Richford)

FIRST CHURCH
ORGANIZED 1821, BUILT 1823
BY PURITAN SETTLERS.
REBUILT IN 1854. ORIGINAL
BELL NOW IN USE

34
(On NY 38, Richford)

SITE OF
THE OLD ABBEY
BUILT 1813 BY SAMUEL SMITH
WHO KEPT A TAVERN HERE.
THE RICHFORD POST OFFICE
ESTABLISHED HERE IN 1830
35
(NY 38 & 79, Richford)

DUNHAMVILLE
EXPERIMENTAL CITY STATE
PROPOSED IN 1828 BY
WM. DUNHAM, MERCHANT
FIRST POSTMASTER, AND
SUPERVISOR OF RICHFORD
36
(NY 38 ½ m. S. of Richford)

TOWN OF SPENCER

SPENCER WAS THE
COUNTY SEAT
1811-1822
ON THIS LOT STOOD THE
OLD COURT HOUSE
DESTROYED BY FIRE 1821
37
(On NY 34, Spencer)

TOMPKINS COUNTY

TOWN OF CAROLINE

OLD TOBEY TAVERN
BUILT 1808. INN KEEPERS
GEORGE VICKORY AND NATHANIEL
TOBEY. ONCE TOBEYTOWN.
NOW VILLAGE OF CAROLINE

1
(NY 79 ½ m. West of Caroline)

SPEEDSVILLE
COMMONS
INCORPORATED STATE PARK, 1858
LABAN JENKS EARLY SETTLER
BUILT HOUSE IN 1819

2
(County rd. at Speedsville)

DEERLICKS
ON '76 ROAD EXTENSION
INDIANS AND EARLY SETTLERS
HERE OBTAINED THEIR SALT
'76 ROAD BUILT BY
AUGUSTINE BOYER, 1804
3
(NY 330 2 m. E. Brooktondale)

Howard S. Ford

SETTLER'S CABIN
BUILT BY BENONI MULKS
NEAR SPRING 1798-1801
ORIGINAL FIREPLACE STAND-
ING. BOYCEVILLE'S
FIRST SETTLEMENT

4
(NY 79, Slaterville Springs)
south of Caroline)

SPRINGFARM
OLD PLANTATION HOME OF
DR. JOSEPH SPEED, VIRGINIA
PIONEER, 1805
LEVEL GREEN ROAD
CAROLINE ONCE CALLED SPEMCER

5
(Level Green Rd. ¾ mile
west of Slaterville Springs)

SLAVE BURYING GROUND
45 RODS EAST OF THIS POINT
IN EDGE OF WOODS ARE
BURIES 14 SLAVES
OWNED BY RESIDENTS
OF TOWN OF CAROLINE

6
(Ellis Hollow Rd., 1 mile

1ST TOWN MEETING
HELD HERE IN BUSH
TAVERN, MADE OF HEWN LOGS;
APRIL 1811
WILLIAM ROUNSVELL, SUPERVISOR
CAPT. LEVI SLATER, TOWN CLERK
7
(NY 79 ½ m. W of Slaterville Spr.)

CAMPING GROUND
CHIEF WHEELOCK
ONEIDA INDIAN
KILLED IN ACTION
WAR OF 1812

8
(NY 79 1 ½ m. W.Slaterville Spr.)

BLAIR HOMESTEAD
BIRTHPLACE OF AUSTIN BLAIR
CIVIL WAR GOVERNOR OF MICHIGAN
SON OF GEORGE BLAIR
PIONEER SETTLER 1809

9
(TR 2 m. N. Speedsville)

OLD RICH TAVERN
BUILT AND CONDUCTED BY
CAPTAIN DAVID RICH WHO
EMIGRATED HERE FROM
VERMONT 1795. ALSO SITE
OF CAPT. RICH'S LOG CABIN
10
(NY 79 ½ m. E Caroline)

CABIN SITE
CABIN BUILT BY MARIA
EARSLEY, 1794, FOR HOME.
FIRST SETTLER IN CAROLINE.
FIRST TRIP FROM ROXBUTY, N.J.
ON HORSEBACK WITH SON, JOHN
11
(NY 79 at Caroline)

QUICK HOMESTEAD
BUILT IN 1823 BY HENRY
QUICK AND WIFE SALLY
EARSLEY, WHO CAME WITH
FIRST SETTLER FROM ROXBURY
(MONTCLAIR) NEW JERSEY, 1794
12
(NY 330 2 ½ m. E Brooktondale)

WEST OWEGO CREEK, N.W.
BOUNDARY "BOSTON PURCHASE"
230,400 ACRES OF INDIAN LAND
CEDED BY NEW YORK TO MASS.
1787, TO SETTLE BOUNDARY
DISPUTE
13
(CR 2 ½ m. E of Slaterville Spr.)

SOUTH ENTRANCE TO
"SIX HUNDRED FOREST"
GORGE OF UPPER SIX MILE
CREEK. SITE OF OLD "BOTTOM
MILL", SAWMILL BUILT 1808

14
(CR 1 m. E Slaterville Spr.)

HOME OF
NATHANIEL TOBEY
WHO EMIGRATED FROM BRISTOL
CO. MASS. BUILT MANY NEW
ENGLAND STYLE HOMES HERE, 1810

15
(NY 79 at Caroline)

SLATERVILLE
MAGNETIC MINERAL SPRINGS
DISCOVERED IN VALLEY BY
DR, WILLIAM C. GALLAGHER
WHO SUNK THE FIRST ARTESIAN
WELL HERE IN 1871
16
(NY 79, Slaterville Springs)

EAST BOUNDARY
CANTINE MILITARY TRACT
THIS FARM CEDED TO JOHN
ROBINSON BY GEN. JOHN
CANTINE IN 1801

17
(NY 79 2 m. W of Caroline)

OLD GENUNG FARM
LOT 93 WAS CLEARED BY
MOSES AND BENJAMIN GENUNG,
BROTHERS, NEW JERSEY REV.
SOLDIRS. CABIN BUILT IN
1800. OWNED BY FAMILY 125 YEARS
18
(NY 79 2 ¼ miles west of
Slaterville Springs)

TOWN OF DANBY

SITE OF
SPEED BLOCKHOUSE
BUILT 1806 OF SQUARED LOGS
BY JOHN JAMES SPEED.
POST OFFICE HERE 1806 CALLED
SPEEDSVILLE. CATSKIL TURNPIKE
FROM CATSKILL TO BATH, 1804
19
(NY 79 1 ½ m. west of Caroline)

DUTCH REFORMED
CHURCH SITE-CEMETERY-1820
FIRST CHURCH IN CAROLINE
BUILT 1820-ORGANOIZED 1810
BY THE FIRST DOMINIE
REV. GARRET MANDEVILLE

20
(NY 79 1 m. west of Slaterville Springs)

THIS WAS THE
FIRST CHURCH
IN THE TOWN OF DANBY
ORGANIZED 1807
ERECTED 1813

21
(NY 96 at Danby)

TOWN OF DRYDEN

NEW JERUSALEM
CHURCH SITE
ORGANIZED 1816, BUILT 1824
FOUNDED BY DR. LEWIS BEERS
PHYSICIAN, PASTOR, JUSTICE
AND PIONEER SETTLER, 1797
22
(NY 96 1 m. SE of Danby)

UNDERGROUND
RAILROAD
HOME OF WILLIAM HANFORD
AND WIFE ALTHA C. TODD,
WHO SHELTERED FUGITIVE SLAVES
ON WAY TO CANADA AND FREEDOM
23
(TR, ½ m. west of Etna)

FIRST ROAD
IN TOMKINS COUNTY FROM
EAST. USED BY MANY EARLY
SETTLERS. STARTED BY JOSEPH
CHAPLIN; CONTRACTOR, MAY 5,
1792. COMPLETED IN 1795
24
(CR. at Malloryville)

FIRST ROAD
IN TOMPKINS COUNTY FROM
EAST. USED BY MANY EARLY
SETTLERS. STARTED BY JOSEPH
CHAPLIN; CONTRACTOR, MAY 5,
1792. COMPLETED IN 1795
25*
(NY 13 4 m. NE of Dryden)

MALLORYVILLE
SETTLED BY SAMUEL MALLORY
IN 1826 WHO OPERATED HERE
CHAIR AND CLOTH FACTORIES.
ONCE SITE OF HOWE AND WATSON
AND WADE COOPERAGES
26
(Co. Rd. at Malloryville)

MALLORYVILLE
ABOUT 1845 WILLIAM TRAPP
HERE INVENTED THE FIRST
SUCCESSFUL BARREL-MAKING
MACHINE. HAMLET LATER
BECAME COOPERAGE CENTER
27
(Co. Rd. at Malloryville)

ONE MILE EAST ON HILL LOG CABIN
SITE OF BIRTHPLACE JOHN MC GRAW,
1815-1877. DONOR MC GRAW HALL,
CORNELL UNIVERSITY
FATHER OF JENNIE MC GRAW FISKE,
CORNELL BENEFACTRESS

28
(CR 4 m. S. Willow Glen)

BIRTHPLACE OF
WILLIAM R. "DADDY" GEORGE
1866-1936
FOUNDER OF
GEORGE JUNIOR REPUBLIC

29
(CR 1 ½ m. W. of W. Dryden)

WAGONSHEAD
WILLIAM R. GEORGE CONCEIVED
OF THE JUNIOR REPUBLIC HERE.
THE YOUTHFUL VILLAGE WHOSE
MOTTO IS "NOTHING WITHOUT
LABOR" WAS FOUNDED JULY 10, 1895
30
(CR 3/4 m. W. of W. Dryden)

Howard S. Ford

JOHN MILLER
FIRST GOVERNOR OF
NORTH DAKOTA
BORN HERE IN
TOWN OF DRYDEN
INAUGERATED 1889
31
(CR 3 m. South of Willow Glen)

INDIAN CAMP
HUNTING AND FISHING
GROUNDS ON DRYDEN LAKE.
ARROWS, SINKERS, AND
FLINTS AROUND IN
GREAT NUMBERS
32
(CR 2 m. SE of Dryden)

1ST BAPTIST CHURCH
DRYDEN, 1830. ORGANIZED 1804
1ST CHURCH BUILT, 1807
REV. JOHN LASURE, FIRST PASTOR

33
(County Road at Etna)

UNDERGROUND
RAILROAD
HOME OF HANANIAH WILCOX
AND WIFE NANCY ANN PRICE
WHO SHELTERED AND ASSISTED
FUGITIVE SLAVES ON WAY TO CANADA
34
(On town Road at Etna)

CHARLES W. SANDERS
1805-1889
AUTHOR OF SCHOOLBOOKS
RESIDED IN WEST DRYDEN
AND COMPLETED HIS
"FIRST SPELLER" HERE
35
(On town Road at Peruville)

BRIDLE ROAD
VIRGIL TO ITHACA 1795
BUILT BY JOSEPH CHAPLIN
DRYDEN CENTER HOUSE
BUILT BY BENJ. ALDRICH
TOWN MEETINGS HELD HERE
36
(NY 13 2 ¼ m. W of Dryden)

TOWN OF ENFIELD

INDIAN SITE
EARLY IROQUOIAN VILLAGE
ARROWS, CRACKED BONES, BEADS,
COOKING STONES, FLINT, PIECES
OF IROQUOIAN POTTERY FOUND

37
(On Schuyler-Tompkins Co. line
1 mile north of NY 79)

INDIAN VILLAGE
CIRCULAR PALISADE AROUND
POND. WALL SOUTH FROM GATE
IMMENSE EARLY IROQUOIAN SITE
HERE THE INDIANS
OBTAINED CLAY FOR POTTERY

38
(On Schuyler-Tompkins Co.
2 miles north of NY 79)

WALLENBECK INN
ROUTE OF CATSKILL TURNPIKE
FIRST ROAD BUILT IN TOWN.
OLD POST ROAD AND STAGE
ROUTE USED FROM MECKLENBURG
TO KIRBY'S, 1826

39
(Schuyler-Tompkins County line
1 mile south of NY 79)

TOWN OF GROTON

APPLEGATE TAVERN
BUILT BY JOHN APPLEGATE
1807. SETTLED IN TOWN 1805.
1ST SCHOOLHOUSE IN TOWN
N. OF TAVERN, ERECTED 1809
APPLEGATE'S CORNERS
40
(NY 79 5 m. W. of Ithaca)

VAN DORN
TAVERN SITE
BUILT BY PETER VAN DORN
A CATSKILL TURNPIKE
MILESTONE STOOD AT
VAN DORN'S CORNERS
41
(NY 79 4 m. W. of Ithaca)

CUMMINGS HOME
GURDON CUMMINS AND WIFE
ABIGAIL PETTIS FROM MANSFIELD
CONN. SETTLED HERE IN 1810
OWNED AND OCCUPIED BY FOUR
GENERATIONS OF CUMMINGS
42
(On CR 2 m. s. of Summer Hill)

SYLVESTER PENNOYER
1831-1902
BORN HERE; GOV. OF OREGON
1886-94
MAYOR CITY OF PORTLAND,
OREGON
1896; OWNER AND EDITOR OREGON
HERALD 1868-71
43
(NY 38 at Groton)

INDIAN VILLAGE
FAVORITE HUNTING GROUND
OF CAYUGA INDIANS
AND OTHER LOCAL TRIBES
NEAR OWASCO CREEK

44*
(NY 38 3 m. S. of Groton)

OLD BAPTIST
CHURCH-1828
FOUNDER REV. BENJ. WHIPPLE
1ST PASTOR REV. P.L. PLATT
MEETINGS HELD SINCE 1805

45
(County rd. at McLean)

OLD EAST GROTON
CEMETERY AND 1ST CHURCH
KNOWN AS E. CONGREGATIONAL.
ORG. 1805. SITE AT STICKLES
CORNERS. BUILT OF LOGS 1810
1ST PASTOR, JOSHUA LAND, 1809
46
(NY 222 2 m. east of Groton)

OLD MILL SITE
LAFAYETTE GRISTMILL
BUILT BY GEORGE FISH, 1818
NAMED SAME DAY GENERAL
MARQUIS DE LAFAYETTE
VISITED AUBURN, 1825
47
(NY 222 at Lafayette)

ELM TREE INN
SITE OF FIRST LOG TAVERN
IN MCLEAN BUILT BY AMASA
COBB, 1796. GIANT ELM WAS
NATIVE FOREST SAPLING
WHEN TAVERN WAS BUILT
48
(On county Rd. at McLean)

CITY OF ITHACA

CONGREGATIONAL CHURCH
ORGANIZED 1816, BUILT 1832
FIRST SERVICE MAY 3, 1833
CENTENNIAL JULY 16, 1916
WEST GROTON, N.Y.

49
(On county Rd. West Groton)

OWEGO-ITHACA
TURNPIKE 1811-1841
R.R. INC 1828, OPENED 1834
2ND R.R. CHARTERED IN STATE
INCLINED PLANE 480 FT. EAST

50
(NY 96, south end of Ithaca)

OLD HOMESTEAD
REV. DR. SAMUEL PARKER AND
MARCUS WHITMAN, PLANNED
HERE IN 1833 JOURNEY WHICH
SAVED OREGON TO THE UNION.
INDIAN CEMETERY ON ESTATE
51
(On Parker Place)

SITE OF
FIRST COURT HOUSE
A PRIMITIVE HALL OF JUSTICE
BUILT OF WOOD IN 1818
ERECTION PREVENTED TOMPKINS
CO. BEING REANNEXED TO
SENECA AND CAYUGA COUNTIES
52
(On Court St.)

SIMEON DEWITT
HOME SITE AND BURIAL PLACE
1756-1834
SURVEYOR GEN. OF N.Y. STATE.
REMAINS MOVED TO ALBANY
RURAL CEMETERY 1854
53
(On DeWitt Place)

OLDEST HOUSE
IN TOMKINS COUNTY, BUILT
ABOUT 1800 BY ABRAM MARKLE
SOLD TO SIMEON DEWITT AND
USED AS INITIAL POINT OF
SURVEY FOR EARLY TURNPIKES
54
(On Linn St.

Howard S. Ford

TURNPIKE
FROM CATSKILL TO BATH
RAN ORIGINALLY THROUGH
STATE (OWEGO) ST. MAIL TO
WESTERN SETTLEMENT CARRIED
OVER THIS TURNPIKE
55
(On East State St.)

CAYUGA INDIAN
WINTER QUARTERS
LOCATED ON EXPOSED
FLATLANDS OF THIS GORGE
BELOW WELLS FALLS

56
(On Columbia St.)

ORIGINAL LANE
USED BY FIRST SETTLERS:
YAPPLE AND DUMOND NEAR
STATE ST; HENNEPAW ON
CASCADILLA CREEK

57
(On East Buffalo St.)

SITE OF FIRST
WHITE SETTLEMENT 1789
BEGINNING OF SOUTHERN
CAYUGA INDIAN TRAIL

58
(On East State St.)

END OF TURNPIKE
WEST TO OLD BOAT LANDING
EAST THROUGH LANSING
"ENTERPRISE" FIRST STEAMBOAT
LAUNCHED ON LAKE 1820
ROUND TRIP TWO DAYS
59
(Aurora & Lincoln St.)

TOLLGATE HOUSE
ONCE STOOD UPON ROAD
AND TRAFFIC PASSED THROUGH
OWEGO-ITHACA TURNPIKE
SURVEYED AS EAST ROAD 1792
ON INDIAN TRAILS
60
(NY 34 on north bank of Fall
Creek at Lake St. bridge)

FROM THIS SITE
THE ITHACA CONSERVATORY
OF MUSIC FORMED IN 1892
AND ITS SUCCESSOR ITHACA
COLLEGE CHARTERED IN 1931
OPERATED FROM 1911 TO 1966
61
(Buffalo St bet. Cayuga & Tioga)

TOWN OF ITHACA

OLD STONE HEAP
DAVENPORT'S TAVERN–LOT 87
HERE ABNER TREMAN SPENT THE
NIGHT ON HIS RETURN, 1793–
1794, TO HIS CLAIM, NOW THE
VILLAGE OF TRUMANSBURG
62

CATSKILL
TURNPIKE
STAGE COACH ROUTE FROM
CATSKILL TO BATH 1815. OLD
POST ROAD AND MAIL ROUTE
BETWEEN WATKINS AND ITHACA
63
(NY 79 ½ m. west of Ithaca)

LINDERMAN TAVERN
BUILT BY CORNELIUS LINDERMAN
SETTLED IN TOWN 1802
SITE OF LOG CABIN
PANORAMA OF CAYUGA LAKE
AND CITY OF ITHACA
64
(NY 79 ½ m. west of Ithaca)

TOWN OF LANSING

FISHER'S TAVERN
JACKSON'S TAVERN AND
TOLLGATE SITES 3/10 MILE
SOUTH IRISH HILL ROAD
CORDUROY UNTIL 1853
RENAMED NEWFIELD ROAD 1903
65
(NY 13 & 34 2 m. SW Ithaca)

COREORGONEL
(WHERE WE KEEP PIPE OF PEACE)
CAYUGA INDIAN VILLAGE
IROQUOIS SIX NATIONS
DESTROYED BY SULLIVAN'S ARMY
SEPTEMBER 24-25, 1779
66
(NY 13 & 34 2 ½ m. SW Ithaca)

LUDLOWVILLE-MYERS
DETACHMENT OF GEN. JOHN
SULLIVAN'S ARMY UNDER
COL. BUTLER CAMPED ON THESE
HEIGHTS SEPT. 24, 1779
ANDREW MYERS, PIONEER, 1779
67
(NY 34 B between Ludlowville and Myers)

TOWN OF NEWFIELD

LUDLOW INN 1795
FIRST LOG TAVERN, 1792
LOG GRISTMILL 1795
BUILT BY MAJOR THOMAS LUDLOW
EARLY SETTLERS—SILAS, HENRY
AND THOMAS LUDLOW, 1791
68
(County Road at Ludlowville)

ROGUES HARBOR INN
1830, BUILT BY D.D. MINIER
SON OF GEN. ABRAM MINIER
WHO LOCATED IN TOWN 1788
AND LIVED ON SITE 1792
LIBERTYVILLE NOW SOUTH LANSING
69
(NY 34 & 34 B at South Lansing)

CONNECTICUT HILL
BORN HERE, JULY 22, 1855, TO
FOREST ERVAY AND WIFE, FOUR
CHILDREN, KNOWN AS ERVAY
QUADRUPLETS; ON EXHIBITION
FOR SEVERAL YEARS
70
(TR 3 m. W. of Trumbull Corners)

TOWN OF ULYSSES

CONNECTICUT HILL
EARLY CALLED SAXTON HILL
HIGHEST ELEVATION 2097.2 FT.)
IN TOMPKINS COUNTY. ONCE
OWNED BY STATE OF
CONNECTICUT
71
(TR 3 m. W. of Trumbell Corners)

CAMP HOUSE
BUILT IN 1840 BY
HERMAN CAMP
COLONEL OF CALVARY
NIAGARA FRONTIER
WAR OF 1812
72
(Lawn St. Trumansburg)

ABNER TREMAN
FIRST SETTLER AND
FOUNDER OF TRUMANSBURG
BUILT HIS LOG HOUSE
NEAR THIS SPOT
IN 1792
73
(NY 96 at Trumansburg)

ALGONKIAN SITE
INDIAN CAMP
EXTENDING FROM MOUTH OF
CREEK TO FALLS
OF HALSEYVILLE

74
(Taughannock Falls St. Pk.)

HALSEY HOUSE
BUILT 1829
BY NICHOLL HALSEY
FIRST SETTLER AND FOUNDER
WITH EXPLORING EXPEDITION
CAMPED HERE IN JUNE 1788
75
(NY 96 at Halseyville)

CAMP SITE
CAPTAIN JONATHAN WOODWORTH
REVOLUTIONARY SOLDIER,
NAVIGATOR AND SURVEYOR

76
(Taughannock Falls St. Pk.)

Howard S. Ford

| SAMUEL WEYBURN
SETTLED HERE IN 1790
THE HOSPITALITY OF HIS LOG
CABIN HOME SAVED LIFE OF
ABNER TREMAN, REV. SOLDIER
CAUGHT IN BLIZZARD 1793-4
77
(Taughannock Falls St. Pk.) | OLD COOPER INN
BUILT BY THOMAS COOPER 1823
PIONEER SETTLER, 1799
ITHACA-GENEVA TURNPIKE
STAGE COACH ROUTE
AND POST ROAD, 1811
78
(NY 96 at Jacksonville) | CAYUGA INDIAN
FORT AND BURIAL GROUND
EARTH WORK ON NORTH SIDE
BURIAL GROUND OPPOSITE
CIRCULAR EARTH WORKS S.E.
BLUFF SUPPORTED PALISADE
79
(TR ½ m. W. of Waterbury) |

WAYNE COUNTY

TOWN OF LYONS   TOWN OF MARION

| FIRST SCHOOL
A LOG SCHOOL HOUSE WAS
BUILT ON THIS SITE BEFORE
1808. BRICK STRUCTURE
REPLACING IT WAS USED
AS A CATHOLIC CHURCH
1
(On Butternut St., Lyons) | NAMING OF LYONS
ABOUT 1796 NEAR THIS SPOT
THE RIVER VIEW RESEMBLING
THAT OF LYONS, FRANCE, LED
CHARLES WILLIAMSON TO
RENAME THE "FORKS"
SETTLEMENT–LYONS
2
(On Water St., Lyons) | 1800
FIRST TAVERN
KEPT IN MARION
WAS LOCATED
ON THIS SITE
3
(On Main St., Marion) |

| FIRST LOG HOUSE
IN MARION WAS ERECTED
ON THIS SITE
IN 1795
BY HENRY LOVELL
4
(NY 21 in Marion) | MARION
SETTLED IN 1795-6
BY PIONEERS FROM RHODE
ISLAND AND MASSACHUSETTS,
WAS ORGANIZED AS A
TOWN APRIL 15, 1826
5
(On Main St. Marion) | THIS HOUSE
ERECTED IN 1830
WAS A STATION OF THE
UNDERGROUND RAILWAY
IN THE DAYS OF SLAVERY
6
(NY 21 ½ m. S. of Marion) |

TOWN OF PALMYRA

| JOSEPH SMITH HOME
WHERE HE LIVED IN 1827
WHEN HE TRANSLATED
PART OF BOOK OF MORMON
7
(CR 1 m. S. of Palmyra) | ------
4 MILES SOUTH
CUMORAH
FAMOUS MORMON HILL
AND
ANGEL MORONI MONUMENT
8
(NY 31 & 21 in Palmyra) | ------
1/4 MILE
SACRED GROVE
9
(CR 1 m. S. of Palmyra) |

MARTIN HARRIS
FARM
MORTGAGED FOR $3000 IN
1829 TO PROVIDE FUNDS
FOR THE FIRST PUBLICATION
OF BOOK OF MORMON
10
(CR 1 m. N. of Palmyra)

1793-1805
FIRST SCHOOL HOUSE
IN PALMYRA BUILT HERE ON
LAND GIVEN BY GENERAL
JOHN SWIFT

11
(On Church St. Palmyra)

ROPE WALK
HERE ROPE WAS MANUFACTURED
IN 500 FOOT LENGTHS. IT
WAS USED ON THE ALBANY
SCHENECTADY R.R.

12
(CR ½ m. E. of Palmyra)

HERE IN 1790
FIRST LOG HOUSE
IN PALMYRA
BUILT AND OCCUPIED BY
THE PIONEER SETTLER
GENERAL JOHN SWIFT
13
(NY 31 & 21 in Palmyra)

SITE OF
FIRST CHURCH
IN PALMYRA
1811-1832
LAND GIVEN BY
GENERAL JOHN SWIFT
14
(Church St. Palmyra)

THIS HOUSE
BUILT BY PLINY SEXTON IN
1827 WAS A STATION OF
THE UNDERGROUND RAILWAY
IN THE DAYS OF SLAVERY

15
(Main St. in Palmyra)

SITE OF
PIONEER HOME
OF GIDEON DURFEE
BUILT 1811

16
(CR ¼ m. E. of Palmyra)

SITE OF
ORTHODOX QUAKER
MEETING HOUSE
FIRST ONE ERECTED IN WESTERN
NEW YORK 1800-1830

17
(TR 2 m. N. Of Palmyra)

EAST PALMYRA CHURCH
FIRST TO BE ORGANIZED
IN STATE, WEST OF PRE-EMPTION
LINE, 1793

18
(CR ½ m. E. of East Palmyra)

TOWN OF SAVANAH

SAW MILL BROOK
LONG ISLAND COLONY
SETTLED HERE MAY 2, 1792

19
(CR 1½ m. W. of E. Palmyra)

SAMPSON HOUSE
BIRTHPLACE OF REAR ADMIRAL
WILLIAM T. SAMPSON
COMMANDER OF FLAGSHIP
IN SPANISH-AMERICAN WAR
1840-1902
20
(S side Vienna St. Palmyra)

INDIAN TOWN
ON HILL TO EAST WAS
ONONTARE, A FORIFIED
TOWN OF CAYUGA NATION.
IN 1670 THE SITE OF
MISSION OF ST. RENE
21*
(NY 414 1 m. S of Savannah)

Howard S. Ford

TOWN OF WALWORTH

SITE OF FREEWILL BAPTIST CHURCH 1834-1875 BUILT AT A COST OF $2000 22 (CR 2 m. NW. of Walworth)	SITE OF LOG SCHOOL HOUSE BUILT IN 1804 23 (on CR at Walworth)	SITE OF THE FIRST ACADEMY IN WALWORTH INCORPORATED 1842 BUILT OF LAKE STONES AT A COST OF $4000 24 (on CR at Walworth)
ON THIS SITE ISAAC BARNHART BUILT DAM IN 1813, GRIST MILL IN 1818. CRAGGS ROLLER MILLS 1862-1930 25 (CR nr Walworth-Macedon line)	SITE OF FIRST CHURCH IN WALWORTH, BUILT PRIOR TO 1809; IN USE UNTIL 1825 26 (NY 350 1 m. W. of Walworth)	SITE OF TANNERY BUILT BY LUTHER FILLMORE IN 1805 27 (TR 1 m. N. of Walworth)

TOWN OF WILLIAMSON

WALWORTH KNOWN AS DOUGLAS CORNERS 1801-1825 HERE STEPHEN DOUGLAS OF CONN. BUILT FIRST HOUSE 28 (On CR at Walworth)	FIRST ROAD IN WILLIAMSON BUILT BY CHARLES WILLIAMSON IN 1794 CALLED THE OLD SODUS ROAD BETWEEN PALMYRA AND SODUS BAY 29 (US 104 at East Williamson)	INDIAN TRAIL THIS ROAD, SECOND IN TOWN WAS INDIAN TRAIL, LATER CANANDAIGUA-PULTNEYVILLE POST ROAD, BUILT OF PLANK, HERE STOOD TOLL GATE 30 (NY 21 2 m. N. of Williamson)
SITE OF UNDERGROUND RAILROAD TERMINUS HOME OF SAMUEL CUYLER USED AS TERMINUS OF UNDERGROUND R.R. DURING SLAVERY PERIOD 31 (CR ¼ m. E. of Pultneyville)	SITE OF UNION CHURCH ERECTED 1825, OPEN FOR USE OF ANY DENOMINATION, DEDICATED TO TOLERANCE AND PROMOTION OF GOOD ORDER AND RELIGION 32 (NY 21 at Pultneyville)	FIRST WHITE MEN FROM 1687 FRENCH BATEAUX MEN STOPPED HERE TO TRADE WITH INDIANS. FIRST SETTLER "YANKEE BILL" WATERS, A HUNTER LIVED HERE 1804 33 (NY 21 at Pultneyville)

TOWN OF WOLCOTT

SITE OF
FIRST LOG HOUSE
BUILT 1807 BY MAJOR WILLIAM
ROGERS. USED FOR TAVERN,
STORE AND POST OFFICE.
SETTLEMENT WAS CALLED
ROGERS CORNERS

34

(NY 21 & 104, East Williamson)

WOLCOTT FALLS
CALLED BY INDIANS
"CANADASGUA", LEAPING
WATERS ABOVE THE LAKE.
SITE OF MELVIN'S MILLS
ESTABLISHED 1809

35

(US 104 at Wolcott)

YATES COUNTY

TOWN OF BENTON

METHODIST CHURCH
BENTON CLASS FORMED 1793
EZRA COLE PREACHED 1792
OLDEST EXISTING RELIGIOUS
SOCIETY IN YATES CO. AND OF
METHODISM IN WESTERN N.Y.

1

(NY 14A, Benton Corners)

TOWN OF BRANCHPORT

RED JACKET
NEAR THIS SPOT STOOD
CABIN HOME OCCUPIED BY
PARENTS OF NOTED SENECA
CHIEF RED JACKET, 1752
HIS MOTHER'S GRAVE IS NEAR

2

(NY 54 A, ½ m. S., Branchport)

TOWN OF JERUSALEM

BUILT ABOUT 1790
FRIEND'S HOME
HERE LIVED
JEMIMA WILKINSON
KNOWN AS
THE UNIVERSAL FRIEND

3

(CR 4 m. N., Branchport)

HERE LIVED
GU-YA-NO-GA
INDIAN CHIEF OF THE
SENECA NATION
FRIEND OF THE REVOLUTION

4

(CR 2 m. N., Branchport)

TOWN OF MIDDLESEX

INDIAN BURIALS
HERE IS AN INDIAN BURIAL
PLACE OF THE PERIOD PRIOR
TO THE COMING OF EARLY
SENECAS. EXCAVATED BY
STATE MUSEUM 1922

5

(In Vine Valley)

TOWN OF POTTER

BUILT ABOUT 1790
POTTER MANSION
HOME OF ARNOLD POTTER
PIONEER AND EARLY SETTLER
AFTER WHOM TOWN IS NAMED

6

(CR 3 ½ m. NW., Penn Yan)

Howard S. Ford

TOWN OF TORREY

**THE UNIVERSAL FRIEND
JEMIMA WILKINSON
HER SETTLEMENT
1788–1794
7*
(TR. 1 m. S., Dresden)**

This list of markers has been provided by the courtesy of Philip Lord, Jr. of the

New York State Museum, division of the State Department of Education.

Bibliography

Anklin, Karen Richards and Barbara B. Spain, "Pioneers and Prominent Citizens of Skaneateles", Artcraft Press, Skaneateles, N.Y., 1979, 178 p.

Bakeless, John, "America As Seen By Its First Explorers", Dover Publications, Inc., New York, 1961, 178 p.

Bashant, Nancy, General Editor, History of Oneida County, County of Oneida, 256 p.

Beauchamp, William Martin, "The Life of Conrad Weiser", Syracuse: Onondaga County Historical Association, 1925

—, "The History of the New York Iroquois", AMS Press Inc New York 1905

Bowen, Catherine Drinker, "The Most Dangerous Man in America", Little, Brown and Company, Boston, 1974 261p.

Bridgwater, William and Elizabeth J. Sherwood, Editors, "The Columbia Encyclopedia", Columbia University Press, New York, 24 volumes

Cardamone, Helen and Emily Williams, "Cherry Valley Country", Brodock Press Inc. Utica, 1978.

Carmer, Carl, Editor, "The Tavern Lamps Are Burning", an anthology, David McKay Company, Inc. New York, 1964, 550 p.

—, "The Susquehanna", Rinehart & Company, Inc. New York, 1955, 456 p.

—, "The Hudson", Farrar and Rinehart, New York, 1939, 421 p.

Central New York Society of Land Surveyors, "Highway History"

Chamberlin, John, "The Enterprising Americans: A Business History of the United States" Harper & Row Publishers, New York, 1963

Clark, Dr. Geoffrey, "Engineering and Entrepreneurship of the Stevens Family", from a talk to the Stevens Old Guard Alumni Association

Clarke, T. Wood, "Émigrés in the Wilderness", Ira J. Friedman, Inc., Port Washington, N.Y., 1967, 238 p.

Clune, Henry W.,"The Genesee", Holt, Rinehart, and Winston, New York, 1963, 338 p.

—, "The Rochester I Know", Doubleday & Company, Inc., Garden City, N.Y. 1972, 384 p.

Colden, Cadwallader, "History of the Five Indian Nations" 1727 and 1749.

Cooper, Charles B., "The Story of the Steamboats on Skaneateles Lake", Privately printed, Skaneateles, N.Y.,1979, 15 p.

De Voto, Bernard, "The Course of Empire", Houghton, Mifflin Company, The Riverside Press, Cambridge, 1952, 635 p.

Dohan, Mary Helen, "Mr. Roosevelt's Steamboat", Dodd, Mead & Company, New York, 1981, 172 p.

Eckert, Allan W., "Wilderness Empire", Little, Brown and Company, New York, 1969, 737 p.

—, "Wilderness War", Bantam Books, New York, 1982, 564 p.

Edmonds, Walter D., "The Musket and the Cross", Little Brown and Co., Boston, 1968, 499 p

Delavan, Elizabeth, "Upstate Village", North Country Books, Lakemont, N.Y. 1975, 96 p.

Ellis, C. Hamilton, "The Lore of the Train", Allen and Unwin, London, 1971, 1971, 240 p.

Ellis, David M, "New York State: Gateway to America, Windsor Publications, Inc., 1988, 397 p.

—, James A. Frost, Harold C. Syrett, and Harry J. Carman, "A Short History of New York", New York Historical Association, Cornell University Press, 1957, 690 p.

Emmons, E. Thayles, "The Story of Geneva", The Finger Lakes Times, Geneva, 1982, 475 p

Flexner, James Thomas, "Mohawk Baronet: Sir William Johnson of New York",Harper & Brother, New York 1959.

Frazier, Ian, "Family", Farrar Straus Giroux, New York, 1994, 386 p.

Friedenberg, Daniel M. "Life, Liberty, and the Pursuit of Land: The Plunder of Early America", Prometheus Books, Buffalo, New York 1992 407 p.

Galpin, William F., "Central New York; An Inland Empire", Lewis Historical Publishing Co., Inc., New York, 1941, Vol. 1, 319 p.

Goodenough, Simon, "The Fire Engine An Illustrated History", Chartwell Books, Inc., Secaucus, N.J., 1978, 158 p.

Graymont, Barbara, "The Iroquois in the American Revolution", Syracuse University Press, Syracuse, 1972, 359 p.

Hamilton, Edward P., "The French and Indian Wars", Doubleday & Company, Inc., Garden City, N.Y. 1962, 318 p

Hawke, David Freeman, "Nuts and Bolts of the Past", Harper and Row, Publishers, New York, 1988, 293 p.

Hertzler, Arthur E., M.D., "The Horse and Buggy Doctor", University of Nebraska Press, Lincoln, 1938 322p.

Holbrook, Stewart H., "The Golden Age of Railroads", Random House, 1960

Hosmer, Howard C., "Monroe County", Rochester Museum and Science Center, Flower City Printing, Inc. Rochester, N.Y., 1971, 305 p.

Jennings, Francis, "Benjamin Franklin, Politician: The Mask and the Man", W.W. Norton & Company, New York, 1996 231 p.

Jennings, Francis, "Empire of Fortune", W.W. Norton & Company, New York 1988, 509 p.

Johansen, Bruce E. and Grinde, Donald A., Jr., "The Encyclopedia of Native American Biography", Henry Holt and Company, New York 1997, 437 p.

Kammen, Carol, "The Peopling of Tompkins County", Heart of the Lakes Publishing, Interlaken, N.Y. 1985, 245 p.

Keller, Jane Eblen, "Adirondack Wilderness", Syracuse University Press, Syracuse, N.Y. 1980,

Lamb, Wallace E., "New York State and its Communities", American Book Company, 1942,

Lancaster, Bruce and J.H. Plumb, "The American Heritage Book of the Revolution", Dell Publishing Co., Inc. New York, 1963, 367 p.

Mau, Clayton Dr., "The Development of Central and Western New York", F. A. Owen Publishing Co., Dansville, N.Y. 1958, 451 p.

Mellick, Andrew D.,Jr., "Lesser Crossroads", Edited by Hubert G. Schmidt, Rutgers University Press, New Brunswick, 1948, 391 p.

Merrill Arch, "Land of the Senecas", Vail-Ballou Press, Inc. Binghamton, N.Y., 1975, 146 p.

—, "Slim Fingers Beckon", American Book-Stratford Press, Inc., New York, 184 p.

—, "Southern Tier", Volume 2, American Book-Stratford Press, Inc. New York, 210 p.

Morgan, Ted, "Wilderness at Dawn: The Settling of the North American Continent", Simon & Schuster, New York, 1993

Morison, Samuel Eliot, "The Oxford History of the American People" 1965, 1150 p.

New York State Historical Association, "An Informal Guide to the Museums of the New York Historical Association", Cooperstown, N.Y. 1975, 96 p.

O'Connor, Lois, "A Finger Lakes Odyssey", North Country Books, Inc., Lakemont, N.Y., 1977, 108 p.

Ogburn, Charlton, "Railroads The Great American Adventure", National Geographic Society, Washington, D.C., 1977, 200 p.

Parkman, Francis, "La Salle and the Discovery of the West", Frontenac (11th) Edition, Little, Brown, and Company, Boston, 1905, 489 p.

Porter, Roy, "The Greatest Benefit to Mankind: A Medical History of Humanity" W.W. Norton & Company, New York, 1997, 764 p.

Pound, Arthur, "Lake Ontario", the Bobbs-Merrill Company, New York, 1945, 363 p.

Roberts, Ellis H., "American Commonwealths: New York", Houghton, Mifflin & Co. Boston, 1895, 2 Volumes

Scheer, George F. & Hugh F. Rankin, "Rebels and Redcoats", A Mentor Book, World Publishing Co., The New American Library of American Literature, Inc., New York, 1959, 587 p.

Schramm, Henry W., "C E N T R A L NEW YORK: A Pictorial History", The Donning Company, Norfolk, Va., 1987, 227p.

Howard S. Ford

—, "The Rivers of Time: A Bicentennial History Chronology of Onondaga County", Cultural Resources Council of Syracuse and Onondaga County, 1994, 93 p.

—, "Empire Showcase", North Country Books Inc., Utica, N.Y. 1985, 182 p.

—, and Roseboom, William F., "They Built a City", Manlius Publishing Corporation, Fayetteville, N.Y., 1976, 178 p.

Seaver, James, "The Life of Mary Jemison", The American Scenic and Historic Preservation Society, New York, 1982, 182 p.

Shaw, Ronald E., "Erie Water West: A History of the Erie Canal, (1792-1854)", University of Kentucky Press, 1946, 449 p

Sobel, Robert, "I. B. M. Colossus in Transition", Truman Talley Books, New York, 1981,.

Staufer, Alvin F., "New York Central's Early Power",

Stinson, Donald J., "The Burning of the Frontenac", Heart of the Lakes Publishing, Interlaken, N.Y., 1985, 104 p.

Taylor, Alan, "William Cooper's Town", Alfred A. Knopf, New York, 1995, 537 p.

Tunis, Edwin, "Frontier Living", The World Publishing Company, Cleveland, 1961, 161 p.

—, "Colonial Craftsmen", The World Publishing Company, Cleveland, 1965, 159 p.

—, "Wheels", The World Publishing Company, Cleveland, 1955, 96 p.

Van Every, Dale, "Forth to the Wilderness", William Morrow and Company, New York
369 p.

van Wagenen, Jared, "The Golden Age of Homespun", Cornell University Press, Ithaca, N.Y.,1953, 270 p.

Van Zandt, Roland, "Chronicles of the Hudson", Black Dome Press Corporation, Hensonville, N.Y., 1992, 346 p.

Wallace, William M., "Appeal to Arms, A Military History of the American Revolution", Harper and Brothers, 1951

Walter, George W., "The Loomis Gang", Fay Edward Faulkner Printing Company, Sherburne, N.Y., 1968, 271 p.

Watson, Winslow C., "Men and Times of the Revolution; or Memoirs of Elkanah Watson,", Crown Point Press, Inc., Elizabethtown, New York, 2nd edition, 1968, 527 p

Wellikoff, Alan, "The Historical Supply Catalogue", Rough-Hewn Books, Baltimore, Md. 1993,

Wyld, Lionel D., "40'x28'x4': The Erie Canal-150 Years", Rome, N.Y., Oneida County Erie Canal Commemoration Commission, 1967 54 p.

Printed in the United States
27444LVS00001B/99-188